PRAISE FOR *AMERICAN JESUS*

"For the general reader, *American Jesus* offers a fascinating *tour d'horizon*. For believers, it's testimony to Jesus' everlasting power and glory. For skeptics, it's proof positive there's a sucker born every minute."
—DAN CRYER, *Newsday*

"[*American Jesus*] offers a kaleidoscopic vision that strives to dismantle the separation between theology and popular culture."
—SHARON ULLMAN, *The Boston Globe*

"Prothero conducts his quest for the American Jesus with broad and imaginative research, and reports his findings in a lucid and lively prose that will appeal outside the academy. Sifting through a vast assortment of material—books, pictures, films, sermons, hymns—Prothero offers a generous and often witty panoramic view of the Jesus 'who belongs . . . to all of us, Christians and non-Christians alike.'"
—EUGENE McCARRAHER, *Chicago Tribune*

"Prothero's chapter on Judaism's changing attitudes toward Jesus is worth the price of the book."
—JACK MILES, *Jerusalem Post*

"A frequently fascinating romp through American culture with the emphasis on pop culture (some would say there is no other kind), showing the myriad ways in which the figure of Jesus has been detached from theological or churchly connections to become an icon for the promotion of almost anything."
—*First Things*

"A witty, entertaining, and eye-opening romp through American cultural history."
—*Library Journal*

"Nearly every page offers a fresh portrait of some corner of American religious history."
—*Publishers Weekly*

M. STEWART

STEPHEN PROTHERO

AMERICAN JESUS

HOW THE SON OF GOD BECAME A NATIONAL ICON

Stephen Prothero is the chair of the Department of Religion at Boston University. He is the author of *The White Buddhist: The Asian Odyssey of Henry Steel Olcott* and *Purified by Fire: A History of Cremation in American Culture*. *American Jesus* was named one of the best religion books of 2003 by *Publishers Weekly*, and one of the year's best nonfiction books by the *Chicago Tribune*. Prothero has written for *The New York Times Magazine*, *The Boston Globe*, *The Washington Post*, *The Wall Street Journal*, *Salon*, and other publications. He lives in East Sandwich, Massachusetts.

ALSO BY STEPHEN PROTHERO

Purified by Fire:
A History of Cremation in America (2001)

The White Buddhist:
The Asian Odyssey of Henry Steel Olcott (1996)

AMERICAN JESUS

AMERICAN

𝕵𝖊𝖘𝖚𝖘

★

How the Son of God Became

a National Icon

STEPHEN PROTHERO

FARRAR, STRAUS AND GIROUX

NEW YORK

For S. Richard and Helen Anderson Prothero

Farrar, Straus and Giroux
18 West 18th Street, New York 10011

Printed in the United States of America
First edition, 2003

The Library of Congress has cataloged the hardcover edition as follows:
Prothero, Stephen R.
American Jesus : how the Son of God became a national icon / Stephen Prothero.— 1st. ed.
p.   cm.
Includes bibliographical references (p.   ) and index.
ISBN-13: 978-0-374-17890-1 (hardcover : alk. paper)
ISBN-10: 0-374-17890-9 (hardcover : alk. paper)
1. Jesus Christ—Person and offices.   2. United States—Religion.   I. Title.

BT203 .P76 2003
232'.0973—dc22

2003006947

Paperback ISBN-13: 978-0-374-52956-7
Paperback ISBN-10: 0-374-52956-6

Designed by Debbie Glasserman

www.fsgbooks.com

14   16   17   15   13

CONTENTS

Illustrations follow page 180

NOTE ON CAPITALIZATION

Pronouns used to refer to Jesus are often capitalized by Christians, to indicate Jesus' divinity. Here I follow that practice only in direct quotations. Otherwise I use lowercase pronouns, in keeping with the custom in many Bible translations, including the King James.

AMERICAN JESUS

INTRODUCTION

𝕰very Christmas, in towns and cities across the United States, Jesus is reborn in Nativity scenes erected on public property. Almost as regularly, civil libertarians challenge the constitutionality of these public displays of religion, forcing the courts to consider yet again how to interpret the First Amendment. Underlying this question of constitutional jurisprudence is the equally vexing matter of the religious character of the nation: Is the United States a religious country or a secular state? Is it Christian? Judeo-Christian? Or, as President George W. Bush has suggested, an Abrahamic nation under one Judeo-Christian-Islamic God?

What makes the matter of America's religious character intriguing—and the debates it stimulates enduring—is that evidence abounds on all sides. In a treaty with Tripoli (now in Libya) signed in 1797, the United States pledged, as its leaders would more than two centuries later, that the nation has no quarrel with Islam. "The Government of the United States of America," the treaty read, "is not in any sense founded on the Christian religion." Liberal advocates of the separation of church and state repeatedly cite this obscure treaty. Of course, conservative critics of church-state separation have proof texts of their own, including an 1892 U.S. Supreme Court opinion that lauds "the Redeemer of mankind" and calls the United States a "Christian nation."[1]

Away from the official rhetoric of jurisprudence and diplomacy, in the field of American religious history, the debate goes on, though there it is typically framed around the axes of Protestantism and pluralism. For generations, historians of American religion wrote almost exclusively about American Protestants. Robert Baird, who served as a Presbyterian missionary before becoming the first great chronicler of American religion, called his 1844 classic *Religion in America* but his subject was really Protestantism in America—Puritans who settled New England and revivalists who yanked Puritan theology (kicking and screaming) into an evangelical age. The drama those Puritans and revivalists played out was for Baird a sacred errand to a promised land set aside by a providential God: America the beautiful and the Protestant.

In the 1950s, the Jewish sociologist Will Herberg looked out over a different country, radically transformed by more than a century of Catholic and Jewish immigration from Europe. Could these immigrants and their religions be integrated into the Protestant myth of America? In *Protestant, Catholic, Jew* (1955), Herberg answered that question with an emphatic yes. Protestantism, Catholicism, and Judaism, he argued, had become three branches in a shared patriotic piety that revered God and cherished democracy. Herberg's "triple melting pot" theory circulated widely during the 1950s, the same decade that saw the U.S. Congress insert the words "under God" into the Pledge of Allegiance. By the 1960s, however, that theory was starting to look parochial. In 1965, legislation opened up immigration from Asia, prompting U.S. Supreme Court Justice William Douglas to observe that the United States was no longer merely Christian or even Judeo-Christian but "a nation of Buddhists, Confucianists and Taoists" too.[2]

Over the last few decades, scholars have been exploring that nation of religions, expanding our understanding of Hinduism and Buddhism, Transcendental Meditation and Santeria, Theosophy and Mormonism. In the process, the old Protestant paradigm of Baird and his progeny has given way to a new pluralist paradigm in which America's city on the hill is topped with church spires and minarets: America the beautiful and the pluralist.

This new interest in religious "outsiders" is most prominent in the work of Harvard professor Diana L. Eck, who contends in *A New Religious America* (2001) that recent immigration from Asia has transformed the United States into "the most religiously diverse nation on earth." In Eck's America, Hindu priests and Muslim imams open U.S. congressional sessions, and Jains crowd into sanctuaries once occupied by Lutherans. This pluralistic reality, moreover, is all for the good, since in her view "the ideal of a Christian America stands in contradiction to the spirit, if not the letter, of America's foundational principle of religious freedom."[3]

In a review of *A New Religious America*, Pennsylvania State University professor Philip Jenkins has written that the only problem with Eck's book "is that it is flat wrong." Yes, the post-1965 immigration boom is reshaping the religious landscape, Jenkins argues, but it is making the United States more rather than less Christian. After all, the vast majority of immigrants from Latin American countries are either Catholics or Pentecostals, and Christianity is widespread among Asian immigrants too. American religious diversity, Jenkins concludes, is a myth perpetuated by liberal academics and other eggheads troubled by the conservative Christian commitments of the American people.[4]

Historians like to believe that their work is exempt from the rough and tumble of contemporary concerns. But objectivity is a casualty on both sides of the Christian America debate. Participants often oscillate between the descriptive and the normative, confusing what is (or was) with what ought to be. They also routinely conflate demographic, legal, and cultural questions, forgetting that a country may be Christian in one respect and secular in another. Typically those who understand the United States as a multireligious country focus on the law and cheer on religious "outsiders," while those who emphasize its Christian character focus on demography and cast their lot with the "insiders." While for one group Christian dominance (either real or perceived) is the problem, for the other it is the solution.

Each of these approaches misses much. The Christian nation

camp overlooks the vitality of non-Christian religions in the United States, while the multireligious camp turns a blind eye to the public power exercised by the Christian majority. Both sides fail to see how extensively insiders and outsiders are improvising on one another— how Buddhists, Hindus, and Muslims are adopting Christian norms and organizational forms, and how Methodists, Baptists, and Presbyterians are taking up, however stealthily, the beliefs and practices of Asian religions. (Nearly one-quarter of the Christians in the United States now believe in reincarnation.)[5]

Today the country boasts a sprawling spiritual marketplace, where religious shoppers can choose among all the world's great religions, and from a huge menu of offerings inside each. There are about two thousand mosques in the United States, and more than six hundred Hindu congregations. In the Los Angeles area alone, there are at least two hundred Buddhist centers—for American-born converts, and for the Vietnamese, the Japanese, the Taiwanese, the Burmese, the Koreans, and the Tibetans. Inside these sacred spaces, adherents adapt their religious traditions to American circumstances. But as recent *Time* magazine cover stories on Buddhism (in 1997), yoga (in 2001), and meditation (in 2003) attest, Asian religious traditions are also influential outside temple walls—in meditation and yoga classes, and among practitioners of feng shui and the martial arts.

All this religious diversity should not obscure the fact that the United States now boasts more Christians than any other country in world history. Following his now-famous tour of the United States in 1831, the Frenchman Alexis de Tocqueville wrote, "There is no country in the world where the Christian religion retains a greater influence over the souls of men than in America."[6] But this is no antiquated observation. Today the top ten denominations in the country are all Christian, as is roughly 85 percent of the population. And Christians enjoy a privileged place in the public square. While there are likely more Muslims than Episcopalians in the United States, there are infinitely more Episcopalians than Muslims (44 to 0, to be exact) in the 108th United States Congress. As a nation, Americans celebrate Christmas, not the Buddha's birthday. And whatever religious diversity they enjoy is always being negotiated in what can only be described as a Christian context. In the United States, Buddhists are free to be Buddhists, but invariably they yank their traditions around to Christian norms and organizational forms—calling their temples "churches," voting for Zen masters, singing hymns such as "Onward, Buddhist Soldiers," tending to the hungry and the homeless, and otherwise following their consciences wherever they might lead.

The only way to make sense of all these facts—on both sides of the ledger—is to refuse to make a Solomonic choice between Christian America and multireligious America, between the country's de facto religiosity and its de jure secularity. American culture has long been both Christian and plural, both secular and religious, and much of the dynamism of U.S. religious history derives from that paradox. Any story of religion in the United States that fails to take seriously both Christians and non-Christians is bound to obscure as much as it illuminates.

A QUEST FOR THE CULTURAL JESUS

The subject of this particular story of American religion is Jesus, more precisely Jesus as Americans have understood him. So on its face, this book would appear to fall in the Christian nation camp. Yet many of the most interesting appraisals of Jesus have emerged outside the churches: in music, film, and literature, and among Jews, Hindus, Buddhists, and people of no religion at all. To explore the American Jesus, therefore, is not to confine oneself to Christianity. It is to examine how American Christianity has been formed by Christians and non-Christians alike, and how the varieties of American religious experience have been shaped by the public power of the Christian message. Finally, to see how Americans of all stripes have cast the man from Nazareth in their own image is to examine, through the looking glass, the kaleidoscopic character of American culture.

There are many places to begin this search for the American Jesus, but the fourth-century Council of Laodicea may be the most appropriate. At that gathering, early Christians met to close the canon of the still evolving Christian Bible. Some, following the second-century theologian Marcion, insisted that the one true Church should have only one true Gospel. Others, citing Marcion's contemporary Irenaeus, fought for four (one for each corner of the earth). Inexplicably,

Irenaeus got his way. Long before postmodern faddishness turned intellectuals on to polysemy and multivocality, Christians at the Council of Laodicea incorporated into their canon four different perspectives on the life of Jesus. So it should not be surprising that when Jesus asks (in each Gospel, except for John), "Who do people say that I am?" he doesn't get a simple answer. Some say John the Baptist. Some say Elijah. Some say one of the prophets. Peter, of course, says the Christ, but that doesn't settle the matter. And as the New Testament proceeds, the options multiply.

The proliferation of Jesus images did not end with the canonization of the Bible, or even the Crusades or the Reformation. Jesus may be "the same yesterday and today and forever" (Hebrews 13:8), but American depictions of him have varied widely from age to age and community to community. As the chapters that follow should make clear, the friendly Jesus who abided in the hearts of Victorian evangelicals would scarcely have been recognized by stern Puritan divines, and there is a world of difference today between the Elder Brother of Mormonism and the Black Moses of the black church. At least in the United States, Jesus has stood not on some unchanging rock of ages, but on the shifting sands of economic circumstances, political calculations, and cultural trends. Like the apostle Paul, who once wrote that he had become "all things to all men" so that he "might by all means save some" (1 Corinthians 9:22), the American Jesus has been something of a chameleon. Christians have depicted him as black and white, male and female, straight and gay, a socialist and a capitalist, a pacifist and a warrior, a Ku Klux Klansman and a civil rights agitator.

This American Jesus has not been solely a Christian concern, however. To be sure, most American conceptions of him have been produced and consumed by Christians. But the power of Christians to put Jesus on the national agenda has compelled Americans of all faiths to weigh in on him. Speaking of Judaism in late-nineteenth-century America, the New Testament scholar Samuel Sandmel observed that "no Jew breathing the free air of America could refrain from coming to grips in some way with Christianity and with Jesus."[7] And American Jews have not been alone. Atheists and agnostics, Black Muslims and white Buddhists have also reckoned with America (and with their own identities) by wrestling with Jesus. Moreover, outside the churches, synagogues, mosques, and temples, the American Jesus has insinuated himself into supposedly secular venues, including television and the movies. In the process, he has become an athlete and an aesthete, a polygamist and a celibate, an advertising man and a mountaineer, a Hindu deity and a Buddha-to-be.

All this is to say that Jesus has an American history. To hold Jesus up to the mirror of American culture is to conduct a Rorschach test of ever-changing national sensibilities. What Americans have seen in him has been an expression of their own hopes and fears—a reflection not simply of some "wholly other" divinity but also of themselves and their nation.

This book examines those hopes and fears, exploring not only what Americans have said about Jesus but also what their malleable and multiform Jesus has to say about the United States. Its subject is neither the "living Christ" of faith nor the "historical Jesus" of scholarship. It says nothing about who Jesus really is, and distinguishes itself from stacks of recent Jesus quest books by remaining silent about who he really was. My quest is for the cultural Jesus, who belongs neither to ancient Palestine nor to Christian America but to all of us, Christians and non-Christians alike. More specifically, I am searching for the American Jesus—Jesus as he has been interpreted and reinterpreted, construed and misconstrued, in the messy midrash of American culture.

I use the name *Jesus* here advisedly, since my focus is on Jesus the person, not Christ the theological sign. It is common to refer to "Jesus Christ" as if Jesus were his given name and Christ his surname. But Christ, of course, is a title: the English equivalent of the Greek term (*kristos*) for Messiah. To invoke Jesus Christ, therefore, is not simply to name a person but to affirm that person's status as the liberator long awaited by the Jewish people. More broadly speaking, the title Christ is a theological term that invites christological arguments about, among other things, his relative place in the Trinity alongside the Father and the Holy Spirit, the hypostatic union of his divine and human natures, and the meanings of related appellations such as *Son of God* and *Son of Man*. None of these matters lies at the heart of this project.

Though the christologies of theologians do come into play here, this book is not a history of American theology. It is a cultural history—a quest for the cultural Jesus—that draws on images of Jesus in missionary tracts and theological treatises, to be sure, but also in novels, films, biographies, musicals, hymns, spirituals, and the visual arts. In these sources, I have looked for evidence of the character and personality of Jesus the man, not the nature and function of Christ the messiah. I want to understand how Americans relate to Jesus, not how he relates to this theological system or that. I want to know what Americans see in him—whether he is aloof or friendly, dour or merry, masculine or feminine, homely or handsome. I am interested in the man, not the metaphysics.

AMERICA'S RELIGIOUS REVOLUTION

Though this may be difficult to believe, Jesus has not always been a household name, even in Christian households. Before the Revolutionary War, church members were in a distinct minority. In New England and the Middle Colonies (today's New York, New Jersey, Delaware, and Pennsylvania), only about one in every five people was affiliated with a church. That ratio was considerably lower—roughly one in eight—in the South, because slaves, who accounted for more than two out of every five inhabitants, had not yet converted in significant numbers. Moreover, even those colonists who were church members did not have any notable reverence for Jesus. Influenced by the Reformed theology of John Calvin, which emphasized the absolute sovereignty of God and the total depravity of human beings, Christians in the colonies typically focused their piety largely on the First Person of the Trinity, whom they feared as a distant yet powerful potentate. In their religious training, the Old Testament trumped the New, and Jesus the Son cowered in the shadow of God the Father. True, Jesus was the mediator who died on the cross to pay for human sins and satisfy the righteous judgment of his angry Father. Yet he functioned more as a principle than a person. Jonathan Edwards, one of the finest theologians North America has ever produced, fretted that this radical subordination of the Son to the Father might undermine the long-standing Christian commitment to the parity of the Trinity's three Persons. But even he described Jesus more often via abstract nouns—paired "excellencies" such as "infinite justice and infinite grace" and "infinite majesty and transcendent meekness"—than personal qualities.[8] In Puritan theology, Christ had a limited role to play; Jesus had almost none.

Today things are very different. Church membership is the norm— roughly three out of five Americans are affiliated with a church—and Christians of all stripes lavish their love on Jesus. In most European countries, Christianity is passé and Jesus a mere curiosity. In Sweden, for example, there are roughly twice as many atheists as there are active members of the Church of Sweden. In England, more than half of the population claims no religious affiliation and more than one out of five deny that Jesus existed. In the United States, by contrast, more than two out of every three citizens say they have made a "personal commitment to Jesus Christ" and approximately three out of four report they have sensed his presence.[9]

Yet Jesus is not the exclusive property of Christians. Polls reveal that Americans of all faiths view Jesus "overwhelmingly in a favorable light" and that he has "a strong hold even on those with no religious training." Amazingly, nearly half of the country's non-Christians believe that Jesus was born from a virgin and raised from the dead. Here atheists and Buddhists are active producers and consumers of images of Jesus, who in many respects functions as common cultural coin. Talk to a Hindu and she might tell you that Jesus is an avatar of the god Vishnu. Ask a Jew and you might be told that he was a great rabbi. In a bestselling novel from 1925, Bruce Barton described Jesus as *The Man Nobody Knows*. Today he is the man nobody hates.[10]

Jesus is also ubiquitous in American popular culture. On the radio, Mick Jagger and Bono sing about looking for the Buddha but finding Jesus Christ. In movie theaters, Jesus films open every few years, as do Jesus plays and musicals on and off Broadway. Readers also have a voracious appetite for Jesus. The Library of Congress holds more books about Jesus (seventeen thousand or so) than about any other historical figure, roughly twice as many as the runner-up (Shakespeare), and Jesus books there are piling up fast.

Finally, Jesus is a fixture on the American landscape—on highway billboards, bumper stickers, and even tattooed bodies. A hot-air balloon Jesus, complete with a purple robe identifying him as "King of

Kings, Lord of Lords," can be seen flying across western states. Not far from Disney World, there is a Jesus theme park called The Holy Land Experience. "Christ of the Ozarks," a seven-story statue of a risen Christ, lords over Eureka Springs, Arkansas. This statue, like the dream of televangelist Oral Roberts to construct a 900-foot Jesus (abandoned in the early 1980s for lack of funds), testifies to the tendency of some Americans to confuse bigness with greatness. Yet it testifies as well to Jesus' cultural reach, which extends from coast to coast and deep into the national psyche.

How did this happen? How did the Son of God become a national icon beloved by Jerry Falwell and the Dalai Lama alike? How did the United States become a Jesus nation? These are the guiding questions of this book, which charts the development of the American Jesus from an abstract principle into a concrete person, and then into a personality, a celebrity, and finally an icon.

The prelude to that story—a tale of captivity and freedom—starts in the ancient Mediterranean, where Jesus was sustained in the scriptures, creeds, and rites of Roman Catholic and Orthodox Christians. Over time, theologians made of Jesus the man a metaphysical abstraction whose divinity overwhelmed his humanity. As a result, Jesus receded from popular view, overshadowed by God the Father and, among many Roman Catholics, by saints such as the Blessed Virgin Mary. During the Renaissance and the Reformation, Christians rediscovered the humanity of Jesus, yet the form of Christianity that came to dominate the British colonies in North America continued to hold fast to a metaphysical Christ. The architecture of John Calvin's theology depended entirely on maximizing the tension between a sovereign God and fallen humanity. In the house that Calvin built, there was little room for a guest who was both divine and human.

Beginning with the Enlightenment of the eighteenth century, skeptics in Europe and America started to chip away at the traditions of the Church, employing reason and experience to undermine confidence in the Bible and the creeds. This assault on tradition might have killed Jesus, but it did not. On the contrary, it freed him up to be a hero to those who could not embrace the beliefs and practices of traditional Christianity. Thomas Jefferson would have been forced to reject Jesus if he had seen him as a take-it-or-leave-it proposition. But

Jefferson, as bold in religion as in politics, refused to grant Christians the right to serve as his exclusive interpreters. Christ he could not accept, but he was determined to revere Jesus. As Jefferson sat down in the White House, razor in hand, and began to cut and paste his own Bible, the American Jesus was born.

Soon Christians too were emphasizing Jesus' humanity over his divinity. In the free-wheeling spiritual marketplace opened by the ratification of the First Amendment in 1791, populist preachers competed for the hearts of parishioners by humanizing Jesus. Gradually they disentangled him (and themselves) from beliefs and practices that made them uncomfortable. Inspired by the revolutionary rhetoric of liberty, equality, and fraternity, evangelical Protestants popularized Jefferson's revolt against Calvinism by Christianizing it. Whereas Jefferson had embraced Jesus without Christianity, they embraced Christianity without Calvinism, rejecting the doctrine of predestination as an offense against human liberty and divine mercy. Jesus had come to earth not for some but for all, they insisted, and each was free to accept or reject the salvation he so graciously offered. Through the revivals of the Second Great Awakening of the first third of the nineteenth century, these evangelical enthusiasts democratized Christianity and Christianized America. So began America's religious revolution, which liberated Jesus from Calvin as surely as the Revolutionary War had liberated the colonists from George III. The early political uprising had given birth to a new nation, and this spiritual revolution gave birth to a new form of American religion, centered no longer on a wrathful Father but on a loving Son.

This American revolution proceeded in three overlapping stages. In the early nineteenth century, evangelicals liberated Jesus first from Calvinism and then from creeds. Though few rejected his divinity, Americans emphasized his humanity, transforming him from a distant god in a complex theological system into a near-and-dear person, fully embodied, with virtues they could imitate, a mind they could understand, and qualities they could love. In the process, they emboldened their Jesus to rise up and overthrow his Father as the dominant person in the Trinity.

The second stage culminated in the decades immediately following the Civil War. This time liberal Protestants were in the vanguard. Informed by Darwinism, comparative religion, and biblical criticism, they disentangled Jesus from the Bible, replacing the *sola scriptura* ("Bible alone") rallying cry of the Reformation with *solus Jesus*: Jesus alone. Instead of basing their faith on scripture and tradition, like Roman Catholics, or on scripture, as earlier Protestants had done, they took Jesus as their one and only authority. Their new slogan was "Back to Christ" and their new hymn "Jesus Only."

The third stage in this revolution fulfilled the promise of Jefferson's vision for Jesus, liberating him from Christianity itself. This stage, which began with Jefferson, the founding father of America's extra-Christian Jesus piety, was forcefully advanced by Jewish writers and rabbis between the 1860s and the 1930s. It came to fruition in the midst of the post-1965 immigration boom, as Hindus and Buddhists boldly adopted Jesus as one of their own, unbinding him (at least for their purposes) from the Christian tradition.

In *From Jesus to Christ* (1988), Paula Fredriksen has described how the early Church transformed Jesus the man into the Christ of the creeds. In the United States, Americans reversed that process. As they made it possible to reject the Calvinist Christ, the creedal Christ, and the biblical Christ, Jesus became accessible to Americans who could not believe in predestination, the Trinity, or the inerrancy of the Bible. As they disentangled Jesus from Christianity itself, Jesus piety became possible even for non-Christians. To be sure, not all Americans went this far. After the American Jesus—born in Jefferson's White House and raised by evangelical and liberal Protestants—turned his back on his Christian upbringing and struck out on his own in multireligious America, conservative believers beckoned him back to what many still believe is a Christian nation. But the genie was out of the bottle, and Americans of all religious persuasions (and none) now felt free to embrace whichever Jesus fulfilled their wishes.

RESURRECTIONS AND REINCARNATIONS

Artifacts of the American Jesus number in the millions, and one book obviously cannot cover them all. So this project is by necessity selective and by admission idiosyncratic. Here I ignore Native American and Hispanic Jesuses, and devote scant attention to liturgical traditions such as Roman Catholicism, Episcopalianism, and Lutheranism. I say nothing about the gay Jesuses who appear in the Robert Goss book *Jesus Acted Up* (1993) and the Terrence McNally play *Corpus Christi* (1998). Neither do I explore the claim of Mary Baker Eddy, the founder of Christian Science, that Jesus was "the most scientific man that ever trod the globe," nor the provocation in *The Last Temptation of Christ* (1988) that Jesus had sex with Mary Magdalene (or at least dreamed about it).[11] Another author taking up this vast subject would no doubt produce a very different volume.

As for this book, it is divided into two parts. The first, "Resurrections," proceeds chronologically in four chapters that explore reawakenings of Jesus among Christian insiders, especially white Protestants. The second, "Reincarnations," proceeds thematically, focusing on rebirths of Jesus in outsider communities, including the black church, the Church of Jesus Christ of Latter-day Saints, and American Judaism, Hinduism, and Buddhism.

The doctrine of the resurrection originated in the Jewish tradition, but it is most commonly associated with Christians, who made Jesus' triumph over death a centerpiece of their liturgy and theology. The resurrection stories in the New Testament describe Jesus appearing in Galilee to Mary Magdalene, Peter, and other members of the nascent Christian community. They interpret his miraculous rising from the dead as evidence of his unique status as the Risen Lord, a status underscored by his glorious ascension to heaven. My first four chapters explore resurrections of this sort—efforts to give Jesus new life inside the Christian community, though this time in the United States. Although the Christians highlighted in these chapters often disagree about just who Jesus is, they all affirm his standing as a unique figure in sacred history. Their Jesus is a New Testament Jesus, and their interpretations arise from a combination of American circumstances and biblical texts. Moreover, because these communities are typically defending public power rather than grasping for it, their reinterpretations of Jesus often support existing social and political arrangements rather than calling them into question.

Reincarnation presents a very different picture of life after death. Common in Asian religions, this doctrine describes the human situation as a cycle of life, death, and rebirth in which the individual soul, after each successive death, seeks out a new body in a new place and time, typically in accordance with the moral theory of karma. The four chapters in this part of the book deal with communities that operate outside the confines of white Protestantism. Most of these communities refuse to bring Jesus to life inside the body of the Church, making a new home for him inside other religions instead. Furthermore, they typically set him alongside (rather than above) other religious virtuosi, rejecting his putative standing as the one-and-only savior of the world. Some of the believers included in these chapters, notably members of black churches and the Church of Jesus Christ of Latter-day Saints, have much in common with the white Protestants emphasized in the first part of the book. They too draw on the New Testament to interpret Jesus, but they rely far more on the Hebrew Bible. As a result, they transport Jesus to worlds that are often as Hebraic as they are Christian. Moreover, their interpretations of Jesus may criticize the dominant culture rather than championing it.

Such an approach to America's Jesus attempts to do justice to both the country's Christian majority and its religious minorities, and to the sacred and secular commitments of its people. Jesus became a major personality in the United States because of the ability of religious insiders to make him culturally inescapable. He became a national icon because outsiders have always felt free to interpret him in their own fashion. To put it another way, while Christian insiders have had the authority to dictate *that* others interpret Jesus, they have not had the authority to dictate *how* these others would do so. In the United States, thinkers from Frederick Douglass and Rabbi Stephen Wise to Swami Yogananda and Malcolm X have boldly distinguished between the religion of Christianity and the religion of Jesus. And while they have rejected the former, they have embraced the latter as their own. Some have been even more audacious, insisting that they understood Jesus better than did the Christians themselves. To be sure, not all Americans went this far. The vast majority of U.S. citizens today are committed Christians. Yet no one group has an interpretive monopoly. Everyone is free to understand Jesus in his or her own way. And Americans have exercised that freedom with wild abandon.

PART ONE

Resurrections

One

ENLIGHTENED SAGE

Thomas Jefferson is revered in the United States today as the author of the Declaration of Independence, the architect of the First Amendment, and one of the saints of American civil religion. Though questions persist regarding his views on race and his relationship with his slave Sally Hemings, he is widely respected nonetheless as one of the nation's great champions of individual freedom. Jefferson's reputation was quite different in his own time. In fact, the country's third president was one of the most polarizing politicians of his day. At the turn of the nineteenth century, you either loved him or you hated him, and for his enemies there was nothing more odious about the man than his unconventional religion (or lack thereof).

New England's ministers denounced Jefferson as an atheist during his failed bid for the presidency in 1796. In his successful 1800 effort to unseat President John Adams, he endured personal attacks that plumbed depths seldom seen in U.S. politics. Jefferson's Federalist opponents smeared him as an idiot and a coward whose antediluvian nostalgia for agrarian life would kill the mercantile economy. But much of the character assassination focused on Jefferson's unusual

faith. According to the Federalists, Jefferson was an infidel and Ja-
cobin whose damnable flirtations with the French goddess of reason
were sure to bring down the country. The election "of a manifest enemy to the religion of Christ, in a Christian nation, would be an awful
symptom of the degeneracy of that nation, and . . . a rebellion against
God," warned the Reverend William Linn, a Dutch Reformed minister from New York. It would "destroy religion, introduce immorality,
and loosen all the bonds of society." Not all the religious politicking
broke the same way, however. Following Jefferson's victory, Abraham
Bishop, a Republican supporter, likened "the illustrious chief, who,
once insulted, now presides over the union" to "him who, once insulted, now presides over the universe." He then compared those who
voted against Jefferson with Jews who refused to accept Jesus as their
Messiah.[1]

Today we know as much about Jefferson's faith as we do about the
faith of any other Revolution-era statesman. In his own time, however, Jefferson's piety was a closely guarded secret. The man who appended to the First Amendment the metaphor of a "wall of separation
between church and state" also believed in a wall of separation between the public and the private, and he relegated religion (religiously, we might say) to the private realm. "Our particular principles
of religion are a subject of accountability to our god alone," Jefferson
wrote in an 1814 letter. "I enquire after no man's, and trouble none
with mine."[2]

This "don't ask, don't tell" policy made it difficult for opponents to
criticize Jefferson for what they suspected was infidelity, so they dug
around for clues in Notes on the State of Virginia (1782), his only published book. There Jefferson attacked religious establishments and
defended religious freedom, arguing in a now-famous passage that "it
does me no injury for my neighbor to say there are twenty gods or no
god. It neither picks my pocket nor breaks my leg." Seizing on this
passage, partisans of Adams insisted that heterodoxy and anarchy
were the closest of kin. "Let my neighbor once persuade himself that
there is no God," Linn fumed, "and he will soon pick my pocket, and
break not only my leg but my neck. If there be no God, there is no
law." A "Christian Federalist," no less alarmed, viewed the prospect of
Jefferson's election as the beginning of the end of his Christian na-

tion. "Can serious and reflecting men look about them and doubt," he wrote, "that if Jefferson is elected, and Jacobins get into authority, that those morals which protect our lives from the knife of the assassin—which guard the chastity of our wives and daughters from seduction and violence—defend our property from plunder and devastation, and shield our religion from contempt and profanation, will not be trampled upon and exploded." Such vituperations did not prevent Jefferson from winning the White House, but they did send Federalists into a postelection frenzy. After a rumor circulated that President Jefferson had decreed a bonfire of the biblical vanities, housewives in New England reportedly squirreled away their scriptures in wells, to prevent them from being burned by the flames of Jeffersonian free thought.[3]

Characteristically, Jefferson refused to reply directly to his critics, but he did organize a defense. In a series of letters to friends such as the Philadelphia physician Benjamin Rush and the British scientist Joseph Priestley, he described his faith in considerable detail. This private correspondence, which includes most famously a "Syllabus of an Estimate on the Merit of the Doctrines of Jesus, Compared with Those of Others" (enclosed in an 1803 letter to Rush), demonstrates that Jefferson may have been, as one biographer has put it, "the most self-consciously theological of all America's presidents."[4] It also illustrates Jefferson's deep devotion to Jesus or, to be more precise, to Jesus' moral teachings, which constituted for Jefferson the essence of true religion. Some interpreters have described these private missives as politically inspired leaks meant to counter criticisms of Jefferson's atheism. That judgment is too harsh. Jefferson probably knew that news of his unorthodox creed would not remain entirely private. But the letters themselves testify eloquently to the sincerity and depth of his Jesus piety.

"THE FIRST OF HUMAN SAGES"

Jefferson (1743–1826) was born and raised an Anglican, and he never formally renounced that connection. But as a boy, he began to question fundamental Anglican tenets, including the doctrine of the Trinity. After immersing himself in theological works by Enlightenment rationalists, he considered jettisoning religion altogether in his late teens. But works by the British Unitarian Joseph Priestley, particularly *An History of the Corruptions of Christianity* (1782), *An History of Early Opinions Concerning Jesus Christ* (1786), and *Socrates and Jesus Compared* (1803), convinced him that he did not have to choose between religion and reason, faith and common sense.

Priestley, whom Jefferson befriended after the scientist-turned-theologian came to the United States from England in 1794, prided himself on approaching religious questions in the light of reason and common sense. He built his theological system, however, on what can only be described as a myth. According to that myth, the religion of Jesus was as simple as it was sublime. It affirmed one God, taught the afterlife, and insisted on moral living. But beginning with Paul and the writers of the Gospels, later Christians hijacked his simple religion, overlaying it with complex dogmas and empty rites. The solution to this problem was to get up a new coup. In the distant past, Christianity had overthrown Jesus; now it was time for partisans of Jesus to overthrow Christianity.

In his private writings on religion, Jefferson followed Priestley closely. He praised Jesus as "meek, benevolent, patient, firm, disinterested, and of the sublimest eloquence," and his system of morals as "the most perfect and sublime that has ever been taught by man." Then he blasted "the corruptions of schismatising followers, who have found an interest in sophisticating and perverting the simple doctrines he taught, by engrafting on them the mysticisms of a Grecian Sophist, frittering them into subtleties, and obscuring them with jargon, until they have caused good men to reject the whole in disgust, and to view Jesus himself as an imposter." Jefferson's list of these corruptions was long, extending to dogmas such as original sin, the virgin birth, the atonement, predestination, salvation by faith, transubstantiation, bodily resurrection, and above all the Trinity. "It is too late in the day," Jefferson wrote in 1813, "for men of sincerity to pretend they believe in the Platonic mysticisms that three are one, and one is three; and yet the one is not three, and the three are not one." The only interests such Trinitarian sophistries served were the interests of entrenched priests and ministers, who played the same villainous role in Jefferson's spiritual world that kings occupied in his republican politics. In an effort "to filch wealth and power to themselves," Jefferson wrote, these tyrants had perverted the pure morals of Jesus into "an engine for enslaving mankind."[5]

The antidote to this illness, Jefferson argued, was a religious revolution as radical as the events of 1776: a repudiation of the spiritual slavery of creeds and rites and a return to the pure, primitive teachings of Jesus. So far this was pure Priestley. But in at least one important respect, Jefferson was more radical than his Unitarian friend. He rejected Priestley's Socinian position that God had empowered Jesus to perform miracles and even to rise from the dead. Miracles, Jefferson insisted, were an affront to the demands of reason and the laws of nature, and Jesus had performed not a one. Jefferson's refusal to view Jesus as a miracle worker might have marked him as a Deist, but his anti-supernaturalism did not detract a whit from his appraisal of Jesus. In fact, if anything, Jefferson heaped more praise upon the man than did his British colleague. Jesus was, in Jefferson's words, "the first of human Sages."[6]

Given his views of the corruptions of the religion of this preeminent sage by Paul and his heirs, it should not be surprising that Jefferson saw the New Testament as corrupt too. Noting that Jesus had written nothing himself, he argued that the Gospels were drafted by "the most unlettered, and ignorant of men." As a result, Jesus' teachings had come down "mutilated, mistated, and often unintelligible." It took a discerning man to dig back through "the metaphysical abstractions of Athanasius, and the maniac ravings of Calvin" to the true teachings of Jesus, but Jefferson saw himself as just the fellow for the job.[7]

JEFFERSON'S RAZOR

On January 20, 1804, Jefferson ordered from a Philadelphia bookseller two copies of the King James Version of the New Testament, each of the same translation and edition. Roughly two weeks later, he received a pair of nearly identical volumes, each published by George Grierson in Dublin in the 1790s. As the sitting president, Jefferson

had plenty of things to do other than read scripture. He had just dou-
bled the size of the United States with the Louisiana Purchase, and
England was at war with France. But somehow he found time to sit
down in the White House with his two Bibles, razor in hand. His goal
was to excise from the New Testament the corruptions of Paul and his
"Platonizing successors," leaving behind a complete record of the simple gospel of Jesus the enlightened sage. So he began to cut the authentic passages out of his Bibles, pasting them into two columns on
46 octavo sheets (the size favored at the time by ministers). The de-
tritus left behind literally fell to the White House floor.

Dividing the biblical wheat from the chaff might have been an impossible task for lesser minds. In fact, a nearly identical effort some
two centuries later by the Jesus Seminar would take hundreds of re-
searchers nearly a decade. But for Jefferson the project took only two
or three evenings (and then only after he had done the correspondence for his day job). In fact, he found the task "obvious and easy";
the true sayings, he later wrote, were "as easily distinguishable as diamonds in a dunghill."[8]

Jefferson called his micro-Testament "The Philosophy of Jesus of
Nazareth" and indicated in a lengthy subtitle that the book was intended "for the use of the Indians unembarrassed with matters of fact
or faith beyond the level of their comprehension." Some have taken
the subtitle literally, imagining that Jefferson compiled the book for
the edification of Native Americans. But the subtitle was really a jab
at his Federalist critics, particularly the ministers of New England
Congregationalism whose unquestioning allegiance to Calvinist com-
plexities blinded them in his view to the simple faith of Jesus. For no
purpose other than self-aggrandizement, these "Pseudo-Christians"
had dressed Jesus up "in the rags of an Imposter." Jefferson's book
stripped off those rags, garbing Jesus once again in the simple robes
of a Galilean sage.[9]

Jefferson did not make plain the principles of inclusion and exclu-
sion he employed to distinguish the voice of Jesus from later corruptions, but they are easy enough to discern. He excised all miracles and
eliminated all legends surrounding Jesus' virgin birth, crucifixion, resurrection, and ascension. In other words, he left on the White House

floor any passage with even a whiff of supernaturalism. What survived was a severely abridged text that, like the apocryphal Gospel of Thomas (not known to Jefferson), consisted entirely of Jesus' sayings. In Jefferson's book, Jesus prayed to God and affirmed the afterlife, but he was not born in a manger and he did not die to atone for anyone's sins. In fact, he did little more than wander around Galilee delivering pithy moral aphorisms. Jefferson characterized "The Philosophy of Jesus of Nazareth" as a "precious morsel of ethics" and it was a thin book.[10] In fact, only about one in ten Gospel verses survived Jefferson's razor.

In 1819 or 1820, Jefferson compiled a second scripture by subtraction, calling it "The Life and Morals of Jesus of Nazareth." Popularly known as the Jefferson Bible, this text is often confused with "The Philosophy of Jesus of Nazareth," in part because it too is a cut-and-paste job and because the earlier book has never been found.[11] But the two Jefferson Bibles are actually quite distinct. In the later work, published by the U.S. Congress in 1904 and now held in the National Museum of American History in the Smithsonian Institution in Washington, D.C., Jefferson again excised passages "of vulgar ignorance, of things impossible, of superstitions, fanaticisms, and fabrications."[12] But this time he included, in addition to the genuine sayings of Jesus, his authentic actions. Unlike "The Philosophy of Jesus of Nazareth," which was executed in English only, "The Life and Morals of Jesus of Nazareth" presented its passages in Greek, Latin, and French as well as English. Finally, while the former effort had been arranged topically, the latter was structured chronologically.

Jefferson's second Bible put some skin on the bare bones of "The Philosophy of Jesus of Nazareth," but it too was a skimpy work. At least to readers familiar with the New Testament, it begins and ends abruptly. Rather than starting, as the Gospel of John does, with Jesus the eternal Word, Jefferson raises his curtain on a political and economic matter: Caesar's decree that all the world should be taxed. He concludes his story with this hybrid verse taken from the Gospels of Matthew and John: "There laid they Jesus, and rolled a great stone to the door of the sepulchre, and departed." Between these scenes, there are no angels, no wise men, and not a hint of the resurrection.

CHRISTIANITY, TRUE AND FALSE

After he completed "The Philosophy of Jesus of Nazareth," Jefferson claimed in correspondence with a friend that his Bible demonstrated his bona fides as a Christian: "It is a document in proof that *I* am a *real Christian*, that is to say, a disciple of the doctrines of Jesus." Earlier he had told Benjamin Rush, "I am a Christian, in the only sense in which he wished any one to be; sincerely attached to his doctrines, in preference to all others; ascribing to himself every human excellence, and believing he never claimed any other." Whether Jefferson really was a Christian has been much debated, both in his time and in ours. Over the last two hundred years, Jefferson has been called an atheist and an infidel, a theist and a Deist, a Unitarian and an Anglican, an Epicurean and a secular humanist. In fact, the list of historical Jeffersons is nearly as long (and creative) as the list of historical Jesuses.[13]

What is most clear about Jefferson's faith is what he was not, and what he was not was a traditional Christian. Jefferson unequivocally rejected the Nicene Creed, which has defined orthodoxy for the overwhelming majority of Christians since 381, as well as the Council of Chalcedon (451) formula of Jesus as "truly God and truly man." He sneered at Calvinist verities such as predestination, which throughout his political career dominated American religious thought, and was particularly contemptuous of the doctrine of the Trinity ("mere Abracadabra" and "hocus-pocus phantasm," he said, distinguishable from paganism "only by being more unintelligible"). The sleight of hand clerics had used to split the one true God into three had also been employed, in Jefferson's view, to substitute the real Christianity of Jesus for the false "Platonic Christianity" of the so-called Christian churches.[14]

Later in U.S. history, thinkers as different as the abolitionist Frederick Douglass and the fundamentalist J. Gresham Machen would draw sharp distinctions between the false Christianity of the churches and the true Christianity of Jesus. In *Narrative of the Life of Frederick Douglass, an American Slave* (1845), Douglass professed his love of "the pure, peaceable, and impartial Christianity of Christ" and his hatred of "the corrupt, slaveholding, women-whipping, cradle-plundering, partial and hypocritical Christianity of this land." He observed a vast gulf dividing the "slaveholding religion" of America from "the Christianity of Christ." In fact, that gulf was "so wide, that to receive the one as good, pure, and holy, is of necessity to reject the other as bad, corrupt, and wicked." Machen, who raged against modernism rather than slavery, drew his line in the sand between the supernaturalistic Christianity of fundamentalism and the naturalistic faith of Protestant modernists (whom he called liberals). These two options were not two different types of Christianity, he argued in *Christianity and Liberalism* (1923), but two entirely different forms of religion. Liberalism, he insisted, was "anti-Christian to the core."[15]

For Jefferson, the choice between genuine Christians and the Platonizing deceivers was equally stark. Anticipating Douglass and Machen, Jefferson claimed to represent real Christianity, dismissing his detractors as imposters peddling a counterfeit faith. Athanasius (the defender of the Nicene Creed) and Calvin were "mere Usurpers of the Christian name, teaching a Counter-religion, made up of the deliria of crazy imaginations, as foreign from Christianity as is that of Mahomet." The nation's Federalist ministers were no better. These "Pseudo-Christians" and "mountebanks," Jefferson fumed, were "the real Anti-Christ."[16]

Jefferson's religious genius was his ability to imagine Jesus apart from historical Christianity. If he had been living in another country, where a powerful religious establishment could define how its key symbols were to be interpreted, Jefferson probably would have rejected both Christianity and Jesus (as so many of his French friends had) and left it at that. But in his America, religious establishments were outlawed at the federal level and moribund in the states. So he was able to imagine a Jesus piety that was not beholden to the churches. "The religion-builders have so distorted and deformed the doctrines of Jesus, so muffled them in mysticisms, fancies and falsehoods, have caricatured them into forms so monstrous and inconcievable, as to drive them rashly to pronounce it's founder an imposter," Jefferson contended.[17] But Jefferson himself would not be duped.

Had they been privy to it, Jefferson's opponents would have denounced such rhetoric (and such chutzpah) as uncharitable and unchristian. So it is with some justification that conservative Christians and secular humanists alike now see the "Virginia Voltaire" as a harbinger of secular America. Yet twenty-first-century America is anything but secular, and Jefferson was a deeply religious man. To be sure, Jefferson was no traditional Christian. But he was no atheist either. In fact, he saw atheism as irrational, and monotheism as the only natural faith. In this respect, he typified not the radical Enlightenment of France but the moderate Enlightenment of his home country. While the freethinker Thomas Paine bragged that he went "through the Bible as a man would go through a wood with an axe on his shoulders and fell trees," Jefferson went through the New Testament with shears and pruning hooks, cutting away the dead wood so the remaining text could live and breathe. True, his rational religion ran in rivulets outside the American mainstream, but heterodoxy is faith of a different form and, like orthodoxy, should be recognized for what it is: a way of being religious. Jefferson has been called an infidel, an atheist, and even the anti-Christ. What he was was a follower of Jesus, or at least of the rational sort of Jesus a leader like Jefferson could follow.[18]

A GREAT MORAL TEACHER

In an 1822 letter to Jefferson, the Unitarian James Smith called Jesus "the most perfect model of Republicanism in the Universe." Jefferson's Jesus was a republican too: a great moral teacher who spread the gospel of liberty, fraternity, and equality across ancient Palestine and, via apostles such as Jefferson, through the United States as well.[19]

To Jefferson, Jesus was a man rather than a god, and he was a man after Jefferson's own heart. "Fear God and love thy neighbor," Jefferson wrote in an 1816 letter, is the "sum of all religion." And so his Jesus was first and foremost an ethical guide. He was not sent by God to die on a cross and atone for humanity's sins. He came not to save, but to teach. Or, he came to save by teaching. Jefferson's Jesus, in short, was an enlightened sage. His moral philosophy was "more pure, correct and sublime than those of the antient philosophers." And nothing in that philosophy contradicted either religion or science.[20]

Because Jesus' understanding of religion was at odds with the religious authorities of his time, he was by necessity a reformer of Judaism as well as a teacher of moral philosophy. While Moses had worshiped "a being of terrific character, cruel, vindictive, capricious and unjust," Jesus worshiped a God of "wisdom, justice, goodness." While Moses ignored the afterlife, "Jesus inculcated that doctrine with emphasis and precision." While Moses "had bound the Jews to many idle ceremonies, mummeries and observances," Jesus "exposed their futility and insignificance," shifting the locus of true religion from rites to ethics, acts to intentions. This "great Reformer of the Hebrew code" also proved himself the superior of Moses in his preaching of "universal philanthropy." Rejecting the parochialism of the chosen people ideal, he demanded that we offer our love "not only to kindred and friends, to neighbors and countrymen, but to all mankind," insisting that all human beings were part of "one family, under the bonds of love, charity, peace, common wants, and common aids."[21]

Everyone reads the Bible selectively, employing a "canon within the canon," which emphasizes certain books and passages while neglecting others. The tendency of evangelical Christians, who accept the entire Bible as the Word of God, to emphasize the New Testament over the Old is well known—the religious equivalent of the major league pitcher who rarely ventures over the inside half of home plate. But you don't have to be an evangelical to wear out some pages of the Bible without cracking others. Liberation theologians prefer the prophetic books over the Psalms, and Luke over John; fundamentalists focus on the Passion and Revelation more than Exodus and Leviticus. Jefferson's "canon within the canon" consisted of the Gospels, principally the synoptic accounts of Matthew, Mark, and Luke. Inside those books, Jefferson emphasized the sayings of Jesus. And among those sayings, his favorites came from the Sermon on the Mount.

Jefferson once received a letter containing a sermon called "What Think Ye of Christ?" His coy reply described one possible answer to that question, but that answer was clearly his own. Jesus, Jefferson wrote, was "the Herald of truths reformatory of the religions of mankind in general, but more immediately of that of his own countrymen, impressing them with more sublime and more worthy ideas of the Supreme being, teaching them the doctrine of a future state of rewards and punishments, and inculcating the love of mankind." The marrow of his teaching, Jefferson added, could be found in the Sermon on the Mount, which he characterized as "the stamp of genuine Christianity."[22]

Though remembered today as a champion of the separation of church and state, Jefferson shared with virtually all of his contemporaries the view that no society could survive without a shared system of morality, and that "no System of morality however pure it might be" could survive "without the sanction of divine authority stampt upon it." But his profession of faith was not merely pragmatic—a bone tossed to the masses to keep them from growling. Jefferson was convinced of the existence of God by the argument from design, which affirmed that the universe, so exquisitely crafted, must have sprung from the mind of an intelligent designer. He was also convinced that God had stamped Jesus' character with his divine imprimatur. Jesus, Jefferson confessed, was "the most innocent, the most benevolent the most eloquent and sublime character that has ever been exhibited to man."[23]

In 1812, Monticello's sage heeded Jesus' admonition to love one's enemies when he reconciled with his longtime political foe John Adams. Soon the two men were exchanging a remarkable series of letters on a wide range of topics, religion included. In one telling exchange, Adams wrote wryly of his wish that Jefferson might live until he became a Calvinist, and Jefferson responded that, if granted, such a wish would make him immortal. Calvin, Jefferson added, "was indeed an Atheist, which I can never be; or rather his religion was Daemonism. If ever man worshipped a false god, he did."[24]

Adams worshipped no such God. Like Priestley, he was a Unitarian, and he corresponded with Jefferson while the Unitarian Controversy of the early nineteenth century was at its height. That controversy, which ran from 1804 until the establishment of the American Unitarian Association in 1825, touched on the doctrine of the Trinity, but centered on human nature. While traditionalists affirmed Calvin's dogma of the total depravity of human beings, Unitarians defended the more optimistic view that human beings were essentially good. Jefferson followed this controversy closely, and he was solidly in the anti-Calvinist camp. In an 1818 letter thanking a

New Hampshire congressman for sending him pamphlets related to that debate, Jefferson aligned himself with the reformers. After praising the Unitarians for continuing the "half reformation" of Christianity begun in the sixteenth century, he expressed his hope that the recovery of "the plain and unsophisticated precepts of Christ" begun by German Reformers would be completed by American Unitarians. Three years later, Jefferson received from Thomas Pickering, a onetime Federalist foe, a copy of the definitive statement of American Unitarianism, William Ellery Channing's 1819 discourse on "Unitarian Christianity." One year after that a Unitarian physics professor named Benjamin Waterhouse wrote Jefferson about the Unitarian Controversy. In his reply to Waterhouse, Jefferson provided this succinct summary of the Jeffersonian creed:

1. That there is one God, and he all-perfect.
2. That there is a future state of rewards and punishments.
3. That to love God with all thy heart, and thy neighbor as thyself, is the sum of religion.

He then closed by prophesying that "there is not a *young man* now living in the U.S. who will not die an Unitarian."[25]

Unitarians have pointed to this passage in an effort to prove that Jefferson was one of their own. Others have read the letter, particularly its threefold creed, as quintessentially Deistic. In his private writings, Jefferson repeatedly affirmed his belief in a nominal religion that distilled true religion down to God, the afterlife, and moral living. Deists typically invoked this same holy trinity, so there is some justification for aligning Jefferson with them. Yet in his writings on religion, Jefferson repeatedly, even obsessively, invoked the name of Jesus, something Deists were generally loath to do. Surely Jefferson was closer to Deism than he was to atheism, but he was closer still to Unitarianism. If Jefferson were to wander today into a Unitarian Universalist church—the American Unitarian Association merged with the Universalist Church of America to form the Unitarian Universalist Association in 1961—he would no doubt be greeted with open arms, though he would likely be one of the most theologically conservative people in the pews. But Jefferson was not exactly a standard-issue Unitarian, since he rejected the miracles, which those "supernatural rationalists" affirmed.[26]

Toward the end of his life, Jefferson wrote, "I am of a sect by myself, as far as I know."[27] This is a wonderfully American conceit, and it has been repeated by multitudes, among them Ralph Waldo Emerson, Henry Adams, and generations of post-sixties undergraduates. But like most conceits it has a lie in it. Jefferson did not feel comfortable labeling himself a Unitarian for the same reason he did not call himself a Baptist or an Episcopalian. According to his own meticulous account books, Jefferson contributed regularly to religious causes, including $200 to the building of an Episcopal church, $60 for a Presbyterian church, and $25 for a Baptist church in one year alone. From a strictly economic perspective, these figures may prove that Jefferson was more of an Episcopalian than a Presbyterian, and even less of a Baptist. Yet they demonstrate as well that Jefferson saw denominational infidelity as a virtue, not a vice.

Though surely something of a religious independent, Jefferson was first and foremost a partisan of Jesus. And in that party he had many fellow travelers. Yes, Jefferson was unfaithful to traditional Christianity, and he was to that extent an infidel. But his infidelity to traditional Christianity was motivated by his admiration of Jesus, whose moral teachings were to Jefferson as self-evidently true as the proposition that all men are created equal.

THE JESUS SEMINAR

Jefferson's legacy in American religion is at least as long as it is in American politics. More than anyone else, Jefferson was responsible for setting the ground rules for religious practice in the United States. His commitment to voluntarism, enshrined today in the First Amendment, transformed his nation into the world's most Christianized country. But it also opened that country to the religious diversity we see today.

Though Jefferson kept his religious views largely to himself, his understanding of Jesus as an enlightened sage spread as the nation expanded, most notably among Unitarians, Reform Jews, and liberal

Protestants. By the end of the nineteenth century, many Americans, both Christian and otherwise, had begun to disentangle Jesus from rites and creeds, affirming that his exemplary life was more important than his atoning death. Today, U.S. suburbs are filled with "Golden Rule Christians" who, like Jefferson, believe that the essence of true religion lies in right living rather than right thinking, and that service to others is the highest form of prayer.[28]

Jefferson's influence is particularly apparent in the case of the Jesus Seminar, which conveyed Jefferson's Jesus into the twenty-first century. Like Jefferson himself, the Jesus Seminar is quintessentially American. Its method is democratic, its goal is freedom, and its obsession is Jesus. The animating spirit of this group, which first met in Berkeley, California, in March 1985, is the renegade New Testament scholar and self-styled agent provocateur Robert Funk. A one-time child evangelist and Bible college student from rural Texas, Funk turned from preaching the gospel to researching its origins while still a young man. After receiving his Ph.D. from Vanderbilt University, he taught New Testament at a series of institutions, published a grammar of Hellenistic Greek, and served as president of the Society for Biblical Literature, the leading professional association for Bible scholars. By his own account, he grew tired of the insular world of New Testament scholarship and its jargon-filled journals. He watched in horror as the Reverend Jerry Falwell and other "televangelists" helped to elect Ronald Reagan president in 1980, and was dismayed when his religious studies colleagues remained as mum as Trappists while the Christian Right attempted to draft Jesus as a Reagan Republican. All the while, Funk longed for a broader audience for his work. And with the Jesus Seminar, he found it.

Though no friend of modern-day Republicans, Funk described the Jesus Seminar in the rhetoric of classical republicanism. Its quest for Jesus was a "quest for freedom," and it had three different emancipations in mind. The first was to free the real Jesus of history from the fetters of traditional Christian creeds—to enable Jesus to be himself rather than playing the roles forced upon him by Peter or Paul or the writers of the Nicene Creed. A second aim was to liberate the real Jesus from the chains of born-again mythology. "There are thousands, perhaps millions, of Americans who are the victims of a mythical Jesus conjured up by modern evangelists to whip their followers into a frenzy of guilt and remorse—and cash contributions," Funk declared. "I have a residual hankering to free my fellow human beings from that bondage, which can be as abusive as any form of slavery known to humankind." Finally, the Seminar sought to free Jesus from the cloistered confines of the academy, by bringing cutting-edge research about him to the attention of the mass media.[29]

In the drama that was the Jesus Seminar, Funk played Abraham Lincoln and Robin Hood, casting his Fellows as Union soldiers and
. Merry Men. Together they would emancipate Americans from their slavish devotion to dogmatic Christianity, and transfer the riches of biblical scholarship from the Ivory Tower to ordinary Americans. In the process, the false Christs of Catholic creeds and the Christian Right would give way to the real Jesus of history. The result, Funk claimed, would be nothing less than a "new reformation" and a "new gospel." Jesus would be born again on American soil.[30]

·Although Funk described his project in revolutionary terms, it was really more of a revival of the spirit of the Enlightenment philosophes, who began in the eighteenth century to apply their beloved precepts of reason and common sense to the study of the Bible. Das Leben Jesu (1835) by the German theologian David Friedrich Strauss and Vie de Jésus (1863) by the French skeptic Ernest Renan popularized this approach, prompting the first quest for the historical Jesus that occupied many European scholars, most of them liberal Protestants. In 1909, the Irish Catholic writer George Tyrrell evaluated their contributions, observing that whenever liberal Protestants tried to dig down the well of Catholic history to the real Jesus they succeeded only in finding their own reflections. "Whatever Jesus was," Tyrrell demurred, "he was in no sense a Liberal Protestant."[31]

Such criticisms suspended the hunt for the historical Jesus for roughly a half a century, until the discovery of the Dead Sea Scrolls in the late 1940s prompted a second search, announced most prominently in A New Quest of the Historical Jesus (1959) by James M. Robinson, now professor emeritus at Claremont Graduate University. Chastened by Tyrell's skepticism—and by similar criticisms from the German scholar Albert Schweitzer—the scholars in this "New Quest" (mostly German and American Protestants) did not attempt to construct a complete biography of Jesus. Instead they focused on comparing what little they could know about the historical Jesus with what the Church proclaimed about the living Christ. The New Quest came to an end in the early 1970s as the existential philosophy and neo-orthodox theology that pervaded Jesus research in this period went out of fashion. What Funk and the Jesus Seminar helped to get going in the 1980s was, therefore, a third quest. By the time they started searching for the historical Jesus, the hunt had been on for over a century, and they were stalking old prey.

Still, the Jesus Seminar was not entirely imitative. Two things distinguished its work from earlier quests. First, it was an American rather than a European enterprise. Ernest Renan was French and David Strauss was German, as was Rudolph Bultmann, the famed "demythologizer" whose interest in existentialism inspired the second quest. Funk, by contrast, is an American, as are almost all of his Seminar's Fellows. The second distinguishing mark of the Jesus Seminar was its obsession with publicity. Nineteenth-century "lives of Jesus" sold well, and many were controversial. But Strauss and Renan came by their notoriety honestly—by accident. Funk, by contrast, courted controversy like a lover. Instead of simply denying the virgin birth, he called Jesus a "bastard messiah." Instead of saying the parables were witty as well as wise, he said Jesus was "the first Jewish stand-up comic." Funk believed that Jesus was an iconoclast, and he too wanted to stir the pot. So when rumors began to circulate in the midnineties that Paul Verhoeven, the director of Basic Instinct and Showgirls (and a Seminar Fellow), was planning a feature film based on the group's findings, Funk did nothing to still the storm.[32]

The first project of the Seminar took six years and focused on the sayings of Jesus. Fellows read and debated papers concerning both canonical and non-canonical sayings. Then they voted to determine what Jesus really said. Voting on the sayings of Jesus requires considerable chutzpah, but the way the Seminar voted was particularly provocative. Fellows were not asked for a simple yea or nay. They were instructed instead to cast one of four colored beads into a ballot box. They were to choose red if "Jesus said it or something very close to it" and pink if "Jesus probably said something like it, although his words have suffered in transmission." The two final alternatives were

gray ("These are not his words, but the ideas are close to his own")
and black ("Jesus did not say it; the words represent the Christian
community or a later point of view").[33]

THE JESUS WARS

The Jesus Seminar was designed to provoke, and provoke it did. It
presented Jesus as a "subversive sage" who defied not only the religious authorities of his day but also the expectations of contemporary
Christians. Its Jesus did not claim to be either God or the Messiah.
And he did not recite the Lord's Prayer or deliver the Sermon on the
Mount. More at home in the Greek forum than the Jewish synagogue,
he was essentially an oracle of moral wisdom, a sage more important
for what he said than for what he did. And what he said was to a
great extent what Thomas Jefferson put into his mouth two centuries ago.

Many Christians were astounded that anyone would be presumptuous enough to vote a single saying of Jesus out of the Word of God.
Others objected to the Seminar's findings rather than its methods.
"Who was Jesus?" asked one Letter to the Editor. "I'll stand by the
Bible's answer. Isaiah 9:6 describes him: 'Wonderful Counselor,
Mighty God, Eternal Father, Prince of Peace.' No liberal think tank
can improve on this truth." Another letter writer wrote, "Rather than
make Jesus conform to pop culture, let's accept him as who God said
he was: his son."[34]

The sharpest attacks came from New Testament scholars, whose
railing against the Seminar's methods and assumptions helped touch
off the Jesus Wars of the 1990s. Boston University's Howard Clark
Kee called the Seminar "an academic disgrace" hell-bent on finding a
Jesus "free of such features, embarrassing to modern intellectuals, as
demons, miracles and predictions about the future." The Reverend
Carl Henry, an evangelical theologian, objected to the Seminar's
methods. "You don't settle scholarly issues," he said, "by democratic
vote." Another evangelical, the Asbury Theological Seminary professor
Ben Witherington III, called the Jesus Seminar to task for obsessing
on the teachings, not the Teacher. Rather than a crucified Savior, he

argued, the Seminar offers a comic "Talking Head" who "seems a much better candidate for a late-night visit with David Letterman or Jay Leno" than for crucifixion on Golgotha. In 1994, a group calling itself the Fellowship of Merry Christians gave the Jesus Seminar its Scrooge Award, presented annually to the group "whose humbug most insistently dampens the Spirit of Christmas at Christmastime."[35]

Perhaps the most serious critique was that the Jesus Seminar was plumping for a non-Jewish Jesus. Birger A. Pearson, a New Testament professor at University of California at Santa Barbara, argued that the Seminar was "driven by an ideology of secularization" that caused it to overlook a whole generation of scholarship on the Jewishness of Jesus. The result was an ahistorical and anachronistic Jesus, divorced from Jewish practice. "To put it metaphorically," Pearson wrote, "the Seminar has performed a forcible epispasm on the historical Jesus, a surgical procedure removing the marks of his circumcision."[36]

As fundamentalists and scholars fumed, the media took it all in, covering Seminar votes like presidential primaries and the mayhem that ensued like a heavyweight prize fight. "Lord's Prayer Isn't His," ran one New York Times headline, while Lingua Franca called its sardonic feature on the group "Away with the Manger." In 1993, a group of ministers in Gary, Indiana, were so incensed by a piece on the Jesus Seminar published in their local newspaper that they burned copies in protest.

Media coverage only intensified as the Seminar racked up its findings, and it reached a crescendo in 1993 with the publication of The Five Gospels: The Search for the Authentic Words of Jesus. This "red-letter edition" of the four canonical Gospels plus the apocryphal Gospel of Thomas became a bestseller, and put Funk and the Jesus Seminar on the map. In earlier Bibles of this sort, all the sayings of Jesus appeared in red. This book printed those same sayings in either red, pink, gray, or black, depending on the votes they had received in the Seminar. Only 18 percent of the reputed sayings of Jesus received the coveted red or pink ratings; the remaining 82 percent were deemed inauthentic (gray or black). At least in these Gospels, Jesus did not say "I am the way, the truth, and the life" (though thanks to a new colloquial translation called the Scholars Version he did say "damn"). In fact, in the Gospel of John, where the "I am" sayings appear, Jesus said nothing at all. Not one of the sayings attributed to him by John received a red rating.

Beginning in 1991, the Jesus Seminar turned from the sayings of Jesus to his actions. Just as the "What Would Jesus Do?" craze was building among young evangelicals, the Seminar posed the same question in a more scholarly fashion. Members heard papers on 176 different events described in the Bible, and voted on the authenticity of each. Ultimately they determined that Jesus did even less than he said. Out of all the events the Fellows considered, only 29 (16 percent of the total) received red or pink ratings. According to *The Acts of Jesus: What Did Jesus Really Do?* (1998), which reported on this second phase of the Seminar's work, Jesus was not born in Bethlehem, did not walk on water, and was not raised from the dead. In a final coup de grace, the Fellows even doubted the story of doubting Thomas.

Funk has described himself as a revolutionary, and he may be. But he is also a foot soldier in a campaign begun two centuries ago by Jefferson. In fact, when seen in the light of Jefferson's bibles, the work of the Jesus Seminar looks like a tortured second draft. Like Jefferson, Funk and his Fellows produced a volume on the sayings of Jesus, then moved on to a volume on his sayings and actions. They too crafted their Jesus largely by subtraction, whittling away all extraneous material from the biblical block in an effort to reveal the real Jesus within.

Their Jesus was a cross between a 1770s philosophe and a 1970s hippie: He was an enlightened sage, but a groovy one. According to the *Acts of Jesus*, Jesus was no desert ascetic. In fact, he was a "socially promiscuous" "urban partygoer" who loved a good wedding and could eat, drink, and carouse with the best of them. Funk's Fellows "admonished themselves repeatedly to be wary of finding a Jesus that is entirely congenial or congruent with the interests and concerns of the present age." They aimed at scrupulous objectivity and historical accuracy. But most of them came of age either during the Beat movement of the fifties or the youth movement of the sixties, and as a group they were not able to escape the penumbra of countercultural icons such as Jack Kerouac and Timothy Leary. They called Jesus a "subversive sage," and while they borrowed the noun from the Enlightenment they stole the adjective from the counterculture. Their gospel was reminiscent of Kerouac's roman à clef *On the Road*, and their Jesus seemed possessed by the spirit of Kerouac's bad-boy hero Neal Cassady. Like Cassady (and Kerouac for that matter), he was a "social deviant," "troublemaker," and "non-conformist" who quit his job and disrespected his mother only to take up with an "entourage of undesirables" "on the road." He preferred to hang out with "the lowly, the poor, the undeserving, the sinner, the social misfits, the marginalized, the humble"—the same people the Beats romanticized as the *fellaheen*. More poet than prophet, more iconoclast than icon, he was a Dharma Bum of the Galilean variety. No wonder his mother thought he was mad.[37]

Funk called his Jesus "irreligious, irreverent, and impious"—a "secular sage." He also admitted that the Seminar offered "a wholly secular account of the Christian faith." But his agenda was more than strictly intellectual, and when he says he is on a "spiritual trek" it is hard not to take him at his word. Clearly Funk has moved far beyond what he calls the "secondhand faith" of his born-again youth, but he has not traded that in for secondhand secularity.[38]

Funk's rhetoric has the ring of the "Death of God" theology of the early 1960s, and his first book, published in 1966, plainly engages with that approach to theology. In that same year, in *Radical Theology and the Death of God*, Thomas Altizer and William Hamilton put a modern spin on the ancient doctrine of *kenosis*, or the self-emptying of Jesus in the incarnation. What kenosis really signifies, they argued, is that God has emptied himself of transcendence so that Jesus can become fully immanent in the world. At least for Altizer and Hamilton, this radical reinterpretation of the incarnation abolished the distinction between the sacred and the profane, freeing Jesus to be fully human and allowing Christians to celebrate life in the world as he did—wholeheartedly and without reservation. In *Honest to Jesus*, Funk speaks of "giving Jesus a demotion" and emptying him of his iconic status. His purpose, however, is not so much to secularize Jesus as to invest him with new spiritual import. The "creedal Christ" must die, Funk argues, so that the real Jesus can rise again. Funk's effort to liberate Jesus from the shackles of creeds, clergy, and churches seems to be an effort to liberate himself as well. His post-resurrection Jesus, like the Jesus of Altizer and Hamilton, encourages everyone "to celebrate life, to suck the marrow out of existence, to explore, and probe, and experiment, to venture into uncharted seas, without fear of a tyrannical and vindictive God."[39]

Funk has posted on his Web site "Twenty-one Theses" that beg to be compared to the 95 theses against indulgences that Martin Luther reportedly nailed to the door of Castle Church in Wittenberg in 1517. "The God of the metaphysical age is dead," Funk's manifesto begins. It then dismisses original sin, miracles, the virgin birth, the atonement, the resurrection, and the Second Coming of Jesus. It is hard to know what to make of this "Coming Radical Reformation." Surely the rhetoric is part provocation, part publicity. But it is difficult to read Funk's work without seeing hope and faith behind it too. Funk does reject most of the traditional beliefs and practices of traditional Christianity. He denies Jesus miracle-making power. He cuts the Gospels down to a sliver of themselves. Yet he does all that in the service of faith (an alternative faith, to be sure, but faith nonetheless). Although Funk talks of giving Jesus a demotion, his "new gospel" is radically Jesus-centric, focusing squarely on the historical Jesus and the spiritual liberation he promised. Christianity is "anemic and wasting away," he writes. But this former child evangelist is not trying to euthanize it. In fact, he is hoping to shake it back to life, by redirecting Christians to the pure, primitive teachings of Jesus himself.[40]

Funk might have dedicated The Five Gospels to Kerouac (or, as one critic recommended, to P. T. Barnum), but he did not. He dedicated it instead to three fellow revolutionaries: Galileo, "who altered our view of the heavens forever"; David Friedrich Strauss, "who pioneered the quest of the historical Jesus"; and Thomas Jefferson, "who took scissors and paste to the gospels."[41] Of these three, the real spirit animating the Jesus Seminar was Jefferson, who, nearly two hundred years before Funk's Fellows first gathered, had declared his independence not only from George III and England but also from the irrational creeds and empty rites of historical Christianity. Like Strauss and other pioneering Bible scholars, Jefferson approached the New Testament with skepticism. But he produced "The Philosophy of Jesus of Nazareth" before Strauss was even born. Though he was not a trained Bible critic, he was America's first real scholar of the Bible, and the first U.S. citizen to go on a quest for the historical Jesus.

JESUS NATION

Thomas Jefferson's influence on American religion can be overstated. His theological views, unorthodox upon his death in 1825, remain unorthodox today; the overwhelming majority of Americans are now Christians who affirm the creedal view of their Savior as fully divine and fully human. Nonetheless, they have inherited from Jefferson a strategy for understanding Jesus and Christianity that continues to drive religious change, from both the left and the right.

That strategy begins with a bold refusal. It starts when a religious reformer refuses to equate Jesus with the Christian tradition. The religion *of* Jesus, the reformer asserts, is not the same as the religion *about* Jesus; and what really matters is what Jesus did and taught. The second step is to isolate certain beliefs or practices in the Christian tradition as unreasonable or antiquated or immoral. The next step is to use the cultural authority of Jesus to denounce those beliefs or practices as contrary to true Christianity—to call for religious reform. As these alternative understandings gain ground, Jesus is gradually unmoored from the beliefs, practices, and institutions that in the past had restricted his freedom of movement. He loses no authority among the traditionalists, who continue to see him as they had, but he gains authority among the innovators. As his authority expands, Christians are all the more likely to champion reforms in his name, and the cycle repeats itself over and over again.

But this dynamic does not operate merely inside the Church. It operates inside American culture as well. Non-Christians too can isolate Christian beliefs and practices for criticism, and enlist the authority of Jesus against them. And they need not stop there. In fact, many press on, employing Jesus against Christianity itself. The true religion of Jesus, they argue, was not Christianity at all. It was Judaism. Or Hinduism. Or Buddhism. Or maybe the true religion of Jesus wasn't religion at all. Maybe Jesus was an agnostic or even an atheist. In this way, Jesus is disentangled not just from certain Christian beliefs and practices, but from Christianity (and, in some cases, religion) itself.

This strategy too feeds on itself in a grand cycle, as each time it succeeds Jesus acquires more cultural authority.

It is certainly possible to see Jefferson's faith, which says no to Christianity but yes to Jesus, as an enigma, to view Jefferson, who has been called the "American Sphinx," as a paradox not only on race but also on religion.[42] Yet Jeffersonian religion is not paradoxical at all. In fact, it represents an impulse that courses through American religious history and is with us today. Jefferson hated what Christianity had become, not despite his love of Jesus, but because of it. And he was able to admire, respect, and perhaps even love "the first of all Sages" only because he was able to separate the religion of Jesus from the religion of Christianity. Jefferson was not of a sect by himself. Millions of Americans today, Christian and otherwise, harbor similar sentiments. In this sense, Jefferson was a Founding Father not only of the United States of America but also of today's Jesus nation.

Two

SWEET SAVIOR

In the United States today, virtually all Christians are Jesus people. The connection between Jesus devotion and Christian faith is unmistakable at evangelical revivals, where new believers answer altar calls by accepting Jesus as their personal Savior and Lord. It is also clear among liberal Protestants and Catholics, who express their devotion to Jesus by caring for the poor and the needy. In fact, Jesus is so closely allied with Christianity that it is hard to imagine a form of the religion that does not revere him as the Alpha and Omega of the faith. But American Christianity has not always been a Jesus faith, and the United States has not always been a Jesus nation.

Christianity was not particularly popular in the New World colonies. Spiritual indifference was the rule in seventeenth-century Virginia, Maryland, New York, New Jersey, Delaware, and North and South Carolina. In all these places, churchgoers were rare and churches scarce. Many babies went unbaptized, and children uncatechized. Quaker Pennsylvania was more pious, and Congregational New England more pious still. But even in New England towns, membership rates varied considerably—from more than two-thirds of adults to less than a fifth. Moreover, the piety of New Englanders waxed and waned, leading late-seventeenth-century divines such as Increase and Cotton Mather to lament a declension of Christian belief and practice from the heady days of John Winthrop's vision of the New World as a spiritual "city upon a hill." The celebrated Great Awakening of the 1740s powerfully reversed that decline in many locales, but its revivals were not as widespread as many historians have claimed. As Jon Butler has observed, the revivals that ·burned over Massachusetts, Connecticut, Rhode Island, Pennsylvania, New Jersey, and Virginia largely bypassed New Hampshire, Maryland, and Georgia, and were lukewarm at best in New York, Delaware, and the Carolinas. On the eve of the Revolution, only 17 percent of adults were church members, and spiritual lethargy was the rule.[1]

Even church members were relatively uninterested in Jesus. Of course, not all Christians thought alike. Congregationalism predominated in New England and Anglicanism in Virginia, while Maryland was established by a Roman Catholic and Pennsylvania was celebrated (and despised) for its tolerance of dissenters. Nonetheless, there was a reigning theological school. According to Sydney Ahlstrom, "Puritanism provided the moral and religious background of fully 85 percent of the people who declared their independence in 1776." And for the Puritans Jesus was at best a marginal figure.[2]

Puritanism emerged out of the Calvinist wing of the Protestant Reformation, and its distinctive beliefs and practices were at least as Hebraic as they were Christian. For generations, New World Puritans sang nothing but a cappella versions of the Old Testament Psalms in their congregational worship. Their covenant theology took its cues from Israel more than Galilee, focusing not on the individual's relationship with God the Son but on the community's covenant with God the Father. In 1827 Ralph Waldo Emerson would famously describe his time as "the age of the first person singular."[3] Puritans lived in a world of the first person plural.

During the Great Awakening, Jesus hymns by the Calvinist Isaac Watts and the Methodist Charles Wesley won acceptance in isolated congregations, and some pro-revival preachers began to focus more on Jesus. John Wesley (Charles's brother and Methodism's transatlantic powerhouse) preached a strikingly modern form of Jesus piety, which he derived from the hymns of German Moravians about Jesus the Suffering Servant. But Wesley's heart-to-heart connection with "Christ and him crucified" was by no means popular, and George Whitefield, the "Grand Itinerant" of the age, was a staunch Calvinist. Few colonists saw Jesus as a person who could be understood or who might understand them. Few loved him and expected love in return. Most could not even conceive of imitating him. Colonial sermons referred to Christ regularly, of course, but in them he remained more an abstract principle than a concrete person. Jonathan Edwards, the theological dynamo linking Puritanism and evangelicalism, came closer than most Puritan thinkers to the sort of intimate Jesus piety that characterizes American churches today, referring on occasion to Jesus as a "friend." But as Nancy F. Cott has noted, the term *friendship* at the time often connoted, simply, kinship. And even Edwards seemed to get along quite well without a lot of Jesus talk.[4]

The Puritans, in short, were a God-fearing rather than a Jesus-loving people, obsessed not with God's mercy but with His glory, not with the Son but with the Father. The logic of Puritan theology turned on what the theologian Karl Barth, in *The Epistle to the Romans*, would later describe as an "infinite, qualitative distinction" between a righteous God and sinful humanity.[5] In that system, there was some space for Christ, though that space was carefully circumscribed. He was the incarnate God who came to earth to suffer and die on the cross in order to reconcile the sinful elect to his angry Father. He was also technically a person—the second of three persons in the godhead, according to the doctrine of the Trinity. But naming is different from being, and in the colonial period, Christ was a person in name only.

All that began to change in the half century after the Revolution. During this defining era in American religious history, the spiritual landscape in the United States started to take the shape we see today. Following the ratification of the First Amendment in 1791, religion became a matter of individual choice rather than federal mandate. Though state establishments lingered as late as 1833, when the Congregational standing order finally came to an end in Massachusetts, they were shadows of their former selves. Disestablishment supplanted the European-style state church system with a market model that continues to characterize American religion. This new spiritual marketplace produced unprecedented religious creativity and intense religious competition.

Historians now debate when the United States first exhibited real religious diversity. Some see it as a recent development—a consequence of the opening of immigration from Asia in 1965. Others track it to colonial times, particularly to the middle colonies, where Dutch Mennonites and German Baptists mixed with French Huguenots and black Anglicans. But American religion really confronted diversity—and took its current shape—during the first decades of the nineteenth century, a period William Hutchison has described as the "Great Diversification." According to Hutchison, 95 percent of Europeans in the colonies were at least nominally Protestant and 90 percent traced their heritage to the Calvinist wing of the Reformation. Eighty-five percent were *"English speaking* Calvinist Protestants." After the Revolution, and particularly after the turn of the nineteenth century, the demographics changed dramatically. As the frontier opened to the west, immigration from Europe skyrocketed, driving the U.S. population up from 3 million in 1790 to 13 million in 1850. This time the new arrivals came from the Continent as well as England, and now there were Lutherans in the mix.[6]

This period also witnessed the first great influx of non-Protestant immigrants. The U.S. Jewish community remained small but expanded considerably in proportion to the overall population. Roman Catholics arrived in what appeared to worried Protestants to be a tidal wave. In 1800, there were about fifty thousand Catholics in the United States. Over the next half century, the Catholic community expanded five times faster than the general population, hitting at least a million, or roughly 5 percent of all Americans, by 1850.[7]

Along with these transplanted European religions, Americans cultivated a variety of homegrown hybrids. In the 1830s, the Transcendentalists split from the Unitarians, insisting on the sovereignty of the individual soul, the sacredness of the wild, and the truths of Asian religions. During that same decade, the Disciples of Christ formed in an attempt to restore Christianity to its pre-creedal purity, vowing to speak "where the Scriptures speak" and to remain silent "where the Scriptures are silent." One decade later, Spiritualists began to harken to messages from the dead. Meanwhile, utopians were establishing more than one hundred different intentional communities during the first half of the nineteenth century, including the Church of Jesus Christ of Latter-day Saints (the Mormons), far and away the most popular of these "American originals."[8]

Across these diverse religious communities, a new spirit of liberty took hold. After their successful revolt against England, Americans thought nothing about rebelling against traditional Christianity. For obvious reasons, they rebuffed the Anglicanism of the crown, sending what came to be known as Episcopalianism on a long downward slide. Peace churches such as the Quakers, Mennonites, and Moravians also suffered after the war. Americans did far more than reject the denominations of loyalists and pacifists, however. Inspired by republican rhetoric of liberty and equality, and by a popular revolt against deference and hierarchy, they rejected as well the authority of ministers, the veracity of creeds, and the importance of theology. The Bible remained authoritative, of course, but now Americans insisted on interpreting it for themselves. In that effort, they were assisted by a new culture hero: the populist preacher, who combined evangelicalism and egalitarianism in daring new ways. As Nathan Hatch has argued in *The Democratization of American Christianity*, these religious entrepreneurs thrilled their populist parishioners with declarations of religious independence from elitist ministers, established churches, and outmoded creeds. Not surprisingly, this new combination of individual conscience and populist preaching led to a wide variety of interpretations, and First Amendment guarantees of religious freedom saw to it that those interpretations flourished.

Not everyone embraced what disestablishment had wrought. Frances Trollope, who sojourned to the United States in the 1820s and described her misadventures in *Domestic Manners of the Americans* (1832), was unimpressed. "The almost endless variety of religious factions," she lamented, had "the melancholy effect of exposing all religious ceremonies to contempt." This chaotic situation confirmed her already sturdy faith in the benefits of religious establishment (particularly of the Anglican variety), yet one did not have to be British to despair over the situation. Many Americans worried that their new nation seemed destined to divide into religious factions.

This concern quickened as the frontier and the market economy expanded, stimulating unprecedented geographical and social mobility and making the early republic, in Hatch's terms, "the most centrifugal epoch in American church history."[9]

THE EVANGELICAL CENTURY

What spun out of this centrifuge, however, was Christianization rather than chaos. Americans indulged their new religious freedom not by becoming freethinkers or Deists, but by embracing Christianity with a passion rarely seen in the colonies. This new spiritual vigor was most visible on the landscape, where church spires arose alongside factories and farms. The number of Baptist congregations ballooned nearly twentyfold from 497 in 1776 to 9,375 in 1850. Methodist growth was even more explosive, leaping from only 65 congregations to 13,280 over the same period. Somehow a country that was wrestling for the first time with radical religious diversity was also Christianizing its people.

Though it was difficult for early Americans to find a religious center amidst the swirl, in hindsight it is clear that during the first third of the nineteenth century a new breed of Protestants seized center stage. As the new nation embraced Christianity, a new style of Jesus-friendly Christianity emerged as the country's unofficial religious establishment, dominating American religious life into the Civil War. Tocqueville called this new style "democratic and republican religion."[10] We now call it evangelicalism, and by the 1830s its unique combination of enthusiasm and egalitarianism, revivalism and republicanism, biblicism and common sense had come to dominate the private and public lives of most Americans. The Presbyterians, the Congregationalists, and the Disciples of Christ were all evangelicals. So were many African Americans, who embraced Christianity en masse for the first time during late-eighteenth and early-nineteenth-century revivals. Evangelicalism predominated as well among the Methodists and the Baptists, who did more than any other denomination to spread the evangelical impulse across the early republic. Their "holy 'knock-'em-down' power" appealed to a wide variety of ordinary Americans, including blacks, women, and an up-and-coming class of artisans, merchants, and farmers that Methodist historian John Wigger has described as "middling people on the make." While clergy in other denominations hunkered down at one church, typically for a lifetime, Methodist circuit riders and Baptist farmer-preachers moved with the expanding population. As restless as the new nation itself, these peripatetic pioneers turned the Methodists and the Baptists into the country's top two Protestant denominations, positions they continue to enjoy today.[11]

Through this orgy of activism, evangelicalism became not only the dominant religious impulse in the nation but also a major cultural force. According to Richard Carwardine, evangelicals constituted by mid-century "the largest, and most formidable, subculture in American society." In the words of Mark Noll, "No other organized promoter of values, no other generator of print, no other source of popular music or compelling public imagery, no other comforter (and agitator) of internal life . . . came anywhere close to the organized strength of the evangelical churches in the three-quarters of a century after the dawn of the republic." For good reason, the hundred years that spanned from Jefferson's election in 1800 to the publication of Theodore Roosevelt's *The Rough Riders* in 1899 have been widely referred to as "the evangelical century."[12]

Evangelicals followed their Puritan forebears in affirming the divine inspiration of the Bible. For some evangelicals, however, biblicism and creedalism were incompatible. Early in the nineteenth century, Restorationists began preaching "No creed but the Bible." "We neither advocate Calvinism, Arminianism, Arianism, Socianism, Trinitarianism, Unitarianism, Deism, or Sectarianism," Alexander Campbell explained, "but *New Testamentism*." And when Bishop Daniel Alexander Payne of the African Methodist Episcopal Church promised to root his faith in "the Bible, the whole Bible, nothing but the Bible," most of his evangelical brethren—both black and white—said "Amen."[13]

The Puritan emphasis on heartfelt conversion—the "new birth"—was another hallmark of evangelicalism. Even more than the Puritans, however, evangelicals made faith subjective, redirecting it from doctrines to experience, and rooting it in the private stirrings of the individual heart. W.E.B. Du Bois once wrote that slave religion was characterized by three things: "the Preacher, the Music, and the Frenzy."[14] The same could be said of evangelicalism itself, which, at least in the first half of the century, poured a large measure of frenzy into its sermons and its songs.

Evangelicals moved away from their Puritan heritage when they softened or rejected the Calvinist dogmas that Jefferson had derided as "maniac ravings."[15] Some evangelicals, particularly in the South, held fast to Calvinism until late in the century, but most drifted toward Arminianism. The namesakes of the sixteenth-century Dutch theologian Jacob Arminius criticized double predestination (which taught that God assigned all people before birth either to election to heaven or damnation to hell) as an insult to divine love, human freedom, and common sense. In a liberty-loving nation committed to making kings into citizens and citizens into kings, Calvin's fatalism seemed oddly out of place. So evangelicals cast Calvin's God as the new George III, declaring their independence from yet another distant and capricious king, and placing Jesus at the center of the Christian life. Jesus had died for all, not just the high and mighty. And each individual was at liberty to accept or reject his gracious offer of salvation.

In order to give Americans the opportunity to exercise that all-important choice, evangelicals worked hard to spread the good news. They published Bibles and distributed tracts. They cultivated Christian character in the home. They sent missionaries to the frontier. Above all else, they got up revivals. Of course, revivals were nothing new. However, during the First Great Awakening they were typically received, in Jonathan Edwards's terms, as "surprising works of God." During the Second Great Awakening of the early nineteenth century, revivals surprised no one. According to Charles Grandison Finney, the Billy Graham of his day (and, like Graham, a staunch Arminian), revivals were human endeavors, brought on by good planning, hard work, and savvy advertising. Conversions were all but assured for evangelists willing to employ the sound revivalist techniques that Finney referred to as "new measures."

Not everyone welcomed the new revivalism. John W. Nevin, a defender of the sacraments and a leading light of Mercersburg Theology, denounced "new measures" such as Finney's famous "anxious bench" (front row seats designated for sinners ripe for the picking) and his practice of allowing women to testify in public about the private stirrings of their souls. Also opposed were Protestants from liturgical traditions such as Lutheranism and Episcopalianism, who believed that revivals diminished the value of the sacraments. But nay-sayers were the exception to the rule, and as a rule Protestants enthusiastically embraced revivalism as a necessity in a country where persuasion had replaced coercion as the main avenue to the Christian life.

One distinguishing mark of the new revivalism was what Nathan Hatch has called the "sovereign audience." To be sure, populist preachers such as the Methodist Lorenzo Dow and the Baptist John Leland played an important role in winning souls. But the Second Great Awakening was driven by consumers rather than producers, demand rather than supply. Populist preachers such as Dow and Leland took their marching orders from demanding listeners who, as Hatch writes, "wanted their leaders unpretentious" and "their doctrines self-evident and down-to-earth." In what was quickly becoming a market-driven society, preachers in the early nineteenth century were forced to compete for souls not only with other preachers but also with the secular pleasures of the camp and the city. In this way, preachers entered the world of entertainment, tailoring their performances to not only the eternal truths of the Bible but also the shifting desires of a fickle public.[16]

Much has been written about how these preachers moved from the old style of reading a sermon to a more engaging style of extemporaneous speaking. Less attention has been paid to a more momentous shift—the rise of pulpit storytelling. Writing in 1826, a New England clergyman named Timothy Flint attested to a "revolution" in sermonizing on the frontier. "The ten thousand," wrote Flint, were fleeing from preachers who "dogmatize, define, and dispute" to those who employed "many low words, and images and illustrations." As dogma yielded to narrative in the pulpit, preachers and parishioners alike increasingly attended to the life of Jesus more than the dogmas of theology. The story sermon did not catch on as fast in New England as it did in the South and the West, but even there believers grew weary of the predictable eighteenth-century style of chapter-and-verse preaching that aimed "to expound a text and to unfold the divisions and subdivisions of meaning of *Grace*, of *Justification*, of *Atonement*, of *Sanctification.*" (Ralph Waldo Emerson left Unitarianism for Transcendentalism in part because the text/exposition/proof preaching of its ministers left him cold.)[17]

In the early republic, preachers who didn't let theological niceties get in the way of a good story became celebrities of a sort, and it seemed the more they cried and sweated and carried on the more celebrated they became. In this way, the "sovereign audience" produced not only entertaining enthusiasts but also a new form of Protestantism. Hatch is right when he says that Americans in the early nineteenth century wanted unpretentious leaders and self-evident doctrines. But they also wanted a God they could call their own. When Methodists sang these popular lyrics—"God's ministers like flames of fire / Are passing thro' the land, / The voice is here; 'Repent and fear / King Jesus is at hand!' "[18]—they were harkening back to Calvinist views of Jesus as King. They were also announcing the arrival of a new Jesus in their new land.

SOLUS JESUS

During the Renaissance of the fourteenth, fifteenth, and sixteenth centuries, Christians had emphasized Jesus' humanity. Inspired by a rediscovery of the doctrine of the incarnation, artists gloried in his body, including (as art historian Leo Steinberg has provocatively demonstrated) his penis. Their purpose, however, was not so much to sexualize Jesus as to humanize him—to rescue Jesus the man from the shackles of creedal abstractions, in order to allow him to live and breathe among real people in the real world. Although evangelicals were obviously heirs of the Reformation, they saw Jesus more in the light of Renaissance humanism.

Like their Renaissance predecessors, nineteenth-century evangelicals focused on the Second Person in the Trinity more than the First. While Calvinists were ever straining to maximize the distance between God and humanity, evangelicals worked to narrow that gap—by making humans more divine and God more human. Humans remained sinners, but increasingly evangelicals saw their own sin as a matter of choice, not inheritance. More important, they came to see

God in human terms. Taking their cues from the New Testament rather than the Old, they refused to see God as wrathful and distant. Any God worth worshiping, they argued, had to be loving and near.

The more evangelicals associated God with love rather than wrath, the more God the Father receded and God the Son stood out. Ralph Waldo Emerson was no critic of Jesus (who belonged, in Emerson's words, "to the true race of prophets"), but by 1838 he had grown tired of "noxious exaggeration about the person of Christ." More a reincarnator than a resurrector of Jesus, Emerson believed that all human beings were essentially divine. What distinguished Jesus from the rest of humanity was his ability to realize that potential. Fawning over Jesus was, therefore, an affront to spiritual self-reliance, and criticizing him, something of a sacred obligation. "It might become my duty," Emerson mused in his journal in 1840, "to spit in the face of Christ as a sacred act of duty to the Soul, an act which that beautiful pilgrim in nature would well appreciate." Then he added in 1843, "You name the good Jesus until I hate the sound of him."[19]

Whether his countrymen's fawning over Jesus was exaggerated or noxious cannot be settled here. Yet Emerson was right to sense a growing emphasis among American Christians on Jesus. "By the 1840s," Donald Scott has argued, "preaching and worship increasingly centered on the figure of Christ." In 1855, the Baptist firebrand from Nashville, James Robinson Graves, vowed "to serve no master but Jesus." In 1867, E. P. Powell, a Congregationalist from Michigan, noted that "the days yearn for a platform and organs of simple piety, instead of dogmas; less of Calvin, and Beza, and Edwards, and everybody else, and more of Christ." In his 1879 autobiography, the Reverend Nathaniel Bouton of Concord, New Hampshire, reflected on the changes visited on American Christianity since his conversion in 1815. "Very little is said at the present day of the condemning power of the law. God's mercy is magnified, while his adorable justice is kept out of view," he wrote. "Sinners were called upon to 'submit to God.' Now 'Come to Jesus' is the song—'Come just now, Jesus loves you.' "[20]

In a study of the private diaries of nineteenth-century American evangelicals, Richard Rabinowitz has unearthed considerable evidence for a broad shift in religious sensibilities from "doctrinalism" to "devotionalism." The "central fantasy" of this devotionalism, Rabinowitz has argued, was "an intimate walk with Jesus." The importance of that intimate walk was plain in nineteenth century devotional manuals and theological works, which increasingly placed Jesus at the heart of the spiritual life, defining that life not as submitting your mind to God but as inclining your heart to Jesus.[21]

Away from the diaries of ordinary folk, in theological treatises and popular novels, Jesus' star was also rising. Horace Bushnell, a Congregationalist minister deeply indebted to the Romantic vision of the indwelling of God in nature and humanity, described Jesus as "the central figure and power" of Christianity. "Christianity is not so much the advent of a better doctrine," he explained, "as of a perfect character." Later figures echoed Bushnell. The Social Gospel pioneer Washington Gladden defined "the Christian life" as "devotion to a person," not allegiance to a creed. Harriet Beecher Stowe made the same point in her novel Dred (1856). When asked by a preacher what her theology was, one of Stowe's female characters replied, "I hadn't any views of anything but the beauty of Christ." Henry Ward Beecher, the "Minister Plenipotentiary" of late-nineteenth-century America (and Stowe's brother) found "the very genius of Christianity" not in its dogmas or rites or institutions but in the person of Jesus. "When I read the Bible, I gather a great deal from the Old Testament, and from the Pauline portions of the New Testament," Beecher told his Plymouth Congregational Church congregation, "but after all, I am conscious that the fruit of the Bible is Christ. The rest to me is just what leaves are on an apple-tree. When I see the apple I know that there must have been a tree to bear that fruit; but after that I think of the fruit, and nothing else." While *sola scriptura* ("Bible alone") had been the mantra of the Protestant Reformation for nearly three centuries, Americans seemed to be gravitating toward a new slogan: *solus Jesus* ("Jesus alone").[22]

This emphasis on Jesus—his life on earth and his enduring personality—is one reason why evangelicals remained as united as they did during the evangelical century. Colonial Puritans had coalesced around a theology, but in the decades after the Revolution the old Calvinist consensus frayed badly. The yeoman efforts of Yale's New Divinity (or Modified Calvinist) theologians to adapt Calvinism to the democratic realities of the new nation extended Calvinism's life but were not able to sustain its hegemony. As hymns such as "What a Friend We Have in Jesus" (1855) drowned out "Before Jehovah's Awful Throne" (1719), Calvinist theology gave way to Jesus piety.

Why this happened is hard to say. Important historical changes are rarely driven by a single cause, and here the causes are particularly difficult to disentangle. The emergence of a consumer-driven economy and a new middle class were no doubt important, as were shifting conceptions of the American self, transformations of the family, and developments in science, biblical criticism, and comparative religion. Jesus piety also emerged out of the dynamics of the new free market in religion. The Mormon founder Joseph Smith, Jr., admitted to tremendous confusion as he sampled the religious wares offered to him in upstate New York in the first quarter of the nineteenth century. Denominations abounded, and each had its own interpretations of the Bible. "Who of all these parties are right?" Smith wondered, "and how shall I know it?"[23] Smith responded to the "Great Diversification" in American religion with a new scripture and a new church. But for most Americans that was not an option. At least in the early decades of the nineteenth century, most felt compelled to choose between the Baptists and the Methodists, the Presbyterians and the Disciples of Christ, the Millerites and the Mormons. Sometime around the middle of the nineteenth century, however, preachers began to respond to the new Babel of denominations by offering a simpler message. Instead of marketing predestination or free will, the Bible or the Baptists, they began to offer religious shoppers a new relationship with Jesus.

This relationship was personal, so preachers had to make Jesus into a person. And they did so with glee, disentangling him not only from the complex theologies of Calvin but also from the complicated polities of the denominations. As evangelicals placed more of their faith in him, Jesus became more human and less divine. Rather than cowering before Jesus as the King of Kings, evangelicals increasingly approached him as a person who could, in the words of St. Bonaventure, "be known and loved and imitated." No longer a signpost in a vast theological system, Jesus emerged in the mid-nineteenth century as a living, breathing human being.

This was the real revolution in nineteenth-century American religion. Far more than the rise of Arminianism or the emergence of the populist preacher and his demanding audience, the reawakening of Jesus was the main religious story in the first century of U.S. history.

Once Americans began to see Christianity as a Jesus faith, they were well on their way to transforming their country into a Jesus nation. But first they had to figure out precisely who Jesus was. Who was this man nineteenth-century evangelicals felt compelled to know and love and imitate? What sort of person was he?

FEMINIZING AMERICAN RELIGION

To answer these questions it is necessary to look at the sort of people who knew and loved and imitated Jesus in early-nineteenth-century America. As has been noted, these people were for the most part evangelical Protestants who believed in the authority of the Bible, the necessity of individual conversion, and the efficacy of revivals. And the great majority were women. A preponderance of women in the pews is not anything unusual, of course. As Ann Braude has noted, in virtually every religious group in every era in U.S. history, women have outnumbered men. As early as 1691, Cotton Mather was complaining that "there are far more godly women in the world than there are godly men." But the portion of women in the churches rose after the Revolution, and climbed in the early nineteenth century. What truly distinguished the early republic from the colonial period was that women began translating their numerical predominance into influence. While in the 1700s congregations were feminized, in the 1800s Jesus was.[24]

How the "feminization of American religion" came to pass is a matter of some debate. The standard story begins in the colonial period, when boys were raised to be patriarchs, lording over families and farms as steadfastly as the Calvinist God lorded over the universe. In the Industrial Revolution of the early nineteenth century, however, men began to work in factories rather than family farms. Gradually, women took charge of their homes, which ceased to be places of paid labor and instead became havens from it. In the process, families became less patriarchal and more companionate. Especially among white, middle-class Protestants in the Northeast, a new "separate spheres" ideology of rigid gender separation took hold. From there it spread to a variety of other groups aspiring for middle-class status, including African Americans, working-class Protestants, Roman Catholics, and Jews.[25]

This ideology assigned women to the private realm of the home and men to the public realm of politics and business. While men had once been guardians of virtue, they increasingly came to be associated with aggression, competitiveness, and guile—virtues in the business world but vices in the home. Women were now thought to exemplify Christian values such as submissiveness. No longer the lustful and seductive Eve, the stereotypical woman was associated with the pious, pure, and passionless Mary. In the house that domesticity built, women used their wits to Christianize their children. In their hands they held not an apple but a Bible, and in their laps sat America's future, to say nothing of the future of Christianity itself.

Alongside this separate-spheres ideology came a new form of piety that provided a powerful challenge to both Calvinism and revivalism, and a new context for devotion to Jesus. Beginning around the 1830s, Protestants and Catholics alike transformed the home into the center of Christian life, and the mother into a high priestess of domestic piety. Christians of all stripes decorated their homes with religious engravings and lithographs of Jesus. As mothers taught their children about Jesus, they emphasized the Sermon on the Mount, which offered God's blessing to the meek rather than the strong, and the crucifixion, which demonstrated to them the virtues of submission and sacrifice.[26]

This combination of "separate spheres" ideology and domestic piety might have confined women entirely to the home, but it did not. Drawing on the authority of that ideology even as they defied it— What would become of the country if the public square were given over entirely to the avarice and cunning of men?—women gathered in women's clubs, women's colleges, and women's political and labor organizations. Because women were now seen as morally and spiritually superior to men, their influence became more and more prized in society. Women were major forces in the rise of a variety of transdenominational voluntary associations designed to define and sustain a Protestant center to a culture that seemed to many to be swirling out of control. Some of those associations, including the American Bible Society (established in 1816), the American Sunday School Union (1824), and the American Tract Society (1825), had explicitly religious aims. Others, such as the American Temperance Society (1826) and the American Anti-Slavery Society (1833), focused on social reform. In this "Benevolent Empire" of voluntary associations, women did the vast majority of the work.

Women also ventured out of their homes to participate in prayer circles and revivals, and, of course, to go to church. Some even became preachers themselves. But thanks to their new status as the prime guardians of Christian virtue, even lay women exerted tremendous influence in the churches (influence that, in turn, reinforced their moral and spiritual authority). Under the old state church system, ministers might have ignored the concerns of their parishioners. But in the new spiritual marketplace, clergy were predisposed to supply them with what they demanded. "The female part of every congregation have, in general, an influence which, while it cannot be defined, cannot, at the same time, be resisted," the Princeton professor Samuel Miller observed in 1827. And that influence was magnetic, attracting women even as it repelled men. "I never saw, or read, of any country," Frances Trollope wrote in 1832, "where religion had so strong a hold upon the women, or a slighter hold upon the men."[27]

As the influence of women rose in homes, churches, and society, evangelicals began to associate God with feminine rather than masculine virtues. Preachers delivered sermons based on New Testament mercy rather than Old Testament militance, and harsh Calvinist doctrines such as original sin and infant damnation beat a hasty retreat. Some even began to imagine God as a warm and caring Mother. The Shakers said the divine was both male and female, and cast their founder, Mother Ann Lee, as a female coming of Jesus Christ. Later in the century, Helena Blavatsky and her Theosophists would fancy divinity as an impersonal, gender-free Absolute, while Mary Baker Eddy and the Christian Scientists would send their prayers up to a "Father-Mother God."

FEMINIZING JESUS

One important effect of the feminization of American religion was the eclipse of the Trinity's First Person by the Second. Apologists for Hinduism have long argued that even adept polytheists can worship only one God at a time. The same seems to be true of trinitarian Christians. Though they affirm the divinity of the Father, the Son, and the Holy Spirit, they seem to focus most of their devotion on one of the three. For the Puritans of the colonies, that person was the Father; for many contemporary Pentecostalists it is the Holy Spirit; for nineteenth-century evangelicals it was the Son. Antebellum Protestants did far more than send their devotion Jesus' way, however. They also made him over in the light of Victorian ideals of the feminine. Applying to Jesus and his Father the same stark contrasts that other Americans were drawing between women and men, they described Jesus as pious and pure, loving and merciful, meek and humble.

This was a major transformation in American Christianity, but it was no sudden coup. Throughout the Second Great Awakening, many revivalists continued to preach fire and brimstone. Reducing the person of Jesus to the office of Christ, they defined their Savior almost entirely in terms of his atoning death, which they described as the payment of a debt owed to God. They also continued to sing Calvinist hymns, proving, as Stephen Marini has put it, that "there was plenty of Puritan left in the early American evangelical."[28] The feminization of American culture may have started earlier, but the feminization of American religion did not kick in until after the Second Great Awakening. In fact, it was first articulated by ministers not altogether enamored of revivals.

Henry Ward Beecher was torn as a boy between the paternal Protestantism of his demanding father, the Calvinist preacher Lyman Beecher, and what he imagined was the maternal Protestantism of his loving mother, who died when he was only three. Well into his adulthood, he struggled for an authentic conversion experience that would confirm his standing before his father as one of the elect without betraying the affection he felt for his mother. He had that experience one May morning in the woods in Ohio, though it did not take the precise shape Lyman Beecher might have imagined. The best account

available is from late in Beecher's career, so it is colored by the liberalism of his mature theology, but it testifies nonetheless both to
Beecher's transformation and to the transformations American religion was undergoing in this period. It merits quoting at some length:

> It pleased God to reveal to my wandering soul the idea that it
> was his nature to love a man in his sins for the sake of helping
> him out of them; that he did not do it out of compliment to
> Christ, or to a law, or to a plan of salvation, but from the fullness
> of his great heart; that he was a Being not made mad by sin, but
> sorry; that he was not furious with wrath toward the sinner, but
> pitied him—in short that he felt toward me as my mother felt
> toward me, to whose eyes my wrong-doing brought tears, who
> never pressed me so close to her as when I had done wrong, and
> who would fain with her yearning love lift me out of trouble.
> And when I found that Jesus Christ had such a disposition, and
> that when his disciples did wrong he drew them closer to him
> than he did before—and when pride, and jealousy, and rivalry,
> and all vulgar and worldly feelings rankled in their bosoms, he
> opened his heart to them as a medicine to heal these infirmities;
> when I found out that it was Christ's nature to lift men out of
> weakness to strength, out of impurity to goodness, out of every-
> thing low and debasing to superiority, I felt that I had found a
> God.[29]

While Beecher found his sweet Savior in nature, some of his contemporaries found him in images. Advances in printmaking made lithographs affordable in the first half of the century and halftone
engravings inexpensive in the last half. The demise of Calvinism (and,
with it, prohibitions against Christian visual culture) permitted the
broad distribution of popular religious art, which lent an aura of the
sacred to American households during this era of domestic piety. As
images of Jesus proliferated in illustrated books and prints suitable for
display in the home, Americans increasingly approached God through
images as well as texts, and those images in turn reinforced their devotion. In these mass-produced prints Jesus regularly appeared as a
helpless baby and a cherubic child. The emergence of Christmas as "a

major religious event in American culture," also in the mid-nineteenth century, reinforced this identification. So did popular Christmas hymns such as "It Came upon a Midnight Clear" (1849) and "O Little Town of Bethlehem" (1868).[30] But Jesus was also widely represented in a maternal pose. Bernhard Plockhorst's *Christ Blessing the Children* (1885), one of the most popular religious images in nineteenth-century America, borrowed from European paintings of the Madonna and Child, but in this case the cherubic babe is sitting on the lap of an adoring Jesus.

This maternal Jesus was marketed particularly effectively by the venerable lithography firm of Currier & Ives. Remembered today largely for its popular prints of steamboats and presidents, Currier & Ives also produced hundreds of different religious lithographs—540, according to art historian David Morgan. While most of those images were sold to Protestants, a sizeable minority (229 by Morgan's count) were marketed to Roman Catholic buyers.[31] One image produced for Spanish-speaking Catholics, *El Señor, Andando Sobre el Mar* (Christ Walking on the Sea) depicts a hyper-feminine Jesus walking on the water and rescuing Peter from the sea. His hair, framed by a bright halo, is elegantly coiffured. His face is beautiful and his neck and fingers long and delicate. Beneath a long, flowing robe, his wide hips jut out toward the center of the image, as if to accentuate his roundness. This is an unmistakably feminine Savior.

CHRISTIAN NURTURE

Horace Bushnell, arguably the most influential theologian in Victorian America, was another early feminizer of Jesus. Like his contemporary Beecher, Bushnell worked to accommodate evangelicalism to the modern world. While Jonathan Edwards had straddled Calvinism and the Enlightenment, integrating heart religion and head religion, Bushnell's "Progressive Orthodoxy" mediated between the Romanticism of Emerson and Coleridge he delighted in as a boy and the New Divinity theology he learned as a Yale Divinity School student. With the Romantics, Bushnell luxuriated in the ambiguities of language, insisting that the creeds and even the Bible should be read as poetry. With the New Divinity theologians, he preached sin and the vicarious atonement, though he rejected the reigning view of the crucifixion as a substitutionary payment satisfying a debt to a meddling God. Instead of equating the atonement with a ransom, Bushnell saw it as an act of love by a Savior whose willingness to suffer with humanity illustrated the love of God even as it provided a model for the moral life.

Bushnell's most distinctive theological position was his understanding of self-development. Bushnell had no interest in the republicans' self-made man. He was equally unimpressed by the "lunatic airs" of the popular revivalists (who, in the evocative words of Abraham Lincoln, often gesticulated as if they were "fighting bees"). Good character was not developed on its own, or by crazy evangelists, or by well-meaning librarians. It was cultivated by nurturing mothers. In *Discourse on Christian Nurture* (1847), Bushnell argued that it was foolish to abandon children to their own devices, and then to try to implant in them a new heart under the artificial pressures of the revival tent. Getting to know Jesus was a process rather than an event, and it was performed most effectively by mothers at home.[32]

Like the term *personality*, which would emerge as an ideal later in the century, *character* carried with it intimations of individuality— character as the sum of qualities that distinguish one person from other human beings. Yet at mid-century the term typically connoted conformity rather than nonconformity. At least as it was used by leading Protestant thinkers, a person of character was someone who conformed to Christian ideals, demonstrated Christian virtues. More precisely, character meant conformity to Protestant ideals and virtues. In fact, much of the energy that fueled the cultivation of Christian character in the early republic came from fear of Catholic immigrants, whose divergence from Protestant norms of temperance, for example, seemed to many to threaten the stability of the nation. Seizing on this notion of character (and anticipating the later theories of Freud), Bushnell argued that trying to foist new birth on unruly adolescents was a losing battle. You needed to make Christians while they were still young and under the tutelage of their mothers. But how were mothers to cultivate Christian character in their children? And what exactly was Christian character? Bushnell answered those questions by turning to Jesus.

Like so many other Americans in the evangelical century, Bushnell was obsessed with Jesus. To him, Christianity was Jesus and Jesus was Christianity. What was important about Jesus, however, was neither his theology nor his power. "It is the grandeur of his character which constitutes the chief power of his ministry, not his miracles or teachings apart from his character," Bushnell wrote. "Miracles were useful at the time to arrest attention, and his doctrine is useful at all times as the highest revelation of truth possible in speech; but the greatest truth of the gospel, notwithstanding is Christ himself."[33] According to Bushnell, to be a Christian was not to understand the metaphysics of Jesus' dual nature as God and human. It was to ponder the character of Jesus and then to conform to it. In this process of *imitatio Christi*, thinking took a back seat to feeling. What mattered was developing a bond of friendship with Jesus: "We want no theologic definition of God's perfection; but we want a friend, whom we can feel as a man, and whom it will be sufficiently accurate for us to accept and love. Let him come so nigh."[34]

Bushnell occasionally followed the revivalists of the Second Great Awakening in describing Jesus in populist terms—as "the rustic tradesman of Galilee," for example. Still, he emphasized Jesus' feminine virtues far more than his masculine attributes. In *The Character of Jesus* (1861), Bushnell described Jesus repeatedly via metaphors from nature. In keeping with his organic understanding of the cultivation of Christian character, he compared the development of Jesus to the unfolding of a flower. His childhood was "a kind of celestial flower." In his youth, he was a "sacred flower" emitting "a fragrance wafted on us from other worlds." At death, he was "a bruised flower, drooping on his cross."[35]

The compliant character nurtured by Mary and realized by Jesus was gentle, humble, and patient. It endured suffering without complaint or resistance, submitting always to God's will. Bushnell's Jesus sympathized with the poor, who "knew him as their friend." He did not crave worldly success, and he utterly lacked guile. As his character unfolded, he became wholly innocent, not only of sin but also of selfishness. He was, according to Bushnell, "a perfectly harmless being, actuated by no destructive passions, gentle to inferiors, doing ill or injury to none." At death, he was "holy, harmless, and undefiled." In

short, Jesus was a compassionate and companionate human being
who exhibited a full measure of what Bushnell termed "the passive
virtues."[36]

Bushnell's call for mothers to imitate their Savior and for children
to imitate their mothers helped spawn a spate of advice manuals and
children's books that translated Bushnell's views into popular culture.
Still, Bushnell remained a theologian, and in the nineteenth century
theology was to many Americans a dirty word. Like Jefferson, who jettisoned theology for morality, evangelicals during Bushnell's lifetime
were rapidly turning from theology to experience and from experience
to storytelling. Historians from Henry Steele Commager to Ann
Douglas have lamented the "loss of theology" in this era—the shift in
religious circles from thinking to feeling.[37] Whether you agree with
them depends on what you think of Calvinist theology. It may also depend on what you think of women because, at the time, doctrines
were widely associated with male theologians and stories with "scrib-
bling women." At any rate, during the evangelical century Americans
increasingly came to view theology as a distraction from true religion.
In order for the feminine Jesus of Bushnell and Beecher to become
truly popular in nineteenth-century America, he was going to have to
incarnate in a form far more accessible than the theological treatise.
He would have to die to dogma and rise again in narrative form.

"MAD FOR STORIES"

Like so many other Americans before and after them, evangelical
preachers worked from a "canon within the canon," picking and
choosing biblical passages that met their needs and fulfilled their desires. Rather than homing in on the ethical sayings of Jesus, evangelical preachers emphasized stories about him—especially stories about
his interactions with women—which they believed would reveal the
life that lay at the heart of the gospel. Ministers embellished these
biblical narratives with fresh details and new conflicts to entertain
their audiences. They also pressed beyond scripture to anecdotes
about their own relationships with Jesus. "It appears to me that the
world is returning to its second childhood, and running mad for Stories," Harriet Beecher Stowe wrote in 1872. "Soon it will be necessary

that every leading clergyman shall embody his theology in a serial story, to be delivered from the pulpit Sunday after Sunday." Five years later, Phillips Brooks, Boston's beloved preacher and one of the "Princes of the Pulpit" of the postbellum period, conceded that "competition of print" (from Stowe, among others) had all but eliminated the "monotonous reiteration of commonplaces and abstractions" that once dominated American sermons.[38]

Accompanying this new homiletic style were new tracts and new Bibles, many of them illustrated with images of Jesus surrounded by children, or as a child himself. Drama trumped dogma in the handouts of the American Tract Society, which aimed to entertain as well as edify. Aping the promoters of the penny presses, tract colporteurs pitched their wares as "authentic narratives."[39] The American Tract Society drew on cutting edge techniques in papermaking, printing, and distribution in order to carpet the country with Jesus. The American Bible Society used similar techniques in an effort to place a Bible in every home.

Voracious Bible buyers, Americans were initially quite happy with the simple and inexpensive texts of the American Bible Society, but eventually they began to fancy more lavish offerings, such as Harper's *Illuminated Bible*, which boasted 1600 illustrations (many of women) and a gilt-stamped morocco binding when it first appeared in 1846. Many of the most popular new Bibles published in the nineteenth century—and they appeared in thousands of different editions—included extensive notes, charts, commentaries, study guides, maps, and illustrations. According to Paul Gutjahr, Americans gradually grew to demand those extras, and in many cases preferred gazing at them to reading the text itself. While only 16 percent of the Bibles produced in the decade starting in 1810 came with illustrations, by the 1870s 59 percent did.[40]

From the new story sermon, the narrative tract, and the illustrated Bible it was only a short step to a popular new literary genre: the religious bestseller. This new marriage of the sacred and the secular was a match made in heaven: Religious themes made novels respectable, and fiction made religion entertaining. While earlier Protestants had aligned fiction (in fact all works of the imagination, including visual art) with the devil, their preoccupation with personal exhortation about the conversion experience opened the door to religious story-telling. During the first half of the nineteenth century, evangelicals came to see that fiction too could be used for spiritual ends. By mid-century, they enthusiastically embraced religious novels for the same practical reason they had accepted Finney's "new measures"—be-cause they worked to bring sinners to Jesus.

The result was a new form of American popular culture, and a flurry of bestselling novels with religious themes. Most of these nov-els were written either by clergymen or by women—the two groups Ann Douglas identified as the leading feminizers of religion in *The Feminization of American Culture*. These novels all put a premium on experience over doctrine, feelings over formulas. Many became pow-erful vehicles for the dissemination of sentimental Protestantism. Elizabeth Stuart Phelps's *The Gates Ajar* (1869), for example, de-scribed heaven as a scene of middle-class domestic bliss, complete with kitchens and gingersnaps, libraries and symphony orchestras.

Many popular novels of the nineteenth century included heroines who were explicitly Christ types. The most famous were Little Eva and Tom of Harriet Beecher Stowe's *Uncle Tom's Cabin* (1852). This bestselling novel of the nineteenth century was, among other things, an abolitionist tract. It demonstrated the human costs of slavery so ef-fectively that Abraham Lincoln reportedly called its author "the little woman who wrote the book that started this great war." But given Stowe's pedigree, it should not be surprising that *Uncle Tom's Cabin* was a religious as well as an abolitionist classic, and a leading example of the feminization of American religion.

In the novel, which occurs "beneath the shadow of American law, and the shadow of the cross of Christ," Stowe depicts the Christian home as a haven where nurturing mothers serve love along with pan-cakes for breakfast. The women who inhabit the book are far more virtuous than the men, whose salvation plainly hangs more on the subtle influence of their mothers than the pulpit-pounding excesses of fire-and-brimstone preachers. One woman is said to be "a direct embodiment and personification of the New Testament," but the real Christ figures in the book are Little Eva, an angelic five-year-old white girl, and Uncle Tom, a black slave. Both characters exemplify the feminine qualities attached to Jesus in nineteenth-century America. They are pious and passive, submissive and sacrificial. They feel more than they think. They give more than they take. They are also devoted companions. In fact, despite the gulfs of age and race that divide them, the two become fast friends. In the end, both die Christ-like deaths, recapitulating the passion and spreading the gospel of the self-giving love of God. Tom, writes Stowe, is "all the moral and Christian virtues bound in black morocco, complete." Little Eva (Evangeline, formally) is the "evangel," the good news itself.[41]

To sentimental novelists such as Stowe, that good news was that God is love. Moreover, because humans are created in the image of God, they are themselves capable of loving one another, and Jesus too. This form of Christianity is not about correct doctrines of divinity. It is about heartfelt personal relationships—between the individual and Jesus and among humans themselves. In *Uncle Tom's Cabin* and other sentimental novels of the period, the drama quickens when those relationships are severed: when death takes a son from his mother; when a slave auction steals a father from his family; when atheism separates creature from Creator. At the end of *Uncle Tom's Cabin*, the slaveholding atheist Simon Legree brings all these elements together when he brutally beats and kills Tom. Tom triumphs, however, by refusing to hate. What makes him Christlike is not so much that he dies a brutal death but that he forgives his murderer and loves to the end. That love saves two friends, Cassy and Emmeline, from slavery, and gathers two other slaves, Sambo and Quimbo, into the Christian fold. Like the Calvinism that preceded and provoked it, the Christianity preached in this novel is about sin, suffering, and salvation. Here too the suffering of the innocent saves the wicked from their sins. But it does not do so according to the logic of the substitutionary atonement, by transferring the sins of the guilty to the innocent. Like Stowe's Jesus, Tom and Eva save by demonstrating the paradoxical power of self-giving love. When you see the examples of Eva and Tom, you do not just see the evils of slavery. You see God indwelling in humanity. It is not an accident that the only explicit descriptions of Jesus himself in the novel refer to him healing a blind man and receiving the little children. In the gospel according to

Stowe, Jesus exemplifies the sacrificial self of Victorian womanhood. If you truly feel his presence in your heart, you are reborn from hatred to love, sin to salvation.[42]

Other novels fictionalized Jesus more explicitly, and they too sold exceptionally well. The Unitarian minister William Ware was the first to produce a bestseller in the face of a powerful Puritan bias against mixing religion and the imagination. His *Julian: Or, Scenes in Judea* (1841) developed the basic outline for many Jesus novels to come. Rather than taking the measure of Jesus himself (at least for a time, that remained the exclusive province of sermons and scripture), Ware focused on Julian, a skeptic who eventually accepted Jesus as his Savior (though on Unitarian terms). The next novel to capitalize on Jesus' newfound popularity was *The Prince of the House of David* (1855), also written by a minister, in this case Joseph Holt Ingraham, an Episcopal priest from Mississippi. Like Ware's *Julian*, Ingraham's novel averted its gaze from Jesus himself, as if staring at him presented the same dangers to the soul as presented by an eclipse to the eyes. It too focused on the pilgrimage of a skeptic from unbelief to faith, in this case Episcopalianism, but it developed the character of Jesus more fully. For Ingraham, Jesus was a sympathetic God-man, who suffered physically as well as spiritually, enduring (among other things) excruciating headaches.

The capstone of this new genre was *Ben-Hur, a Tale of the Christ* (1880) by the Civil War general Lew Wallace. By some accounts, Wallace's epic outsold even *Uncle Tom's Cabin*, leading some to mock him as "the Homer of Sears-Roebuck fiction." Like *Ben-Hur* the film (whose famous chariot scene lives on in *Star Wars: Episode I*), the novel is a real swashbuckler, the product of an era when religion and entertainment were no longer dizzy about dancing so close. In the novel, as in *Julian* and *The Prince of the House of David*, Jesus waits patiently in the wings, appearing in the climactic pages only to facilitate a conversion. Though *Ben-Hur* is often described as a macho novel, General Wallace's Jesus is a feminine sort. He possesses a "tearful woman-like face" and "a slender, stooping figure, with long hair." When provoked to fight (by supporters and detractors alike), this preacher of "love and non-resistance" refuses to take up the sword. He is, Wallace observes, a "most unmartial figure."[43]

All of these Jesus novels offered readers vicarious spirituality. For many, they supplemented Sunday services, providing yet another way to relate to the Sweet Savior. For others, they provided a substitute for church, and for the Bible.

LIVES OF JESUS

Along with these Christ-type and Jesus-in-the-wings novels, American authors produced more straightforward lives of Jesus. This genre first came to the United States with the publication of *The New and Complete Life of Our Blessed Lord and Saviour, Jesus Christ* (1795) by the Anglican Paul Wright, but it was refined in Europe at the hands of skeptical scholars who were close enough to the church to care about Jesus yet sufficiently independent from it to believe they could improve on Matthew, Mark, Luke, and John. Pioneering works such as Strauss's *Das Leben Jesu* and Renan's *Vie de Jésus* were translated into English quickly (the former by George Eliot), but neither seemed to capture the American imagination. Products of the radical European Enlightenment, both were too skeptical for American tastes. So over the course of the nineteenth century, American writers produced an endless stream of pious and popular lives of Jesus. Many were copiously illustrated—to assist mothers in telling the Jesus story to their children, and to entertain adult readers. The Hall of Christ at the religious resort in the New York town of Chautauqua (a bastion of the liberal Protestant establishment that Teddy Roosevelt once called "the Most American Place in America") collected Jesus lives by the thousands. Like the sentimental novels of the period, most of these books were written either by male clergy or female authors. The Unitarian Henry Ware, Jr. (William Ware's father), the Transcendentalist James Freeman Clarke, the Presbyterian Thomas DeWitt Talmage, and the Congregationalist Lyman Abbott all crafted lives that suited their parishioners. Harriet Beecher Stowe and Elizabeth Stuart Phelps (another best-selling author) weighed in with *Footsteps of the Master* (1877) and *The Story of Jesus Christ* (1897).

The most influential of these Victorian lives of Jesus was Henry Ward Beecher's *The Life of Jesus, the Christ* (1871). Beecher broadcast his views from the pulpit of Plymouth Congregational Church in

Brooklyn Heights, New York, where he served from 1847 until his death in 1887. A prolific writer, Beecher edited the *Independent* and the *Christian Union*, both interdenominational periodicals, and wrote a bestselling religious novel, *Norwood* (1867). Though he began his career as a conservative evangelical after the manner of his father, he grew quite liberal, particularly after his father died in 1863.

Beecher was not an original thinker—his theology has been rightly called "second-hand Emersonianism"—but this quintessential "liberal evangelical" helped to popularize liberal Protestantism as it gradually distinguished itself from evangelicalism proper after the Civil War. Drawing on Romantic poets and American Transcendentalists, he gloried in the essential divinity of human beings and the possibility of personal relations between Christians and Jesus. "A human soul is not something other and different from the Divine soul," he wrote. And so intimate relationships between God and humans were not unimaginable to him. In fact, "the vital union" of our souls with Jesus was for Beecher the essence of Christianity. At times, Beecher described this "vital union" in mystical terms. The "marrow" of Christianity, Beecher wrote, is "to live in him, to have him dwelling in us, to lose our personal identity in his, and have it return to us purified and ennobled." This interpretation of what Beecher called "the very genius of Christianity" blurred the distinction between divine love and human love, transforming human love too into a channel of divine mercy and divine grace. It also blurred the distinction between the supernatural and the natural, since Jesus could now be found in nature as well as scripture. Divinity was immanent, Beecher affirmed, in the flowers and the trees. All nature was a miracle.[44]

In *Norwood*, Beecher's alter ego Reuben Wentworth gives voice to the author's mature theology. Taking aim at the Calvinist preference for theology over personality, Wentworth (a Harvard man with a weakness for Coleridge) tells a local Calvinist pastor: "You have little help from your affections; less from ideality; none from taste and beauty; and, really, you worship an *abstract thought*—a mere projection of an *idea*—not a whole Mind, a *Living Being!*" Against this propositional religiosity, Wentworth offers faith in a ubiquitous Jesus (again punctuated with an exclamation point). "My Savior is everywhere—in the book and out of the book. I see Him in Nature, in human life, in my own experience as well as in the recorded fragments of His own history. I live in a Bible. But it is an unbound book!"[45]

History has not treated Beecher kindly. In fact, he seems to be one of those figures who fits so precisely his own time that he is out of place in any other. Critics of sentimental religion have pinpointed him as the foremost evangelist for the gospel of gush, a pathfinder on the road to New Age platitudes. Critics of consumer culture have damned him for tailoring the gospel to the materialism of his middle-class parishioners. And historians seem to relish his tryst with Elizabeth Tilton, which led in 1875 to the most publicized trial of the nineteenth century (and ended in a hung jury). Nonetheless, Beecher was almost universally beloved during his time. In fact, he was likely the most popular American preacher of the nineteenth century, and his biography of Jesus captured, as perhaps only Beecher could, the sentimental spirituality of the age.

Beecher's *Life of Jesus* followed Jefferson in setting the true religion of Jesus against the false religion of the institutional church. Beecher too sneered at ecclesiasticism, creedalism, and ritualism, imagining Jesus as an antihierarchical and antiecclesiastical hero. Unlike Jefferson, however, Beecher refused to reduce the religion of Jesus to the Sermon on the Mount. It was Jesus himself, Beecher claimed, who set Christianity apart. "Every system, whether of philosophy or of religion, that was ever propounded before Christianity, might be received without any knowledge, in the disciple, of the person of its teacher," he wrote. "The Parsee and the Buddhist believe in a system more than in a person. What Plato taught is more important than what Plato himself was. . . . Not so Christianity. Christianity is faith in Christ." To have this faith was not to affirm a moral system or a systematic theology. It was to cultivate in your own being the feelings Jesus felt, above all the overflowing sympathy he had for all human beings. "It is a psychological kingdom that he came to found," Beecher concluded. "He aimed not to construct a new system of morals or of philosophy, but a new soul, with new capabilities, under new spiritual influences."[46]

Beecher's design for his *Life of Jesus* highlighted the "new spiritual influences" of that "psychological kingdom." Rather than shaping his biography around the teachings of Jesus (as Jefferson and, for that matter, Matthew had done), Beecher organized it around the intimate encounters of human beings with Jesus. In these encounters, Beecher presents Jesus as a sympathetic companion, sharing his love with his friends and cultivating love in each in the process..To be a Christian, the book seems to say, is to love well.

Following Luke more than any of the other Gospel writers, Beecher emphasizes his hero's interactions with women. In fact, he devotes an entire chapter to the story of Jesus and the Samaritan woman at the well. "There are certain experiences which stand for the whole of one's life," Beecher writes, and as he parses this story it becomes clear that for him this particular experience sums up the whole life of Jesus. Jesus' acceptance of the Samaritan woman is for Beecher a clear rebuke to the religious establishment of his time—its tribalism, its legalism, and above all its lack of love. By accepting this foreigner into his family of love, Jesus demonstrates that true religion "requires neither altar, nor priest, nor uttered prayer, but only the grateful heart." The story also demonstrates Jesus' sympathy for all human beings, especially the poor, women, and social outcasts. Beecher's Jesus comes into the world not to die on the cross but to establish a new way to relate to God and other human beings. Following revivalists from Edwards to Finney, Beecher emphasizes the experience of new birth. But for him to be born again is to be initiated into a family of sympathy in which each loves the others as brothers and sisters and treats Jesus as a friend. When Jesus embraces the Samaritan woman as a fellow human being rather than sneering at her as a sinner, he invites her into that family, that "kingdom of love." He also makes himself her "companion."[47]

This companionate Jesus was, to be sure, divine. Yet Beecher portrayed him as an American Everyman. Unlike John the Baptist who stood aloof from individuals, judging their faults, Jesus drew close:

> Jesus was a citizen. He knew the fatigues of labor, the trials which beset poverty, the temptations arising from the practical conduct of business. He lived among men in all the innocent experiences of society life, a cheerful, companionable, and most winning nature. There was no gayety in his demeanor, but much cheerfulness. He did not assume the professional sanctity that

was much in esteem. He was familiar, natural, unpretentious, loving that which was homely and natural in men, rather than that which was artificial and pretentious.[48]

Beecher's unpretentious Jesus was also a domestic Jesus. The piety he exemplified and inspired in his followers was a close kin to the domestic faiths that Beecher's sister, Catharine, had championed in *A Treatise on Domestic Economy* (1841) and Stowe had presented in *Uncle Tom's Cabin*. But Beecher's feminized piety stressed sacrifice far less than either of his sisters, and love far more. Or, to be precise, Beecher presented a different understanding of Jesus as love. While his sisters (and, for that matter, Horace Bushnell) saw the suffering of Jesus on the cross as the embodiment of love, Beecher gravitated toward a more mystical and romantic understanding. For him, love was more about self-fulfillment than self-denial, more about feelings than ethical obligations. To love was to find your true self through union with another. To follow Jesus was to live abundantly, not to lay down your life for a friend.

In *The Life of Jesus, the Christ*, the first thing Jesus does after he starts his ministry is to go home to his mother. "Through the household, as through a gate, Jesus entered upon his ministry of love," Beecher writes. "Ever since, the Christian home has been the refuge of true religion. Here it has had its purest altars, its best teachers, and a life of self-denying love in all gladness." In Jesus' "invisible household of the heart," no one was berated as a sinner, and God was worshiped "no longer . . . as a monarch, but as a Father." As for Jesus, he exhibited all the characteristics of the mother Beecher never knew. Repeatedly, Beecher describes Jesus as a wellspring of sympathy. Jesus exhibited a "tender sympathy for others" and was "sympathetic to a remarkable degree." He repeatedly demonstrated his sympathy through heartfelt acts of love. He touched the blind, the deaf, and the sick. He pulled children close, blessing them not just with "bosom words" but also with "love-pressure." Even his miracles were "glowing expressions of sympathy."[49]

Though Beecher affirmed the divinity of Jesus, his interpretation accented his humanity. "To insert two natures," Beecher explained, "is to dissolve the charm."[50] To more conservative Christians, wringing the charm out of Jesus might have seemed a duty. But Beecher was by all accounts a charming man, and he felt honor bound to find in Jesus the charm his parishioners plainly loved in their pastor. Like so many evangelicals of his century, he emphasized Jesus' humanity and his femininity, approaching his Savior as a loving and sympathetic friend.

"WHAT A FRIEND"

Jesus the friend came alive for nineteenth-century Americans first and foremost in song. Singing about Jesus was rare during the colonial period, because the Puritans confined church singing to the Old Testament psalms. During the eighteenth century, Isaac Watts scandalized his fellow Calvinists by injecting folk melodies and non-scriptural lyrics into Christian hymnody, but he paved the way for the popularization of the hymn by holding fast to Reformed orthodoxy, injecting Jesus into his songs, and somehow managing to stir the passions without letting them get out of control. During the Second Great Awakening, robust hymn singing helped fuel the frontier revivals. After the Civil War, as the "boiling hot religion" of the frontier cooled off, hymns became only more emotional. As new technologies enabled publishers to print complete song lyrics underneath the notes on a page, hymnbooks became huge sellers, with hundreds of volumes selling millions of copies. Most Protestant denominations produced their own hymnbooks, but each borrowed from the others, and many of the most popular hymns appeared in multiple books. Whatever unity evangelicals enjoyed was to a great extent a product of singing to their Lord these new songs. "Evangelicalism found its collective voice," Stephen Marini has argued, "not through any single leader, but through the hymns it sang day and night, in season and out, everywhere and always."[51]

Marini is right that evangelicalism had no single leader, but it did have a single hero. Jesus was the subject of more evangelical hymns than the Father and the Holy Spirit combined. In fact, while evangelical hymns largely ignored the church, the sacraments, and the Trinity, they were obsessed with Jesus. In a massive database based on two hundred evangelical hymnbooks compiled by Marini, Jesus hymns are among the most popular. "All Hail the Power of Jesus'

Name" is the most-printed hymn overall. Hymns about Jesus also top the most printed lists for the classical era (1737–1860) and the modern era (1861–1970). Both John Cennick's "Jesus My All to Heaven Is Gone" (from the former list) and Charles Wesley's "Jesus, Lover of My Soul" (from the latter) tell stories of intimate encounters with Jesus. "Come hither, soul, I am the Way," Jesus coos' in the Cennick lyrics, which end with the believer walking alongside his "dear Savior." In the Wesley song, the singer dreams of hiding in the bosom of her lover, her "defenseless head" safe "in the shadow of Thy wing."[52]

Evangelical hymnody swelled in popularity over the course of the nineteenth century. In the Second Great Awakening and the "businessman's revival" of the 1850s, hymns became an important supplement to revival preaching. During the urban revivals of evangelist Dwight Moody (1837–99) and his chorister Ira Sankey (1840–1908) in the 1870s and 1880s they became at least as important as the sermon itself. Rather than scaring his congregants with the terrors of hell, Moody wooed them with the love of Jesus. Like Beecher, Moody was a master of the everyday anecdote and the commonplace illustration. In fact, he was so enamored of sentimental stories about rescued sinners that he repeatedly claimed he didn't have any theology at all. Whatever theology he had, however, was Jesus-centric to the core. "If there is one word above another that will swing open the eternal gates it is the name of Jesus," Moody once said. "There are a great many passwords and by-words down here; but that will be the countersign up above. Jesus is the 'Open Sesame' to heaven."[53] Moody invoked that magic password repeatedly, but it was Sankey's singing that really opened American hearts. Many who accepted Moody's altar call attributed their decision to "Come to Jesus" primarily to Sankey's "gospel hymns."

For all his fame as a chorister, Sankey was more influential as a publisher of the most popular hymnals of the nineteenth century. Sankey boasted that his hymnals sold as well as any book except the Bible, and they were extraordinarily well-received (selling 50 million copies by one account).[54] Many of the hymns that found their way into Sankey's hymnals (and, through them, into evangelical hearts) were written by women. In fact, Fanny Crosby, a blind woman who wrote roughly 8,000 hymns under 200 pseudonyms, may be the most prolific hymnist of all time. Yet even hymns written by men struck the chords of domestic piety. They too presented a form of Christianity that was relational rather than juridical, focusing on the intimate love of Jesus rather than the awesome power of his Father. References to the home were ubiquitous in the Sankey volumes, and while home often connoted heaven it also referred to domesticity itself, that refuge from grief and danger that cultural critic Christopher Lasch has called a "haven in a heartless world."[55]

Whereas the earlier classics of Isaac Watts typically focused on the exposition of Calvinist dogmas (including the substitutionary atonement and the depravity of the human "worm"), Sankey's hymns told simple stories of individual encounters with Jesus. Like African-American spirituals, they seemed to erase the time/space continuum, extracting Jesus out of first-century Palestine and inserting him into nineteenth-century Boston or Chicago. As one writer observed, Sankey's songs "seem now to bring Jesus of Nazareth right down into the streets of our own city, or, again, to take us right up to the gates of heaven."[56] Moody repeatedly called his own work a lifeboat operation. Sankey's hymns also drew on modern-day metaphors, depicting Jesus not as an abstruse divinity but a real-life rescuer, saving lost souls from danger, guiding them to safety, and piloting them home.

Rather than casting Jesus as a sacrificial lamb as Isaac Watts repeatedly did (in order to emphasize the doctrine of the substitutionary atonement), Sankey's lyricists cast Jesus as a sweet and gentle shepherd calling his lost sheep by name. Human beings were no longer hateful sinners bound for hell but innocent sheep searching for home. "The Ninety and Nine," Sankey's signature hymn, describes Jesus as a compassionate shepherd who will not rest until he has brought a lost lamb back into his fold. Other hymns, including "The Wandering Sheep," "Weary Wanderer," "Come, Wander, Come!" and "Tenderly Guide Us," focus on the stray lamb rather than the shepherd, but they too cast Jesus as a "Shepherd of love." Even "Amazing Grace," by some accounts the most popular hymn of all time, fits into this lost sheep genre, moving from exodus to wandering to home, all thanks to the loving ministrations of Jesus the shepherd. The genius of these Jesus-the-shepherd hymns, and one reason for their enduring popularity, is their emphasis on encountering Jesus one-on-one. While the shepherd may have a flock of ninety-nine, these hymns are not about the flock. They are about one loving shepherd seeking (and finding) one lost sheep.[57]

Another popular metaphor for describing the personal encounter of the believer with Jesus has roots in the Bible, and perhaps in African-American culture. Echoing the call-and-response motif of black sermons and spirituals, these hymns describe Jesus as a preacher of sorts, issuing a call and pleading for a response. In keeping with the ascendant Arminian emphasis on free will, Jesus issues his call to everyone, but he is careful to call "softly and tenderly" (sometimes even in a whisper), leaving the response up to each listener. A variation on this theme describes Jesus knocking. Instead of calling for the hearer to enter his heart, now he is the one doing the knocking. Unlike earlier hymns, which positioned Jesus at the gates of heaven as Judge (or, for that matter, the "Door" controlling all access to the Father), these hymns locate Jesus at the door to each person's heart, beckoning everyone to let him in. Calling and knocking hymns no doubt resonated at revivals, which evangelists traditionally ended with an altar call. In fact, Sankey often sang "Softly and Tenderly Jesus Is Calling" during Moody's invitations.

While the dominant theme of Isaac Watts's hymns was the vast distance between sinful humans and a sovereign God, the overriding theme of the Sankey hymnals was the closeness of Jesus. "If modern Evangelical hymns can be reduced to a single term," Marini has argued, "it would be nearness to Christ rather than the otherness of the sacred."[58] In the Sankey hymns, Jesus was a human being who could be known and loved and imitated. Hundreds of other popular evangelical hymns described the encounter with Jesus in personal terms— as a walk, a conversation, or even an embrace. That encounter is private and secret in some lyrics. "I Come to the Garden Alone," an evangelical classic, describes a devotee meeting Jesus secretly (and alone) at dawn:

> *I come to the garden alone*
> *While the dew is still on the roses*
> *And the voice I hear falling on my ear*
> *The Son of God discloses.*

And He walks with me, and He talks with me,
And He tells me I am His own;
And the joy we share as we tarry there,
None other has ever known.

"In the Secret of His Presence," by the Indian Christian Ellen Lakshmi Goreh, describes with unusual detail another intimate experience of secret communion with Jesus in "the secret place."[59]

These hymns express a religion of love—what Hindus call *bhakti marga*, the path of devotion that also culminates in a face-to-face encounter with divinity. But what sort of love is Jesus giving and receiving here? Some commentators have found in these hymns sublimated sexuality as well as sentimentality. When the believer sings "I am thine, and Thou art mine," she is giving voice to desires that could not otherwise be expressed by a properly passionless Victorian woman. In these hymns, believers lay down their heads on their Savior's breast and rest in the shadow of his sheltering wings. Jesus responds by putting his loving arms around them, and in some cases the embrace lasts until dawn. Clearly there is plenty of evidence here for what Beecher termed "love-pressure." It is possible to read the erotic into these lyrics. In fact, after Freud, who can avoid it? But such interpretations say more about contemporary interpreters than evangelical hymnody itself. The love Jesus and nineteenth-century evangelicals exchanged in these hymns was more *philia* than *eros*. As with the True Woman of "separate spheres" ideology, piety overwhelms passion here. Or, to put it another way, the passion is filial rather than sexual.

More than a lover, the Jesus of popular evangelical hymnody is a friend. In fact, references to Jesus as friend seem to outnumber references to Jesus as lover by at least ten-to-one in Sankey's hymnals. Cyberhymnal.org, an Internet site devoted to evangelical hymnody, lists twenty-eight different hymns under the "Christ the Friend" theme, including "The Best Friend to Have Is Jesus," "Friendship with Jesus," and "I've Found a Friend," all nineteenth-century standards. "What a Friend We Have in Jesus" gained public attention when it appeared in the first edition of *Gospel Hymns* in 1875. Today it remains one of the most beloved hymns in American evangelicalism. But this classic is by no means alone in depicting Jesus as a sweet and tender companion, willing to bear our grief and sorrow as well as our sin. Dozens of hymns popularized in the Victorian era describe Jesus as a divine companion—"our never changing Friend," a "Friend so true," "our dearest Friend." Others urged listeners to return the favor—to "Make Jesus Your Friend."[60]

Black spirituals also described Jesus as a friend. Born in the slave communities of the South long before the Civil War and brought to white Americans beginning in the 1870s by the Fisk University Jubilee Singers, spirituals were powerful vehicles for creating intimacy between believers and Jesus. These "sorrow songs" bridge the divides of time and space that often separate people from one another, and individuals from God. Characters from the Old and New Testaments interact among themselves and with modern believers; Jesus lives not only in ancient Palestine but also in contemporary America. Though he appears as a sovereign in "Ride On, King Jesus," and is conflated with Moses in "Ride On, Moses," spirituals portray him as well in more familiar terms—as brother and friend. Here, as in evangelical hymns, Jesus walks and talks with individual believers. He listens. He promises both eternal life and freedom from oppression. He knows the troubles they see. Finally, he offers an ongoing, intimate relationship: "He have been wid us, Jesus / He still wid us, Jesus / He will be wid us, Jesus / Be wid us to the end."[61]

LIBERAL PROTESTANTISM

Jesus-focused Christianity took root in evangelicalism but flowered in liberal Protestantism, a postbellum theological movement that adapted to the challenges of modernity by stressing the goodness of humanity, the inevitability of progress, the necessity of good works, and the immanence of God in nature, culture, and the human heart. Evangelicals had championed the Bible over the creeds, downplaying or denying doctrines long considered essential to the Christian faith. Liberals jettisoned even more. While evangelicals continued to affirm the twin authority of Jesus and the scriptures, liberals weaned themselves off the Bible, which they increasingly viewed as a good book rather than God's Book. Ultimately, their faith came to rest on the authority of Jesus alone.

When the Puritans set sail from England and Holland in the early seventeenth century, they had vowed to establish in the New World a "Biblical Commonwealth." Their hope for a godly society in which church and state would work hand in glove was dashed with the passage of the First Amendment. Yet their commitment to the Bible lived on. Americans began printing Bibles in 1777, and the American Bible Society spread biblical literacy far and wide. By the time of the Civil War, whites and blacks, Northerners and Southerners were, as Abraham Lincoln recognized in his Second Inaugural Address, reading the same scripture. The Bible had become, in the words of church historian Martin Marty, an "icon in mind, home, church, and culture."[62]

The Bible's iconic status owed much to the Reformation slogan *sola scriptura*. While Roman Catholics had always read the Bible through tradition (and, at least theoretically, deferred to priests and popes in interpreting it), Protestants insisted on reading the Bible fresh, without reference to church tradition. "*Quod non est biblicum, non est theologicum*," the Reformers averred: "What is not biblical is not theological." In matters of faith and practice, the Bible alone was authoritative. So went the Reformation.

Over the course of the nineteenth century, American Protestants effected a second Reformation. As biblical criticism, evolutionary science, and comparative religion chipped away at the authority of the Bible, and the Civil War dealt it a near-lethal blow, some turned to alternative sources of authority, including reason and experience. Many more turned to their Savior—the Jesus of history for some, and the Jesus of experience for others. While Reformation standard-bearers had retreated from tradition to the Bible, evangelicals began to retreat from the Bible to Jesus. By the time liberalism emerged out of evangelicalism in the decades after the Civil War, this retreat had become an all-out withdrawal.

Other interpreters of nineteenth-century American religion have described the rise of Arminian theology or Christian populism as the main story in nineteenth-century American religion. But the real religious revolution of the century was the emergence of Jesus as the all-important religious symbol in American culture. In the colonial period he had cowered in the corner like a timid son before an angry Father. During the first half of the century, he grew up. In the aftermath of the Second Great Awakening, he overthrew God the Father as the dominant person in the Trinity. Evangelicals, instead of defining Jesus in terms of God, increasingly came to define God in terms of Jesus. God was loving and merciful, they argued, and His character was most clearly manifest in Jesus. During the second half of the century, liberal Protestants took this revolution one step further. Boldly declaring Jesus' spiritual independence, they overthrew the Bible as the key source of religious authority. God's real revelation, liberals now argued, was not scripture but Jesus.

Protestant liberals defined conversion as a process rather than an event, so perhaps it is fitting that this transformation from Bible Christianity to Jesus Christianity was gradual. Jesus played an important role in the Second Great Awakening, when populist preachers began to tailor their sermons around his atoning work on the cross. He was prominent in the books of liberal evangelicals such as Horace Bushnell and Henry Ward Beecher. Not until the "United Evangelical Front" broke down after the Civil War, however, did the typical American Protestant put Jesus at the center of the Christian life—inside individuals and society, and leading both onward and upward to the kingdom of God on earth.

Evangelicalism had been a big tent in the antebellum period, but as evangelicals weighed the challenges of modernity, two distinct positions emerged. Those positions began to harden as evangelicals debated the proper role of Christianity in society. Conservatives faced modernity by holding fast to the inspiration of the Bible. Liberals responded by carving out a mediating position (often referred to as the "New Theology") between capitulation to modern thought and rejection of it. By the 1880s, liberal Protestants had left the evangelical fold, and evangelicalism had come to refer not to the broad center of American Protestantism but to the conservative right. At the turn of the century, liberals began to take over the mainline Protestant denominations. By the Scopes "Monkey Trial" of 1925, the conservatives who opposed them had become religious pariahs.

As liberal Protestantism ascended, Jesus did too. In fact, the more these liberal Protestants disentangled Jesus from controversial Calvinist dogmas and restrictive creeds, the more prominent and popular he became. When liberals said "yes" to Darwin and to European biblical critics, they jettisoned even more from the Christian tradition. Horace Bushnell had criticized Darwinian evolution. Virtually all of the leaders of the New Theology of the 1880s and beyond eagerly embraced Beecher's self-definition as a "cordial Christian evolutionist." Most gave up on Beecher's defense of miracles, and on Bushnell's effort to rehabilitate the doctrine of the vicarious atonement. None regarded the Bible as the literal word of God. As evangelicals did battle with the Bible critics, liberals made peace with their methods, insisting that Christians could live with the likes of Renan and Strauss.

This truce vitiated the Reformation slogan of *sola scriptura*. How could Christians base their beliefs and practices on scripture alone once it was believed that the books of the Bible contradicted not only science but also one another? Happily, the liberals' found a different foundation for their faith. And that foundation was *solus Jesus*. "A theology which is not Christocentric," argued Andover Theological Seminary professor Egbert Smyth, "is like a Ptolemaic Astronomy, it is out of true relation to the earth and the heavens, to God and the Universe." The Reverend George A. Gordon of Old South Church in Boston agreed. "Nothing can be so surely fatal to the pulpit," he wrote, "as a meagre Christology." William Adams Brown lent the New Theology its rallying cry, "Back to Christ," and Christianity its new bottom line: "Let no theology call itself Christian which has not its center and source in him."[63]

It is now commonplace to refer to liberal Protestants as christocentric, and as these quotations demonstrate *Christ* continued to be a standard term for Jesus. But few Protestant liberals actually focused on the messianic role of their Savior—his status as the Christ. Liberal Protestants were far more interested in recovering the historical Jesus than in tweaking the Christic formulas of the creeds. Their thinking was Jesus-centric rather than christocentric; they focused far more on the person of Jesus than on the Christ of the cross.

While Calvinists had maximized the distance between God and humanity and evangelicals had narrowed it, liberal Protestants all but obliterated it. Drawing on the doctrine of the *imago Dei*, they argued that humans were created good, in the image of God, not sinful, in the image of a fallen Adam. As for God, He dwelled in the world, rather than standing aloof from it. "The idea of God as transcendent," the Episcopal theologian A.V.G. Allen wrote in 1884, "is yielding to the idea of deity as immanent in His creation."[64]

Given their emphasis on the immanence of God, liberals refused to recognize the sharp dualisms—between the sacred and the secular, divinity and humanity, the supernatural and the natural, the world and the church—that had given Calvinism its dynamism. They also followed Henry Ward Beecher (who had regularly preached against slavery) in defying an old taboo against politics in the pulpit. Their Jesus was not restricted to the church or even to the heart. He could be found in novels and nations, science and society. "The spirit of benevolence, and even of evangelization, is no longer confined to the Church of God," the Black Episcopalian Alexander Crummell wrote. "It is the spirit of the age. Our Lord Jesus Christ has put this spirit into insurance companies, and mercantile ventures. It stimulates adventure. It prompts geographical research. It vitalizes science. It gives coloring and tone to literature."[65] This blurring of the boundaries between what Augustine had called the kingdom of God and the kingdom of the world opened American culture up to the influence of Jesus. But it also opened Jesus up to the influence of American culture. It should not be surprising, therefore, that liberal Protestants shaped Jesus in their own image. And as they disenchanted the cosmos, they disenchanted Jesus too.

JESUS WEPT

All but the most radical Protestant liberals affirmed the divinity of Jesus, but they emphasized his humanness. Though some focused on the Jesus of history, most spoke of Jesus in experiential terms, placing him not in first-century Palestine but in their own hearts. They emphasized his birth instead of his resurrection, the incarnation rather than the atonement, his immanence rather than his transcendence. More a moralist than a miracle worker, their Jesus came to earth not to satisfy a legal judgment or to pay a debt owed to an angry Father but to reveal to human beings the loving character of God, and to prompt them to develop that same character in themselves. His death saved sinners not from hell (which few liberals believed in anymore) but from selfish solitude. The new birth he offered was essentially moral, an awakening to a life of sympathy with all of God's children. "In life and death," wrote the Baptist theologian William Newton Clarke, "Jesus is the supreme illustration of the truth that God is served in serving men."[66]

Like their evangelical forebears, liberal Protestants also feminized Jesus. They typically steered clear, however, of the antebellum emphasis on his sacrifice and submission. For liberals, the life of Jesus was a story of the loving union of God with humans and humans with one another. Elizabeth Stuart Phelps's *The Story of Jesus Christ* epitomized this view. Prepared while Elizabeth Cady Stanton was working on *The Woman's Bible* (1895–98), Phelps's biography was a love story of sorts. It was also the first full-length feminist interpretation of Jesus. "The story of the Gospels was written by men," Phelps wrote, "Men have studied and expounded it for two thousand years. Men have been its commentators, its translators, its preachers." Her goal was to supplement that record with a female voice, and according to that voice Jesus was a "great democrat" who undertook a "social revolution" on behalf of women. Convinced "that men and women stood before God upon the same moral plane, and that they ought so to stand before human society," he always showed the utmost "respect for womanhood." He was, Phelps concluded, "the only man who ever understood" the plight of women.[67]

Phelps's "sacred romance" lauded Jesus in language almost as lofty as the hymns to the Cosmic Christ that begin the New Testament books of Ephesians and Colossians. "He himself is Christianity," she wrote. "He is the greatest force in civilization: the highest motive power in philosophy, in art, in poetry, in science, in faith. He is the creator of the human brotherhood." Her Jesus was no self-made man, however. His character was formed by "the loveliest of mortal mothers." (Joseph—an unsympathetic character here—died while Jesus was still young.) A lover of nature, Jesus grew "to manhood in a world of flowers," his eyes trained from his youth "to the tints of narcissus, iris, and the red tulip . . . the pink convolvulus and daisy . . . the cyclamen and asphodel." He was a sensitive man with fine features—a delicate throat, a soft beard, and curly hair. "His lips, exquisitely cut, trembled to every stir of feeling." His smile was radiant and his voice sweet. His sermons were music instead of thunder, promises instead of threats, love instead of law. During his public ministry, Jesus "received into his heart one class of people—the most miserable," and so revealed himself as "the greatest Master of human sympathy." There was no crying in Jefferson's Jesus. But Phelps's Jesus wept.[68]

ANDROGYNE

This was about as far as the feminization of Jesus went. A few theologians portrayed Jesus as a feminist in the 1970s.[69] In 1975, Edwina Sandys created a sculpture of a bare-breasted Jesus on the cross to celebrate the United Nations' Decade of Women. *Christa* was later displayed at the Cathedral of St. John the Divine in New York and at the Yale Divinity School. But she was always better at stirring controversies than moving the masses. She lives on (barely) in obscurity, tucked away in the undercroft of Christ Church in New Haven, Connecticut.

If Americans today are unreceptive to a female Jesus, they were even less interested during the nineteenth century. In fact, for the overwhelming majority of Victorian Americans a female Jesus was literally unthinkable. No one during the evangelical century seriously contested Jesus' maleness. What evangelicals and liberals did was nuance his undeniable maleness with a heavy dose of femininity. In sermons and novels, prayers and hymns, lithographs and half-tones, evangelical and liberal Protestants alike depicted Jesus as a feminine male—what we would now call an androgyne. In her Jesus biography, Phelps called Jesus "sweet because strong." His "exquisite compassion," she wrote, was "tenderer than woman's, stronger than man's"—a combination "undreamed of before in the world." That same alluring combination was at work in the rare hymns that referred to Jesus in maternal terms. "Jesus, Savior, Pilot Me" compared Jesus' stilling of the storm with a mother shushing her child. "My Rock" spoke of leaning on Jesus like a "child on mother's breast." Yet both hymns supplemented these maternal metaphors with images of manly strength. In "My Rock," Jesus was "strong to save" and "my Rock and Righteousness." In "Jesus, Savior, Pilot Me," he was the "Wondrous Sov'reign of the sea."[70]

Church historian Philip Schaff, an influential advocate of Mercers-

burg Theology, also endowed Jesus with an intriguing mix of masculine and feminine virtues. In *The Person of Christ* (1865), Schaff
wrote: "He combined childlike innocence with manly strength, all-
absorbing devotion to God with untiring interest in the welfare of
man, tender love to the sinner with uncompromising severity against
sin, commanding dignity with winning humility, fearless courage
with wise caution, unyielding firmness with sweet gentleness." This
same mix of unyielding yang and yielding yin appeared regularly in
nineteenth-century lives of Jesus. Henry Ward Beecher outfitted Jesus with a full array of feminine virtues, yet even he insisted that
Jesus did not shirk from a fight. Though Beecher's Jesus spoke "the
natural language of affection and sympathy," he was also capable
of using "warrior words." And when provoked, his love could be
"equipped for conflict" as surely as his benevolence could be "arrayed
against evil." "My Christ was a lamb," Beecher told his congregation
in a sermon in 1863, "but he was also a lion of the tribe of Judah."[71]

Jacob Abbott, the father of Lyman Abbott and an author of the
popular Rollo book series for boys, took up the gender of Jesus in *The
Cornerstone* (1855). "Jesus Christ," he wrote, "was, in some respects,
the most bold, energetic, decided, and courageous man that ever
lived; but in others he was the most flexible, submissive, and yielding;
and in the conceptions which many persons form of his character
there is a degree of indistinctness and confusion, from want of clear
ideas of the mode in which these seemingly opposite qualities come
together."[72] This is a delicious quotation, not only for its yin-yang description of Jesus (as both energetic and yielding, courageous and
submissive) but also for its articulation of the confusion Abbott and
his contemporaries felt as they attempted to know and love and imitate their Jesus. Especially during the heyday of separate-spheres ideology, it simply did not make sense to find the masculine and the
feminine cohabiting in one body. One of the great mysteries of Jesus
has been his ability to bring divinity and humanity together in one
person. To Victorian Americans his ability to display feminine virtues
in a male body must have been almost as mysterious. Eventually it
would become disquieting too.

Three

MANLY REDEEMER

On November 15, 1898, a major exhibition of Jesus art debuted at the American Galleries in New York City. Lives of Christ are typically textual, but *Life of Our Saviour Jesus Christ* by the French artist James Jacques Joseph Tissot was executed in watercolors. Tissot's 365 gouaches (one for each day of the year) told the story of Jesus from birth to death to resurrection, and while New Yorkers did not feel moved to kneel down in the gallery and pray, as the Parisian faithful had in an earlier showing, the city was captivated. The exhibition's popularity prompted similar shows in Boston, Philadelphia, Chicago, St. Louis, and Omaha, and buoyed sales of a variety of multivolume coffee table books of Tissot's visual gospel. All this attention won Tissot renown he never enjoyed in Europe (and a generous payment of $60,000 from the Brooklyn Museum of Art, which purchased the paintings).

Born in France, Tissot (1836–1902) moved in 1871 to England, where he made a reputation as an illustrator for *Vanity Fair* and a realistic painter of high-society Londoners. But a life dedicated to flattering fashionable women and dandy men can wear on anyone, and apparently it wore on Tissot. After returning to Paris, he attended a mass at the Church of St. Sulpice while researching a painting called *Sacred Music*. To get there, he would have had to wade past shops laden with the sort of mass-produced religious art that made Paris's Left Bank the nation's Mecca for the sale of crucifixes, rosaries, and holy cards—kitsch so identified with that particular church that it was known across Europe as *l'art Saint-Sulpice*. In the Church of St. Sulpice, Jesus reportedly appeared to Tissot in a vision. Realizing that all was vanity, including his prior work, Tissot dedicated his life to the Church and his art to biblical subjects. He left Paris suddenly, leading friends who knew of his newfound piety to speculate that he had joined a Dead Sea monastery. He had actually fled to Palestine, a pilgrim on an artistic and spiritual quest.

As a Roman Catholic, Tissot was determined to create a life consistent with both scripture and tradition. As a realist, he was determined to avoid the anachronisms he knew beset other Jesus paintings. So he read widely in the history of the region, spoke with local rabbis, took scores of photographs, and filled sketch books with drawings of the faces and finery of Jewish men and women. He then spent nearly a decade creating his masterpiece. The result was a visual version of Ernest Renan's *Life of Jesus*, minus the skepticism. Like his countryman Renan (who had also researched his master work on site), Tissot was committed to capturing the historical Jesus. Unlike Renan, he did so in the service of faith.

Tissot's gouaches are as sumptuous as the Cecil B. DeMille film *King of Kings* (1927)—no accident since DeMille based the cinematography for his Jesus masterpiece on Tissot's work. Although Jesus lords over these pictures as plainly as he does over American Christianity itself, the local landscape (both demographic and geographical) is clearly on show. In *Sermon on the Mount*, for example, Tissot takes up a vantage point above both Jesus and the multitudes. Here Jesus' face is not visible; his body, painted in earth tones, seems to grow out of the landscape. Behind him is nothing but red earth, a blue sea, and a black sky. Before him is a turbaned sea of humanity, the folds and shadows on their mantles matching exquisitely the forms of the mount itself.

Reviews of the New York show were favorable without being fawning. *The New York Times* praised Tissot's "pluck," his "workmanlike determination," and his "marvelous industry" only to go on to inform viewers that they would find "no special masterpiece" in the galleries. The *Times* did laud Tissot, however, for his cosmopolitan treatment of Jesus' face and figure. "He has made Him of a high type that suits European as well as Asian, Greek as well as Hebrew," its critic wrote, "and very rarely allows the face to degenerate into the namby-pamby effeminate look so often seen."[1]

While Tissot's Jesus pictures were hanging in New York, Kate Hampton, a writer for the liberal Protestant magazine *The Outlook*, happened by. At least to her, Tissot's Jesus did not seem particularly manly. In fact, the gouaches looked like the kitsch derided across Europe as *l'art Saint-Sulpice.* She wondered, however, what others would think. Soon *The Outlook* was conducting a survey of New York City clergy, asking, "Does the face of Christ, as depicted in ancient and modern art, realize your idea of a strong face?"

Responses flooded in from priests, ministers, and rabbis, and the verdict was all but unanimous: "The soft, curled, hermaphroditical" Jesus decried half a century earlier in Herman Melville's *Moby Dick* (1851) was alive and well. A Presbyterian minister called traditional images of Jesus "weak" and "repulsive." A Unitarian said the hundreds of paintings he had seen presented a "lackadaisical and gelatinous" personality. A Reform Jew told *The Outlook* that he had not once seen a picture of a strong Jesus. An Episcopal priest said that "feeble, mawkish, sickly portraits of Christ" were the rule rather than the exception, while another clergyman of the same denomination said that Jesus images were utterly lacking in the strong features routinely found "among college athletes, among soldiers, young business men, and even city roughs." A third Episcopalian concluded that not even the great Tissot had been able to give late Victorian Americans the manly Christ they so plainly coveted. No Mormons were consulted in this survey, but they probably would not have dissented. Writing around the same time, a Mormon writer complained that artists had misrepresented Jesus as a "somewhat effeminate and sentimental young man with long flowing locks, a weakling in body and with few traces on his face of the strength of character within."[2]

"The Face of Christ in Art" appeared in *The Outlook* in April 1899.

That same month, two influential Americans spoke out against the feminization of American culture. G. Stanley Hall, president of Clark University and one of America's foremost psychologists, gave his talk before a national kindergarten teachers' convention. The United States was suffering from an epidemic of effeminacy among males, he argued, and the cure was to allow them to act like the primitive savages they were. At least for boys, Hall said, self-restraint was counterproductive. They needed to release their anger, not sublimate it. They needed more passion, not less, and less civilization, not more. Boxing, he told an aghast audience of schoolmarms, was not just a spectator sport but a pedagogical tool, which forward-looking parents and teachers should employ to raise young boys up to manhood. Though vilified in the press as a "preacher of pain and pessimism" and an advocate of "boxing for babies," Hall earned accolades from New York Governor Theodore Roosevelt, who praised his contributions to American manliness. "Over-sentimentality, over-softness, in fact washiness and mushiness," Roosevelt wrote in a letter to Hall, "are the great dangers of this age and of this people."[3]

The second influential American to decry the dangers of the effeminacy epidemic that month was Teddy Roosevelt himself. Only recently back from his exploits in Cuba in the Spanish-American War, Governor Roosevelt delivered his now-famous "Strenuous Life" speech at the Hamilton Club in Chicago on April 10, 1899. He decried both the "over-civilized man" and "that cloistered life which saps the hardy virtues in a nation," and, like Hall, he was convinced that nothing less than the future of the United States hung in the balance. If the country were to cultivate another generation of "weaklings" who "fear work or fear righteous war," he warned, it would (and should) "vanish from the earth."[4]

The age of Teddy Roosevelt witnessed major shifts in American cultural, social, economic, and religious life. Historians disagree on precisely how to characterize the Progressive era of the 1890s through World War I. Some see a transition from a producer-driven society of small businesses to a consumer-driven society of large corporations. Others detect a passage from a culture of scarcity (with its values of thrift, hard work, and self-denial) to a culture of abundance (and its focus on consumption, leisure, and self-gratification). The cultural historian Jackson Lears has detected a shift from Protestantism to secularity, "salvation to self-realization."[5] Among these historians there is broad agreement, however, that right around the turn of the century the country was made new.

THE CURSE OF FEMININITY

With this new era came a crisis in masculinity (a term widely used for the first time in the 1890s). *Crisis* may be too strong a word, but clearly the roles assigned to men and women in the American drama were being rewritten. Right around the time that the feminization of American culture became firmly entrenched in the 1880s, opposition arose, particularly among middle-class white men. As early as 1864, the Transcendentalist-turned-Catholic Orestes Brownson was decrying the feminization of American culture. "The curse of the age is its femininity, its lack, not of barbarism, but of virility," Brownson lamented. "It is the age of woman-worship. Women are angels; men are demons." In 1886 in *The Bostonians*, Basil Ransom spoke for the novelist Henry James when he complained, "The whole generation is womanised; the masculine tone is passing out of the world; it's a feminine, a nervous, hysterical, chattering, canting age." Men responded to predictions of their demise—and James's call for the preservation of "the masculine character"—by joining all-male fraternal orders such as the Odd Fellows, Freemasons, Knights of Pythias, and Red Men. They read novels about the adventures of cowboys and Indians. They took up outdoor activities such as fishing and hunting. Once again, they insisted on raising their boys to manhood—as coaches of sports teams and as leaders in groups such as the Boy Scouts of America (established in 1912). Perhaps more than anyone else, Frederic Remington seared into the nation's consciousness images of this passionate man, incarnated in *Harper's Weekly* woodcuts as the soldier in battle, the cowboy on the frontier, and the gritty footballer, throwing himself into a sport that during Roosevelt's presidency became a national obsession.[6]

There are a variety of explanations for the resurgence and redefinition of masculinity in the 1890s and beyond. The Civil War was no doubt a factor. Without the manly courage of fallen Union fighting men, the United States would not have remained one nation; in the South, the sacrificial deaths of valiant Confederate soldiers became a key ingredient in what Charles Reagan Wilson has called "the religion of the Lost Cause."[7] Another factor was the rise of Social Darwinism: If only the fittest survive, it must be a personal and patriotic duty to muscle up. The proliferation of white-collar labor was also important. In earlier eras of American history, work itself had kept men fit. However, as the ranks of managers and administrators swelled in the decades after the Civil War, muscles once honed in factories, battlefields, and farms began to atrophy. The expansion of the middle class and the contraction of the working day made leisure pursuits possible, and increasingly middle-class men (and those who aspired to middle-class status) chose to fill their time off with strenuous activities such as hiking and body building.

Perhaps the most important factor behind the masculinization of American culture was a creeping sense that women were beginning to encroach on what in the past had been all-male preserves. As has been noted, during the late nineteenth century, women entered the workplace in force and took up important positions in reform societies. But they also attended colleges in large numbers, and began knocking on the doors of professional schools in law and medicine. Some became preachers, while others agitated for the right to vote. Finally, and most ominously from the perspective of fin de siècle men, a few began to meddle in sacred domains such as business, men's clubs, and sports. As muckrakers began to expose the immorality of corporations, other social reformers tried to close down fraternal organizations and ban boxing (even as women themselves were taking up smoking).

Many American men responded to these perceived assaults on all-male turf by attempting to overturn the "separate spheres" doctrine. While in the past such men had valued "civilization" and identified it with supposedly feminine values such as passivity and self-denial, they now gloried in the savage and the primitive, and reinterpreted traditionally male vices such as assertiveness as necessities, even virtues. If America had been inspired in the nineteenth century by pious women, they reasoned, it would be led in the twentieth century (as it had been during the Civil War) by passionate men.

This broad cultural shift was particularly visible in the religious arena, where earlier efforts to cultivate "muscular Christianity"—in the Great Revival of 1857–58 (also known as the "businessmen's awakening") and via groups such as the Young Men's Christian Association (YMCA)—apparently had not done enough to stem the tide of feminine religion. As early as 1892, the conservative evangelical magazine *The Watchman* was reporting on a survey of eight churches that found membership rates of only 28 percent men. In an effort to gauge the depth of that fall into feminization, the YMCA conducted a study in 1910 that determined that U.S. churches were only one-third male. Roughly 3 million men were missing from the pews.[8]

JESUS THE SCRAPPER

American Christians responded to this dire news with a series of books intended to make their faith more manly. While many of the sentimental classics of the mid-nineteenth century were written by women, virtually all of these new volumes were written by men. In *The Masculine in Religion* (1906), Baptist pastor Carl Delos Case argued that Christianity needed to recover its masculine side (and its manly metaphors). The church, he wrote, "is a factory to turn out products for a modern civilization; it is a laboratory in which an expert examination is made of soul life; it is an arsenal where are found all sorts of armor for warfare; it is a foundry where is forged the armor for defense; it is a fort from which the soldiers sally forth to victory." In 1911, the newly formed Men and Religion Forward Movement devoted itself to luring men back to the churches with the slogan "More Men for Religion, More Religion for Men." Jason Pierce's *The Masculine Power of Christ* (1912) and *Manhood of the Master* (1913) by Harry Emerson Fosdick, one of the most influential liberal Protestant preachers of the first half of the twentieth century, gave that same theme book-length treatments. The common denominator here was what *Century* magazine called a "vigorous, robust, muscular Christianity . . . devoid of all the et cetera of creed." Doctrine was for sissies, and the meek weren't going to inherit the earth.[9]

When the Men and Religion Forward Movement faded after a whirlwind campaign in 1911–12, the "baseball evangelist" Billy Sunday (who had once patrolled center field for the Chicago White Sox) stepped up to the plate. He was the hottest act in the country in the years preceding World War I, in part because he gave voice to a more virile form of revivalism that proved attractive to both men and women. While other Protestant preachers were displaying their erudition, Sunday displayed his muscles, sliding across the stage as if barreling into home plate. "Lord save us," Sunday prayed, "from off-handed, flabby-cheeked, brittle-boned, weak-kneed, thin-skinned, pliable, plastic, spineless, effeminate, sissified, three-caret Christianity." Instead of urging fellow Christians to turn the other cheek, he challenged his male listeners to fight the good fight and his female listeners to embrace macho men, including the Manly Redeemer. While Homer Rodeheaver (Sunday's answer to Ira Sankey) sang hymns such as "Onward Christian Soldiers" and "The Battle Hymn of the Republic," Sunday railed against the sissified Jesus of the feminized crowd. Jesus "was no dough-faced, lick-spittle proposition," he insisted. "Jesus was the greatest scrapper that ever lived." Sunday then dared his audiences to fight alongside Jesus. "The manliest man," Sunday said, "is the man who will acknowledge Jesus Christ."[10]

As Billy Sunday crisscrossed the nation converting Americans to this scrappy Jesus, evangelicalism began to split into two camps, the fundamentalists and the modernists. The publication of the landmark series of pamphlets on "The Fundamentals" between 1910 and 1915 and the Scopes trial of 1925 made plain the deep divisions inside American Protestantism. Yet the emergence in American Protestantism of what church historian Martin Marty has referred to as a "two-party system" (of "private party" conservatives and "public party" liberals) did not produce any real disagreement over either the centrality or the personality of Jesus. When Sunday tried to portray modernism as "emasculated Christianity," modernists fought back with a masculine Jesus of their own. Not everyone agreed with the writer and Civil War veteran William Elliot Griffis, who called war "the story of our race" and championed "Jesus the Soldier," but almost everyone now seemed to believe that Christianity was first and foremost about the person of Jesus, and that his personality packed a powerful punch. As Jesus stepped down from his pedestal and became a real man, he was prodded by liberals and conservatives alike.[11]

THE SOCIAL GOSPEL

In his 1906 essay on "The Moral Equivalent of War," psychologist William James called upon the churches to give real men something important to do other than wage war. Answering that call, Social Gospel advocates such as Washington Gladden (1836–1918) and Walter Rauschenbusch (1861–1918) challenged men to become Christian "knights" in a brotherhood Rauschenbusch called the "Holy Chivalry." Fighting on behalf of their women, their families, their country, and their Savior, these knights would achieve a just social order they called the Kingdom of God. The separate-spheres ideology, which had confined virtue to women and women to the home, was in their view outmoded. Men too could exhibit Christian virtues, and could enact them in the battlefield of society.[12]

The Social Gospellers stood in a long line of socially concerned evangelicals obsessed with the example of Jesus. Because they understood the kingdom of God in familial terms—as the goal of a "brotherhood of man" operating under the "Fatherhood of God"—they did not jettison the First Person of the Trinity. When it came to acting in the world, however, they followed the footsteps of the Second. Wary of creeds and skeptical about the Bible, they built their ethics on Jesus. Lyman Abbott, a Social Gospel thinker who succeeded Henry Ward Beecher at Plymouth Congregational Church in Brooklyn (and also wrote a popular life of Jesus), epitomized this Jesus-centrism. "Suppose that all your life you dreaded an awful god," he wrote, "and suddenly the curtain were rent aside and you saw the luminous figure of the living Christ, and over his head were written the words, 'This is thy God, O man.'" Walter Rauschenbusch's spiritual world also revolved around a friendly Son rather than a wrathful Father. "The God of the stellar universe is a God in whom I drown," he explained. "Christ with the face of Jesus I can comprehend, and love, and assimilate, so I stick to him."[13]

Social Gospel thinkers initially described Jesus in the sentimental language of domestic piety, focusing on his self-sacrifice on the cross. After the century turned and the new cult of masculinity emerged in full force, however, their Jesus muscled up. Sentimental hymns that appeared in early YMCA hymnals disappeared in a revised hymnal issued in 1904. A 1910 songbook called *Manly Songs for Christian Men* praised "the manly man of Galilee." Gradually the story of Jesus' cleansing of the Jerusalem Temple became the paradigmatic gospel story. "There was nothing mushy, nothing sweetly effeminate about Jesus," Walter Rauschenbusch insisted. "He was the one that turned again and again on the snarling pack of His pious enemies and made them slink away. He plucked the beard of death and He went into the city and the temple to utter those withering woes against the dominant class."[14]

Although Rauschenbusch agreed with Billy Sunday on the masculinity of Jesus (and the importance of the Temple cleansing story), the two did not agree on just what sort of man Jesus was. Jesus was for both preachers a courageous man of action. But while Sunday's Jesus was a street fighter, putting up his dukes against individual sin, Rauschenbusch's Jesus was a progressive activist going into battle against the collective sins of a capitalist society. His hero lorded over not only the home and the church but also the shop and the factory.

Social Gospelers followed the evangelical tradition in speaking about Jesus as a friend, but to them he was more comrade than companion, a coworker for the Kingdom of God. Rauschenbusch called him a hard-working carpenter and "a man of the common people." He was a man of power, "virile, commanding, and strong," according to the Social Gospel theologian Francis Greenwood Peabody. But instead of using his muscles to bully people into converting, as Billy Sunday's Jesus had done, the progressive Jesus of the Social Gospel used his power "to crush the Wrong, uphold the Right." After Teddy Roosevelt's death in 1919, the Boy Scouts of America described the Trust Buster like this: "He was frail; he made himself a tower of strength. He was timid; he made himself a lion of courage. He was a dreamer; he became one of the great doers of all time." These same words capture the martial Jesus of the Social Gospel.[15]

In addition to theological works by the likes of Gladden and Rauschenbusch, the Social Gospel produced a library of Jesus novels. Some described Jesus as a socialist. In Archibald McCowan's *Christ, the Socialist* (1894), Jesus stands on the steps of New York City Hall and denounces corporations as Pharisees. In Elizabeth Stuart Phelps's *A Singular Life* (1894), a Christlike figure named Emanuel (with a mother named Mary, a father named Joseph, and fishermen for disciples) trades in his seminary lessons on "predestination, foreordination, sanctification, election, and botheration" for a life devoted to saving prostitutes and alcoholics in a seaside town.[16] He dies at the age of thirty-three, stoned by a man named Judas. Upton Sinclair's *They Call Me Carpenter* (1922) is a bit more subtle, but it too stars a Christlike socialist, in this case 'a "Bolsheviki Prophet" named "Mr. Carpenter" who runs into trouble for supporting his local trade union.

Social Gospel writers also produced a series of "Jesus in" books and stories that imagined Jesus taking up residence in U.S. cities (and not liking what he sees). W. T. Stead's *If Christ Came to Chicago* (1894) and W.E.B. Du Bois's "Jesus Christ in Georgia" (1911) both fit this genre. So does the most popular and enduring Social Gospel novel of all time: Charles M. Sheldon's *In His Steps: "What Would Jesus Do?"* (1897). In this novel, which inspired the "What Would Jesus Do?" craze in the late twentieth century, the Reverend Henry Maxwell of First Church in the fictional small town of Raymond challenges his parishioners to ask themselves, in every situation for a year, "What would Jesus do?" Sheldon then follows the lives of a newspaper editor, a businessman, and a society girl (among others) as they try to apply the ancient discipleship practice of *imitatio Christi* to modern America.

Sheldon was a liberal Congregationalist minister, and the good news in his novel was quintessentially liberal. While by the end of the century most evangelicals had accepted a division of society into secular and sacred spheres, liberals followed the Puritans in rejecting that division, insisting that God could not be confined merely to the church and the home—that religion was a public as well as a private matter. In the novel, Sheldon brings "the Christianity of Christ" to bear on all segments of society, including the seemingly secular arena of business. He describes the Christian life as a valiant fight. He also draws on earlier themes in sentimental evangelicalism, including its emphases on individual piety, self-sacrifice, and the cultivation of character. In that respect, *In His Steps* was a transitional work.[17]

BEYOND THE BEARDED LADY

In His Steps sold by the millions and was translated into over twenty languages, but Sheldon was not the most important evangelist for the gospel of the manly Christ. That title belongs to a layman named Bruce Barton (1886–1967). Although Barton's bestseller, *The Man Nobody Knows: A Discovery of the Real Jesus* (1925), is usually seen as a tract for consumer capitalism, it was first and foremost a brief for the manly Christ. It was also an homage to the author's father, the Reverend William E. Barton, who had been decrying the feminization of Jesus for decades when *The Man Nobody Knows* appeared.

Barton the elder, a Congregational minister who like other liberal Protestants of his generation did not shirk from the intellectual and social challenges posed by modern life, was a prolific author. He wrote scores of books, including a well-regarded biography of Abraham Lincoln and a series of imaginative gospels told from the perspectives of, among others, John the Baptist, Judas Iscariot, and James the brother of Jesus. In *Jesus of Nazareth* (1903), a lavishly illustrated octavo, Barton denounced Tissot's Jesus as a "wan, weak figure"—"an impotent Christ." He also railed more generally against the "womanly sweetness" of Jesus in art. According to Barton, it was as if artists through the centuries had said to one another, "We will make our Christ with a woman's face, and add a beard."[18]

Barton did praise some Jesus art. He called a French painting of a crucifixion set against the Paris skyline "an anachronism of the most daring kind." "If at first thought it seems irreverent," he wrote, "it certainly is not so intended, and there is a sermon in it." Barton also found a sermon in "Behold, I Stand at the Door and Knock!" (1902) by the American illustrator Frank Beard, who pictured Jesus attempting to gain entry into the office of a businessman poring over his accounts. That same sermon would be expounded at length two decades later by Barton's own son.[19]

In his youth, Bruce Barton considered going into the family business, but he decided to forgo the ministry for a series of secular callings, in part because of his liberal Protestant conviction that God was immanent in culture as well as the church. After graduating from Amherst College in 1907, he worked for a series of magazines. The slogan for the Harvard Classics he devised during a stint in marketing at *Collier's Weekly*—"the essentials of a liberal education in only fifteen minutes a day"—was a hit, and launched him into a career in advertising. Before his death in 1967, Barton was the second "B" in BBDO, one of the country's largest advertising agencies.

Although Barton would go on to market products for Macy's, General Motors, and United States Steel, he is remembered today for marketing Jesus. That effort began with the appearance of his first major book, *A Young Man's Jesus*. Published in 1914, when Barton was a young man himself, *A Young Man's Jesus* was written for a confused generation of American men who came of age with pictures of the Sweet Savior in their bedrooms and photographs of Teddy Roosevelt's Rough Riders in their basements. The frontispiece, "The Master" by Darius Cobb (another preacher's son), underscored the roughness and toughness of the book's protagonist, complete with massive, deep-set eyes and a steely stare. *A Young Man's Jesus* opened with this manifesto:

> It is time for those of us who are this side of thirty-five to unite and take back our Jesus . . . We have surrendered his statues to cathedrals and hospitals and—Heaven forgive us—even to monasteries. We have looked on unprotestingly while painters have made Him soft-faced, and effeminate; and hymn-writers have written of His sufferings as though that were all in His life worth writing about. We have only ourselves to blame, if out of all the repellent medley of hospitals and monasteries and weak pictures and spiritless hymns, the public has formed its own conception of a tired, unhappy, martyred Jesus who lived without a real laugh and looked forward to dying in a sort of fanatical eagerness.[20]

Barton's Jesus, by contrast, was "a young man glowing with physical strength and the joy of living." He had a strong handshake and a good sense of humor. His muscles, honed for years in a carpenter's shop, "stood out like knots of iron," and his shoulders were as broad as his chest was deep. This "man's man" was also "a woman's man" who possessed in abundance the "manly strength" that "since the world began" has been a "magnet" attracting the weaker to the stronger sex. Barton's Jesus was not merely physically attractive, however. He was also decisive and authoritative and, above all, courageous. At least in Barton's telling, Jesus began his public career in the Temple in Jerusalem, where, with "eyes aflame" and "cheeks red with righteous anger," he overturned the tables of the hypocritical and the greedy (to say nothing of the expectations of Barton's more gentle readers). And while this Jesus did not preach either economic or social revolution, he was "athrill with the protest of youth against oppression and intolerance."[21]

Between the publication of *A Young Man's Jesus* in 1914 and the appearance of *The Man Nobody Knows* in 1925, a variety of American writers celebrated Jesus' manliness. In *The Virility of Christ* (1915), Warren Conant resurrected the bearded lady metaphor of Barton's father, protesting against artists who "subjoin a silky, curly beard to a woman's face and hair and label it 'The Christ.'" Against this "insipid portrait" he offered a vision of a "Fighting Christ" who "came not to send peace, but a sword." "The men of a strenuous age," Conant observed, "demand a strenuous Christ." And Conant's Jesus was the epitome of strenuousness—a great athlete with "big lung capacity," a "well developed torso," and the "free, swinging stride of the mountaineer."[22]

The most high-profile advocate of this muscular Jesus was G. Stanley Hall, the Harvard-trained psychologist who advocated "boxing for babies" in 1899. In *Jesus, the Christ, in the Light of Psychology* (1917), Hall praised Jesus as the "world's master psychologist," and so joined a long line of Jesus experts who saw in the man from Nazareth a reflection of themselves. Hall also saw Teddy Roosevelt's reflection in Jesus, whom he lauded as a "manly man" and the perfect model of virile masculinity for American boys.[23]

Echoing the Reverend Barton, Hall lamented the feminization of Jesus in American culture and called for new representations of Jesus, both visual and textual, that would be more faithful to the original. *Jesus the Christ, in the Light of Psychology* began with a critique of Jesus art. "Most pictures of Jesus during the last century give him a distinctly feminine look," Hall wrote. Then he conjured up the bearded lady (which was rapidly becoming a cliché): "The beard is usually, though not always, light, exposing the upper part of the chin, and its scantiness, with the usual very copious hair of the scalp and the feminine features, sometimes almost suggests a bearded lady." Unhappily, things were no better on the page than on the canvas. "In literature, as in art," Hall wrote, "Jesus is represented with feminine as well as with masculine traits of both body and soul. He is meek, passive, intuitive, a lover of children, and perhaps a little deficient in some of the attractions of virility."[24]

Hall was more of a pedagogue than a literary critic or an art historian, so it should not be surprising that he proposed a solution to the problem of the effeminate Jesus. Repeatedly, Hall challenged producers of Jesus art and literature to craft images that captured his strength, beauty, and "personal magnetism." The challenge was to make Jesus modern—to invite him not just into our hearts but into every corner of modern life—and in so doing to provide red-blooded American boys with a spiritual hero to emulate. "Could we not have Jesus as an athletic champion, illustrating perhaps the ideal of doing the prodigies that athletes so admire?" Hall asked. "Could Jesus be knight, priest, banker, sailor, landed proprietor, society man, manufacturer, actor, professor, editor, etc.?"[25]

THE UNKNOWN MAN

At least in the United States, the answer to that question was an unequivocal yes. In 1925, Bruce Barton toed the rubber and delivered in *The Man Nobody Knows* a manly Jesus who, like the modern-day relief pitcher, is both athlete *and* businessman (to say nothing of a savior of the game). But why did Barton call his popular hero "The Man Nobody Knows"?

The answer to that question lies in the book's preface, a set piece about a confused boy in Sunday School. Jesus is a "lamb of God" who is "weak and unhappy and glad to die," the boy's teacher proclaims. But this "sissified" christology bores the child, while pictures of Old Testament heroes—Daniel in the lion's den, David and his sling, and Moses with his snake—thrill him. As he is daydreaming about how David would have fared in a fight with the heavyweight boxing champion Jim Jeffries (pretty well, he thinks), he gazes up at a picture of "a

pale young man with flabby forearms and a sad expression." Jeffries
could have dropped that Jesus with one punch, he thinks. Then, in a
flash of liberation, the boy realizes that the Sunday School Jesus is a
fraud. The "real Jesus" had been obscured for centuries by the theol-
ogizing of cloistered monks and the feminizing of Sunday School
teachers, who had conspired to reduce Jesus from a lover of life to a
self-flagellating "killjoy."[26]

The Man Nobody Knows is easily parodied. While Billy Sunday
turned Jesus into the captain of his revival team and the Social
Gospelers made him into a chivalrous social reformer, Barton presented Jesus as a savvy executive who "picked up twelve men from
the bottom ranks of business and forged them into an organization
that conquered the world." Like Barton, this Jesus was an adman
whose parables were "the most powerful advertisements of all time."
Like Abraham Lincoln, he possessed "the personal magnetism which
begets loyalty and commands respect." Like Henry Ford, he understood that service is the key to business success.[27]

Yet business success is by no means the only concern of the book.
Far more than a tract for capitalism, the book is a manifesto for manliness which casts Jesus as the man all males should mimic. As has
been noted, the preface attends to gender, not economics: "A physical
weakling! Where did they get that idea? Jesus pushed a plane and
swung an adze; he was a successful carpenter. He slept outdoors and
spent his days walking around his favorite lake. His muscles were so
strong that when they drove the money-changers out, nobody dared to
oppose him!" Blessed with "steel-like" nerves and "muscles hard as
iron," the Jesus Barton knew played hard and worked hard. He was
both an "outdoor man" and a "sociable man." People (particularly
women) were drawn to him, and he was drawn to people. He had a
hearty laugh, and he preached joy, not condemnation. His Father was
neither a "stern Judge" nor a "vain King" but a "happy God" who
wanted nothing but happiness for His children. Jesus was what we
now call a people person. In fact, he was "the most popular dinner
guest in Jerusalem."[28]

Barton began The Man Nobody Knows with an epigraph that continues to incense liberal critics: "Wist ye not that I must be about my
Father's *business*." The passage was from Luke 2:49 but the italics

were Barton's own, and critics of the business-friendly Christianity that steel magnate Andrew Carnegie dubbed "The Gospel of Wealth" have for generations seized upon them to argue that Barton's book was first and foremost a pitch for capitalism. In 1925, *The New Republic* ridiculed Barton for writing up Jesus as a "Brother Rotarian." In the 1950s, Samuel Sandmel, a Jewish New Testament scholar, judged the book an "atrocity." In the 1960s, the Catholic novelist Walker Percy blasted Barton in *Commonweal* for reading the Gospels "as a sort of primitive Dale Carnegie course" in positive thinking. Of course, *Commonweal* only offered Percy an occasion to vent because . *The Man Nobody Knows* was that rarest of publishing creatures: an overnight sensation with legs. Barton's book topped the nonfiction bestseller list in 1925 and 1926 and has remained in print ever since.[29]

In part because of this popular success, Barton has become a whipping boy for American Studies scholars, who over the last few decades have argued that Barton transformed Jesus into a shill for self-realization through consumption, and in the process helped to usher in a secular age. Such criticisms wrongly assume that contemporary America is secular, an assumption refuted by, among other things, the enduring popularity of Jesus. More to the point, they suggest that *The Man Nobody Knows* is a book nobody reads—no scholars, at least—since a careful exploration of the text reveals that the business of Barton's Jesus was by no means the business of Calvin Coolidge's America.

When it comes to understanding Barton's "Father's *business*" epigraph, context is key. That context is the story of a trip to Jerusalem by Mary, Joseph, and their twelve-year-old boy. Mary and her husband are on their way home when they discover that their boy is missing. Doubling back, they find him in the Temple, as Luke has it, "sitting in the midst of the doctors, both hearing them, and asking them questions" (Luke 2:46). Grabbing her son's arm, Mary asks Jesus why he had worried them so, adding that she and Joseph had "sought thee sorrowing." "How is it that ye sought me?" Jesus replies. "Wist ye not that I must be about my Father's *business*?"[30] These words sting Mary in more ways than one, since in Barton's telling she wants her son to be about Joseph's business—toiling in his "prosperous carpenter shop." But Jesus has more important things to do than chase the almighty denarius.

Barton's subsequent treatment of Jesus as a pioneering CEO is comically anachronistic. But there is a sermon in it too. God, Barton insists, is not in the business of religion alone. "Ask any ten people what Jesus meant by his 'Father's business,' and nine of them will answer 'preaching,' " he writes. But that definition is far too narrow, since "*all* business is his Father's business." Here Barton is aligning himself not so much with laissez-faire capitalism as with Protestant liberalism, which by the 1920s had rejected the distinction between the secular and the sacred, the natural and the supernatural. He is also dismissing the "separate spheres" ideology, which had built an impenetrable divide during the nineteenth century between not only home and work but also work and religion, the public and the private. While earlier in his career Barton had felt compelled to choose between the dirty business of business and the pure calling of the ministry, he eventually came to believe that he could go into the ministry of business, so long as he dedicated his work to the glory of Jesus. Much earlier Horace Bushnell had written that "toil is liturgical." Barton's book said as much, though not as economically. "We have been taught that a man's daily business activities are selfish, and that only the time which he devotes to church meetings and social activities is consecrated," he wrote. But in truth "all work is worship; all useful service prayer. And whoever works wholeheartedly at any worthy calling is a co-worker with the Almighty in the great enterprise which He has initiated but which He can never finish without the help of men."[31]

THE REAL THING

The State Historical Society of Wisconsin now houses a large collection of letters written to Barton about his most popular book. Tellingly, the letters ignore almost entirely Barton's depiction of Jesus as a successful executive. Apparently what moved readers of the book was not his dream of Christianizing capitalism as much as his talent for bringing Jesus to life. Like so many Americans before him, Barton made Jesus real by emphasizing his humanity. "I am grateful for the human Jesus you have so wonderfully provided," wrote a man from Little Rock, Arkansas. An eighteen-year-old girl echoed this sentiment in a prize-winning book review published in the *Detroit Free Press*. "The book points out to us how very human Jesus was," she wrote. "Mr. Barton awakens the dormant minds and hearts of those who read this book to the fact that Jesus was a leader of men, a meek but powerful human being and a just judge of humanity." Other readers thanked Barton for emphasizing Jesus' assertive masculinity. Barton's Manly Redeemer—"a rugged man of action" in the words of one minister—was according to another Barton fan an effective antidote to "the squeamish, whimpering, weak-kneed God Jesus of the churches."[32]

Works of art become popular when they express the inchoate sentiments of their public. *The Man Nobody Knows* did just that, offering Americans (oddly enough) a man whom they already knew before they met him anew on its pages. The book also charted a course between agnosticism and fundamentalism that was appealing to a wide swath of the American public. Barton's presentation of Jesus as both human and masculine was so persuasive that many readers concluded that his Jesus was the real thing—that Barton had captured the "real character" and the "real personality" of Jesus. One fan said the book depicted "the Nazarene as he really was," while another said it "made the Son of Man *real* to people, and not merely . . . an actor in a theological drama." Yet another (who presumably was familiar with the New Testament) deemed the novel "the truest picture of the Master" in existence. Some of Barton's most enthusiastic readers went further, claiming that *The Man Nobody Knows* was divinely inspired. "I feel the Great Ones have inspired you at just this critical time to give people a more rational idea of the Man," wrote one woman. Another fan concluded Barton had functioned as a "channel" for the Spirit of the divine. "I have a very strong feeling," yet another wrote, "Jesus dictated that book to you."[33]

Barton's Jesus seemed real to many Americans for a variety of reasons, but Barton's Gospel of Wealth was not high on the list. Though Barton was a political conservative who would go on to serve two terms as a Republican U.S. Representative from New York, he was a theological liberal who believed that Christians were duty-bound to adapt their beliefs and practices to changing circumstances, that God was immanent in culture, and that culture was ever progressing. This cluster of modernist convictions—"adaptation, cultural immanentism, and a religiously based progressivism"—had already inspired Social Gospel advocates such as Walter Rauschenbusch to Christianize the economy by socializing it. To those advocates and their heirs in the academy, Barton could be understood only as a corporate shill, and his book as compelling evidence for the secularization of American culture. Those critics may be right when they argue that Barton's work has been used in efforts to jam the round peg of Christianity into the square hole of capitalism, but such was not Barton's aim. To go down that interpretive road is to misunderstand the author—to turn Barton himself into an unknown man. Like Walter Rauschenbusch before him, Barton was sincerely committed to adapting Christianity to modern economic circumstances. That commitment led Barton not to throw out capitalism (as Rauschenbusch had done) but to try to Christianize it, by drafting Jesus as "the silent partner in every modern business."[34]

While Bushnell and Beecher had welcomed Jesus into nature and the human heart, and Rauschenbusch had welcomed him into society, Barton invited him into the business world. Barton's aim was unabashedly Christian: to seize in the name of Jesus territory ceded to Satan in the era of separate spheres. Businesses don't have to be corrupt, Barton was saying, and neither do the men that run them. This view may have been optimistic, even naive. But it was sincere, and theologically motivated.

History is replete with irony, at least for historians with ironic sensibilities. So it should not be altogether surprising that Barton's novel likely contributed more to the dechristianization than to the Christianization of American culture. Rather than heeding Barton's call for a new form of business conducted in the spirit of Jesus, many businessmen used the book to baptize the status quo as Christian. In the process, they undermined the ability of Christians to call consumer capitalism to task. All this can be admitted, however, without stripping Barton of his faith, or pretending that he would have endorsed such an outcome.

More than a decade before he wrote *The Man Nobody Knows*, Barton wrote a revealing piece called "My Father's Business." Subtitled "A Preacher's Life as Seen by a Preacher's Son," this 1914 article is part autobiography, part confession. In it, Barton tells his readers that he once wanted to go into the ministry, but after he realized that he would never be as successful a minister as his father, he opted for advertising instead. "I try to convince myself that I am doing as important a thing in my business as he did in his," Barton confesses, but he falls far short of sweet assurance: "It is one thing to have contact with lives as I have it in business, but quite another thing to reach one's hand down into the soul of man; to reshape a life, as he every day has done." As of 1914, Barton believed there was a world of difference between the ministry and advertising. As far as he was concerned, his father's business was the Father's only business.

By 1925, Barton the younger had changed his tune. He now viewed his earlier understanding of God's work as too narrow, and the gulf he had seen between the Reverend Barton's career and his own as a mirage. Like his father, Bruce Barton had become a writer, and at least in that capacity he had become far more successful than his progenitor. More important, Barton had also become a minister of the gospel, preaching a virile Christ to hundreds of thousands of readers in their bedrooms, and a gospel of service to thousands more in the boardrooms.

The Man Nobody Knows spawned a variety of derivative projects, including The Book Nobody Knows (1926), about the Bible. An illustrated version of the original called The Man from Galilee (1928) first ran as a series in Good Housekeeping, proving that Barton's Jesus was not only a man for all seasons but a man for all genders. Barton's work was popular not because it secularized Christianity or justified consumer capitalism but because it offered to everyday Americans a human (and manly) Jesus they could know and love and imitate. In The Man Nobody Knows, Barton presented a spiritual rather than a religious Jesus. Like Thomas Jefferson, he tried to leapfrog over the metaphysics of Catholicism and Calvinism to the pure, primitive gospel of Jesus. He too wanted "to free the mind from the numbing grip of ancient creeds." But while Jefferson focused on Jesus' sayings, Barton focused on Jesus' actions. Rather than presenting Jesus as a subversive sage, a teacher of unsettling yet immortal moral truths, he

presented Jesus as a muscular man of action, leading his manly followers onward and upward. "He did not come to establish a theology,"
Barton wrote, "but to lead a life."[35]

Evangelical critics jumped on Barton for treating Jesus, as one
Methodist wrote, "as casually as he would a candidate for Sheriff."[36]
Fundamentalists, beleaguered by the Scopes trial, which captivated
(and scandalized) the country the same year Barton's bestseller appeared, blasted Barton for sidestepping crucial doctrines such as the
miracles and the atonement. So did conservative Catholics. But that
move was the genius of the book. While a lesser writer might have
mucked himself up in christological controversies, Barton danced
deftly around those debates, as any pragmatic advertising man would.
He also gave contentious matters such as evolution and biblical criticism (two key sources of the Scopes controversy) a wide berth, focusing instead on stories about Jesus' life that could be affirmed by
Christians of any denomination, and by lovers of Jesus with no
church at all.

FROM CHARACTER TO PERSONALITY

In 1923, two years before the appearance of Barton's bestseller, another life of Jesus sold more copies in the United States than any
other nonfiction book (with the exception of Emily Post's *Etiquette*).
In 1924 and 1925, Giovanni Papini's *Life of Christ* was once again a
top-five nonfiction bestseller. Papini, an Italian and a recent convert
to Catholicism, wrote with the glee (and, at points, the bigotry) of a
man of unshakeable faith. But Papini too steered clear of christological disputes. Distinguishing itself from Jesus novels of the previous
century, which had gazed upon Jesus indirectly (as if looking at an
eclipse), Papini's *Life of Christ* took direct aim at its subject, focusing
unabashedly on what a *Catholic World* reviewer called "the spell of
Christ's personality."[37] That personality was, in Papini's telling, strong
and confident, without doubts or weaknesses of any kind.

The cultural historian Warren Susman has described America's
great turn-of-the-century transition as a shift from a "culture of character" to a "culture of personality." At the time Bruce Barton's father
was born, in the middle of the nineteenth century, most Americans

saw the self as a danger to social order and the ego as a threat to individual salvation. When mothers set their children on their laps and read them the Bible, they were passing on lessons about self-control and submission to parental and divine authority. To raise children in this way was to cultivate sentimental virtues such as patience, gentleness, and above all sympathy. Character was comprised of those virtues, which were the same for every human being. This "culture of character" was visible in theologians such as Horace Bushnell and in post-Christian thinkers such as Ralph Waldo Emerson, who provided his century's most succinct definition of character: "Moral order through the medium of individual nature."[38]

This culture of character did not come to an end with the nineteenth century. In fact, it is still present today. By the turn of the century, however, it was giving ground to a culture of personality. If the culture of character was a response to the dangers of social chaos lurking on the edges of a rapidly urbanizing republic, the culture of personality was a response to the fear of the loss of the individual in ever-growing crowds. This fear, as old as Romanticism, was deeply felt by Henry David Thoreau, who elevated nonconformity, first, to a virtue and then to a necessity. By the first decade of the twentieth century, however, the fear Thoreau had confronted in solitude at Walden Pond was endemic. Between 1850 and 1900, the U.S. population more than tripled—from 23 million to 76 million. Cities expanded, and work life become increasingly bureaucratic. By 1900, many Americans (especially men) worried more about the obliteration of their individuality than they did about social chaos, Susman argues. In this new culture of personality and the new consumer society that accompanied it, middle-class Americans developed themselves not through self-control but through self-fulfillment. Self-assertion was a virtue, and denying the self a mortal sin.

Parents now taught their children not to follow the crowd but to stand out from it. "Personality" was the quality of doing just that—"the quality of being Somebody." Be yourselves, the Protestant modernist Shailer Mathews wrote in *The Message of Jesus to Our Modern Life*, "rather than copies of someone else." While old advice manuals had hammered into children keywords such as "citizenship, duty, democracy, work, . . . honor, reputation, morals, manners, integrity," the keywords of the new how-to books were "fascinating, stunning, attractive, magnetic, glowing, masterful, creative, dominant, forceful."[39]

Theologians responded to this new culture of personality by endowing God with Somebody status. Boston Personalism, a new school of liberal Protestantism led by Boston University's Borden Parker Bowne, saw personality as the master key to philosophy, theology, and even God Himself. Harry Emerson Fosdick of New York City's Riverside Church went even further, writing that "the key to the understanding of all life is the value of personality."[40]

In addition to new theologies, the culture of personality gave rise to new heroes, virtually all of them men. Before the Civil War, Americans had respected refined gentlemen who knew how to control themselves and lauded mothers who gently influenced their children. They now praised men of power who knew how to sway others. Magnetism, in other words, was more important than morality. As T. J. Jackson Lears has pointed out, crowds in this era were coded as female.[41] Therefore, the fear of becoming swallowed up in mass culture was also a fear of being emasculated, and the quest for personality was a quest for masculinity. This conjunction of manliness and personality was clear in The Man Nobody Knows. What set Barton's Jesus apart from the crowd were the martial virtues, but those same virtues were also the hallmarks of personality: vigor, strength, originality, courage, power, and, above all, "the personal magnetism which begets loyalty and commands respect."[42]

Henry Ward Beecher may have been the first of these new manly heroes. Ever sensitive to the twists and turns of American culture, Beecher began his career as a champion of character and ended it as a champion of personality. His adultery trial in 1875 seemed only to increase his stature, showing how far the culture of character had already declined, at least among Beecher's white, middle-class admirers. Beecher anticipated the culture of personality when he insisted on preserving the charm of Jesus in The Life of Jesus, the Christ. By the time he delivered his lectures on preaching at Yale in 1892, he was urging new preachers to "thrust" and "lunge" in the pulpit. "It takes a man," Beecher said, "to refashion men."[43]

The real heroes of the culture of personality came into prominence a generation later, however. Revivalists such as Billy Sunday and Social Gospel ministers such as Walter Rauschenbusch fit the bill. So did robber barons such as Andrew Carnegie and John D. Rockefeller, whose oversized wallets made them larger than life.

New notions of the hero and a new emphasis on personality produced a new understanding of Jesus as a man of action with a magnetic personality. Shortly after the turn of the century, books such as *Who Then Is This? A Study of the Personality of Jesus* (1905), *The Personality of Jesus* (1906), and *The Significance of the Personality of Christ for the Minister of To-day* (1907) proliferated. In Horace Bushnell's classic, *The Character of Jesus* (1861), the man from Nazareth had been first and foremost an exemplar of Christian virtues. In these new books, Jesus became a personality par excellence—someone his followers could imitate only by endeavoring to discover in themselves their own true selves.

Once it was decided that Jesus had a personality, disagreements arose about what sort of personality it was. As Christian thinkers began reading Sigmund Freud, books on the mind of Jesus proliferated. The first decade of the twentieth century alone saw the publication of *The Mental Condition and Career of Jesus of Nazareth Examined in the Light of Modern Knowledge* (1904), *Studies in the Inner Life of Jesus* (1907), *The Psychology of Jesus* (1908), and *The Psychology of Christ* (1909). Some authors wondered whether D. F. Strauss had been right when he diagnosed Jesus as a fanatic who lived in a house of his own illusions. But that interpretive line had little life in the United States, and G. Stanley Hall put an end to it when he gave Jesus a clean bill of health in *Jesus, the Christ, in the Light of Psychology*.

One effect of all this speculation about the mind of Jesus was to propel his personality ever closer to the epicenter of Christian life. Liberal Protestantism had been Jesus-centric for decades, but during the Progressive era it became even more obsessed with Jesus. Harry Emerson Fosdick ran all of his theology through Jesus. He even refused to recite the historic creeds, preferring to pledge his spiritual allegiance to Jesus alone. The main argument of his best-known sermon, "Shall the Fundamentalists Win?" (1922), was that conservatives cared more about "the tiddledywinks and peccadillos of religion" than they did about the person of Jesus. "Whenever I say 'God'," Fosdick wrote, "I think Christ."[44]

FROM PERSONALITY TO CELEBRITY

Embraced as person in the early nineteenth century and a personality early in the twentieth, Jesus became in the 1920s an American celebrity. Celebrity is notoriously difficult to define, but at a minimum it is personality magnified and applauded. Celebrities are people with personality, but their personalities are larger than life, and are recognized as such by their society. If personalities stand out from the crowd, celebrities are seen as unique. If personalities can sway the masses, celebrities are able to get crowds up on their feet and bring them to tears.

While the rise of the culture of personality was tied to the emergence of a consumer society, the culture of celebrity was made possible by the rise of mass communications. Jesus had benefitted in the nineteenth century from the invention of new printing technologies and new modes of transportation that enabled the mass production and distribution of Bibles and tracts. The emergence in the first quarter of the twentieth century of new national media such as radio and moving pictures made it possible for particularly magnetic personalities to be recognized as celebrities nationwide. While in the past great personalities could be admired by local communities and subcultures, now they could be beloved by the nation itself.

Hollywood and its "star system" are often credited with creating the American celebrity, and the death of Rudolph Valentino in 1926 lent the type considerable currency. But sound did not come to movies until 1927, and by that time sports heroes were the driving force behind the new culture of celebrity. The most magnetic personalities in the twenties were Walter Hagen in golf, Bill Tilden in tennis, Jack Dempsey in boxing, and Babe Ruth in baseball. Each of these men lorded over his realm as surely as Henry Ford did over the automobile industry, but with far more aplomb. "The Haig," as Hagen was known, drove a Rolls-Royce and once hit off the first tee in a pro tournament in a tuxedo. Babe Ruth had an appetite for life as gargantuan as his home runs. He was, in the words of sportswriter Bill McGeehan, "our national exaggeration." Grantland Rice, the Babe Ruth of 1920s sportswriters, had this to say about these flamboyant new heroes: "They had something more than mere skill or competitive ability.

They also had in record quality and quantity that indescribable asset known as color, personality, crowd appeal, or whatever you may care to call it."[45]

These men had more than mere personality, however. Sports pages debuted in mass circulation newspapers in the 1890s, so by the twenties they had Rice and McGeehan and other sportswriters around to elevate their accomplishments into myths, their personalities into celebrity. Unlike heroes of prior generations, they also had radio and movies to broadcast their personalities to mass audiences, and new business strategies such as advertising to reinforce them. In an era of magnetic sports personalities, Babe Ruth was the greatest magnet of them all. If he had been born a generation earlier, however, "the Sultan of Swat" would have been merely the apple of New York's eye. Radio, film, advertising, and mass circulation magazines and newspapers magnified Ruth's personality and expanded his fan base, transforming him into a national icon.

Jesus also benefitted from the revolution in communications and the emergent culture of celebrity. Americans continued to portray him as a Manly Redeemer—attractive and athletic, fascinating and forceful. But now they had the persuasive power of the new mass media behind them. Barton's popular portrait of Jesus was reinforced by advertising for the book depicting its star as a muscular carpenter. Aimee Semple McPherson, the darling of American evangelism, used her radio license (the first ever granted by the FCC to a woman) to preach her own "Foursquare Gospel" of the four roles of Jesus: as Savior, Baptizer, Healer, and Coming King. Paul Rader, a Chicago-based evangelist, preached Jesus over his station WJBT ("Where Jesus Blesses Thousands"). *The Man Nobody Knows* came to the screen in 1925, as did *Ben-Hur*. *King of Kings* premiered in 1927. While *Ben-Hur* followed the cautious nineteenth-century model, casting Jesus as a supporting actor, the other two films made Jesus the star. Of the two, Cecil B. DeMille's *King of Kings* was most popular. In fact, it remained the most watched Jesus movie of all time until the 1970s, in part because of its use of the close-up literally to distinguish Jesus from the madding crowds. DeMille was probably right when he boasted in his autobiography that only the Bible brought Jesus alive for more people than did his film.

At the time Jesus was coming to life as an American celebrity, mainline Protestantism seemed to be dying. Historian Robert Handy has traced "the second disestablishment" of liberal Protestantism to the 1920s. While the First Amendment had robbed the leading Protestant denominations of government support, Handy argues, this second disestablishment robbed them of public power. Earlier efforts to make the United States into a Christian nation effectively ground to a halt after World War I ended, science emerged as a major cultural force, and another immigration wave made the country more pluralistic than ever. Building on Handy's argument, Grant Wacker has dated "the demise of Biblical civilization" to the 1920s and 1930s. While intellectuals were viewing the Bible as a product of human history in the decades immediately following the Civil War, that approach began to trickle down to ordinary Americans in the 1920s.[46]

This comeuppance had been in the works for some time. As Protestants adapted to American culture from the American Revolution through World War I, they had shorn from Christianity much of what Christians had historically held dear. The creeds, the sacraments, even the Bible had come under attack. At least among liberals, supernaturalism yielded to naturalism; Jesus became an exemplary human being rather than a miracle-working God. Traditional teachings about heaven and hell, sin and the devil lost their saliency for many, and fell away entirely for others. Moreover, the refusal to distinguish between the sacred and the secular diminished rather than augmented the public power of Protestantism. American Catholics chipped away at their tradition too, earning condemnations from the Vatican for Americanizing and modernizing all too eagerly. During the 1920s Harry Emerson Fosdick described the churches as "intellectually chaotic, ethically confused [and] organizationally challenged" but much of that chaos and confusion was due to the gains made by modernists like Fosdick, who were pushing Christianity more boldly away from its roots than ever before. No wonder the fundamentalist theologian J. Gresham Machen, in a vigorous defense of miracles and biblical inerrancy in *Christianity and Liberalism* (1923), called modernism pretend Christianity. "What the liberal theologian has retained after abandoning to the enemy one Christian doctrine after another is not

Christianity at all," he wrote, "but a religion which is so entirely different from Christianity as to belong in a distinct category."[47]

For Protestant liberals, the self-appointed denizens of American culture, hand-wringing was the gesture of the day. In *Does Civilization Need Religion?* (1927), Reinhold Niebuhr spoke of fundamentalism and modernism alike as symptoms of a new "psychology of defeat" in the churches. Niebuhr and his brother H. Richard emerged in the 1920s and 1930s as the leading advocates of neo-orthodox theology, which tried to chart a middle path between those two extremes. Focusing anew on human sinfulness and the sovereignty of God (and on the distinction between the sacred and the secular), the Niebuhrs and other neo-orthodox theologians redirected attention from Jesus the loving friend to God the inscrutable Father. They chastised Christians for their naive faith in progress and their attempts to reshape God in their own image. The effort to Christianize the secular order, they argued, had resulted only in the secularization of Christianity. By the mid-thirties, H. Richard Niebuhr was calling for "the liberation of the church from its bondage to a corrupt civilization."[48]

One of the puzzles of American religion is that, as mainline Protestantism lost public power, Jesus only gained in stature. When supernaturalism was everywhere in Puritan New England, Jesus was close to irrelevant, except as a metaphysical marker in a complex theological system. As evangelicals downplayed his divinity and made him into a real person, Jesus became an important character in the American drama. As liberals undercut the authority of the Bible, they came to define Christianity in terms of *solus Jesus*. The movement from theologies of salvation to therapies of self-realization strengthened Jesus' standing even more. "The Modernist," Shailer Mathews wrote of Jesus, "knows no other center for his faith."[49]

A NATIONAL ICON

When Americans closed their eyes and prayed to Jesus in the twenties and thirties, some likely conjured up the face of H. B. Warner, who played the lead role in *King of Kings*. Others probably saw something like Heinrich Hofmann's popular *Head of Christ*. In keeping with a centuries-old tradition of depicting Jesus in scenes from the Bible, Hofmann did not produce his *Head of Christ* as a freestanding picture. The image first appeared in a larger narrative painting called *Christ and the Rich Young Ruler* (1889), which tells the story of a wealthy young man unwilling to follow Jesus into a life of voluntary poverty. Demand for an icon of Jesus led printmakers to extract the portrait from the painting, and the popularity of that portrait led John D. Rockefeller, Jr., to purchase the original painting of *Christ and the Rich Young Ruler* and donate it (along with *Christ in the Garden of Gethsemane* (1890), another popular narrative painting by Hofmann) to Riverside Church. During the first decades of the twentieth century, reproductions of Hofmann's works appeared in hundreds of books and hung in countless homes and churches across the United States. They also provided Americans with their most vivid and enduring images of Jesus.

In 1940, an obscure graphic artist from Chicago created a picture that would become more popular than Hofmann's *Christ and the Rich Young Ruler*, Barton's *The Man Nobody Knows*, and DeMille's *King of Kings* combined. *Head of Christ* by Warner Sallman would eventually be reproduced in almost every imaginable form—on prints, plaques, bookmarks, funeral cards, church bulletins, buttons, calendars, clocks, lamps, coffee mugs, stickers, billboards, and key chains. As it multiplied, among Christians and non-Christians alike, this picture helped to transform Jesus from a celebrity into a national icon. As of the turn of the twenty-first century, over 500 million copies had been produced, making *Head of Christ* the most common religious image in the world.

Like Barton, Sallman (1892–1968) was an advertising man. Like Tissot, he applied his artistic talents initially to secular work, including posters supporting the U.S. cause in World War I. Unlike either of these men, however, Sallman was an evangelical Protestant. Sallman's parents were both members of the Swedish Evangelical Covenant Church, a revivalist denomination transplanted to the United States by Swedish immigrants during the mid-nineteenth century. In 1908, Sallman had a born-again experience at a revival conducted by the Chapman-Alexander Evangelistic Campaign. He would eventually return to his parents' denomination, but his 1908 experience, like Tissot's vision in the Church of St. Sulpice, led him to commit his career to creating sacred art, and to see that career as a Christian calling.

Sallman said he was first inspired to attempt a portrait of Jesus in 1914 by a teacher at Chicago's Moody Bible Institute. Upon learning that Sallman was an artist, that teacher reportedly encouraged him to paint "a virile, manly Christ." "Make him a real man!" he told Sallman. "Make him rugged, not effeminate. Make Him strong and masculine, so people will see in His face that He slept under the stars, drove the money changers out of the temple, and faced Calvary in triumph." In 1924, Sallman says, he was blessed with a vision of just such a man, who appeared to him while he was struggling to create a Christ picture commissioned for a church monthly called *The Covenant Companion*. "All I did," Sallman later reported, "was to reproduce as faithfully as I could what I had seen in my dream." The charcoal he drew appeared as *Son of Man* on the cover of *The Covenant Companion* in February 1924. More important, it became the basis for Sallman's celebrated oil painting of 1940, *Head of Christ*.[50]

Head of Christ prints sold briskly. An initial run in early 1941 of one hundred thousand copies was gone in two months. By the end of the year, over a million had been sold, and three million more were snapped up in 1942, thanks to efforts by the USO, the Salvation Army, and the YMCA to distribute the image to American soldiers fighting overseas in World War II. Soon individual fans of Jesus were also pitching in. Through a program called "Christ in Every Purse," Carl H. Duning distributed wallet-sized prints from his home in Richmond, Indiana, to individuals, libraries, public schools, and city halls around the country. Supported by a variety of civic and religious groups, this effort to create "card-carrying Christians" (Dunning's quip) quickly spread outside the United States. President and Mrs. Eisenhower praised the program, as did J. Edgar Hoover of the FBI.[51]

During the postwar revival of the 1940s and 1950s, as Protestants and Catholics downplayed denominational differences in order to present a united front against the menace of godless Communism, Sallman's Jesus became far and away the most common image of Je-

sus in American homes, churches, and workplaces. Thanks to Sallman (and the savvy marketing of his distributors), Jesus become instantly recognizable by Americans of all races and religions.

Art historian David Morgan has argued that "when devout viewers
see what they imagine to be the actual appearance of the divinity that
cares for them," the image that fosters their imagination "becomes an
icon." For some Americans, Sallman's picture was iconic in that tech-
nical sense. Just as the bread and wine in the Catholic mass convey
the essence of Jesus through the mouth, *Head of Christ* conveyed his
essence to the eyes. During the 1990s, Morgan solicited opinions
from a variety of Americans on Sallman's *Head of Christ*. One woman
told him that the picture was "an exact likeness of our Lord Jesus
Christ." Another reported, "When I look at it in prayer, and when I am
the most in need, I see not only a painted portrait, but the face of the
real, the living Christ." Others saw *Head of Christ* as the true image of
Jesus—a twentieth-century version of the Shroud of Turin that captured not only his personality but also the shape of his nose and the
cut of his beard. At least a few attributed miracles to the picture.
While one pocket-sized *Head of Christ* was said to secrete oil, blood
reportedly flowed from another. Some who had visions of Jesus said
the picture was his spitting image. Most Americans lavished upon
Sallman's image more modest devotion. But even for them *Head of
Christ* became normative—the best picture available in a culture that
increasingly longed for a glimpse of his true face.[52]

Sallman's *Head of Christ* was not the first image of Jesus to circulate widely in the United States. As has been noted, Heinrich
Hofmann was the pre-Sallman Sallman. Other artists also produced
popular images that captured the American imagination. *Jesus Blessing
the Children* and *The Good Shepherd*, both by Bernard Plockhorst,
were widely reproduced. The former likely inspired another of Sallman's oil paintings, *Jesus, the Children's Friend* (1946), while the latter
probably informed yet another Sallman oil, *The Lord Is My Shepherd*
(1942). Also widely viewed were works by the Hungarian artist Mihaly Munkácsy. The Presbyterian retailing magnate John Wanamaker
acquired two massive works by Munkácsy—*Christ Before Pilate*
(1881) and *Christ on Calvary* (1884)—and put them on display at the

World's Columbian Exposition in Chicago in 1893 and at his department store in Philadelphia.

One reason *Head of Christ* supplanted pictures by Munkácsy, Plockhorst, and Hofmann is that Sallman divorced his subject entirely from biblical narratives. Instead of interacting with his disciples or his mother or even with God, Sallman's Jesus engaged the viewer directly, and he did so in a way that was inviting, reassuring, comforting, and intimate. Severing Jesus from the Bible stories reinforced the image of Jesus as friend. It also advanced the cause of *solus Jesus*. Depicting the baby Jesus at his mother's breast evokes in many viewers the doctrine of the incarnation; representing Jesus suffering on the cross evokes the doctrine of the atonement. A head-and-shoulders portrait, however, evokes Jesus alone. Although Sallman was a Bible-believing evangelical, his Jesus stood apart, even from the Gospels themselves.

Yet another reason for the popularity of *Head of Christ* was its masculinity. An article called "Did Christ Look Like This?" published in 1948 in the evangelical magazine *Christian Life* placed Hofmann's and Sallman's most famous portraits side-by-side. Hofmann, the author argued, "portrayed Christ as an appealing, almost feminine character." Sallman's depiction was in her view more scriptural and more manly—"a firm, more masculine figure."[53] At least to contemporary eyes, it is hard to see either the firmness or the masculinity in Sallman's Jesus. His skin is movie-star perfect. His hair is flowing. And the light that bathes his beautiful face begs to be described as dreamy. While the subject is clearly male, he is not self-evidently masculine. This ambiguity, however, may have been one source of the picture's success. Different Americans could read different Jesuses into it, and apparently they did just that. The picture sold spectacularly well among evangelicals, who claimed Sallman as one of their own. It was also popular among liberal Protestants and some Roman Catholics, in part because (like Barton's book) it was not identified with any one denomination or any particular theological stance.

To the delight of his admirers, Sallman continued to produce new Jesus pictures until his death in 1968. *Christ at Heart's Door* (a 1942 oil reprising the "Jesus knocking" theme of evangelical hymnody) and

Christ Our Pilot (a 1950 oil showing Jesus guiding a boy at the helm of a ship) are according to Sallman biographer Jack R. Lundbom the most popular of those later works. For Catholics looking for more traditional images, Sallman also produced a portrait of the *Sacred Heart of Jesus*.

SINKING SALLMAN

Following World War II, Sallman's images came under attack as American Christians mounted another campaign against the feminization of Jesus. During the war, women had moved into the labor force at an even faster pace than they had in the late nineteenth century. Once again men were concerned that they were losing their grip on the public sphere, and once again they pointed to female-dominated congregations as evidence for the hyper-feminization of American Christianity (and the demise of American civilization).

American Catholics were particularly concerned about the feminization of Christianity. Some Catholic critics thought that "excessively old-maidish" architecture was chasing men away from the mass but, as historian Colleen McDannell has noted, many focused on outdated depictions of Jesus. Father E. M. Catich, an art professor at St. Ambrose University in Iowa, recalled respondents to the 1899 *Outlook* survey when he blasted popular depictions of the Sacred Heart of Jesus as effete: "What emerges is a young man in flowing gowns, with soft face, large eyes, small delicate mouth, slightly parted lips, small thin nose, downy beard, long curly hair parted in the middle and falling gracefully to the shoulders, slender dainty hands, narrow shoulders, long neck, [and] a slight tilt of the head and neck as if beseeching the viewer." Richard Muehlberger, an artist writing in the Catholic periodical *Liturgical Arts*, added some snappy rhetoric to this interpretive line when he criticized the typical Sacred Heart of Jesus as "a biological Valentine." He saved his fiercest words, however, for Protestant artists who had turned Jesus into "a bearded woman with as much dignity as a movie-house billboard."[54]

One effect of all this agitation was the gradual eclipse of *Head of Christ*. As poster artists flooded the country during the 1940s with macho images of American war heroes, the ability of Sallman's art to conjure up the real Jesus faded. Sallman himself repeatedly described his *Head of Christ* as masculine, and it was marketed as "manly," but now critics began to deride it as effeminate kitsch. In a 1948 piece called "Not Frail, Not Pale," *Time* magazine quoted a man who said the picture presented to Sunday school children a "sissified" image of Jesus who was not only frail and pale but "piously smirking" and "actorishly barbered"—a "teacher's pet." Sallman's Jesus was "a pale and posturing person with immoderately long, silky hair . . . who clutched a kind of diaphanous drapery gracefully about him with an expression of simpering vapidity," he complained. "It was into this hand, so unmistakably the limp and clammy hand of an effeminate curate, that little boys were to put theirs trustingly." Robert Paul Roth, a Lutheran evangelical, jazzed up the shopworn "bearded lady" image, calling *Head of Christ* a "pretty picture of a woman with a curling beard who has just come from the beauty parlor with a Halo shampoo." Church historian Martin Marty got in the best jab, dubbing the image "as ugly as a rented bowling shoe."[55]

In the wake of the civil rights campaigns of the 1950s and the Black Power movement of the 1960s, Sallman's *Head of Christ* took criticism from a different quarter. Now the picture looked not too feminine but too white. While *Christianity Today* continued to refer to the picture as "an evangelical icon," the mainline Protestant weekly *Christian Century* pronounced *Head of Christ* "on the way out" in 1962.[56] As multiculturalism spread, both as fact and as value, during the 1970s and 1980s, *Head of Christ* seemed even more anachronistic—an affront not only to African Americans but also to Christian immigrants from Asia and Latin America.

Sallman was a victim of his own success. By the 1960s, *Head of Christ* had become so ubiquitous that it begged to be seen as cheap. This fate is common in today's culture of cool, where city kids routinely move on to new sneakers as soon as they see suburban interlopers tying them on. In the art world, things have worked much the same way: real art is high art and unique; popular art is reproducible and kitsch. Sallman's work, of course, was spectacularly popular, so it should not be surprising that art critics denounced it as *l'art Saint-Sulpice*. Such criticisms may not have cut too deep into sales, but a growing perception among young Americans that *Head of Christ* was their parents' icon no doubt hurt its reputation. So did the unwritten rules of the new culture of celebrity, which demand that celebrities change their look at least every few years.

As Sallman's work lost its power to conjure up the real Jesus, new images arose to fill the vacuum, but none became as dominant as Sallman's *Head of Christ* had been in the decades after World War II. By the sixties, the U.S. population had become too diverse for that. New media, especially television, brought the nation together in ways that were not possible before, but American culture was simultaneously divided into a variety of regional, racial, and religious subcultures. Though virtually all of those subcultures (with the notable exception of the Jewish community) embraced Jesus as a hero, they now saw different faces when they invoked his name. What they did not see were different biblical scenes. Sallman's portrait had defined Jesus as an icon, and even as that particular portrait faded away the portrait genre abided. Subsequent artists understood that Americans want their Jesus straight up. However he was depicted, Jesus the celebrity remained a head-and-shoulders icon.

One leading alternative to Sallman's picture was Richard Hook's *Head of Christ* (1964). Here again the genre is the portrait, so the viewer is confronted with Jesus the person, detached from any particular Bible story or denominational creed. In this case, however, Jesus looks straight ahead, engaging the viewer in an intimate, one-on-one encounter. Caring but not sentimental, manly but not macho, Hook's hero seems to strike a perfect balance between the Sweet Savior of the nineteenth century and the Manly Redeemer of the early twentieth. He has the requisite shoulder-length hair and beard, but is far more scraggly than either Sallman's manicured Jesus. Copyrighted by Concordia Publishing House, a Lutheran publisher, Hook's Beach Boy Jesus initially found an audience among young Lutherans, but now circulates widely among evangelicals.

The proliferation of images such as Hook's *Head of Christ*, along with a variety of new portraits of Jesus as an African American, undermined the ability of Sallman's image to function as an icon in the religious sense. In fact, the diversity of Jesus images made it harder for any one image to convey the reality of Jesus to Americans. But that same diversification helped to turn Jesus into an icon in the more popular sense of that word. Icons in this more commonplace meaning are instantly recognizable; they also stand for abstract realities larger than themselves. The Statue of Liberty stands for freedom, but it also symbolizes America. The Coke bottle and Mickey Mouse stand for the Coca-Cola and Disney corporations, and perhaps even for joy, but they also stand, both at home and abroad, for America. The profusion of images of Jesus in the 1960s and beyond turned Jesus into an American icon too. Extracted from scripture and tradition via the genre of the portrait, Jesus came to stand for Christianity, even the essence of spirituality itself. And he too came to stand for America. Drew University professor Leonard Sweet was joking (and complaining) when he said that Sallman transformed Jesus from "Logos to logo," but there is some truth in the barb. As surely as the Jesus books and films of the twenties made Jesus into a celebrity, Sallman and his rivals turned Jesus into an American icon.[57]

NANCY REDDERER

Four

SUPERSTAR

Shortly before Easter in 1966, John Lennon proclaimed the Beatles more popular than Jesus. Clerics were outraged, and Lennon (uncharacteristically) apologized. But at least in the United States Lennon seemed to be right. Only a month after Lennon prophesied the demise of Christianity, a rush on books by "Death of God" theologians, most notably *The Secular City* (1965) by the Harvard professor Harvey Cox, prompted *Time* magazine to ask, on its April 8 cover, "Is God Dead?" To many, it seemed as if the nation was about to be engulfed in a wave of secularity so gigantic as to drown even God Himself.

By the mid-1960s, Americans had been subtracting elements from Christianity—dechristianizing it, as it were—for nearly two centuries. Jefferson cut out the miracles. Restorationists excised the creeds. Then liberal critics of the Bible took the reins of the mainline Protestantism in the early twentieth century, and Christianity seemed to be running to ruin ever since. True, there was a revival of religiosity and patriotic churchgoing in Eisenhower's America, but it was of the lukewarm rather than the hot-blooded sort. And now God Himself was under attack, and theologians seemed in the mood for dancing rather than mourning.

But just as sociologists of religion and "Death of God" theologians were beginning to take His pulse, God sprang back to life. By 1967, religion was vibrant, and while God the Father remained in hiding, Jesus was ubiquitous. As baby boomers came of age, young people rebelled en masse against their parents and their pursuit of postwar prosperity, insisting that the true quest was spiritual, not material. As their influence coursed through the nation, Americans of all ages seemed drawn to perennial questions, prompting *Time* to reconsider its earlier obituary notice on a 1969 cover: "Is God Coming Back to Life?"

We now know that neither secularization nor dechristianization are unidirectional processes. Both proceed in fits and starts, and each is eminently reversible. We also know that the sixties were as spiritual a decade as the United States has ever seen—an Age of Aquarius *and* of avatars. After the U.S. Congress opened up immigration from Asia in 1965, the country seemed to be flooded with wise men bearing spiritual gifts from the East: A. C. Bhaktivedanta Swami Prabhupāda with Krishna Consciousness, Chögyam Trungpa with Tibetan Buddhism, and the Maharishi Mahesh Yogi with Transcendental Meditation.

Yet "the sixties spiritual awakening," as Robert Ellwood has described it, did not belong entirely to these Asian alternatives.[1] The Beatles sparked a guru vogue when they went as pilgrims to India in 1968, and many baby boomers understood Timothy Leary's famous incantation to "turn on, tune in, drop out" as an invitation to dig Zen and the Buddha. But many more tuned in to the Bible and took Jesus as their guru. In lieu of a mantra, these born-again boomers chanted the "Jesus cheer":

> *Give me a J (J)*
> *Give me an E (E)*
> *Give me an S (S)*
> *Give me a U (U)*
> *Give me an S (S)*
> *What does that spell? (Jesus)*
> *What will get you higher than acid? (Jesus)*

What will keep you up longer than speed? (Jesus)
What does America need? (Jesus)

These Jesus fans were the praying wing of the Woodstock nation and, more than any other group in American history, they boiled Christianity down to Jesus alone. Together they brought to the United States another evangelical revival, and another conception of Jesus tailor-made for its time.

JESUS FREAKS

The Jesus People, also known as "Jesus Freaks" or "street Christians," traced their origins to Jesus and the apostles, notably the day of Pentecost when God poured out His Holy Spirit on the Church. Chroniclers of the movement, however, typically begin in 1967 in San Francisco's Haight-Ashbury district, with Elizabeth and Ted Wise. That year, with financial help from local ministers, these two recent converts from drugs to Jesus opened a coffeehouse called The Living Room. They also established, along with a few like-minded couples, The House of Acts, the first of many Jesus movement communes to come. At their coffeehouse and their commune, the Wises pleaded with speed freaks and heroin addicts to drop out of the drug culture and turn on to Jesus. It looked like a hard sell, since hippies were as allergic to organized religion as the Black Panthers were to politics as usual. But the Wises did not pitch Christianity. In fact, they openly disdained the institutional church. They offered instead a personal relationship with Jesus, and they found a ready audience in San Francisco.

Earlier in the decade, illegal drugs had been widely associated with freedom: nirvana by narcotics. By the time the *San Francisco Oracle* had proclaimed 1967 the "Summer of Love," however, the pharmacologic innocence of the Age of Aquarius was giving way to a string of bad trips, particularly in the Haight. Media hype about this Mecca of the counterculture had already overburdened the district with seekers. After the *Oracle* announced that the youth of the world were converging on San Francisco in a "Gathering of the Tribes," thousands more felt honor-bound to join the pilgrimage. But few found jobs, and not all found homes. As heroin replaced pot as the drug of choice and overdoses multiplied, many came to associate drugs with captivity rather than freedom.

To these addicts, the Wises offered the simple alternative of Jesus. Their Savior rejected marijuana, acid, and heroin, but he embraced enthusiastically the slang, clothes, and music of hippiedom. Like Leary's Buddha, the Wises' Jesus was a dropout, an outlaw, and a revolutionary who scoffed at the religious establishment of his day. He had come to save the disillusioned and the dispossessed; the high, not the mighty. No distant king, he was instead a loving friend—someone who would hold your hand, wipe your brow, and get you through a bad trip. Those who accepted (and returned) that love put a new spin on the Catholic tradition of the imitation of Christ when they began to dress like Jesus (or at least as they imagined he would). They wore their clothes loose and their hair long, and tramped around the Haight preaching Jesus as urgently as their Savior had wandered around the Galilee preaching the Kingdom of God. Critics called them "Jesus Freaks," and soon Wise and his followers had adopted that moniker as a badge of honor.

Active alongside the Wises in the Bay Area was Jack Sparks, who in 1968 started the Christian World Liberation Front (CWLF). A one-time statistics professor at the Pennsylvania State University, Sparks moved west to work at the University of California at Berkeley with an evangelical group called Campus Crusade for Christ. There he heeded Paul's advice to "become all things to all men" (1 Corinthians 9:22) by becoming a hippie among the hippies. Elders at Campus Crusade, a buttoned-up evangelical organization catering to middle-class college kids, objected to Sparks's bell-bottoms, scraggly beard, and long hair. So he struck out on his own, forming the CWLF as a spiritual halfway house between the apolitical Campus Crusade and the secular Third World Liberation Front. While other Jesus Freaks translated the gospel into flower power slang, Sparks worked with the rhetoric of revolution. At rallies and strikes organized by Berkeley radicals, he and his CWLF comrades carried signs proclaiming Jesus "The Real Revolutionist." They also published *Right On!*, an underground newspaper that attended to the social and political questions of the day. Sparks himself wrote a hip version of the New Testament called *Letters to the Street Christians*, which translated biblical truths into street slang. "Do not commit adultery," for example, became "Don't ball anyone you're not married to." Paul's famous brief for faith over law in Philippians became: "Watch out for the law pushers. They'll lay a heavy rap on you about how you got to follow rules in order to keep up your relationship with Jesus. Following a set of rules doesn't make us the Father's children. It's digging on the relationship with Him. Trust Jesus, not what you can do."[2]

JESUS GOES TO HOLLYWOOD

Though born in San Francisco, the Jesus movement came of age in Hollywood, which in the late sixties drew would-be Jesus Freaks like adolescent boys to a Marilyn Monroe film. There the movement picked up a laid-back southern Californian vibe, thanks to groups such as the Christian Surfers, who preached the joy of sharing the perfect wave with Jesus, and the Hollywood Presbyterian Church, which opened Salt Company, the first Jesus movement nightclub, in the summer of 1968. Jesus People continued to focus, however, on offering the "Jesus trip" to young people alienated from the suit-and-tie church. During the 1950s, Jack Kerouac, Allen Ginsberg, and other Beat Generation writers had rebelled against the man in the gray flannel suit (and the clerical collar) by romanticizing the fellaheen: hustlers and hoboes and other social and cultural outsiders who somehow bore inside them the spiritual secrets of an age. Hollywood's Jesus People also focused their energies on these modern-day Samaritans. But rather than imitating them (as Kerouac and Ginsberg had done), they converted them. Had not Jesus himself come to rescue lost sheep?

In Hollywood, the head shepherd was Arthur Blessitt. A Baptist minister who began his ministry to hippies in the North Beach area of San Francisco, Blessitt drifted south to Hollywood's Sunset Strip, where he made a name for himself by preaching in Gazzarri's Hollywood-A-Go-Go strip club. As the title of his 1971 autobiography (*Turned On to Jesus*) indicates, Blessitt was also an eager translator of gospel truths into street screed. He encouraged Hollywood hippies to "drop Matthew, Mark, Luke, and John" and to groove on "Jesus the everlasting high." His homiletic style, however, was not quite so mellow. One observer said his sermons attacked sin with all the nuance of a battering ram, advancing in only two gears: "forte and fortissimo." While other street preachers of the day became famous for mass baptisms in the Pacific, the "Minister of Sunset Strip" worked with whatever water he could find. One celebrated rite at Blessitt's His Place coffeehouse was the toilet baptism. Whenever a druggie turned from pot and LSD to Jesus, Blessitt would dispatch him to the john and instruct him to drop his grass and acid into the bowl. "I don't need this anymore," the initiate would say. "I'm high on the Lord."[3]

Another local Jesus movement institution was the *Hollywood Free Paper*, which debuted in 1969 and hit a peak circulation of close to 500,000 before folding in 1975. Duane Pederson, a ventriloquist from Minnesota, was the editor, and the *HFP* was his Charlie McCarthy. Instead of taking jabs at Edgar Bergen, Pederson's paper preached a bare-bones Christianity focused on Jesus alone. The *HFP*, Pederson wrote, had "only one creed: Jesus Christ." It found social and political questions as repellent as theological debates. Like many other Jesus Freaks, Pederson was burned out on causes. He welcomed a revolution, but only on the battlefield of the individual soul. Although the *HFP's* headlines often hinted at a controversial issue, its articles routinely ended with Jesus. A piece called "How Moral Is War?" brought up Vietnam only to change the subject: "Nope we're not talking about Viet Nam, we're talking about personal warfare inside of the individual. Dig?"[4]

When Pederson opened a mail order store specializing in posters, bumper stickers, T-shirts, and buttons, he intended simply to support the *Hollywood Free Paper* (which as its name indicates was given away for nothing). But he did a brisk trade, and in the process alerted Christian retailers to the commercial possibilities of Jesus stuff. Like the Protestant Reformation, which gave the world slogans such as "justification by faith," "the priesthood of all believers," and "scripture alone," the Jesus movement spread its message through catchphrases. Pederson's store trafficked in them all—"High on Jesus" T-shirts, "Honk if You Love Jesus" bumper stickers, "The Messiah Is the Message" buttons, and "Jesus: Like a Bridge over Troubled Water" posters. While many of the most memorable slogans riffed on the drug culture, others were inspired by advertising slogans. "Jesus Christ: He's the Real Thing" echoed a Coke campaign; "You have a lot to live and Jesus has a lot to give" echoed Pepsi advertising. At least in Hollywood, Jesus was both celebrity and icon, *Logos* and logo.

Another California vigilante for Jesus was Hal Lindsey. Like Jack Sparks, Lindsey was a former Campus Crusade for Christ staffer who left that group in order to minister to hippies, in his case around the UCLA campus. There he began a successful ministry called J.C. Light and Power Company. Lindsey is best-known, however, for his *The Late Great Planet Earth* (1970), which became the best-selling nonfiction book of the 1970s (and paved the way for the phenomenal success three decades later of the *Left Behind* series of rapture novels by Tim LaHaye and Jerry B. Jenkins). More than anyone else, Lindsey captured the millennialist view, widespread among Jesus People, that everything would soon be made new. Together with Blessitt, Pederson, and other Jesus movement leaders, Lindsey helped to reposition Jesus as a hippie and a spiritual revolutionary.

HIPPIE JESUS

This hippie Jesus had much in common with the sentimental Savior of the nineteenth century. Jesus People described him not as a distant divinity but as a near and dear friend they could know and love and imitate. Unlike their counterparts in the nineteenth century, however, they saw their Savior in countercultural terms. A long-haired rebel who somehow tuned in to God long before the Summer of Love of 1967, their Jesus made love, not war. The love he made, however, was more friendly than sexy, more *philia* than *eros*.

Time magazine captured the essence of this rebel with a cause in a "Jesus Revolution" cover dated June 21, 1971. The illustrator was Stanislaw Zagorski, who one year earlier had done an album cover for the alternative rock band the Velvet Underground. Recalling Warner Sallman, Zagorski offered *Time* readers a head-and-shoulders portrait of Jesus with the requisite long hair and beard. But while Sallman's Jesus was straight as an arrow, Zagorski's was a freak to end all freaks. Bedazzled with pink skin and purple hair and framed by a psychedelic rainbow, he bore down on the reader with deep-set brown eyes, exchanging the more typical stare to the heavens for a soul-searching gaze. Whether this Jesus was communing with his people or tripping on LSD is open to interpretation, but he was clearly experiencing an altered state of consciousness.

A "Wanted: Jesus Christ" poster, quoted in the cover story, lent a political edge to this countercultural pose. Produced by the CWLF, this popular poster described the Prince of Peace as a "typical hippie type—long hair, beard, robe, sandals." But he was also a social revolutionary. A "notorious leader of an underground liberation movement," he was wanted for, among other things, "practicing medicine, wine-making, and food distribution without a license" and "associating with known criminals, radicals, subversives, prostitutes and street people." "Warning," the poster concluded, "He Is Still at Large!"[5]

In his story on the Jesus movement, *Time* reporter Richard Hoag argued that Jesus was a father figure to the young people in the Jesus movement. But their Jesus was more friend than father. Though influenced somewhat by the feminized Jesus of Victorian sentimentalism, this friendly Savior was most plainly a product of the masculinity revival of the early twentieth century. More politicized Jesus People depicted Jesus as a Social Gospel hero, a "professional agitator" trying "to overthrow the established government."[6] Less politicized Jesus Freaks accented their hero's fight against the religious establishment. But both groups projected those qualities on a handsome man with rugged good looks. Like the Beat Generation heroes of an earlier decade, this hippie Jesus was not to be domesticated. He gloried in the road and in intimate comradeship with his male friends. "Jesus Christ is no namby-pamby character," Duane Pederson of the *Hollywood Free Paper* testified. "In fact, Christ really socks it to you with some real heavy stuff."[7]

Time magazine's "Jesus Revolution" story captured the centrality of Jesus to the movement that bore his name. "If any one mark clearly identifies them," *Time* wrote, "it is their total belief in [Jesus]." Yet *Time* slipped up when it described their hero as the "awesome, supernatural Jesus Christ, not just a marvelous man who lived 2,000 years ago, but a living God who is both savior and Judge, and Ruler of their destinies." The Jesus People did affirm both the divinity of their Savior and his miracles. And they did not deny his apocalyptic role as end-time Judge. But the Haight's Jesus was no authoritarian ruler. He was an everyday guy who associated, as another Jesus poster put it, "with common working people, the unemployed and bums."[8]

SUPERSTAR AND GODSPELL

The Jesus movement emerged from the underground in 1971, when Jesus Freaks caught the attention of *Time* and other mainstream media. On New Year's Day 1971, Billy Graham, "the Pope of American Protestantism," discovered the power of the Jesus movement while serving as the grand marshal of the Tournament of Roses Parade in Pasadena, California. As he made his way along the parade route, he found himself surrounded by young people pointing their index fingers to heaven and screaming for their Savior. Zen, Scientology, Krishna consciousness, even Satanism had been offered to them, but they had chosen Jesus. While Black Power activists held up their fists, and peaceniks made the peace sign, Jesus Freaks did the "One Way" salute. Soon Graham was gesturing and shouting too: "One Way—the Jesus Way!"[9]

Later that year, *Look, Newsweek, Life, Rolling Stone*, and *U.S. News & World Report* also discovered the Jesus movement. *Christian Century* declared Jesus "in," and proclaimed 1971 the year of Jesus.[10] Recalling Lennon's controversial remarks, the Christian rock star Larry Norman gloated (in his song "Reader's Digest") about the demise of the Beatles (who split up in 1970) and the emergence of Jesus as a pop icon. Not long ago, Norman observed, people kept Jesus at arm's length. But "this year he's a superstar. / Dear John, who's more popular now?"

Jesus' status as a pop icon was confirmed when two rock musicals—*Jesus Christ Superstar* and *Godspell*—opened in 1971. *Jesus Christ Superstar* came first, but it was too controversial for the theater so a record album was released in 1970 as a trial balloon. Lifted by the music of Andrew Lloyd Webber and the lyrics of Tim Rice (both young Englishmen then, and both knights today), that balloon rose to the top of the *Billboard* charts, prompting a minister at Fifth Avenue Presbyterian Church in New York City to conduct a baptism "in the name of the Father, the Holy Ghost, and Jesus Christ Superstar." Despite (because of?) protests that this "anti-Bible" opera preached a "fake Christ," the record sold more than 3 million copies in its first year, making a Broadway production a foregone conclusion and leading *Time* to feature Jesus on its cover for the second time in a year.[11]

Directed by Tom O'Horgan, who had earlier overseen the quintessential sixties musical *Hair* (1968), *Superstar* offended so many kinds of people when it premiered in October 1971 that the opening-night picket line was a model of interfaith comity. Protestants and Catholics claimed the show portrayed Jesus as insufficiently divine and Judas as insufficiently demonic. Jews objected to yet another portrait of them as Christ killers. Critics reported being moved only by the curtain call. The *New York Post* called the production "flat, pallid and actually pointless." "Beyond redemption," *Downbeat* said: "The music is banal, the lyrics infantile, the staging monumentally vulgar, the theological conception of the Passion of Christ a travesty." Still the show was a smash, running for over 700 performances.[12]

Godspell opened off Broadway in 1971, a few months before *Jesus Christ Superstar*, and sold out there for five years. It moved to Broadway in 1976, and ran for over 500 performances before closing a year later. Because it showed the resurrection (*Superstar* did not), seemed to affirm the divinity of Jesus, and did not implicate Judaism in deicide, *Godspell* did not raise the hackles of Jews and conservative Christians. It was also fairly well received by theater critics, perhaps because it was not hyped like *Superstar*. (What was?) *Life* called it "a theatrical miracle," adding that the low-budget *Godspell* was "a carefree beggar" in comparison with *Superstar's* rich "Pharisee."[13] Like *Superstar*, *Godspell* had a life outside New York, with dozens of companies putting on the show across the country and overseas. In 1973, both hits were made into films, bringing the spirit of the Jesus movement back to its Hollywood home.

Though often lumped together as seventies Jesus "rock operas," the theatrical versions of *Jesus Christ Superstar* and *Godspell* are quite different. *Superstar*, confined to the last week of Jesus' life, is a passion play. The show isn't so much about Jesus as it is about reactions to him—by a black Judas (the star of the show), and a sensuous Mary Magdalene (whose lusting after her man transforms Christian love from *philia* back to *eros*). Webber and Rice borrowed their theme from the Gospel of Mark, where Jesus' messiahship remains a secret until his trial (when the high priest asks him, "Are you the Christ, the Son of the Blessed?" and Jesus replies, "I am.") In *Superstar*, "Who are you?" is the question, and even Jesus seems unsure of the answer. A tormented teenager groping, hippie-style, after his own identity, he sulks his way to the crucifixion like only an adolescent could. In the end, why Jesus dies is as unsettled as who he is. He seems to be crucified more for his own failures than for the sins of others, as if, like Jimi Hendrix and Janis Joplin, he had overdosed on his own demons, including perhaps his own lust for superstardom.

Especially when compared with *Superstar*'s angst, *Godspell* is a joy—an upper to *Superstar*'s downer. Inspired by the Gospel of Matthew and a chapter on "Christ the Harlequin" in Harvey Cox's *The Feast of Fools* (1969), *Godspell* portrays Jesus as a jester and his followers as flower children. Everybody wears psychedelic costumes; Jesus sports a Superman logo on his chest and a red heart on his forehead. His main job is not to brood about how no one understands him, but to share the good news of God's kingdom. He performs that job energetically through a series of engaging pantomimes, parables, and puns.

If *Godspell* is more upbeat than *Superstar*, it is also more reverent. John-Michael Tebelak, who wrote the script, was raised an Episcopalian. He reportedly got the idea for the musical after attending a dour Easter service at the Episcopal cathedral in Pittsburgh, where he was both bored (by the liturgy) and accosted (for his long hair and ragged appearance). "I left with the feeling that, rather than rolling the rock away from the tomb, they were piling more on," Tebelak said.[14] So he went home and wrote *Godspell*. His intention was to inject some joy and hope into the Jesus story, and the show does just that. It also injects some old-fashioned theology. While *Superstar* seems to glory in decimating traditional Christian creeds, *Godspell* weaves old-fashioned doctrines into its book and libretto. Many of the songs, including the hit "Day by Day," are based on Episcopal hymns hand-picked by Tebelak. They affirm, among other things, the divinity of Jesus and the truth of the resurrection. This passage from "Bless the Lord" somehow manages to sum up the doctrine of the substitutionary atonement and the spirit of sixties youth culture:

Oh bless the Lord my soul
He pardons all thy sins
Prolongs thy feeble breath
He heals thine infirmities
And ransoms thee from death
He clothes thee with his love
Upholds thee with his truth
And like an eagle he renews
The vigor of thy youth[15]

Superstar and *Godspell* present different pictures of Jesus. Both portray him as a hippie opposed to the hypocrisy of the religious establishment, but they draw on conflicting impulses from the sixties in creating those images. As every student of the decades knows, the sixties went in like a lamb and out like a lion. They were peace and love and flower power: Woodstock. Then they were race riots and overdoses and Vietnam: Altamont. *Superstar* grows out of the sixties' dark side. It ends with the crucifixion, and its Jesus is James Dean. Full of causes but sure of none, he stalks the stage like an angry young man on the eve of his destruction. *Godspell*, by contrast, is a product of the sixties' bright side. True, its Jesus flays lawyers and Pharisees as snakes and vipers, but rather than looking forward to an end-of-time judgment where those hypocrites will get their due, he prays for a day when "Earth shall be fair / And all her people one." Then he sings about love and harmony, thanks God for sunshine and rain, and rejoices in a community of caring friends. And when he dies, he rises again.

After considering the merits of both *Godspell* and *Jesus Christ Superstar*, *Christian Century* wondered "whether the Holy Spirit might be using the commercial stage to rescue Jesus from the church." The magazine was on to something. One of the distinctive features of the Jesus movement was its appeal to those who found church unappealing. *Godspell* and *Jesus Christ Superstar* did the same. Stephen Schwartz said *Godspell* was "not about religion," and Andrew Lloyd Webber insisted that *Jesus Christ Superstar* was "a dramatic work, and not specifically a religious work at all." But both men protested too much. These were not musicals by Christians for Christians, but they

were spiritual nonetheless, vehicles for propagating Jesus piety outside the institutional churches.[16]

JESUS ROCKS

Like earlier revivals in American history, the Jesus movement spread
through music as much as sermons and slogans. During the great urban revivals of the last half of the nineteenth century, the sweet
hymns of chorister Ira Sankey set the stage for the sentimental sermons of evangelist Dwight Moody. Early in the twentieth century,
Homer Rodeheaver's militant hymns provided the soundtrack for Billy
Sunday's muscular revivals. Now *Jesus Christ Superstar* LPs sold by
the millions, and songs such as Judy Collins's "Amazing Grace,"
Ocean's "Put Your Hand in the Hand" (of the Man from Galilee),
Lawrence Reynolds's "Jesus Is a Soul Man," and the Doobie Brothers'
"Jesus Is Just Alright" became Top 40 hits.

As Jesus became a countercultural celebrity, many mainstream musicians got into the act. Pat Boone (cool back then) baptized new
Christians by the hundreds in the swimming pool at his Hollywood
mansion, and rock stars who did not themselves convert praised Jesus
in their own way. In "Mrs. Robinson," Paul Simon promised his sexy
heroine that "Jesus loves you more than you will know." In "Fire and
Rain," James Taylor asked Jesus to help him face death and beat ad-
diction. *Hair* celebrated long hair "like Jesus wore it" (adding, "Hal-
lelujah, I adore it"). The most striking of these pop appropriations was
a haunting hymn recorded by Lou Reed and the Velvet Underground
in 1969. Two years earlier, in a single called "Heroin," Reed (who like
Paul Simon was Jewish) had sung of feeling "just like Jesus' son." Now
he and his group delivered "Jesus" straight up, in a meditative mantra
that begs to be described as a prayer. Invoking Jesus no fewer than
twelve times, Reed described himself as "falling out of grace" and implored Jesus to help him "find my proper place."

The name of Jesus fell far more easily (and frequently) off the lips
of full-time Jesus rockers such as Larry Norman, a long-haired, raspy-
voiced Jesus Freak, who better than anyone in his generation translated the gospel into the lingua franca of the counterculture: rock 'n'
roll. Although born again as a boy, Norman reportedly left the church

because he couldn't stand the hymns. Mimicking Ralph Waldo Emerson, who roughly a century and a half earlier had left Unitarianism because of the "corpse-cold" sermons of his ministers, Norman walked out of his church because of its deathly hymns ("funeral marches" he called them).[17] Unlike Emerson, however, Norman did not reject Christianity. In fact, he devoted his life to spreading Jesus' name. His chosen venue was the stage rather than the lectern; his concerts were church for the unchurched.

Norman broke into the music business as the lead singer with the San Diego–based rock band "People!" Before their first album was released, he ran into the proverbial "creative differences" with their Capitol Records label. Norman had called that inaugural album *We Need a Whole Lot More of Jesus (And a Lot Less Rock 'n' Roll)* and proposed an album cover depicting the Son of God standing in the midst of his "People." Capitol Records released it instead with innocuous cover art of the band and a bland title: *I Love You*. Before the album hit record stores, Norman bolted the group and the label. Seeing a star (and perhaps a new music market) in the making, Capitol executives asked Norman to return. He did, and his first solo LP, *Upon This Rock* (1970), transformed him momentarily into the Bob Dylan of the Jesus set. *Only Visiting This Planet* (1972) gave Jesus rock its theme song (and its apologetic: "Why Should the Devil Have All the Good Music?"), and a new musical genre was born.

Jesus rock benefitted not only from the openness of pop mainstream musicians to Jesus but also from the openness of evangelicals to popular culture. As early as the revivals of the Second Great Awakening, evangelists have been important producers and consumers of popular culture. Voluntary organizations such as the American Bible Society and the American Tract Society helped to usher in the mass media. Ira Sankey married secular tunes with evangelical lyrics. Then came what historians now refer to as the "Great Reversal." As liberal Protestants and Catholics embraced the Social Gospel, evangelicals narrowed the scope of Christian activism to converting individuals. They also began to turn against popular culture. Following the embarrassments of the Scopes trial of 1925, evangelicals followed their fundamentalist kin into a conservative Christian cocoon of their own making. No longer committed to Christianizing American culture, they decided to withdraw from it. This Great Reversal began to reverse itself after World War II, and by the late sixties a new creature had emerged from the old cocoon. The "Neo-Evangelical," as this creature was called, was more open to social action and to popular culture (including mass media). His resurgence, notably in the person of President Jimmy Carter, prompted *Time* and *Newsweek* to anoint 1976 "The Year of the Evangelical" and prepared the way for the powerful entry in the 1980s of born-again Christians into the public square. It also set the stage for Jesus rock.

Jesus rock emerged from the Christian underground at "Jesus tents" at mainstream rock festivals. In the late sixties, Jesus festivals emerged, devoted solely to this new genre. While the Beatles communed with the Maharishi and practiced TM, radio stations adopted Jesus rock formats, featuring groups such as Love Song, Agape, and the All Saved Freak Band. Meanwhile, amateur Jesus rockers strummed guitars in Christian nightclubs, singing hits such as Norman's apocalyptic "I Wish We'd All Been Ready" and Christian take-offs on sixties standards ("Jesus in the Sky with Diamonds").

Churches groovy enough to open their doors to Jesus Freaks and their ears to electric guitars also made a place for Jesus rock. Under the direction of forty-something pastor Chuck Smith and twenty-something youth minister Lonnie Frisbee, Calvary Chapel in Costa Mesa, California, became one of the fastest-growing churches in the country in the early 1970s. One source of Calvary's success was its single-minded emphasis on Jesus. "Why are so many thousands of people flocking to Calvary?" one young convert asked. "They aren't getting religion and church; they're seeing Jesus and the Bible and love."[18] The Jesus preached at Calvary Chapel was a far cry from Calvin's aloof Sovereign. At Calvary, Jesus was intimate rather than intimidating, and Frisbee and Smith spoke about his life as if they were swapping stories about an old college friend. Chuck Girard, a professional musician who accepted Jesus at Calvary Chapel and went on to form the Christian band Love Song, was particularly struck by Smith's preaching:

He just started rapping. It was different. It wasn't like reading a portion from the Bible and then saying a bunch of words. It was like he was sharing someone he knew—Jesus Christ. He wasn't telling me about a God I'd someday find; he was telling me about his personal Friend.[19]

Jesus the friend also came alive in Calvary Chapel's music. Following the injunction of Psalm 96 to "Sing to the Lord a new song," Smith and Frisbee devoted large segments of their worship services to praising Jesus in song. In 1971, the church started its own label, Maranatha Music! (in Greek, "Maranatha" means "the Lord is coming"), which went on to become one of the leading providers of "praise and worship" music in the country. In this way, Chuck Smith became not only a godfather of the Jesus Freaks but also a progenitor of contemporary Christian music.

Squarer Christians denounced Jesus rock as an instrument of Satan, just as traditionalists had once denounced the church organ as "the devil's bagpipe." But Jesus People saw no reason why rock couldn't be used to drive Satan crazy. Martin Luther, they noted, had not apologized for lending Christian lyrics to secular songs. So when it came to music, they too would give no quarter. "Here I stand," they said with Luther, "I can do no other." And then they picked up their guitars and drumsticks and got about the business of praising their Lord in song.

AS CALIFORNIA GOES . . .

Born in California, the Jesus movement quickly spread elsewhere. One favorite verse among Jesus People was Matthew 8:20: "Foxes have holes, and birds of the air have nests, but the Son of man has nowhere to lay his head." To many, these words proved that Jesus was an itinerant dropout who left his job and family in order to seek God. Larry Norman captured this face of Jesus in his 1972 song, "The Outlaw," which presented its hero roaming "across the land / with a band of unschooled ruffians and a few old fishermen." This restless Jesus provided an example for Jesus Freaks to follow, and follow him they did. With the inchoate purpose and passion of Dean Moriarty, the frenetic hero of Jack Kerouac's benzedrine novel *On the Road*, they traveled the country spreading the good news of the hippie Jesus.

Arthur Blessitt, the controversial Minister of Sunset Strip, epitomized this restlessness. After picking a fight with the Los Angeles
Sheriff's Department, which had shut down His Place in response to
local bar owners' complaints, Blessitt chained himself to a cross and
fasted for twenty-eight days in protest. The protest paid off in a new
site, but Blessitt refused to be tied down to anything but Jesus. On
Christmas Day in 1969, he put some wheels on his cross and began
walking to Washington, D.C. Two years later, he launched a world pilgrimage that as of the turn of the millennium had taken him (and his
cross) to 292 countries.

Thanks to migrations by other Jesus Freaks, the Jesus movement
reversed the westward march of most other U.S. new religious movements, moving irrepressibly east. As evangelists and rockers and thousands of Jesus People moved and moved and moved again, the Jesus
movement migrated to Seattle, Milwaukee, Chicago, Atlanta, and
Gainesville. It crossed the border to Montreal and the oceans to Europe and Australia. Soon Jesus People were publishing dozens of papers across North America, including *Truth* in Spokane, *Maranatha* in
Vancouver, *Street Level* in Milwaukee, and *The Ichthus* in Cherry Hill,
New Jersey.

It is tempting to see the Jesus movement through the eyes of Tom
Wolfe and other critics of the "Me Decade"—to find in the Jesus People not only an obsession with Jesus but also an obsession with the
self. This criticism, however, ignores the powerful collective spirit of
the Jesus movement, which helped to instigate an orgy of communi-
tarianism not seen since the 1830s. Historian Timothy Miller, who
has studied sixties and seventies communes, estimates that the
United States was likely home to tens of thousands of communal
groups, with several thousand of them connected to the Jesus movement.[20] Most of the Jesus movement experiments flopped after a few
years, or even a few months, but some evolved into enduring organizations. John Higgins, who worked with Chuck Smith and Lonnie
Frisbee to start the House of Miracles community in 1968, established a commune called Shiloh in Eugene, Oregon, in 1969. From
there, he expanded south and east, establishing outposts in thirty
states under the umbrella of Shiloh Youth Revival Centers. Jesus People USA (JPUSA) began in the early seventies as a traveling band of

Jesus Freaks intent on getting up revivals wherever young people congregated. By the mid-seventies, they had sold their Jesus bus and settled into a Chicago-based community. Today JPUSA publishes a magazine, *Cornerstone*, with a circulation of roughly 35,000. Every summer it sponsors a popular Christian music festival in nearby Bushnell, Illinois.

The Jesus movement also moved in more dangerous directions, spawning authoritarian groups decried by critics as destructive "cults." The most notorious was the Children of God (COG), which, under the leadership of "Moses" David Berg, grew out of a Huntington Beach coffeehouse called the Light Club. COG's aggressive proselytizing tactics earned it media scrutiny and trouble with local authorities, so the group was continually on the run. In 1971, while Berg was living in London, an organization calling itself Free Our Children from the Children of God (FREECOG) formed, devoted to "deprogramming" supposedly brainwashed family members. After a series of quasi-scriptural "Mo Letters" came to light, interpreting the biblical injunction to "love your neighbor" as a command to use sex as a recruiting technique—"Flirty Fishing" it was called—FREECOG added spiritual prostitution to its list of COG sins. Nonetheless, the group spread to dozens of countries. Now known as The Family, it survived Berg's death in 1994, but has not prospered.

As the Jesus movement migrated out of Hollywood and the Haight, it also broadened demographically. Along with the hardcore ex-druggies-for-Jesus who formed the nucleus of the movement, it attracted middle-class youth from Protestant and Catholic families. Some played the role of the Jesus Freak to perfection. Sporting long hair and well-worn Bibles, they walked a middle path between their square parents and countercultural radicals. Another step removed from the Arthur Blessitt and the Lonnie Frisbees of the Jesus movement were the young straights for Jesus: Catholic kids active in charismatic renewal, and Protestants active in interdenominational campus organizations such as Campus Crusade for Christ and Inter-Varsity Christian Fellowship. The movement also attracted Jews, due to the missionizing of groups such as Jews for Jesus. Although the Jesus movement is typically associated with long-haired freaks, it actually attracted (and affected) many straights. The freaks got most of the attention because their hip speech made for great quotes and their colorful couture for memorable photographs.

"ALL YOU NEED IS JESUS"

The success of the Jesus movement invited criticism, and in the early 1970s a wide variety of critics accepted that invitation. A few Jesus People objected to the liberties their friends were taking with their Lord. Breck Stevens, a pastor to the hippies of North Redondo Beach, California, said that all the hip talk about Jesus "lowers Christ to a worldly level. Jesus is not a cool cat; He's not hip; God's not groovy."[21] Stevens also objected to Jesus rock on the theory that the early church never used music to spread the gospel. Outsiders generally reprised time-honored criticisms of revivalism. Piety among the Jesus People was too emotional and experiential, some argued. Others claimed that their emphasis on converting individuals undermined the social side of the gospel. The most common objection was that the Jesus People were theologically shallow—that the movement's focus on experiencing Jesus had led it away from the truths of the Bible and the doctrines of the creeds.

It is difficult to know what to make of these criticisms, since the Jesus People were themselves so diverse. The Jesus movement was never exactly a full-fledged movement. Or, if it was a movement, it was a spasmodic one—a flotilla of rudderless ships captained by no one other than perhaps Jesus himself. Many have described the Jesus People as millennial and apocalyptic. Mammoth sales of Hal Lindsey's *The Late Great Planet Earth*—roughly 35 million in 50 languages—indicate, at a minimum, tremendous popular interest in *fin de toute* prophesies. It must be said, however, that many Jesus People were too busy tripping on Jesus to concern themselves with reading Vietnam, Woodstock, or the Arab-Israeli Six-Day War for signs of the end times. Hal Lindsey's J. C. Light and Power House discouraged UCLA students from using expectations of the second coming to rationalize dropping out of school. Arthur Blessitt's street sermons steered clear of millennialism altogether.

Another distinctive feature of the Jesus movement is said to be speaking in tongues or, more broadly, the exercise of the spiritual gifts (*charismata*) of the Holy Spirit described in the New Testament book of Acts. Pentecostals and charismatics share with evangelicals an emphasis on conversion, but they also believe in a second blessing of the Holy Spirit typically manifest by speaking in tongues. While evangelicals typically believe that the gifts of the Holy Spirit described in Acts ended with the age of the apostles, Pentecostals and charismatics insist that they are available to Christians today. Many Jesus People were charismatics, but here too the movement was divided. Some enthusiastically embraced such spiritual gifts as speaking in tongues and spiritual healing; others, including Jack Sparks's Christian World Liberation Front, did not. Many walked a middle path, allowing charismatic practice in their communities while taking a hard line against the view that Christians who did not speak in tongues were somehow second-class citizens. This middle way continues to be charted at Calvary Chapel, where Chuck Smith insists (following 1 Corinthians 13) that the greatest spiritual gift is love.

Though the Jesus People did not coalesce around apocalypticism or speaking in tongues, they did share a few key tendencies. A preference for spirituality over religion was one of them. Like so many other lovers of Jesus, the Jesus People were hostile to what Christian rocker Keith Green called "Churchianity." Although in many cases Jesus movement pioneers benefitted from financial support from local pastors, they repeatedly drew sharp distinctions between themselves and traditional churches. Following so many earlier Americans, they distinguished between the false Christianity of the institutional church and the true Christianity of their own imagining. Some even claimed that traditional Christians weren't Christians at all. Like Emerson, who derided Unitarian sermons, and Kerouac, who mocked the generic "faith-in-faith" of Eisenhower's America, the Jesus People were desperate to experience divinity, but they could not find God in the churches and synagogues of middle-class America. Similar yearnings had led Emerson to explore Hinduism and Kerouac to experiment with Buddhism, but the Jesus People stayed closer to home, hunting for spiritual diamonds in their own backyards.

A commitment to evangelism also characterized the Jesus movement. None of the baby boomers who became Jesus Freaks in the late sixties and early seventies were born that way. They all had to be made, and they were made through aggressive proselytizing—in Christian coffeehouses, at Jesus rock concerts, and on the streets. Prompted by the Great Commission—the charge of the risen Christ in Matthew 28:18 to "Go therefore and make disciples of all nations"—Jesus People sought to make Christians of the Woodstock nation. They did not insist, however, that their converts cut their hair and don suits and ties. "Seeker sensitive" before seeker sensitivity was cool, they actually exhorted new Christians to continue to dress like hippies in order to convert more of the same. Since the time of Paul, Christian missionaries had debated whether they should preach Christ and civilization or Christ alone. Do Gentile converts need to be circumcised? Do African converts need to dress like proper Americans? In this debate over missions theory, the Jesus People came down firmly for Christ alone.

Given this missiology, it should not be surprising that the Jesus People were radically Jesus-centric. Most affirmed the literal truth of scripture, and hip translations such as *The Living Bible* (1971)—the best-selling nonfiction book in 1972 and 1973 (outpacing even *The Joy of Sex*)—were ubiquitous in the Jesus set. But here *solus Jesus* was a more powerful rallying cry than *sola scriptura*. Like their Reformation forebears, the Jesus People had a talent for sloganeering, and virtually all of their slogans—"Jesus is better than hash," "Freaked out on Jesus," "Join the Jesus revolution"—put Jesus front and center. Their gospel could be summed up in three words ("Jesus Loves You") or two ("Jesus Saves") or even one ("Jesus"). Whereas the Beatles sang "All You Need Is Love," the Jesus People said "All You Need Is Jesus." Whether your problem was drugs, homosexuality, or ennui, Jesus was the answer. If your concern was war or racism, Jesus was the answer too. An article published in the *Hollywood Free Paper* epitomized this emphasis on experiencing Jesus:

Well, we're not rapping about positive thinking or playing religious games. Nope. That's just as phony as the drug trip. We're rapping about a Person—Jesus Christ. And if you can dig Him (that means to depend on Him to put your head together) then you're in for some heavy surprises!! He'll turn you on to a spiritual high for the rest of forever.[22]

GODSTOCK

The Jesus movement seems to have peaked right around the time Jesus became a Broadway superstar. In the summer of 1972, a massive Jesus festival called Explo '72 brought about 80,000 young people to the Cotton Bowl in Dallas for a week of singing and sermons. *Life* magazine, which along with *Time* continued to be animated by the spiritual concerns of its founder, the Presbyterian Henry Luce, described the event in a June 30 cover story as "an emotional high, centering on the figure of Jesus." Billy Graham, who had given the Jesus movement his blessing in *The Jesus Generation* (1971), praised Explo '72 as a "religious Woodstock." Others shortened that to "Godstock." Bill Bright, the irrepressible Campus Crusade for Christ founder who orchestrated the gathering, was less measured. Convinced Explo '72 was the most important Christian happening since Pentecost, he prophesied the evangelization of the entire country by 1976. What Bright saw as the start of an evangelical tsunami, however, now appears to have been the crest of a west-to-east Jesus wave that first surged over California in 1967 and crashed shortly after *Jesus Christ Superstar* and *Godspell* hit the Great White Way.[23]

Life's cover story on "The Great Jesus Rally in Dallas" was one of the last major treatments of the Jesus movement by a national periodical. By 1973, *Eternity* magazine was wondering, "Where Have All the Jesus People Gone?" Two years later, *Christianity Today* asked, "Whatever Happened to the Jesus Movement?" The simple answer was that the party was over and the revelers had gone home. As the seventies aged, some of the seekers who had found Jesus in San Francisco or Hollywood moved on to the Moonies or the Hare Krishnas, and then to est or the Divine Light Mission. Others left religion altogether. Larry Norman once boasted that the Jesus movement was "like a glacier. It's growing and there's no stopping it." By the mid-seventies that glacier seemed to have melted.[24]

Today it is common to view the Jesus movement as a sixties curio—a comic combination of the hip and the square. But it is a mistake to write off the Jesus People as irrelevant eccentrics. The Jesus movement represents a culmination of key trends in American Protestantism rather than a diversion from them. Long before Ted Wise first chanted the Jesus cheer and Duane Pederson did the "One Way" salute, evangelicals and liberals alike were transforming Christianity into a Jesus faith. If the Jesus movement was a glacier, it carried with it debris picked up from earlier Americans—an emphasis on the humanity of their Savior, a preference for Jesusianity over "Churchianity," and above all the conviction that to be a Christian was not to recite a creed but to walk with Jesus. And when it melted it turned large swaths of the country into its moraine.

Like the counterculture itself, the Jesus movement lives on in mainstream America. Many of the Jesus People who abandoned communes and coffeehouses in the early seventies took Jesus with them as they cut their hair, settled down, and started families. Some returned to the churches and synagogues of their youth. Jack Sparks led a contingent of Christian World Liberation Front members into Eastern Orthodoxy in 1975. Other Jesus Freaks settled down in nondenominational churches that sprouted up across the country during the 1970s. But the influence of the Jesus movement goes far beyond the individuals who flushed their drugs down the toilet at His Place in Hollywood or danced to Love Song at Explo '72. Many who turned on to Jesus during the Jesus craze went on to energize parachurch groups such as Campus Crusade for Christ and InterVarsity Christian Fellowship, which both enjoyed strong growth during the seventies. And when evangelicalism, Pentecostalism, and the charismatic movement took off during that same decade, former Jesus People occupied the pews and pulpits.

The Jesus movement also gave a boost to Christian retailing. Americans have been selling Jesus stuff since the early nineteenth century, but the Jesus movement turned Christian retailing into a major industry, which now accounts for more than $4 billion in annual sales. Christian bookstores first appeared in the 1950s, but they proliferated in the 1960s and 1970s. Their stock expanded too, pressing beyond Bibles and other books to record albums, posters, buttons, T-shirts, patches, bumper stickers, and collectibles. In these bookstores, Jesus became not just a national icon but also a profitable brand, his name and likeness festooned on an endless variety of paraphernalia.

SEEKER-SENSITIVE CHURCHES

Nondenominational megachurches may be the most important institutional legacy of the Jesus movement. This influence is ironic, given the opposition of many early Jesus People to the institutional church. But in keeping with their roots in the Jesus movement, the megachurches billed themselves as the 7-Ups of the Christian world—un-churchly alternatives to the vast denominational bureaucracies. Donald Miller describes the startling rise of these "seeker-sensitive" or "new paradigm" churches as nothing less than a "Second Reformation." While the Reformation of the sixteenth century emphasized faith over works and the Bible over tradition, he argues, this reformation emphasizes experience over doctrine, emotion over theology, and spirituality over religion. In place of the old hymns and the old liturgy, "new paradigm" churches sing contemporary songs and worship God in new ways. Given more than a century of historical precedents for each of these developments, the language of reformation is probably not appropriate here. But the combination the megachurches have hit on is clearly working. While membership at mainline churches is declining, these churches are booming, counting their members in many cases by the thousands.[25]

Like the street ministries of Ted and Elizabeth Wise and the concerts of Larry Norman and Love Song, seeker-sensitive churches focus on reaching the unchurched. Given this emphasis on evangelism, it should not be surprising that their congregants share a lot with earlier revivalists. Nathan Hatch has described the spirit of the Second Great Awakening of the nineteenth century as populist: "Increasingly assertive common people wanted their leaders unpretentious, their doctrines self-evident and down to earth, their music lively and singable, and their churches in local hands."[26] The same can be said of these new-paradigm churches, though they add to this populist impulse the concerns of their own generation. In seeker-sensitive congregations, informality trumps hierarchy, ministers go by their first names, and everyone dresses casually. Architecturally, seeker-sensitive churches look more secular than religious, mimicking malls with their large open spaces, flooded with light. Services feature contemporary music played over elaborate sound systems, often with Jumbotron screens and projected lyrics that make singing (and hand raising) easy for newcomers. Though based on the Bible, sermons are mercifully short, particularly in comparison with the singing, which often consumes more than half of the time for worship. Sermons typically entertain as much as they evangelize, and they accent the positive. None of the venom in Jonathan Edwards's notorious fire and brimstone sermon, "Sinners in the Hands of an Angry God," passes the lips of these positive pastors, who focus on offering to their congregants authentic experience rather than correct doctrine. "It isn't a religion, it's a relationship," they say. These are sinners in the hands of a friendly God.

One influential "new paradigm" church is Calvary Chapel. The most dynamic and enduring organization to emerge from the Jesus movement, Calvary Chapel began in 1965 when Chuck Smith accepted a call to a congregation of only twenty-five members in Costa Mesa, California. Smith was in his forties at the time, ancient by sixties standards. When hippies started materializing around him, Smith's first impulse was to throw them in the tub and march them down to the barber shop, but he had three teenagers at the time and they helped him empathize with the burgeoning youth culture. Soon Smith's Pacific Ocean baptisms were making street Christians by the hundreds. Like the mustard seed of the parables, his modest church spawned a worldwide movement of over six hundred congregations (many led by pastors Smith led to Jesus) as well as a Bible college, a Christian school, and a radio station. In keeping with the nondenominational emphasis of most megachurches, Calvary's churches have resisted forming a denomination.

Just as sentimental Protestants of the nineteenth century have been castigated for trading in theology for storytelling, seeker-sensitive churches have been accused of emphasizing experience at the expense of doctrine, and music to the detriment of the Bible. In keeping with Smith's roots in the experiments of the sixties, Calvary Chapel services do emphasize the heart over the head. Affiliated churches continue to view music as central to their mission. Nonetheless, the association has worked hard to make its members both biblically literate and creedally correct. One distinguishing mark of Calvary Chapel services is old-fashioned, verse-by-verse exposition of scripture; the sermons listed on Chuck Smith's Web site are named only by biblical book. In these sermons, Smith takes his listeners through a chapter or two at a time, teasing out his text's meanings line by line. In order to keep their worshipers focused on the love of Jesus rather than the power of the Holy Spirit, Calvary Chapel congregations downplay charismatic gifts and the runaway emotionalism that sometimes accompanies them. Smith was raised in the International Church of the Foursquare Gospel, a Pentecostal denomination started by Aimee Semple McPherson, and his experiences there taught him that spiritual gifts could divide a congregation. In *Charisma vs. Charismania* (1982), Chuck Smith encouraged his readers to keep speaking in tongues a private matter between themselves and God.

The Anaheim-based Association of Vineyard Churches also emerged from the Jesus movement. It began with Kenn Gulliksen, who was ordained by Chuck Smith and tapped to start a sister church in Los Angeles called the Vineyard (because of its interest in planting churches and harvesting Christians). Like Smith and Frisbee, who clashed earlier over the proper use of the gifts of the Holy Spirit, Smith and Gulliksen were soon at loggerheads. While Smith downplayed spiritual gifts, Gulliksen gloried in them. He believed that the full range of spiritual gifts, including prophesy and healing, should be on display in every church. So Gulliksen struck out on his own. As his church grew and his "signs and wonders" theology spread, he followed Smith's example, spinning off sister churches under the Vineyard name. In 1982, Gulliksen joined forces with John Wimber, a Calvary Chapel minister (and former keyboardist for the Righteous Brothers) who had just left that movement for similar reasons. Gulliksen was so impressed with Wimber that he turned over the entire Vineyard operation to him.

During the mid-nineties, the Vineyard movement drew fire after the list of "signs and wonders" expanded at Toronto Airport Vineyard Fellowship to include, first, "holy laughter" and, later, the miraculous transformation of dental fillings into gold. The faithful had proof texts for God's new role as Rumpelstiltskin. (Does not Psalms 81:10 promise, "Open your mouth wide, and I will fill it"?) Most evangelicals, however, were unconvinced, claiming that the Vineyarders' infatuation with miracles and the Holy Spirit had led them away from the Bible and Jesus Christ. In recent years, the group has moderated its stance on charismatic gifts. Its current statement of faith now speaks of fostering churches "where demonstrated purity and character are valued as highly as charisma and rhetorical skills."[27]

There are now over 850 Vineyard churches operating worldwide. Unlike Calvary's congregations, which are only loosely affiliated, these Vineyard congregations have become an official denomination. In addition to its member congregations, the Association of Vineyard Churches includes a nonprofit label, Vineyard Music, specializing in "praise and worship" music.

Part of the appeal of the Vineyard and Calvary Chapel churches is their single-minded focus on Jesus. In the Calvary Chapel parking lot, bumper stickers attest to this Jesus-centrism: JESUS LIVES, MY HEART BELONGS TO JESUS, JESUS ON BOARD, and BEAM ME UP, JESUS! This Jesus, however, never stands alone. He is always in a relationship—walking side-by-side with a Christian friend. At a service at Calvary Chapel Costa Mesa attended by Donald Miller, the lead guitarist announced, "We're not singing about religion tonight; we're talking about a relationship with Jesus." Greg Laurie, a onetime Jesus Freak who took over a small church in Riverside, California, in the early seventies and built it into a 15,000-person congregation (now called Harvest Christian Fellowship), echoes that sentiment. "The answer is not religion," he said. "It is a relationship with Jesus."[28]

Vineyarders also insist on knowing Jesus. One Vineyard pastor says, "The apostles didn't know theology. They just knew Jesus."[29] But who is the Jesus they know? He does not appear to be a hippie. In fact he does not appear, visually, at all. Like the temples of the Church of Jesus Christ of Latter-day Saints, new paradigm churches typically eschew crosses. At Calvary Chapel a dove (an image of the Holy Spirit) has replaced the cross as the key icon. Protestant churches began this effacement of Jesus centuries ago, when they traded in the crucifixes of Catholicism for empty crosses. Now seeker-sensitive churches such as Calvary Chapel are going one step further, by eliminating crosses altogether. Like the apostle Paul, who never saw the historical Jesus, these congregants have experienced only the living Christ. Unlike Paul, who built his theology around the cross, they seem far more interested in the resurrection than the crucifixion, victory than suffering. This shift in visual cues may seem to downplay Jesus, but the effect may not necessarily be to replace one-third of the Trinity with another. In fact, the elimination of the cross may free Jesus up to be everywhere rather than somewhere—to allow him to reside in each believer's heart, in keeping with each believer's needs.

It is tempting to discern a bit of gnosticism here. Disembodied and de-historicized, the evanescent Jesus of these churches seems to exist only in the mind, as an object of believers' feelings, experiences, and desires. It may be more accurate, however, to see the Jesus of the Vineyard and Calvary Chapel as a twenty-first-century baby boomer rather than a first-century gnostic. Smith and Wimber are as fluent in boomer-speak as the *Hollywood Free Paper* was in the vernacular of the hippies. The Jesus they preach isn't just seeker-sensitive, he's boomer-sensitive. To a generation suspicious of organized religion, he offers friendship rather than membership. To a generation skeptical of dogma, he accents experience. To a generation obsessed with the first person singular, he offers self-realization as well as salvation. This is the upbeat Jesus of John 10:10 (and of Bruce Barton's *The Man Nobody Knows*), who comes "that they may have life, and have it abundantly." And that abundant life begins here and now rather than in the by and by.

CONTEMPORARY CHRISTIAN MUSIC

Another important legacy of the Jesus movement is Contemporary Christian Music. Evangelism, entertainment, and the economy have been silent partners in the United States at least since the Second Great Awakening, so it should not be surprising that an industry grew up around the Jesus rock scene. What would come to be known as CCM began in the mid-seventies with the formation of record labels devoted exclusively to Jesus rock, folk, and pop. Consistent with its Jesus movement roots, CCM initially aimed more at selling Jesus than at making money. The acts these labels recorded and promoted played different kinds of music. They shared a commitment to evangelizing the unchurched by transposing the good news of Jesus into new sounds.

Success came slowly for CCM. At first, the music was too Christian for the secular market and too secular for the Christian market. But slowly Christian groups such as the pioneering rock band Petra (Greek for "rock") found an audience. By the late 1970s, the industry was large enough to merit its own monthly. *CCM Magazine* launched in 1978, the same year the Christian music singer Amy Grant released her first album. One year later, Bob Dylan (who had converted to Christianity through the efforts of the Vineyard movement) gave CCM a huge boost when he put out *Slow Train Coming*, the first of three explicitly Christian albums. In 1982, Amy Grant's *Age to Age*, released on the pioneering CCM label Myrrh, became the first album on a Christian label to go platinum. By that time, CCM wasn't just stocked in Christian bookstores; it was on shelves at Kmart too.

From the beginning, CCM was an odd genre, defined more by its lyrical content than its musical style. Nonetheless, the industry focused for at least a decade on rock, pop, and folk. During the mid-eighties, the genre spread its wings. In 1984, Stryper fused Christianity and heavy metal in a debut album released by Enigma, the label that had brought the world Mötley Crüe. Even seasoned CCM observers didn't know what to make of this big-haired band and its yellow-and-black spandex uniforms. The enigma deepened when the band went on a "Heaven and Hell" tour with Mötley Crüe and started pelting its fans with Bibles. Although some denounced Stryper with the same vehemence an earlier generation of critics had shown in denouncing soft rock groups such as Love Song, mainstream vehicles such as *CCM Magazine* made peace with the band. Soon Christian music bins were filled with not only Christian heavy metal but also Christian punk, country, reggae, jazz, blues, alternative rock, rhythm-and-blues, and even Christian hip-hop (thanks to the popularity of "righteous rappers" dc Talk).

As CCM spread its wings in the late 1980s, mainstream record companies began to sit up and take notice. Some started their own Christian divisions. Others inked distribution deals with Christian labels. Thanks to the popularity of Amy Grant, songs by crossover Christian artists began to crack rotations at secular radio stations. "Positive pop" was the neologism for their new music, which was Christian by stealth rather than acclamation. During the 1990s,

CCM really took off. In 1991, Amy Grant's *Baby Baby* became the number-one-selling single in the country. In 1995, an eponymous album by the alternative rock band Jars of Clay went double platinum. "Kiss Me" by Sixpence None the Richer climbed toward the top of the secular singles charts in 1999. Creed, another alternative Christian band, was named rock artist of the year by *Billboard* in 2000. By the early twenty-first century, CCM had become a billion-dollar industry with its own award shows (the Doves), its own Britney Spears (the teen diva Jaci Velasquez), and even its own oldies stations. CCM songs produced by secular conglomerates such as AOL Time Warner could be heard on Hollywood soundtracks and MTV.

This success did not come without controversy. Evangelicals initially criticized rock and roll, including Jesus rock, as an instrument of the devil. But as the genre went mainstream, they attacked CCM's message more than its medium. Crossover artists, the criticism went, were ignoring the cross, worshiping mammon rather than God, and sacrificing Jesus on the altar of the *Billboard* charts. Some were even going the way of Peter, denying they were Christian groups at all. These critics often followed the lead of Christopher Lasch's *The Culture of Narcissism* (1978), chastising Christian musicians for obsessing with the first person rather than the Divine Person. "In the glitz of high-fidelity faith," one critic asked, "who's really being worshiped—Jesus Christ or the superstars?"

Such criticisms may have inhibited sales in the main venue for Jesus rock: Christian bookstores. But they probably boosted sales everywhere else. Just as rock music benefitted from the fulminations of anti-rock parents and pastors—"If Mom hates it, I'll buy it"—Jesus rock seemed more authentic after it was blasted as blasphemous. What could be more enticing to young Christians than a sound that grated on pastors and parents alike?

THE JESUS TEST

The Jesus movement, the megachurch phenomenon, and the CCM industry share more than historical connections. They also share a coterie of Christian critics. According to detractors, the Jesus movement was theologically shallow, megachurches pander to therapeutic culture, and CCM is about entertainment, not evangelism. The core complaint seems to be that all these folks have adapted too much to American culture. Rather than making America more Christian, the Jesus People, the megachurches, and the CCM industry have tried to make Christianity more American. They have molded Jesus to the world instead of molding the world to Jesus.

In *The Modernist Impulse in American Protestantism* (1976), William Hutchison identified adaptationism—"the conscious, intended adaptation of religious ideas to modern culture"—as one of the hallmarks of Protestant modernism. Hutchison's study tracked this impulse in works by liberal Protestants who believed that Christianity needed to change with the times in order to remain a living tradition. But that impulse, rooted as Hutchison notes in "a belief in the interpenetration of religion and culture," animated the Jesus movement too, and it is alive and well in CCM and the megachurches, where a new breed of Christians—call them evangelical modernists—abounds.[30]

The Willow Creek Community Church, a pioneer in the seeker-sensitive approach, epitomizes this born-again modernism. Before he opened his sanctuary in suburban Chicago in 1975, pastor Bill Hybels conducted an informal marketing survey of unchurched residents in surrounding neighborhoods. The goal was to find out why people avoid church, and then to create a congregation designed just for them. Hybels discovered that potential members disliked being hit up for money and being pressured to make a decision for Jesus. They felt awkward when they were asked to stand up and introduce themselves, and guilty when ministers badgered them about their sinfulness. With this research in hand, Hybels planted his seeker-sensitive church. Today the Willow Creek Community Church draws up to 15,000 a week to its massive suburban campus, and the broader Willow Creek Association (established in 1992) boasts roughly 100 similar congregations.

During the 1920s, when Jesus first emerged as an American superstar, secular and religious critics ripped Bruce Barton's *The Man Nobody Knows* for selling Christianity out to capitalism. Barton responded by claiming that his critics had artificially divided the world into the sacred and the secular, and had barred God from much of

His own creation. God was immanent in all human culture, Barton insisted, and Jesus was more desperately needed in the marketplace than in the home.

The Jesus People and their offspring were not Protestant liberals like Barton. But they too said "Amen" to the modernists' call to adapt Christ to culture. If suits and ties were obligatory, how would the hippies be evangelized? If heavy metal was off limits, how would Jesus be preached to eighties youth? If marketing surveys were verboten, how would pastors reach out to unchurched suburbanites? As they threw out their ties, cranked up the volume, and canvassed the neighborhood, these evangelical modernists also refused to restrict their Father's business to the church. "I think everybody should be a full time Christian," Larry Norman said, echoing Barton, "even if they work on cars or sell insurance."[31]

This is no place to settle the debate between the evangelical modernists and their anti-modern critics. In the end, the propriety of any given transformation of the Christian tradition depends on theological calculations about the transcendence and immanence of God. More practically, it depends on where the line is to be drawn between Christian essentials and inessentials. What is intriguing about the history of American Christianity is that no one seems to have drawn that line on the other side of Jesus. No one has seen Jesus as inessential. Over the American centuries, some liberals have given up on miracles, the inspiration of the Bible, and (in the case of the "Death of God" theologians of the 1960s) divinity itself. Some conservatives have given up on creeds, while others have jettisoned doctrines once thought sacrosanct, including predestination, original sin, and the substitutionary atonement. But rather than killing Jesus, these adaptations have only made him stronger. It almost seems as if the Christians who subtracted this doctrine or that rite were beginning to question their own standing, and in order to convince themselves (and their neighbors) of their bona fides they bent over backwards to laud and magnify their Savior. Or perhaps religious practice is a zero-sum game; when you subtract religious energies from one channel of grace (the Bible or the sacraments), those energies immediately flow into another (Jesus).

Scholars have known for some time that the liberals of the late nineteenth century and the modernists of the early twentieth century were all radically Jesus-centric. But as the liberal Protestant mainline lost its public power in the 1920s, Jesus continued to lord over American Christianity. Recalling their roots in the sentimental piety of early Victorianism, evangelicals in the Jesus movement and beyond centered their lives on a personal relationship with Jesus. When asked to describe what he and other pioneering Jesus rockers were doing in the early 1970s, Larry Norman said "the vision was Jesus, Jesus, Jesus." Oddly enough, "Death of God" theologians said the same thing.

Something has been lost as the modernists (evangelical and otherwise) have done what they do best. The modern-day Calvinists who decry the loss of doctrine that has beset even born-again Christianity have a legitimate complaint. But in order to carry the day, they need to take on not only the Jesus movement, the megachurches, and CCM but also Dwight Moody (who advertised aggressively), Ira Sankey (who set Christian songs to popular music), Billy Sunday (who was allergic to theology), and Billy Graham (who perfected the evangelism business). They might need to take on as well the early-nineteenth-century evangelical congregations whose decision to embrace Jesus as a sweet and tender Savior made them the first "seeker-sensitive" churches in the nation.

During the Great Awakening of the early eighteenth century, Jonathan Edwards developed a series of tests for distinguishing true from false religion, true from false Christians. One, which might be called the Jesus test, went like this:

By the sight of the transcendent glory of Christ, true Christians see him worthy to be followed; and so are powerfully drawn after him; they see him worthy that they should forsake all for him: by the sight of that superlative amiableness, they are thoroughly disposed to be subject to him, and engaged to labor with earnestness and activity in his service, and made willing to go through all difficulties for his sake. And it is the discovery of this divine excellency of Christ, that makes them constant to him: for it makes a deep impression upon their minds, that they cannot forget him; and they will follow him whithersoever he goes, and it is in vain for any to endeavor to draw them away from him.

Only a small minority of Edwards's fellow colonists would have passed this test. On a bad day Edwards might have flunked it himself. Today, however, virtually all American Christians would pass with flying colors. U.S. Christianity is divided into two parties: a conservative party that affirms doctrines such as the virgin birth, the inspiration of the Bible, and the bodily resurrection; and a liberal party that does not. American Christians no longer come together around a theology or a book. Yet they are united in their love of Jesus. All seem "powerfully drawn after him," attracted to his "superlative amiableness." And even that small minority that cannot affirm Jesus' "divine excellency" say they are willing to "follow him whithersoever he goes."[32]

PART TWO

Reincarnations

Five

MORMON ELDER BROTHER

The New Testament is silent about much of Jesus' life. Regarding the thirty years between his infancy and the onset of his ministry, it tells only one tale—of a precocious teenager lingering in the Jerusalem Temple, worrying his parents and astounding the scribes. Though this slim record has frustrated some, most Christians have been content to express their frustrations through nothing more radical than clever interpretations of the New Testament. Some have shown less restraint. Certain that God has not left Himself without a witness, even in America, they have uncovered extra-biblical evidence of Jesus—in ancient manuscripts, personal visions, and the disembodied voices of spirits of the dead.

"Copy of a Letter Written by Our Blessed Lord and Saviour Jesus Christ," based on a letter reportedly unearthed under a stone at the base of a cross in the Roman province of Galatia, first surfaced in the Americas in 1761. The contents changed as the copy was copied, weighing in on matters as diverse as keeping the Sabbath (for it), wearing fancy dresses (against them), and working hard (for it). Some believed that copies of the document contained magical properties.

"And whosoever shall have a copy of this letter, written with my own hand and keepeth it in their houses," the 1761 version promised, "nothing shall hurt them, neither pestilence, lightning, nor thunder."[1]

Another popular text, also ostensibly of ancient origin, contained this detailed physical description of Jesus "written by Publius Lentulus, a resident of Judea in the reign of Tiberius Caesar":

> His hair is of the colour of the ripe hazel-nut, straight down to the ears, but below the ears wavy and curled, with a bluish and bright reflection, flowing over his shoulders. It is parted in two on the top of the head, after the pattern of the Nazarenes. His brow is smooth and very cheerful with a face without wrinkle or spot, embellished by a slightly reddish complexion. His nose and mouth are faultless. His beard is abundant, of the color of his hair, not long, but divided at the chin. His aspect is simple and mature, his eyes are changeable and bright. He is terrible in his reprimands, sweet and amiable in his admonitions, cheerful without loss of gravity. He was never known to laugh, but often to weep. His stature is straight, his hands and arms beautiful to behold. His conversation is grave, infrequent, and modest. He is the most beautiful among the children of men.[2]

The diffusion of this letter prompted artists across the country to try their hand at rendering this "most beautiful" man. A Currier & Ives lithograph called *The True Portrait of Our Blessed Savior, Sent by Publius Lentulus to the Roman Senate*, first published in the 1850s, depicts Jesus with brilliant eyes, a forked beard, and hair parted in the middle.

When a Spiritualist vogue swept the country beginning in the 1840s, a new genre of modern apocrypha emerged as mediums claimed the ability to channel American heroes such as Ben Franklin and even Jesus himself. *A Holy, Sacred and Divine Roll and Book* (1843), a Shaker scripture believed to be dictated by an angel to the medium Philemon Stewart, described Jesus' Second Coming in the female form of Shaker founder Mother Ann Lee. Before the century's end, Spiritualists had channeled two different autobiographies of Jesus, and Jesus had overseen (in the spirit) at least one new translation of an abridged New Testament. Today the Library of Congress classifies dozens of books under the author "Jesus Christ (Spirit)," and a few more entries, also attributed to Jesus, under the subject of "Spirit Writing." One of these books, *True Gospel Revealed Anew by Jesus* (1900), led to the formation of a new religious movement called the Foundation Church of the New Birth, which reveres its heaven-sent gospel as holy writ.

Growing interest in Asian religions, particularly after the World's Parliament of Religions brought Hindu and Buddhist representatives to Chicago in 1893, gave rise to a new genre of modern apocrypha, rooted in the religions of the East. The Russian war correspondent Nicholas Notovitch claimed his *Unknown Life of Jesus Christ* (1894) was a translation of an ancient life of Jesus tucked away in a Tibetan monastery. While traveling in Tibet in the 1880s, Notovitch reportedly came across a manuscript called "Life of Saint Issa" (a Tibetan term for Jesus), written shortly after Jesus' death. That text filled in Jesus' "lost years" with a sojourn in India and Tibet, and extensive study of Hindu and Buddhist scriptures. Though dismissed by Albert Schweitzer as "a bare-faced swindle" and G. Stanley Hall as "a crass and naively told story," Notovitch's *Unknown Life* was a popular sensation, not only in Europe but also in the United States, where three independent translations appeared in 1894 alone.[3]

The Aquarian Gospel of Jesus the Christ (1908), by the Civil War chaplain Levi W. Dowling, was even more popular. It also presented itself as a transcription, and it too dispatched Jesus to India and Tibet. Dowling's sources, however, were "the imperishable records of life, known as the Akashic Records." In other words, Dowling was a medium who downloaded his book from the vast storehouse of esoteric knowledge known to occultists as the Akashá. Both Levi's *Aquarian Gospel* and Notovitch's *Unknown Life* were heavily influenced by Theosophy, an esoteric wisdom tradition that views all great religions, Christianity included, as manifestations of one spiritual tradition originating in ancient India. And both fed demand for esoteric lives of an esoteric Jesus. Large sections of Levi's *Aquarian Gospel* made their way (unattributed) into Noble Drew Ali's *The Holy Koran of the Moorish Science Temple* (1920s), which in one of its original passages described Jesus as a redeemer of "His people . . . from the pale skin nations of Europe." George Willie Hurley's Universal Hager's Spiritual Church, another syncretistic black denomination, read reverently from Levi's text in its worship services. Notovitch's *Unknown Life* also had a considerable afterlife, living on in Elizabeth Clare Prophet's *The Lost Years of Jesus* (1984) and in stories of Jesus' past lives by the popular medium Edgar Cayce.[4]

All of this modern apocrypha seeks to orient Jesus to modern times. In that sense, its authors and publishers stand with rather than against Bushnell, Beecher, and other Americans who have shaped Jesus in their own image. But outsider texts such as the *Aquarian Gospel* and the *Unknown Life* differ significantly from the resurrections of Jesus effected by white Protestant insiders. These books, rather than bringing Jesus alive inside evangelical or liberal Protestantism, transport him to very different religious worlds. And rather than restricting their sources to New Testament books, they turn to alternative scriptures for inspiration. As a result, these images of Jesus tend to be culture-transforming rather than culture-affirming. Many are far more countercultural, in fact, than the hippie Jesus of the Jesus movement. Such reinterpretations are best understood, therefore, as reincarnations rather than resurrections. They bring Jesus back to life in a new time and a new place, far away from both ancient Palestine and modern American Protestantism.

A NEW RELIGION FOR A NEW NATION

The most intriguing example of these reincarnations of Jesus is also far and away the most popular, with over 100 million copies in print and another fifteen thousand or so coming off the presses every day. Divinely inspired scripture to members of the Church of Jesus Christ of Latter-day Saints (popularly known as Mormons), the Book of Mormon is, according to the faithful, a translation of ancient gold tablets unearthed in the 1820s in upper New York state by Joseph Smith, Jr. (1805–44). Told in the idiom of the King James Bible and through the genre of the Old Testament chronicle, this epic saga ranges over a millennium—from about 600 B.C.E. to 421 C.E. Lehi, a faithful Israelite, leaves Jerusalem six centuries before Jesus and sets sail for the Americas with his wife Sariah and six sons. Two of those sons, Nephi and Laman, give rise to warring factions: the good (and light-skinned) Nephites and the evil (and dark-skinned) Lamanites. During a final battle that takes place in 421 C.E., the Lamanites butcher the Nephites. One of the last men standing before his clan is extinguished is a righteous Nephite named Moroni. Anticipating *Moby Dick*'s Ishmael, another sole survivor, Moroni leaves behind a tale, written in this case by his father, Mormon. To ensure the survival of his story in what he sees as dark times coming, he etches his words into precious metal—the gold tablets unearthed over a millennium later by Joseph Smith.

While most of this American Bible is devoted to wars and rumors of wars, its enduring popularity lies in its testimony about Jesus, who is reincarnated here neither in Palestine nor in India but in the ancient Americas. Unlike Notovitch and Dowling, who filled in the missing years of Jesus' adolescence and early adulthood, the Book of Mormon homes in on the period immediately following his resurrection and ascension. It locates Jesus' extrabiblical adventures in the Americas rather than Asia—and inside Christianity rather than in Hinduism, Buddhism, or Theosophy. But the most intriguing claim of the book is that Jesus visited the Americas in the flesh, establishing his Church there more than a millennium before Columbus.

Often described as a Fifth Gospel, the Book of Mormon is more like a Second Book of Acts, inasmuch as it describes the post-resurrection appearances of Jesus and his founding of the early Church. According to 3 Nephi, Jesus appeared following his resurrection not only in Galilee but also in a New World land called Bountiful. There the people of Nephi "saw a Man descending out of heaven . . . clothed in a white robe." "Behold, I am Jesus Christ," he said, "whom the prophets testified shall come into the world." Jesus then invited the multitudes to "thrust your hands into my side" and "feel the prints of the nails in my hands and in my feet, that ye may know that I am the God of Israel, and the God of the whole earth, and have been slain for the sins of the world." Over the next three days, Jesus planted his true church in the Americas. He preached a gospel of repentance and salvation. He healed the sick. He taught his followers how to pray. He instituted baptism (by immersion) and what Mormons now call the sacrament of the bread and wine. He commissioned twelve American apostles to carry on his work. He also made it clear that the United States had a special role to play in restoring Christ's true church.

Many scholars have documented the tendency of Americans to make their nation sacred—to view its citizens as God's chosen people and their country, as the Book of Mormon puts it, as "a land which is choice above all other lands."[5] Yet Americans have typically sanctified their society through leaps of the typological imagination, by transforming Washington into an anti-type of Moses, or Lincoln into a modern-day Christ. Colonial place names—New Canaan, Goshen, Hebron—testify to the typological minds of Puritan divines, who transformed a howling wilderness into a new England, and colonial towns into biblical anti-types. Joseph Smith was also capable of typological thought. Yet he was a more concrete thinker than either Cotton Mather or Jonathan Edwards, Puritan divines for whom typological leaps were always at least in part poetic and metaphorical. Like Mather and Edwards, Smith believed that Adam and Eve had literally walked in the Garden of Eden. Unlike his Puritan predecessors, who understood the location of this primordial paradise to be locked away in the impenetrable mind of a sovereign God, Smith believed that Eden's location was eminently knowable. In fact, he traced it to present-day Independence, Missouri. When it came to the Second Coming, Smith was just as specific, pinpointing Jackson County, Missouri, as the "land of promise" where Christ would reign in his New Jerusalem.[6]

Mormonism came into being alongside the social convulsions of the Age of Jackson, the economic upheaval of the Industrial Revolution, and the religious ferment of the Second Great Awakening.[7] While old denominations split over the "new measures" of revivalism, new religious movements emerged in a burst of religious creativity that would not be matched until the 1960s and 1970s. In New England, Transcendentalism emerged out of Unitarianism, thanks to thinkers such as Ralph Waldo Emerson and Henry David Thoreau, who found spiritual inspiration in Hindu scriptures and bean rows. In the "Burned-Over District" of upper New York state, religious enthusiasm burned particularly hot as "Millerites" organized around William Miller's calculations concerning the imminent end of the world. Although this millennialist group dissipated following the "Great Disappointment" of October 22, 1844 (when the earth, by most accounts, kept on spinning), true believers reorganized around Ellen White, forming a new religious movement known today as the Seventh-day Adventists. As Miller and White were hitching their spiritual wagons to a millennial future, another class of innovators justified its inventions by invoking the past. Restorationists such as Barton Stone and Alexander Campbell sought to restore Christianity to the pristine purity (and unity) of the primitive church. Convinced that Christianity had lapsed into apostasy after the apostolic age, they urged modern-day Christians to reject all human creeds and unite instead under the banner of the Bible alone. Of course, this impulse only added to the "Great Diversification" of American religion when Stone and Campbell joined forces in 1832, forming what would come to be known as the Christian Church (Disciples of Christ), now one of American Protestantism's largest denominations.

As the Millerites looked to the future and the Disciples of Christ to the past, utopians of all sorts founded communitarian groups aimed at cultivating the individual soul and reforming society. "We are all a little wild here with numberless projects of social reform," Emerson wrote to a European friend in 1840. "Not a reading man but has a draft of a new community in his waistcoat pocket." He was exaggerating, of course, but many Americans did create spiritual communities in the decades leading up to the Civil War. In the process, groups such as the Oneida Community of John Humphrey Noyes and the Transcendentalists' own communitarian trinity (Fruitlands, Brook Farm, and Hopedale) joined an expanding list of exotic blooms in what Jon Butler has described as "America's spiritual hothouse."[8]

AN AMERICAN PROPHET

No wonder Joseph Smith was confused. Born in Sharon, Vermont, in 1805, Smith had moved at the age of ten with his family to New York's Burned-Over District, first to Palmyra and then Manchester. There he was exposed to a bewildering menu of religious options. Like so many Christians before and after him, Smith fervently desired to be delivered from sin to salvation. Yet he could not find the true path. "In the midst of this war of words and tumult of opinions," he later reported, "I often said to myself: What is to be done? Who of all these parties are right; or, are they all wrong together?"[9]

Had Smith been raised in colonial New England, where Calvinist theology reigned, predestination theology probably would have brought on his adolescent angst. "Am I one of the elect, or one of the damned?" he would have wondered, and then he would have gotten about the business of assuring himself of his own election. In upstate New York in the teens and twenties, however, Smith's anxiety took a different shape. It arose not from the rapidly fading theology of predestination but from the reality of religious diversity or, to be more precise, from a combination of religious diversity and Arminian theology. Religious options in the Burned-Over District were as wide as the frontier, and, according to Arminianism, salvation was a matter of individual choice, not divine fiat. But how to choose? Should you cast your lot with the Methodists? The Presbyterians? The Baptists? And if the Baptists, which ones? The Free Will Baptists, Regular Baptists, General Baptists, or Two-Seed-in-the-Spirit Baptists? Moreover, once you had made your choice, how might you be assured that you had chosen wisely? As sociologist Peter Berger has noted, religious diversity does not necessarily undermine religious belief, yet it undeniably changes its nature. Over the first American century, as religion ceased to be a matter of inheritance and became a matter of preference, the "taken-for-grantedness" of religion began to fall away, leaving individual religious choice as the central spiritual problem.[10]

In Smith's own corner of New York, free will and religious diversity also combined to create unsettled youth. Like the Burned-Over District itself, Palmyra was religiously diverse. Baptists, Methodists, Presbyterians, and Quakers all had churches in or near town. Manchester, where the family moved when Smith was a teenager, was also contested ground. Its environs experienced during Smith's youth "an unusual excitement on the subject of religion" in which "some were contending for the Methodist faith, some for the Presbyterian, and some for the Baptist."[11]

Smith's own household was religiously diverse too. His parents, Joseph Smith, Sr., and Lucy Mack Smith, were by all accounts devout yet unattached Christians. They prayed and read the Bible at home, but attended church sporadically. Joseph's mother went to Western Palmyra Presbyterian Church for a while, but her husband refused to join her. Baptized a Congregationalist, Joseph Smith, Sr., affiliated briefly with Universalism, which built on the foundation of the mercy of God a theology of universal salvation. He also practiced folk magic, heeding dreams and visions as personal revelations from God. Eventually he concluded that all denominations were as hypocritical as they were corrupt, and vowed to make common cause with none of them. The Smith family patriarch was no secularist, however. Though unchurched, he was a committed Christian. In fact, it was the depth of his Christian commitment that compelled him not to attend Sunday services.

All this is to say that Joseph Smith, Jr., came about his status as a seeker honestly. While his parents instilled in him both faith in Jesus and an interest in the Bible, they bequeathed to him more questions than answers. Moreover, in keeping with the shibboleth of free will, they insisted that their son's spiritual choices were his alone to make. Given parents ill-disposed to provide him with the religious answers he was seeking, Smith felt the full weight of the responsibility of religious liberty. Initially he was simply overwhelmed. Then he turned to the Bible.

One of the great hopes of the Protestant Reformation had been that biblical authority and widespread literacy would produce Christian unity. If only the Bible could be snatched from the clutches of the papists and read by ordinary folk, a peaceable (and unified) Christian kingdom would result. Or so went the naive hope of the Protestants. Thomas Jefferson had also hoped that the Bible might produce Christian unity. "If all the Christian sects would rally to the Sermon in the mount," he wrote in an 1824 letter, its moral teachings could become "the central point of Union in religion." Of course, nothing of the sort came to pass. In the absence of a spiritual Supreme Court (or a papacy) to adjudicate competing scriptural interpretations, all believers were free to interpret the Bible for themselves. This new Christian liberty resulted—as Catholics predicted it would—not in unity but in near-anarchy, an endless splintering of Protestantism into a Babel of competing beliefs and practices. It should not be surprising, therefore, that a thorough examination of scripture failed to provide Smith with the answers he was seeking. "The teachers of religion of the different sects understood the same passages of scripture so differently," Smith later observed, "as to destroy all confidence in settling the question by an appeal to the Bible."[12]

At some point during his teenage years, Joseph Smith came to believe that true Christianity could not rest on the authority of the Bible alone. *Sola scriptura* might have worked for Martin Luther in sixteenth century Germany, but it would not work for him. So Smith decided to put his questions straight to God. In some accounts of his youth, Smith's inquiries are cast philosophically or, to be more precise, epistemologically: "Who of all these parties are right? . . . and how shall I know it?"[13] Yet Smith's disquiet was personal as well as philosophical, existential as well as epistemic. He wanted to know which denomination was right, but he wanted to know it because he yearned to be assured that he was headed to heaven rather than hell.

One day while still a teenager, Smith found himself in the woods alone, desperately praying for divine intervention. Just as darkness, despair, and the demonic were about to overwhelm him, he was rewarded with what Mormons describe (and capitalize) as the First Vision. Accounts of the event have changed over time. A canonical version, written in 1838, goes like this:

I saw a pillar of light exactly over my head, above the brightness of the sun, which descended gradually until it fell upon me. It no sooner appeared than I found myself delivered from the enemy which held me bound. When the light rested upon me I saw two Personages, whose brightness and glory defy all description, standing above me in the air. One of them spake unto me, calling me by name and said, pointing to the other—"This is My Beloved Son. Hear Him!" My object in going to inquire of the Lord was to know which of all the sects was right, that I might know which to join. No sooner, therefore, did I get possession of myself, so as to be able to speak, than I asked the Personages who stood above me in the light, which of all the sects was right (for at this time it had never entered into my heart that all were wrong)—and which I should join. I was answered that I must join none of them, for they were all wrong; and the Personage who addressed me said that all their creeds were an abomination in his sight; that those professors were all corrupt; that: "they draw near to me with their lips, but their hearts are far from me, they teach for doctrines the commandments of men, having a form of godliness, but they deny the power thereof." He again forbade me to join with any of them; and many other things did he say unto me, which I cannot write at this time. When I came to myself again, I found myself lying on my back, looking up into heaven.[14]

Critics of Mormonism have delighted in the discrepancies between this canonical account and earlier renditions, especially one written in Smith's own hand in 1832. For example, in the 1832 version, Jesus appears to Smith alone, and does all the talking himself. Such complaints, however, are much ado about relatively nothing. Any good lawyer (or historian) would expect to find contradictions in competing narratives written down years apart and decades after the event. And despite the contradictions, key elements abide. In each case, Jesus appears to Smith in a vision. In each case, Smith is blessed with a revelation. In each case, God tells him to remain aloof from all Christian denominations, as something better is in store.

A few years after this First Vision, when he was only eighteen, Smith reportedly had another theophany. It too began with a near-blinding light. This time, a single figure appeared, dressed in an "exceedingly white and brilliant" robe. He called Smith by name, and gave his own name as Moroni. He then told the future Mormon prophet one of the most astounding tales in American letters: "He said there was a book deposited, written upon gold plates, giving an account of the former inhabitants of this continent, and the source from whence they sprang. He also said that the fulness of the everlasting Gospel was contained in it, as delivered by the Savior to the ancient inhabitants." Buried with the golden book was a breastplate with two seer stones, which would enable the translation (from "reformed Egyptian") of the gold plates. Moroni then quoted extensively from the Bible, though his renditions varied a bit from the King James. Next the angel ascended on a shaft of light, only to return again to Smith's bedside and repeat himself. After ascending again, he returned again, repeating his message once more before disappearing for good. When this visitation was complete, a cock crowed, and Smith's career as an American prophet was under way.

Mormons today typically see in these two visions the origins of their efforts to restore the primitive church, which had lapsed into a "Great Apostasy" at the end of the apostolic age. Yet both visions point beyond themselves to the Book of Mormon. The story they tell is a story about books—an old book that cannot answer the most vexing religious question of the day, and a new one that can: a new New Testament. The crowing cock that punctuates the standard account of the Moroni vision announces the dawn of the Mormon movement even as it positions Smith as the rock upon which God will build His new church. Yet Smith seems fated to play the role of Moses as well as Peter. True, he builds a new church. But that church is as Hebraic as it is Christian, and it is built on a book that Smith brings down from a mountain.

JESUS CELEBRATED: TEXTUAL MORMONISM

At the time the Book of Mormon first appeared, Americans were a "people of the book." "Awash in a sea of faith," as Jon Butler has noted, the American people were also awash in a sea of scripture. References to Bible heroes were as ubiquitous and understandable in popular culture then as references to the sex lives of movie stars are today. The biblical books of choice, however, typically came from the Old Testament. When George Washington died in 1799, ministers compared their fallen hero not to Jesus or Peter but, as Mark Noll has noted, to "Abel, Jacob, Moses, Joshua, Othniel, Samuel, Abner, Elijah, David, Josiah, Jehoiada, Mordecai, Cyrus, and Daniel." And during the early republic the book most frequently cited by American politicians was the Book of Deuteronomy. According to Noll, "Well into the national period, the public Bible of the United States was for all intents the Old Testament."[15]

By 1830, the tide was turning. Some religious upstarts continued to see the Old Testament as the coin of the spiritual realm; a sect called the "Kingdom of Matthias" began when Robert Matthews, a contemporary of Joseph Smith, realized he was a Hebrew rather than a Christian, and set out to build his own Zion in upstate New York. Nonetheless, the scriptural center of gravity in the country was shifting from the Old Testament to the New, and Jesus was emerging from the shadow of Moses and Mordecai, David and Daniel.

Joseph Smith was a product of this biblical nation and its aborning Jesus. Like the Protestants who surrounded him, he read widely in the King James Bible. He distinguished himself from his peers, however, by supplementing that book with new revelations and a new scripture. Drenched in biblical rhetoric and the thee's and thou's of the King James, the Book of Mormon reflected neither America's Old Testament past nor its New Testament future, but the transitional moment of its own time.

Although Mormons now trace their tradition back to 1820 and Joseph Smith's initial vision, Mormonism first came into being in the late 1820s, when some of Smith's acquaintances embraced the Book of Mormon as holy writ. The Mormon movement spread when the Book of Mormon was first published in March of 1830. One month later, "Mormonites" (as Mormons were initially labeled), gathered in Fayette, New York, to form what was then known as the Church of Christ. Most of the early adherents were members of Smith's extended family, and many were attracted to his undeniable charisma, including his ability to communicate with God in dreams and visions. Yet the real drawing card was the Book of Mormon. Given the importance of that new scripture to Smith's new religious movement, it makes sense to refer to early Mormonism as textual Mormonism. Like other Americans, early Mormons were a "people of the book." What made them stand out was their conviction that God continues to speak through prophets.

In order to understand the Jesus of the early Mormon movement, it is necessary to forget much of what you think you know about Mormonism. Today the tradition is linked in the popular imagination with Utah and polygamy, and in the minds of evangelical critics with heterodoxies such as the plurality of gods. Yet in 1830 there wasn't a single Mormon in the Utah Territory, and no Mormon thinker had yet preached a word in favor of either polytheism or polygamy. To be sure, acceptance of the Book of Mormon set Mormons apart from Methodists, Baptists, and Disciples of Christ. Their American testament was something new. Yet the scandal was more its existence than its content.

Hardly any of the doctrines for which Mormonism would become notorious can be found in the Book of Mormon. It does not teach the corporeality or plurality of gods. It does not describe God the Father and God the Son as separate divinities. It does not institute baptism for the dead or marriage for eternity, and it seems to reject polygamy. Following the Christian creeds, the Book of Mormon teaches the Trinity. Like the sermons of Charles Finney, it teaches sin and grace, confession and conversion, salvation and sanctification. In keeping with the democratic spirit of the Age of Jackson, it ridicules Calvinist doctrines such as predestination, limited atonement, and unconditional election. In other words, the Book of Mormon was upon its publication far less radical than it seems today. Thoroughly Arminian in its theology, it insists on the liberty of each individual to choose or reject Jesus. "The Father commandeth all men, everywhere, to repent and believe in me," Jesus says in 3 Nephi 11:32–33. "And whoso believeth in me, and is baptized, the same shall be saved."

Like his new Bible, Smith's new denomination served up fairly traditional Christian fare. Critics chided Smith for dressing up his book in the linguistic finery of the King James, including archaic phrases such as "And it came to pass." Yet those echoes only underscore early Mormonism's ties to Christianity. While Christians appended the New Testament to the Old, Mormons appended the Book of Mormon to the Bible. But the result of that new combination was not nearly as innovative as the Christians' supersession of Judaism. As both its original name, the Church of Christ, and its current name, the Church of Jesus Christ of Latter-day Saints (adopted in 1838) suggest, the organization began as a new genus in the Christian family rather than an entirely new religious species. To be sure, Smith was more enamored of the Hebrew Bible than most of his Protestant contemporaries, and before the Book of Mormon was ever published he received a revelation restoring the Levitical priesthood of Aaron. But his interest in the Hebrew patriarchs did not immediately take him far afield.

(One of the main purposes of the restored priesthood was to legitimize baptism.)

During the first meeting of the Church of Christ, held on April 6, 1830, Smith read to his followers a series of "Articles and Covenants of the Church of Christ." That document, now found in a modified form in the Mormon scripture *Doctrine and Covenants*, functioned as a blueprint of sorts for the denomination. It spoke of grace and faith, sin and repentance, justification and sanctification. It created church offices for "elders, priests, teachers, deacons." It prescribed baptism "in the name of the Father, and of the Son, and of the Holy Ghost" and included a prayer for the sacrament of bread and wine (which it defined as a "remembrance"). It affirmed one God who is infinite and eternal and unchangeable, a Trinity in "which Father, Son, and Holy Ghost are one God, infinite and eternal," and (in language reminiscent of the creeds early Mormons rejected) a Christ who "was crucified, died, and rose again the third day" and then "ascended into heaven, to sit down at the right hand of the Father."[16]

As missionaries fanned out across the country with their new scripture in hand, they too set their sights on Jesus rather than Joseph Smith, preaching far more from the New Testament than from the Book of Mormon. The journals of William E. McLellin, written between 1831 and 1836, provide an extraordinary snapshot of the aborning Mormon movement. There McLellin, who converted to Mormonism in 1831, recorded the topics of hundreds of different talks he and other Mormon missionaries delivered while on the road. Only about a quarter of those subjects were distinctively Mormon. More than half were on Christian beliefs, practices, or texts, or on more generic religious topics such as charity and prayer. Moreover, while McLellin recorded dozens of talks on certain books of the Bible and even particular verses, he recorded only three cases where Book of Mormon texts provided the foundation for a sermon. At least for McLellin, the purpose of the Book of Mormon was not to displace the Bible but to prove its veracity, and its urgency. McLellin's core message was "to come to Christ" and his core text was the Bible.[17]

The Christianness of early Mormonism is also evident in early Mormon hymns, which like McLellin's journals took their refuge in

Jesus. At one of the first Mormon conferences (themselves modeled
on New Testament precedents), believers sang this Jesus-centered
hymn:

> Go on, ye pilgrims, while below,
> In the sure paths of peace,
> Determined nothing else to know,
> But Jesus and his grace.

The first Mormon hymnal, compiled in 1835 by Emma Hale Smith,
Joseph Smith's wife, was filled with hymns extolling Jesus as "the only
name, / In which the saints can trust":

> The wonderful name
> Of our Jesus we'll sing,
> And publish the fame
> Of our Captain and King;
> With sweet exultation
> His goodness we prove
> His name is Salvation
> His nature is love.

In addition to "Captain and King," these hymns described Jesus as
Bridegroom, Shepherd, and "coming Redeemer and friend." They understood the atonement as a vicarious sacrifice, and insisted that the
faithful were saved by the merit of "Christ alone."[18]

Like the Restorationists, early Mormons were Christian millennialists who saw themselves as restorers of what Smith called "the fulness
of the gospel of Jesus Christ."[19] While Stone and Campbell worked to
restore the primitive church of Palestine, however, Smith and his followers aimed to restore the church of the first-century Americas.
They also distinguished themselves from the Restorationists by affirming ongoing revelation and a renewed priesthood. Nonetheless,
the Jesus of this first Mormon era was for the most part the atoning
Redeemer of Second Great Awakening evangelicalism. Yes, Mormons
supplemented Matthew, Mark, Luke, and John with a Fifth Gospel of
Jesus' sojourn in the Americas. But unlike Notovitch and Dowling,

who transported Jesus to Asia in order to transform him into something else (an esoteric and more-than-vaguely Buddhist hero), the Mormons brought him to the New World simply to extend his Old World mission. In the Book of Mormon, Jesus acts and speaks like his New Testament counterpart. He delivers a homily similar to the Sermon on the Mount, and teaches a prayer similar to the Lord's Prayer.

What distinguished the Jesus of textual Mormonism from the Jesus of 1830s evangelicalism was his familiarity with the Jewish tradition. Like the Puritans, the Mormons were fluent in the Old Testament. More than the Puritans, they supplemented Hebraic themes such as priest and temple, covenant and chosen people, and Zion and Israel with Christian themes such as faith and grace, sin and salvation. Yet Mormons did not follow evangelicals over into New Testament territory. They lingered instead in a border zone between the two texts. While their contemporaries were learning to read their Bibles from back to front, early Mormons continued to read New Testament texts through Old Testament types, taking their marching orders not just from Jesus but also from Jehovah (and sometimes conflating the two). All this is to say that Smith and his early followers understood their restoration project in Abrahamic as well as Apostolic terms. In his first sermon in Bountiful, the Book of Mormon Jesus proclaims, "And behold, I am the light and the life of the world." A few chapters later he mixes Old Testament and New Testament metaphors: "Behold, I am the law, and the light." Then, just before ascending to heaven, he promises to his "house of Israel" a "New Jerusalem" in the New World.[20]

Following the example of Protestant preachers who had eulogized George Washington by comparing him favorably to Hebrew patriarchs, early Mormons lauded Jesus by likening him to Jacob and Joshua. The Book of Mormon in no way ignored Jesus as had the Puritan divines. As contemporary Mormons have noted, Jesus' sojourn in America was "the very centerpiece" of the Book of Mormon, which was set down (as its title page indicates) "to the convincing of the Jew and Gentile that Jesus is the Christ." But early Mormons typically kept Jesus at arm's length. Their relationships with him were marked more by reverence and respect than love and intimacy. They offered their Savior their worship rather than their friendship. In fact, while

Calvinists in the colonies had abided a hint of the companion in their Christ, Mormons would have little to do with a sweet and sentimental Savior. William Wines Phelps, who adapted many popular hymns for Mormon use, refused to invoke in his lyrics the feminized Jesus beginning to win the hearts of American evangelicals. His Jesus was unabashedly masculine and unapologetically majestic. In his adaption of "He dies, the friend of sinners dies" by the Calvinist hymnist Isaac Watts, Phelps referred to Jesus as a "great Redeemer" instead of the sinner's friend.[21]

JESUS LOST: TEMPLE MORMONISM

While Mormonism began as a religion of words, it gradually developed into a religion of rites. In the beginning the Mormons saw themselves as a New Israel building a New Jerusalem in the New World. The Book of Mormon provocatively blurred Christian and Hebraic themes in what the historian of Mormonism Jan Shipps has described as a "contrapunctal pattern." Yet the project of renewing ancient Israel had taken a back seat to the project of renewing the church. That changed when the Mormons started practicing temple rites.[22]

The destruction of the second Jerusalem Temple was a crucial event in the development of Judaism. Following the cataclysmic events of 70 C.E., a religious tradition once centered on priests performing temple rites rapidly recast itself as a tradition centered on rabbis interpreting texts—a tradition tailor-made for a diaspora people. Early Mormons reinvented themselves in equally spectacular fashion, but their transformation pivoted around temple construction rather than destruction. Thanks to temples built in Kirtland, Ohio; Nauvoo, Illinois; and, later, Salt Lake City, Mormonism became a religious tradition resting on rites more than words, temples more than texts, gathering more than diaspora.

The notion of gathering God's chosen people out of a corrupt world appears repeatedly in the Book of Mormon, and as early as 1830 Joseph Smith was molding his "peculiar people" around it. In 1831, the year he and his family left New York, Smith called upon all Mormons to gather in "a land flowing with milk and honey" in Kirtland, Ohio. There he began building a Puritan-style kingdom that, in a bold affront to church-state separation, obliterated the boundaries between civil and sacred society. He also received a series of startling revelations, now collected in *Doctrine and Covenants*, including one instructing him to construct a "house of God."[23]

It is tempting to date the origins of temple Mormonism to the dedication of the first Mormon temple, in Kirtland, Ohio. On March 27, 1836, during his dedication prayer, Smith sounded many of the notes that would characterize this more Hebraic form of Mormonism. He invoked the "God of Israel" and referred to fellow Mormons as "children of Jacob" and "children of Judah." His followers sang *The Spirit of God Like a Fire Is Burning*, now a Mormon classic, which cast them as God's New Israel.[24]

The temptation to trace temple Mormonism to Kirtland and the spring of 1836 is especially strong given a vision Smith and his friend Oliver Cowdery reportedly received in the temple one week after the dedication. It began with a visitation of Jesus, whose hair "was white like the pure snow," and whose voice "was as the sound of the rushing of great waters, even the voice of Jehovah." After Jesus looked at the temple and called it good, two Old Testament figures appeared. As Smith later reported, first Moses "committed unto us the keys of the gathering of Israel from the four parts of the earth." Then Elias committed to them "the dispensation of the gospel of Abraham."[25]

Jan Shipps has pointed to this revelation (and what she sees as its displacement of Jesus by Hebrew Bible patriarchs) as a key moment in the transition from "Apostolic" to "Abrahamic" Mormonism. It must be noted, however, that Jesus is the real hero in this story. Of the sixteen verses that describe the vision in *Doctrine and Covenants*, ten are devoted to him and only six to the Old Testament figures. The appearance of Jesus alongside Hebrew patriarchs was perfectly consistent with the "contrapunctal" tendency of textual Mormonism (and, for that matter, Puritanism and African-American Protestantism) to mix Old and New Testament themes. Smith's dedication prayer described the new building as "a house of prayer, a house of fasting, a house of faith, a house of learning, a house of glory, a house of order, a house of God." Significantly, Smith did not describe the temple as a house of ordinances because for years after this "Mormon Pentecost," Smith did not know what to do with his priests or his temple. A temple in name only, the Kirtland building was far more Christian than Jewish. Priests did not perform sacrifices there. In fact, Mormons did little more in it than pray, listen to sermons, sing hymns, and read scripture. The new ordinances introduced there, which included foot washing and the laying on of hands, took their clues more from the New Testament than from the Old. In short, the Kirtland structure was a church, not a temple.[26]

One reason Smith did not craft new rites for his new structure was that Mormons were for most of the 1830s preoccupied with more basic matters, such as survival. Anti-Mormonism was nearly as old as Mormonism itself, and at least as heartfelt. Smith was tarred and feathered by a mob in 1832, and other provocations against Mormon persons and property kept the Mormons perpetually on the run. In Far West, Missouri, Smith laid a cornerstone for a temple on the Fourth of July in 1838. Before construction could begin, an order from Missouri Governor Lilburn Boggs stating that "the Mormons must be treated as enemies and must be exterminated or driven from the state if necessary for the public peace" chased them further, to Nauvoo, Illinois.[27] There a live-and-let-live attitude by Illinois authorities enabled Mormons to build their new gathering place into one of the state's largest cities, with Smith as its mayor and ruling patriarch. It also freed Smith up to reshape Mormonism into a temple-based religion.

In Nauvoo, as in Kirtland, the Mormons built a temple. This time, however, they also developed new rites and new beliefs suited to it. In January 1841, a revelation announced a new temple ordinance called baptism for the dead. In May 1842, less than two months after he was initiated into the rite-rich tradition of Masonry, Smith introduced a lavish ritual called the "endowment," which included washing and anointing, initiation into esoteric mysteries, vows of secrecy, the conferring of special garments, and a dramatic retelling of sacred history—from Adam and Eve to the restoration of Israel and the gospel.[28] One year later he announced to his closest followers the revival of the Old Testament practice of polygamy, which Mormons referred to as plural marriage. He also devised a new rite of "celestial marriage for time and eternity."

Over the next few years, new beliefs came fast and furious. In-

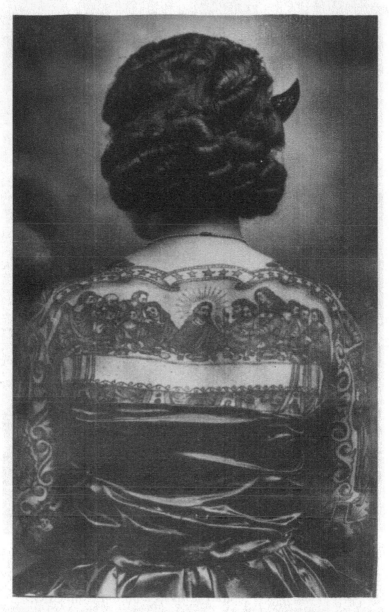

This anonymous photo postcard of a woman with a Last Supper tattoo, likely from the early twentieth century, demonstrates how far some will go to embody their devotion to Jesus.

Clifford Davis's witty painting *The Conformist* recalls both
Warner Sallman's iconic *Head of Christ* and efforts by Bruce
Barton and others to draft Jesus as a buttoned-up CEO.

The accent is on Jesus' femininity in this nineteenth-century
Currier & Ives print, *El Señor, Andando Sobre el Mar*
(Christ Walking on the Sea).

Stephen S. Sawyer's *Undefeated* is one of many efforts to make
Jesus more masculine and Christianity more muscular.

JESUS CHRIST

ALIAS: THE MESSIAH, SON OF GOD, KING OF KINGS, LORD OF LORDS, PRINCE OF PEACE, ETC.

Produced during the heyday of the counterculture of the 1960s and 1970s, this "WANTED: JESUS CHRIST" poster casts the Prince of Peace as an outlaw.

(COURTESY FATHER JACK N. SPARKS AND *RIGHT ON* MAGAZINE)

A popular image among members of the Church of Jesus Christ of Latter-day Saints, John Scott's *Jesus Christ Visits the Americas* depicts a key scene from the Book of Mormon: the shocking appearance of Jesus in the New World.

(OIL ON CANVAS, 1969, COPYRIGHT © INTELLECTUAL RESERVE, INC.)

Janet McKenzie used an African-American woman as the model for *Jesus of the People*, which won the "Jesus 2000" art contest sponsored by the *National Catholic Reporter*.

This untitled woodcut from James Reid's *The Life of Christ in Woodcuts* (1930) depicts an angular Jesus lashing out at money changers in the Jerusalem Temple.

Christ the Yogi, commissioned by the San Francisco Vedanta Society and executed by the Catholic layperson Eugene Theodosia Oliver in the 1920s, portrays Jesus as a peaceable Hindu avatar.

(COURTESY VEDANTA PRESS)

Ralph Kozak's *Jesus Laughing* stands in stark opposition to the medieval "Man of Sorrows" tradition.

(COPYRIGHT © 1977 BY PRAISE SCREEN PRINTS, WWW.JESUSLAUGHING.COM)

spired by a series of rapid-fire revelations, Smith announced the materiality of spirit and the corporeality of the divine. He taught the existence of spirits before birth, dividing human life into premortal, mortal, and postmortal phases. He replaced the bifurcated heaven-hell cosmology of other Christians with a three-story heaven (and a thinly populated hell). He announced a theocratic ideal in which society would be governed by divine rather than human law. He affirmed his church's belief "in the literal gathering of Israel and in the restoration of the Ten Tribes."[29] Most provocatively, he proclaimed a new "Plan of Salvation" that enabled individuals to ascend to exaltation and even godhood through a combination of good works and secret temple rites.

In his famous "King Follett Discourse" (delivered in 1844 at the funeral of a Mormon man named King Follett), Smith boldly distanced his new religious tradition from historical Christianity, and from early Mormonism itself, leading one writer to ask, "Was the Book of Mormon Buried with King Follett?" In a radical reinterpretation of both divinity and humanity, Smith argued that humans have the capacity to progress "from grace to grace, from exaltation to exaltation," even to become gods themselves. In fact, he argued, this was the road once taken by Jesus himself. More than any other great American thinker, with the possible exception of Emerson, Smith blurred the distinction between divinity and humanity. "As God once was, man is," Mormonism now affirmed. "As God is, man may become."[30]

Together these innovations transformed Mormons into true religious outsiders. Rather than aiming at individual salvation, as William McLellin and other early Mormons had done, Mormons now worked for the "exaltation" and "celestial glory" of their families. The means to that goal were temple rites, which enabled married couples and their children "to walk in the presence of the Father." Rather than yoking themselves to Jesus, Latter-day Saints yoked themselves to their families and, through them, to the Mormon tribe. Their veins pulsed with the "believing blood" of Israel. In this way, Mormonism became a religion focused on families rather than individuals, and not simply on the restoration of Israel or the Church but on the "restoration of all things."[31]

As word of Smith's new beliefs and secret rites spread and Mormonism expanded, opposition intensified. Earlier critics had for the most part been content to attack the Mormons as "godless vermin" and the Book of Mormon (in Mark Twain's words) as "chloroform in print." But some Mormons were martyred at the hands of their critics, and now that deadly force turned on Smith himself. In June 1844, just months after he proclaimed his candidacy for President of the United States and days after he ordered the destruction of an anti-Mormon printing press, Mormonism's founder was arrested and taken into custody. On June 27 of that year, a mob broke into the jail in Carthage, Illinois, where he was being held with his brother, Hyrum Smith, shooting and killing both men.[32]

A struggle for succession ensued, splitting the movement into two main groups. One party went with Joseph Smith, his wife Emma, and their son, Joseph Smith III, into what would become the Reorganized Church of Jesus Christ of Latter-day Saints (RLDS). Renamed the Community of Christ in 2001, this group opted for textual Mormonism over temple Mormonism, rejecting most of the doctrinal and ritualistic innovations of Nauvoo, including polygamy and celestial marriage. Members did not aim at eternal progression toward godhood through temple rites. They aimed instead at salvation through the Book of Mormon Christ. Most Mormons, however, rallied around Brigham Young (1801–77), who enthusiastically embraced Smith's Nauvoo innovations, popularizing one new scripture (*Doctrine and Covenants*) and canonizing another (*Pearl of Great Price*).

These Mormon pioneers followed the Puritans in refracting their experiences through the prism of the Exodus story. This time, however, Illinois was Egypt, Utah the Promised Land, and Young the new Moses. During a thousand-plus-mile pilgrimage, undertaken by many on foot with handcarts, Young's Mormons relived both the miracles and the plagues of the biblical Exodus. They rejoiced as they crossed a frozen Mississippi like the Israelites at the Red Sea, wept as a plague of crop-eating crickets attacked their fields around the Great Salt Lake, and rejoiced as hordes of hungry seagulls miraculously descended to consume the crickets and save the faithful from starvation. Together these wonders confirmed the Mormons' identity as a New Israel chosen by their Heavenly Father and gathered out of the world to live under a special covenant with Him.

Only days after Young entered the Salt Lake Valley in 1847, he pinpointed the site for a new temple. In 1852, he proudly proclaimed to the world the Mormon doctrine of plural marriage, an announcement the literary critic Harold Bloom has described as "the most courageous act of spiritual defiance in all of American history." Three years later he oversaw the building of Endowment House, a temporary structure in Salt Lake City's Temple Square dedicated solely to performing Mormon rites (while a permanent temple was being built). Over the next three decades, Mormons would administer 54,170 endowments there. Before his death in 1877, Young would break ground for four temples in Utah, including the signature temple in Salt Lake City that figured so prominently in television coverage of the 2002 Winter Olympics. At those temples, Mormons would perform 38,317 endowments for the living and 486,198 for the dead before the end of the twentieth century.[33]

The gradual transformation of Mormonism from a religion of words into a religion of rites distanced the Latter-day Saints considerably from historical Christianity, and left little room in the religion for Jesus. Although Jesus was by no means repudiated by Mormons in either Nauvoo or Salt Lake City, he was overshadowed. Early Mormonism had been an effort to restore "the fulness of the gospel of Jesus Christ."[34] Mormons had harkened to his words in the Bible and the Book of Mormon, heeded his instructions to repent and be baptized, and trusted that his atoning death on the cross would bring salvation. With the advent of temple Mormonism, all that changed dramatically. In Nauvoo and Salt Lake City, a new Plan of Salvation emerged and solidified, centered on the rites of the Church rather than the words of Jesus. Through practices such as temple endowments, Mormon couples were able to progress eternally from humanity to divinity. Thanks to ordinances such as celestial marriage and baptism for the dead, they were able to take their children with them.

All that spiritual work took place under the watchful eye of a hierarchical church, which in practical terms edged out Jesus as the mediator between God and humanity. Harold Bloom has argued that in contemporary Mormonism "the mediation of the corporately structured LDS church" is "so extraordinarily intense . . . that Jesus becomes pragmatically unnecessary in the work of salvation."[35] As we shall see, that is not the case for Mormons today, but it is a fairly accurate description of temple Mormonism. For Mormons between the 1840s and the 1890s, Jesus had a role to play in salvation, but salvation was no longer the goal of the religious life. Instead, salvation was a step (and a relatively minor one) along the road to exaltation to godhood. In that pilgrimage, rites were more important than words, works more important than faith, and (for all practical purposes) the church more important than Jesus.

For temple Mormons, Jesus was divine. In keeping with the new doctrine of the corporeality of god, he was a fully embodied, flesh-and-blood divinity. However, in keeping with the new belief in the plurality of divinity, he was one god among many—a person entirely distinct from his Father. In a hierarchical organization such as Brigham Young's Church, the separation of God the Father from God the Son naturally prompted questions about the relative importance of each. The Christian creeds had attempted to apportion power equally across the Trinity, but Brigham Young would have none of that. In the new Mormon drama of progression to godhood, God the Father was the leading man and Jesus played only a supporting role—as dutiful Son and Elder Brother. When Young wrote in 1865, "God is our Father, Jesus is our Elder Brother, and we are all brethren, and of one family," he was subordinating Jesus to God the Father in what one critic has called a "chain of command" theory of the Trinity.[36]

Back in 1841, in his notorious sermon on "The Transient and Permanent in Christianity," the Transcendentalist Theodore Parker had, in the eyes of many, damned Jesus with faint praise by referring to him as a brother. "Measure him by the world's greatest sons;—how poor they are! Try him by the best of men,—how little and low they appear! Exalt him as much as we may, we shall yet, perhaps, come short of the mark," Parker had said. "But still was he not our brother; the son of man, as we are; the Son of God, like ourselves?" The "perhaps" here is worth lingering over, since it underscores Parker's hope that other human beings could become Christs—that Jesus was one example of realized humanity rather than a unique God-man. Brigham Young was no Transcendentalist, of course. But like Parker—and Emerson for that matter—he believed that humans could become divine. So with his Transcendentalist predecessors he downplayed Jesus' distinctiveness. During the era of textual Mormonism, Mormons had been determined to know (as the old Mormon hymn put it) "nothing else . . . but Jesus and his grace." Under the leadership of Brigham Young, that Jesus-centrism became a thing of the past.[37]

Now everything in the Mormon tradition revolved around the overriding reality of the patriarchal family. Individuals were not individuals first but sons and daughters, wives and husbands. Divinity too was subject to this master metaphor. So God the Father ruled, and God the Son obeyed. Jesus did not disappear entirely, of course. In 1853, the LDS apostle Orson Pratt invoked him to justify polygamy, arguing on the basis of an esoteric reading of Psalm 45 and the Parable of the Ten Virgins, that "the GREAT MESSIAH who was the founder of the Christian religion, WAS A POLYGAMIST."[38] But even as a polygamist, Jesus was no longer the Mormons' main channel of grace. His atonement was now understood as one scene in the broader drama of the Plan of Salvation. In that drama, Mormons progressed toward divinity not only through faith but more importantly through temple work. Jesus' key function was not to die on the cross but to serve as an example of obedience to God—a job he dutifully fulfilled in the Garden of Gethsemane. By submitting to his superior, even unto death, Jesus demonstrated the obedience that was expected of all Mormons—obedience to God, church leaders, and their own family's patriarch. Those who followed his example became his kin.

While textual Mormonism lasted only about a decade, temple Mormonism had a longer life, dominating the movement for half a century, from roughly 1840 until 1890. The catalyst for Mormonism's first great transformation had been a series of revelations from God to Joseph Smith. Now the catalyst came from the U.S. government, which for the first time made it federal policy to demolish a religion. Beginning in 1862, the U.S. Congress passed a series of anti-polygamy laws, and gave those laws teeth in 1887 when it disincorporated the LDS church and confiscated its real estate. When the U.S. Supreme Court upheld anti-polygamy legislation in 1890, LDS president Wilford Woodruff had a few choices. He could lead his community out of the country in another exodus. He could stay and resist. Or he could accommodate. Woodruff (guided, Mormons believe, by revelation) opted for accommodation. On September 24, 1890, he issued a manifesto advising LDS members not to enter into "any marriage forbidden by the law of the land."³⁹ He also began to dismantle Mormonism's quasi-theocratic kingdom. These two actions opened the door to Utah statehood in 1896. They also ushered in a third period of Mormon history, which once again put Jesus front and center.

JESUS FOUND: TWENTIETH-CENTURY MORMONISM

In the 1890s, Mormons began to reinvent themselves as a model minority. While textual Mormonism had been Apostolic and temple Mormonism Abrahamic, twentieth-century Mormonism was assimilationist. This assimilation proceeded along two tracks. In the past Mormons had thumbed their noses at both the United States and the Protestant denominations. Now they Americanized and Protestantized their tradition.⁴⁰

Certain distinctive practices and propositions were not negotiable. Mormons continued to accept the Bible as God's word only "as far as it is translated correctly." They affirmed ongoing revelation. They insisted that both Jesus and God the Father have bodies made of flesh and blood. They described Jesus as the literal offspring of Mary and God the Father. They affirmed that salvation comes not by faith alone but via faith and "obedience to the laws and ordinances of the Gospel." They asserted that by participating in temple rites individuals "may obtain exaltation and even reach the status of godhood." Finally, Mormons held on to their self-conception as a "peculiar people," though the markers of their outsiderhood noticeably changed. Instead of defining their distinctiveness in terms of community practices such as polygamy and theocracy, they turned inward, adopting strict rules for individual behavior. The "Word of Wisdom," a code of conduct prohibiting the use of tobacco, alcohol, and hot tea and coffee, was ignored for decades after Brigham Young made it a commandment in 1851. During the early twentieth century, it became a key marker of Mormon identity—and as of 1921 observance of it became a prerequisite for admission to the temple. Later in the century, Mormons returned to the Book of Mormon as a marker of difference, inserting study of that text into their Sunday school curriculum in 1972 and transforming it into "the keystone of our religion" in the 1980s and 1990s. But this new emphasis in no way undercut the Mormons' commitment to Jesus. On the contrary, as they dug into their New World scripture they rediscovered, as Susan Easton Black wrote in *Finding Christ Through the Book of Mormon* (1987), that Jesus was "the central focus" of the book.[41]

Still, accommodation was the rule for twentieth-century Mormons. Just as other Americans were transforming Jesus into a national celebrity, the Mormons rediscovered Jesus. In an effort to create a subculture comfortably aside the cultural and religious mainstream, they once again described their restoration project more in Christian than in Hebraic terms. According to Gordon and Gary Shepherd's careful study of sermons delivered at important Mormon meetings called general conferences, distinctive Mormon themes such as the "Great Apostasy" of Christendom declined sharply after 1890. The all-important endowment ceremony was streamlined, and LDS leaders toned down or eliminated controversial elements, including an "oath of vengeance" against enemies of the faith and depictions of Christian ministers as tools of Satan. Mormon hymn books increasingly printed Protestant standards, while Protestantizing the lyrics of popular Mormon hymns. A Hebraicized verse from the Mormon classic *The Spirit of God Like a Fire Is Burning*, which referred to Israel, Moses, Aaron, and Joshua when it was first sung at the dedication of the Kirtland Temple in 1836, was excised from official hymn books, and from versions sung by the Mormon Tabernacle Choir.[42]

In many respects the story of Mormonism's march to respectability is unremarkable. Scholars of religion have for some time observed the tendency of members of new religious movements to cultivate outsiderhood during a period of early growth and then to transform themselves into insiders as their social standing rises. But no other new religious movement in the United States has navigated so adeptly both the rapids of sectarian growth and the still waters of mainstream respectability. Once almost universally hated, Mormons are now lionized as quintessentially American: "thrifty, wholesome, cooperative, industrious, purposeful, patriotic, law-abiding, God-fearing, well-organized, and family-oriented."[43] This acceptance has not come at the expense of growth, however. In 2002, the LDS church bypassed the Evangelical Lutheran Church in America to become the fifth largest religious group in the United States, with more than five million members in its home country and over ten million worldwide. Whether you see Mormonism as a new world religion or a fourth way in world Christianity alongside Protestantism, Catholicism, and Orthodoxy, there is no gainsaying the Mormons' success.

Oddly enough, one secret of that success has been the emergence of multiculturalism. The civil rights movement proceeded under the banner of the universal brotherhood of humanity, but one of its effects has been a rise in racial, ethnic, and religious pride. After black became beautiful, it was also acceptable to glory in your Native American ancestry, your Catholic faith, or your Mormon heritage. In fact, Mormon heritage became not just an identity but an industry as Salt Lake City became a tourist mecca more alluring than the Amish stronghold of Lancaster County, Pennsylvania. Oddly enough, this happened just as Mormonism was expanding beyond its traditional home in the intermountain West, and ceasing to be a provincial faith.

If the Mormons benefitted from the demise of the melting pot myth, they benefitted as well from their renewed love of Jesus. During the era of textual Mormonism, Joseph Smith and his followers had resembled the Disciples of Christ. Now they reemphasized their Restorationist roots, portraying their church as a modern manifestation of the original religion of Jesus. In this new era, Mormons focused on the living Christ more than the historical Jesus. This living Christ did not reside merely in their hearts, however. He was an embodied God who appeared to LDS prophets as surely as he appeared to the apostle Paul and Joseph Smith. For more than six decades after he visited Joseph Smith and Oliver Cowdery in the Kirtland Temple in 1836, Jesus had remained in the shadow of Smith and his successors. In 1898, he appeared to Lorenzo Snow, the fifth LDS president. He appeared to Joseph F. Smith, the sixth president, in 1918. He also became a leading subject in Mormon sermons. According to Shepherd and Shepherd, the relative importance of Jesus in general conference sermons more than quadrupled between the late nineteenth century and the late twentieth.[44]

JESUS AND JEHOVAH

As Mormons rediscovered Jesus, they also reinterpreted him. James Talmage (1862–1933) and Bruce McConkie (1915–1985) were two of the most influential thinkers among twentieth-century Mormon church leaders, and both wrote massive books on Jesus. Talmage's *Jesus the Christ* (1915) ran more than 800 pages, and McConkie's *Messiah* series (1978–82) consumed six volumes. Together these thinkers illustrate some of the tensions that beset the tradition as twentieth-century Mormons reconnected with Jesus.

Talmage, the more moderate of the two, led the first major reevaluation, which took place as Mormons began to consolidate their theology between the 1890s and the 1920s. Since 1842, Mormons had described the Bible as God's word only "as far as it is translated correctly." So they had felt free to criticize and even improve upon it. In an effort reminiscent of Jefferson's Bible, Joseph Smith had produced "translations" of Old and New Testament texts that excised corrupt additions and restored lost material, and Brigham Young had derided parts of Genesis as "baby stories." But Talmage was much more confident about the accuracy of the Bible, especially the Gospel accounts of the life of Jesus. In fact, his quasi-canonical *Jesus the Christ* was a believer's retort to the skepticism that characterized the first quest for the historical Jesus. It drew inspiration more from the pious lives of Jesus by English writers than from the skeptical biographies of German biblical critics. Like Frederic W. Farrar's *The Life of Christ* (1874), Talmage's *Jesus the Christ* harmonized the four Gospels into one account, a strategy that produced, for example, two temple cleansings and two feedings of the multitudes.[45]

In *Jesus the Christ*, some of the most controversial Mormon claims about Jesus fell away, including the view that Jesus was married with children and the more provocative position that he was a polygamist. The most important contribution of the book, however, was its bold thesis that "Jesus Christ is Jehovah." Talmage believed that Jesus and his Father were two separate beings. God the Father was Elohim of the Old Testament while God the Son was Jehovah in his premortal life. Jesus, wrote Talmage, "was the same Being who is repeatedly proclaimed as the God who made covenant with Abraham, Isaac, and Jacob; the God who led Israel from the bondage of Egypt to the freedom of the promised land." This understanding of Jesus, which had been incubating among Mormons since the 1870s, became official Mormon theology in 1916, when LDS authorities adopted it in a formal statement, drafted by Talmage, on "The Father and the Son."[46]

"The Father and the Son" followed Book of Mormon precedent in referring to Jesus repeatedly as a Father of sorts—the Father of all who are "born unto God through obedience to the Gospel." The best thing it had to say about Brigham Young's characterization of Jesus as Elder Brother was that there was "no impropriety" in using it. But Talmage himself used such language sparingly, and "The Father and the Son" warned explicitly against any effort to cut Jesus down to size. "Let it not be forgotten . . . ," the document continued, "that He is essentially greater than any and all" human beings because of his seniority, his sinlessness, and his "selection and foreordination as the one and only Redeemer and Savior of the race."[47]

Jesus the Christ and "The Father and the Son" demonstrated the new interest in Jesus among twentieth-century Mormons, yet both were deeply influenced by temple Mormonism. For Talmage and those in the hierarchy who kept his counsel, Jesus remained subordinate to his Father. Yes, Jesus superintended the creation of the world, but he did so under the authority and instructions of Elohim. In Jesus' life, the resurrection was far more important than the crucifixion. The atonement he effected was but one part in the Plan of Salvation. His defining moment came not on Calvary but in the Garden of Gethsemane, where, his brow dripping blood, he decided to submit obediently to the will of his Father, even unto death.

The cumulative effect of Talmage's widely read work was to make Jesus more important in Mormon belief and practice. Calling Jesus Father blurred the distinction between the first two Persons in the Trinity and elevated Jesus out of his Elder Brother role. Calling him Jehovah gave him a crucial role in religious history—as the God who covenanted in the Old Testament with Abraham and delivered the Ten Commandments to Moses. It also gave him a more conspicuous presence in the endowment ceremony held in Mormon temples. (In that ceremony, Jesus traditionally had no real part, but Jehovah was a major actor.)

As the twentieth century progressed, Mormons gravitated toward evangelicalism and a more evangelical Christ. If in the mid-nineteenth century Mormonism was a bold religious experiment, well on its way to becoming the first great world religion since Islam, by the mid-twentieth century it was far less bold. In fact it looked to be running like a lost sheep (or a Prodigal Son) back into the Christian fold. Twentieth-century Mormons shied away from professing polytheism. They emphasized salvation a bit more and eternal progression to godhood a bit less. They made more of the atonement and less of Gethsemane. A few even adopted the language of being "born again."

In the early 1980s, some students and faculty at BYU began emphasizing the importance of cultivating a personal friendship with Jesus. In *What It Means to Know Christ* (1981), George W. Pace, a popular Brigham Young University professor, called a "dynamic personal relationship with Christ" "the pearl of greatest price." Inspired by Pace's teaching and writing, certain students began praying to Jesus for twenty to thirty minutes each day. Bruce McConkie, a conservative member of the Council of the Twelve, responded in a speech delivered at a 1982 BYU assembly by scolding "erring teachers and beguiled students" for trying to make themselves into "special friends of Jesus." McConkie acknowledged that coming out against Jesus piety would seem like "speaking out against mother love, or Americanism, or the little red school house." But that did not stop him from describing efforts to cultivate "a special relationship with Christ" as "both immature and imperious." Christ, he said, is "our Elder Brother," and "our relationship with the Father is supreme, paramount and pre-eminent over all others." Inside the "Eternal Presidency" of the godhood, the Father ruled supreme. Even the Holy Ghost outranked McConkie's Elder Brother.[48]

What was at stake here was nothing less than the place of Jesus in the Mormon tradition. By the 1980s, American Christianity was focused squarely on Jesus, and in challenging that piety McConkie was, as he recognized, speaking out against something near and dear to most Americans. McConkie, who has been described as a Mormon fundamentalist, was committed to preserving the LDS Church as the key channel of grace, the key avenue for exaltation to godhood. That meant rejecting the *solus Jesus* approach that for decades had characterized much of American Christianity.

McConkie must have scared some of his listeners that day with references to Lucifer spreading false doctrine (a repentant Pace retracted his views only days later), but his formalism did not necessarily carry the day. *Seventh East Press*, a BYU student newspaper, reported that many "traditionally conservative, orthodox, sustaining LDS members" disagreed with McConkie's position. A letter to the editor of that paper quoted a series of Mormon leaders urging "every person to have a personal, ongoing, daily, continuing relationship" with Jesus Christ. One Mormon scholar termed McConkie's attack "spiritual abuse." And a month after McConkie's address, a Mormon teaching manual included a lesson on "Developing a Relationship with the Savior." Given this grass-roots opposition, rumors spread that McConkie had been scolded behind closed doors, and at least one Mormon leader called the talk "a very unfortunate and unchristian thing to do." Even McConkie seemed chastened, gravitating toward more christocentric language as his health failed. In his final testimony, delivered just days before his death in 1985, he said, "The most important doctrine I can declare . . . is one of the atoning sacrifice of the Lord Jesus Christ. His atonement is the most transcendent event that has or ever will occur."[49]

Today Mormons typically approach Jesus with what McConkie called the "required reserve" between themselves and their Savior. But they are increasingly coming to see Jesus rather than the LDS Church as their main channel of grace. Back in 1835, in the original Mormon hymnal, Emma Hale Smith described Jesus "my friend." In 1992, the *Encyclopedia of Mormonism* (1992), an unofficial yet authoritative Mormon text, portrayed Jesus as a "true and merciful friend" who "invites, comforts, answers, exhorts, loves, cries, is troubled over the sins of mankind, and is filled with joy."[50]

ARE MORMONS CHRISTIANS?

As LDS Church members cultivated personal relationships with Jesus and emphasized evangelical themes such as the necessity of being "born again," it became harder to distinguish between Mormons and evangelical Protestants. After a new revelation in 1978 opened the male-only priesthood to blacks, Mormonism moved even closer to the religious mainstream. And by the time the political mainstream jolted to the right after the election of Ronald Reagan as president in 1980, the Mormons were able to slip into it. Soon Mormons and evangelicals were squaring off, in part because it had become difficult to tell them apart.

As each group attempted to proselytize the other, evangelicals began to describe Mormonism as a non-Christian "cult." Southern Baptists led the anti-Mormon offensive, decrying Mormon views of God, Jesus, and salvation as unbiblical and unchristian. In language reminiscent of J. Gresham Machen's fulminations against Protestant modernism in *Christianity and Liberalism* (1923), they granted Mormons the right to be Mormons but insisted that they stop masquerading as Christians. You can believe that God has a body or that humans can progress to godhood, they argued. You can believe that faith needs to be supplemented by works and the Bible with ongoing revelation. You can even call Jesus Jehovah and say he was married. But you can't say such things and call yourself a Christian. In the summer of 1998, Southern Baptists took their annual convention to Salt Lake City. In addition to handing out anti-Mormon tracts, they distributed videos, including *The Mormon Puzzle*, which underscored the differences between Mormonism and Christianity.

Even liberal Protestant denominations spoke out against the Mormons. In 1995, the Presbyterian Church (U.S.A.) adopted a "Report on Mormonism" stating that the LDS Church was not "within the historic apostolic tradition of the Christian Church" and insisting that Mormon converts to Presbyterianism be rebaptized. In 2000, the United Methodist General Conference passed a resolution to the same effect. One year later, the Vatican Congregation for the Declaration of the Faith declared that the Roman Catholic Church would require its converts from Mormonism to be rebaptized.

Mormons might have responded by glorying in their difference. But they did just the opposite. They presented themselves as ordinary Christians, and the most important evidence they provided for their ordinariness was their intense love of Jesus. In 1982, LDS authorities started printing the Book of Mormon with a new subtitle: "Another Testament of Jesus Christ." In 1995, they increased the size of the words JESUS CHRIST on the official logo of the Church of Jesus Christ of Latter-day Saints (used, among other places, on missionaries' name badges) to more than twice the height of the surrounding type. Also during the 1990s, Mormons produced a series of books trumpeting their Christianness. In *Are Mormons Christians?* (1991), BYU professor Stephen E. Robinson answered the question posed in his title with an emphatic yes. But his reasoning had nothing to do with rites or creeds or even the Bible. It had to do with Jesus. "Though all the world may say that Latter-day Saints do not know or love or worship Jesus Christ, I know that we do, and if this is not the issue in question, or if this is not enough to be counted a Christian, then the word has lost its meaning." Daniel Peterson and Stephen Ricks, also BYU professors, boiled Christianity down to Jesus alone in a co-authored 1992 book. "What made a person a Christian in the first century, and what makes a person a Christian today," they argued, "is, simply a commitment to Jesus Christ. Such commitment is central to the religion of the Latter-day Saints."[51]

LDS officials took the same line in a public relations blitz leading up to the 2002 Winter Olympics in Salt Lake City. In a series of television and radio appearances by President Gordon B. Hinckley and other LDS leaders, Mormons emphasized their love of Jesus. Shortly before the 1998 annual meeting of the Southern Baptist Convention in Salt Lake City, Hinckley and Boyd K. Packer, acting president of the Quorum of the Twelve, spoke out on this issue. "Are we Christians?" Hinckley asked. "Of course we are! . . . No one believes more fundamentally that [Jesus Christ] was the Son of God, that He died for the sins of mankind, that He rose from the grave, and that He is the living resurrected Son of the living Father." Packer called efforts to depict Mormons as non-Christians "uninformed and unfair." "I bear witness of the Lord Jesus Christ," he said. "He is our Redeemer and is our Savior. He presides over this church." In an interview for a 1997 *Time* magazine cover story on "Mormons, Inc.," Hinckley said that his church's message "is a message of Christ. He's our leader. He's our head. His name is the name of our church." In 2001, just before the Olympics, LDS asked the media to stop referring to its organization as the "Mormon Church." According to a letter posted on the official LDS Web site, the proper shorthand for the institution had become "The Church of Jesus Christ" or, simply, "The Church."[52]

On January 1, 2000, the LDS hierarchy celebrated the millennium by issuing a new statement affirming their commitment to a high christology. Signed by the members of the First Presidency and the Quorum of the Twelve (and presented in a stylized format that recalls the Declaration of Independence, complete with a facsimile of each man's John Hancock), "The Living Christ" has been accepted by many Mormons as a new revelation. It reiterates Talmage's position that Jesus is Jehovah. It also affirms "that Jesus is the Living Christ, the immortal Son of God. He is the great King Immanuel, who stands today on the right hand of his Father. He is the light, the life, and the hope of the world. His way is the path that leads to happiness in this life and eternal life in the world to come."[53]

Later in 2000, the Museum of Church History and Art in Salt Lake City underscored the importance of this twenty-first-century manifesto when it opened an art exhibition, also called "The Living Christ," organized around the document. "Jesus Christ is the center of our religion," the exhibition text began, "and the focus of our faith." Although the show did not shy away from Jesus' divinity and his authority over the Church—one painting depicted him as Jehovah creating the earth—it described Jesus as a companionate Savior "who cares about us individually and impacts our lives . . . who loves us and is concerned about our welfare." Despite what Jan Shipps has described as a revival of "atonement discourse" in LDS circles in the last quarter century (and the affirmation in the exhibition itself that the atonement is "the central event in human history") none of the images depicted Jesus on the cross. This exhibition demonstrates that Mormons continue to see Jesus not as the Suffering Servant offered as a sacrifice on the cross but as the resurrected and living Christ who appeared to Paul in the New Testament, the Nephites in the Book of Mormon, and Joseph Smith in "the dispensation of the fulness of times."[54]

THE GREAT WHITE GOD

Most of these public relations efforts targeted outsiders, but Mormon leaders also worked to reemphasize and reinterpret Jesus among Mormons themselves. As early as 1961, church authorities were working on a Gospel in Art initiative, which aimed to make available to LDS members "the best in religious art" for display in their ward buildings and homes. At the time, the face of Jesus appeared to most Mormons through the mediation of Heinrich Hofmann, Bernard Plockhorst, James Tissot, and Warner Sallman. Sallman's *Head of Christ* was particularly popular, hung in LDS homes, ward libraries, and Sunday school rooms, and used on calling cards for LDS missionaries. Sallman was not a Mormon, however, so beginning in the 1960s LDS leaders decided it was time to commission some new Jesus art.

Mormons have always imagined Jesus as a white man. According to the Book of Mormon, Jesus' mother was "exceedingly fair and white" (1 Nephi 11:13). A popular Mormon pamphlet calls Jesus "the Great White God" and describes him as "a tall white man, bearded and with blue eyes." At least since the masculine revival of the late nineteenth century, Mormons have also represented Jesus as a Manly Redeemer. "Christ was not red-haired, nor effeminate, neither was he dyspeptic, nor a dreamy sentimentalist," one Mormon wrote in 1904. "The Being who drove the money changers out of the Temple was . . . a vigorous, deep-chested, broad shouldered man, with well cut features and above the medium height." With these traditions in mind, church officials hired Aldo Rebechi to create a massive, eleven-foot-tall, white marble replica of Bertel Thorvaldsen's *Christus*, which now lords over the Visitors' Center in Temple Square in Salt Lake City (and the home page of the official LDS Web site).[55]

In 1983, church officials commissioned a Mormon artist named Del Parson to create a painting of Jesus. Debuting in the Mormon magazine *Ensign* in 1984, *The Lord Jesus Christ* depicts Jesus as a masculine and clearly Caucasian hero. Like Sallman's iconic image, this picture is a head-and-shoulders portrait. Here too Jesus looks above and beyond the viewer, though in this case his line of vision just barely misses eye contact. Parson's Jesus is far more rugged than Sallman's, however. Though draped in a long red robe, he is unequivocally masculine, his chest broad, his neck thick, his face weathered like a pioneer's. Parson has said that he felt the hand of God guiding him when he did the painting, and apparently many Mormons think the same. The Lord Jesus Christ is now the quasi-canonical Jesus image inside the LDS Church.

By all accounts the Gospel in Art program was a huge success. A recent study of material culture in American homes found that, on average, LDS homes had more than four pictures of Jesus, while another study of dormitory rooms found that LDS students had more religious art than either Catholics or Pentecostals. A related study found reproductions of Parson's The Lord Jesus Christ in the majority of Mormon homes and many Mormon workplaces.[56]

As Mormons defended their Christianness against Southern Baptists and other evangelicals, Jesus also became a stronger presence in official Mormon publications. In Church News, stories about the lives of Joseph Smith and Brigham Young gave way to stories about the life of Jesus. Other publications saw an "astounding increase" in Jesus visuals. While Ensign printed an average of 20 Jesus pictures per year in the 1970s, that figure jumped to 37 in the 1980s and 75 in the 1990s.[57]

Perhaps because they emphasized Jesus so much, Mormons did not feel compelled to give up entirely on their distinctiveness. Earlier in Mormon history, Joseph Smith had called his organization "the only true and living church upon the face of the whole earth" and all non-Mormons "Gentiles." Brigham Young had determined that other so-called Christians were "not Christians as the New Testament defines Christianity." Mormons today are more irenic, but they have not entirely given up on their identity as a "peculiar people" with a special relationship to God. When asked whether he believed in the Christ of other Christians, President Hinckley said, "No, I don't. The traditional Christ of whom they speak is not the Christ of whom I speak. For the Christ of whom I speak has been revealed in this the Dispensation of the Fulness of Times."[58]

Evangelicals have seized on such remarks to reiterate their claim that Mormonism is not Christian. "Its theology is as close to Christianity as Hinduism," argues Sandra Tanner, an ex-Mormon who is now a born-again Christian. "It's a totally different view of man and God and creation."[59] This is not the place to settle that debate, which in the last analysis rests on a theological determination of the boundaries of Christianity and Mormonism. What is significant here is the nature of the Mormon response, which defines Christianity in terms of Jesus alone. The fact that Mormons have chosen this course demonstrates their commitment to Jesus. It also demonstrates the importance of Jesus in American Christianity, where Jesus has replaced the churches, the creeds, and even the Bible as the key authority in belief and practice. It must be noted, however, that the Mormon defense in this matter would not have gotten them very far in a debate with Jonathan Edwards in the eighteenth century, or for that matter in a denominational heresy trial in the nineteenth. Thomas Jefferson may have revered Jesus at least as much as President Gordon Hinckley does, but few believe that made him a Christian. And Jonathan Edwards no doubt loved Jesus less than either man, but no one has ever questioned his Christian bona fides. The Jesus-centric arguments Mormons now advance for their Christian status are more than coherent. At least by contemporary American standards, they are close to irrefutable. They carry the day, however, only because the traditional authority of the creeds has so seriously deteriorated.

Mormons have been called the most American of Americans, but it is not just their thriftiness or their work ethic that makes them so. Like millions of Americans from Thomas Jefferson onward, Mormons have pledged their allegiance to Jesus. In fact, in many cases Mormons exceed liberal and evangelical Christians in their adoration of him. But Mormons too have refused to see Jesus as a take-it-or-leave-it proposition. Their Jesus is a flesh-and-blood God, the Jehovah of the Old Testament, and a person quite distinct from God the Father. Although Mormons have gravitated in recent years toward more intimate relationships with Jesus as a companion and friend, most continue to hold him at arm's length, approaching their Savior with at least a modicum of formality. In other words, the Mormon Jesus remains an Elder Brother, who is significant chiefly for charting the path we must follow if we are to attain exaltation and godhood.

With astounding success, Mormons have broadcast these views to the world. But they have done more than that. They continue to insist that their Jesus—who came to America two thousand years ago and still speaks to Mormon prophets today—is the real Jesus, that other Christians have got him all wrong. In making this bold claim, Mormons are not only staking a claim for their Christianness, they are making a case for their Americanness too, because as we have seen this is the American way.

Six

BLACK MOSES

In the wake of the Detroit race riot of 1967, which claimed forty-three lives and injured more than one thousand, a group of African-American men blackened the face of a statue of Jesus at Detroit's Sacred Heart Seminary. Some white men responded by painting the statue white. After a sound truck motored past the school accusing its priests of whitewashing Jesus, the seminarians took matters into their own hands and painted it black.

A few months before the riots, Albert B. Cleage, Jr. (1911–2000) had put the color of Jesus on the city's agenda when he installed in his Shrine of the Black Madonna a massive, eighteen-foot-high painting of a black Madonna and Child. Not long after the riots, St. Cecelia's Roman Catholic Church, also in Detroit, unveiled a striking dome of a thick-lipped, kinky-haired *Black Christ*, surrounded by a veritable United Nations of angels of different races and ethnicities. In 1969, St. Cecelia's *Black Christ* appeared on the cover of *Ebony* magazine. Inside, a story on "The Quest for a Black Christ" devoted considerable attention to yet another Jesus controversy. "We make no claim that Christ is only black," explained Father Raymond Ellis, the

Lebanese-American priest at St. Cecelia's. "We merely wish to affirm that Christ today is also black." But Cleage, a pioneer in the non-denominational Black Christian Nationalist Movement who would later take the name of Jaramogi Abebe Agyeman, would have none of that: "I'm not saying, 'Wouldn't it be nice if Jesus was black? Or 'Let's pretend that Jesus was black.' I'm saying that Jesus WAS black. There never was a white Jesus." Soon citizens across the nation were debating whether Cleage was, as his supporters claimed, black America's next hero or, as his detractors argued, a "religiously illiterate" demagogue.[1]

While this drama was playing itself out, the African-American community was split between civil rights and Black Power. Even after the Reverend Martin Luther King, Jr.'s assassination in 1968, most black churches supported King's strategy of nonviolent civil disobedience and his aim of integration. The Black Power movement rejected King's strategy and his goal. Largely a secular effort, Black Power was led by groups such as the Black Panthers and Stokely Carmichael's Student Nonviolent Coordinating Committee (SNCC). But it too had a spiritual center in a burgeoning black sect known as the Nation of Islam (NOI). Founded in Detroit in 1930 by W. D. Fard, an itinerant peddler of uncertain race, the NOI remained for decades a small organization known less for its political power than for its offbeat interpretations of Islam (including the striking claim that Fard himself was an incarnation of Allah). Under the leadership of Elijah Muhammad, who took over after Fard's mysterious disappearance in 1934, the Nation of Islam became during the 1950s the leading religious alternative in the black community.

Cleage, a friend of the NOI popularizer Malcolm X, symphatized far more with the Black Power revolution than with civil rights reform. Embittered and emboldened by the Detroit race riot, he argued for black separatism in politics and economics. He was convinced, however, that the black revolution would go nowhere without the support of the black church. So he began to create a Christian form of Black Power centered on a Black Messiah.

In an influential collection of sermons called *The Black Messiah* (1968), Cleage argued that the first step toward black liberation was the crucifixion of the white Christ and the resurrection of a Black

Messiah. "Black people cannot build dignity on their knees worshiping a white Christ," he wrote. "We must put down this white Jesus
which the white man gave us in slavery and which has been tearing us
to pieces." Like American religious reformers from Jefferson on, he
began his argument by drawing a sharp line between "the religion *of*
Jesus" and "a religion *about* Jesus." He then characteristically placed
the blame for the corruption of true Christianity at the feet of Paul.
"You have been misled," he told his congregation bluntly. "That which
you believe to be Christianity . . . is not Christianity. The Christianity
which we see in the world today was not shaped by Jesus. It was put
together by the Apostle Paul." Paul's Jesus was, according to Cleage, a
"spiritualized Jesus," and his faith was dangerously individualistic and
otherworldly. The real Jesus was communal, this-worldly, and political. He was also black—literally, biologically black.[2]

Following the Nation of Islam, which had denounced Christianity
as "white man's religion," Cleage ridiculed the hymn "Fairest Lord Jesus" and blasted Sunday school pictures of "the weak little mamby-
pamby white Jesus." But instead of rejecting the Christian Savior,
Cleage reconstructed him as the black hero of a black nation. According to Cleage, the Israelites were a black people. Moses sojourned in
Africa (in Egypt) and married a black woman. Jesus was a black man
born of a black woman who was herself descended from black Israelites. He was also the manliest of men—"a revolutionary black
leader, a Zealot" who had come to bring "not peace but a sword." Judas and the other black Jews who betrayed Jesus were "the Uncle
Toms of their day." The power that crucified Jesus was the "white nation, Rome."[3]

In Cleage's fighting faith, dying on the cross to save individuals
from sin was the last thing on Jesus' mind. Jesus came instead to deliver good news to the captives and lead a national liberation struggle
on behalf of "the Black Nation Israel."[4] Now is the time, he told his
parishioners, for black people to steal Jesus back from white Christianity. Any African American who refused to take up the fight against
white oppression was a modern-day Judas—a honkified Uncle Tom.

After establishing the blackness of Jesus, Cleage established the
blackness of God. His argument began in the beginning, with Genesis 1:27: "God created man in his own image":

If God created man in his own image, then we must look at man to see what God looks like. There are black men, there are yellow men, there are red men, and there are a few, a mighty few, white men in the world. If God created man in his own image, then God must be some combination of this black, red, yellow and white. . . . So if we think of God as a person . . . then God must be a combination of black, yellow and red with just a little touch of white, and we must think of God as a black God. . . . In America, one drop of black [blood] makes you black. So by American law, God is black.[5]

At his Shrine of the Black Madonna, Cleage boldly recast the entire Christian tradition around this black God and his black Son. To celebrate Christmas was to commemorate the birth of a "Black man who came to save a Black Nation." To confess was to admit, "I've 'Tommed' all my life. I've done everything the man wanted me to do." To be baptized was to die to the accommodating black church and the Uncle Tom individualism of "slave Christianity" and then to rise to the new life of the communal Black Nation. To consume bread and wine in the Eucharist was to declare yourself "willing to have your body broken . . . and to shed your blood for the Nation."[6]

Sharply distinguishing himself from other black pastors, Cleage imagined a Nation of Christianity alongside the Nation of Islam. Malcolm X and other NOI leaders had worked hard to transform African-American Baptists and Methodists into Black Muslims (as their members were popularly called). In fact, they regularly conducted what they called "fishing" expeditions outside black churches on Sunday mornings, trolling for converts among Methodists, Baptists, and Pentecostals. In those expeditions, Black Muslims spoke often of Jesus. Jesus, they argued, was not God Himself. He did not die on the cross and he was not raised from the dead. But rather than rejecting Jesus as the central symbol of a corrupt religion, they embraced him as one of their own. Jesus was a prophet of Allah, they told black Christians. He taught "freedom, justice, and equality" and condemned whites as "a race of devils." In short, "Jesus was a Muslim, not a Christian."[7]

Many black ministers chastised the Nation of Islam for its divisive tactics and unchristian and anti-Semitic views. Cleage, by contrast, slammed civil rights leaders as Tomming Scribes and Pharisees who were more formidable barriers to black liberation than racist whites. Then he praised Black Muslim leaders for doing the Black Messiah's work. Malcolm X wasn't just Cleage's "Brother Malcolm"; he was a Christ-like savior who sacrificed his life in the sacred struggle for a Black Nation.[8]

Although Cleage lauded Malcolm X and the Nation of Islam, he did some fishing of his own in ponds stocked with NOI stalwarts. He called loving your enemies impossible and turning the other cheek insane. And he said "Amen" to just about everything Malcolm X preached about Christianity. Malcolm X was right to sneer at the corrupt white Christianity of Paul, Cleage argued, but Paul's Christianity wasn't the real deal. In fact, Paul's letters were not accepted as scripture at the Shrine of the Black Madonna. Like Thomas Jefferson, Cleage worked with an expurgated New Testament, shorn in his case of all writing by the man who had urged slaves to obey their masters (and, by the way, of the Gospel of John too). "The Christian religion you are rejecting, that you are so opposed to," Cleage wrote in a letter to Stokely Carmichael, "is a slave Christianity that has no roots in the teachings of the Black Messiah."[9]

Each of the sermons in Cleage's book ended with a prayer to the "Black Messiah, Jesus Christ." Yet like so many African Americans before him, Cleage read Jesus largely through Old Testament glasses— as a story of collective freedom rather than individual salvation. "The black man's religion," Cleage recognized, "is essentially based on the Old Testament concepts of the Nation Israel, God's chosen people, and our knowledge that the problems of the black Israelites were the same as ours."[10] The Black Messiah was drenched in the Exodus repertory. It included sermons such as "We Are God's Chosen People," "But God Hardened Pharaoh's Heart," "Coming In Out of the Wilderness," and "The Promised Land." It portrayed the Black Messiah as a Black Moses—a liberator from oppression, not a savior from sins. Like King, Cleage believed that Jesus would lead a revolution that would transform the United States from Babylon into Zion. Unlike King, Cleage imagined heaven on earth as a black kingdom, and he championed violence as a path through the wilderness, arming his Black Moses with a sword.

BLACK LIBERATION AND WOMANIST THEOLOGY

Cleage was the most celebrated radical theologian inside the black church in the late 1960s, but he was not the only African American to shape Jesus in his own image. The African-American historian and Mennonite layman Vincent Harding called Jesus the Lord of the Black Power movement as early as 1967. In *Black Theology and Black Power* (1969), James Cone, a young black professor at Adrian College in Michigan, reworked Cleage's rough-hewn rhetoric into a systematic theology that brought the writings of Paul Tillich and other white theologians into conversation with the experiences of African Americans. Almost overnight, Cone became the leading spokesperson for an indigenous version of the Latin American theology of liberation that came to be known as black liberation theology.

Born in segregated Arkansas in 1938, Cone attended the Macedonia American Methodist Episcopal Church in Bearden as a child. "Every Sunday and sometimes on weeknights I encountered Jesus through rousing sermons, fervent prayers, spirited gospel songs, and the passionate testimonies of the people," Cone has written. "Jesus was the dominant reality at Macedonia and in black life in Bearden." Like Cleage, Cone attempted to integrate the Jesus of the black church with the ways and means of Black Power. "Black Theology is the theological arm of Black Power, and Black Power is the political arm of Black Theology," Cone wrote, adding that Black Power was "Christ's central message to twentieth century America." Cone also followed Cleage in coloring Jesus black:

> The "raceless" American Christ has a light skin, wavy brown hair, and sometimes—wonder of wonders—blue eyes. For whites to find him with big lips and kinky hair is as offensive as it was for the Pharisees to find him partying with tax-collectors. But whether whites want to hear it or not, Christ is black, baby, with all of the features which are so detestable to white society.[11]

While Cleage's understanding of blackness was literal and exclusive, Cone's was figurative and open to a more cosmopolitan interpretation. "Being black in America has very little to do with skin color," Cone wrote. "To be black means that your heart, your soul, your mind, and your body are where the dispossessed are . . . It essentially depends on the color of your heart, soul, and mind." This metaphorical interpretation of Jesus' blackness opened up the possibility that well-meaning white liberals (and perhaps even civil rights leaders) could somehow be black too. It also made Cone's work required reading at Protestant and Catholic seminaries eager to introduce students to theology done "from below." If, as Cone argued, blackness was "an ontological symbol for all people who participate in the liberation of man from oppression," then those whites who identified with that symbol could be adopted into the Black Nation.[12]

Black liberation theology grew up around the same time that feminist theology emerged, and this son and daughter of the sixties were close kin. Both black liberation theologians and feminist theologians were radical reformers, rejecting reigning understandings of Jesus and Christianity as racist or sexist. Both groups also devoted considerable attention to the symbol of God. Coining the most famous slogan in feminist theology, Mary Daly observed in *Beyond God the Father* (1973) that "if God is male, then the male is God."[13] Black liberation theologians advanced a similar argument: If God is white, then whites are gods.

Both groups accordingly participated in the American tradition of reimagining Jesus. Whereas black liberation theologians such as Cone and Cleage colored Jesus black, feminist theologians made Jesus into a feminist. To be sure, a few radical feminist theologians eschewed what Daly described as the "Christolatry" of Jesus worship, following Daly as she staged a much-publicized exodus out of the Babylon of Harvard's Memorial Church—and beyond "patriarchal religion" altogether—in 1971.[14] But many more attempted to reform Christianity from within. They too blamed Paul for degrading the egalitarian religion of Jesus into the patriarchal religion of the church. Was it not Paul, after all, who instructed women to obey their husbands (Ephesians 5:22) and to keep silent in the churches (1 Corinthians 14:34)?

Jesus, by contrast, took women as disciples and interpreted Jewish Law in ways that set them free.

During the 1980s, a new group of theologians synthesized feminist theology and black liberation theology. Following the novelist Alice Walker, who had defined the term "womanish" as "referring to outrageous, audacious, courageous or *willful* behavior," these black female thinkers called themselves womanist theologians.[15] They borrowed heavily from Cone and Daly, but chastised both black liberation theology (as sexist) and feminist theology (as racist). They characterized the black experience invoked by Cone and Cleage as black male experience, and the female experience of Mary Daly and her colleagues as white female experience. Then they worked hard to integrate the experiences of black women into the mix. To the pantheon of black male heroes conjured up by Cleage, they added figures such as the biblical slave Hagar and the nineteenth-century African Methodist Episcopal preacher Jarena Lee. The pantheon of white goddesses conjured up by post-Christian feminists they rejected altogether.

Womanist theologians were particularly wary of the flirtation of some radical feminist theologians with goddess worship. Virtually all womanist theologians had grown up in the black church, and moving "beyond Christolatry," as Daly put it, was to them unthinkable. Sojourner Truth, the ex-slave and abolitionist orator, often began her lectures by invoking Jesus, whom she described as "a friend, standing between me and God, through whom, love flowed as from a fountain." Womanist theologians invoked Jesus too and, like Truth, they saw him as both a personal Savior and a political Messiah, an incarnation of God who came into the world to save individuals from sin and deliver his chosen people from captivity.[16]

The most outlandish womanists interpreted Jesus as a black woman. None meant this literally though. The Bible remained authoritative inside the black church, and while that text is extraordinarily malleable, even the most clever hermeneuts couldn't stretch it far enough to uncover a black Jesus in drag. Womanist theologians did insist, however, that the face of Jesus could be seen most clearly in African-American women, who for centuries had struggled against the sins of slavery and segregation, racism and sexism. According to Jacquelyn Grant, a leading womanist theologian, images of Jesus as a white male presented a double offense to African-American women. Drawing on Luke's special concern with women and the poor, and on the resources of earlier theologies of liberation, she embraced Jesus as a "political Messiah." "Christ, found in the experiences of Black women," she concluded, "is a Black woman."[17]

Critics decried the black Jesus of womanist and black liberation theology as an absurd anachronism that turned a universal religion of love into a parochial sect (or cult) of hatred. *Christian Century*, for example, described Cleage as a renegade "who contends that all whites are enemies" and "seems to want to make Christ the exclusive property of blacks and use him as a tool to cause division." More conservative commentators scoffed at any notion, either literal or metaphorical, of Jesus as black, labeling such thinking the effluvia of sixties radicalism gone mad. Whether those critics were right about the dangers of a black Jesus is a matter of debate. But there is no truth to the claim that he (or she) was born in the 1960s. African Americans had been praying to a black Jesus for well over a century before Cleage's *Black Messiah* appeared. In fact, their prayers were so numerous and heartfelt that it makes sense to speak of a black Jesus tradition in the United States.[18]

BLACK MOSES

As has been noted, all interpreters of the Bible work from a "canon within the canon." Paul's letters were verboten in the Reverend Cleage's church, where Matthew 10:34 ("I have not come to bring peace, but a sword") was beloved. The African-American theologian Howard Thurman emphasized the prophetic books of the Old Testament along with the Gospels, but like Jefferson and Cleage he too was wary of the epistles of Paul. In fact, in a striking illustration of the tendency of all biblical interpreters to work from a canon within the canon, Thurman's grandmother, who regularly read the Bible to him while he was a boy, refused to listen to any epistle written by the author of "Slaves obey your masters" (though she did make an exception for 1 Corinthians 13, a chapter she admired on Christian love). As a slave, she had listened to too many sermons by white ministers on the duties owed by slaves to masters. "I promised my Maker that if I ever learned to read and if freedom ever came," she told her grandson, "I would not read that part of the Bible."[19]

The Bible was a holy book in the "invisible institution" of slave Christianity, but most slave Christians could not read it. The slave preachers that could shaped it to fit their circumstances, gravitating toward memorable stories and away from theological arguments. In the New Testament, they emphasized the crucifixion and resurrection along with the mother of all apocalyptic tales, the Book of Revelation. In the Old Testament, they embraced the prophetic books and accounts of the adventures of Israel. Those stories, transmitted orally, became the de facto canon of slave religion, and at the center of that canon was the story of the Exodus.

The basic themes in the Biblical symphony of the Exodus—Egypt, Pharaoh, Moses, Chosen People, Captivity, Persecution, Exile, Diaspora, Wilderness, Deliverance, Promised Land—are well known to most students of U.S. history. The Puritans saw themselves as God's New Israel. Their effort to carve a Biblical Commonwealth out of the forests of New England was, in the memorable words of Perry Miller, "an errand into the wilderness," and on the far side of that wilderness, the Puritans believed, lay their Promised Land. During the American Revolution, patriots looked upon George Washington as a new Moses commissioned by God to liberate his country from the yoke of the Pharaoh, George III. Half a century later, members of the Church of Jesus Christ of Latter-day Saints went on an errand to the West, led by the "American Moses" Brigham Young. Closer to our own time, the Reverend King construed the civil rights movement as a march from captivity to freedom. As he led the bus boycott of Montgomery, Alabama, in 1955 and 1956, and the March on Washington in 1963, his followers cast him as a modern-day Moses. After his assassination, many came to see him as a modern-day Jesus too, a Suffering Servant crucified to set his people free.

As Albert Raboteau has demonstrated, African Americans have been an Exodus people, and their church an Exodus church.[20] Like the Puritans, black Christians have lived to a great extent in an Old Testament world. From the beginnings of the slave trade through the founding of the black church and the marches of the civil rights movement, they have interpreted their experiences in light of Exodus themes, claiming for themselves God's promise to deliver His chosen people from captivity, and finding in their midst a series of Moses figures—from Underground Railroad "conductor" Harriet Tubman and educator Booker T. Washington to black nationalist Marcus Garvey and even Jesus himself.

But rather than distinguishing carefully between Old Testament and New Testament types, and between biblical times and their own, African-American Christians have for centuries fused them all, inviting biblical figures to toil alongside them in the cotton fields of Mississippi and permitting themselves the luxury of walking the Road to Jericho or the responsibility of relieving Simon of Cyrene of the burden of the cross. They also tended to merge Moses into Jesus and Jesus into Moses.

The gospel of Matthew repeatedly compares Jesus to Moses. Matthew's Jesus delivers five major speeches, as a counterpoint to the Pentateuch of Moses (one of them, Moses-like, on a mountain). But Matthew's goal is to prove Jesus is the fulfillment of Hebrew Bible prophesies and the superior of his Israelite predecessors. Slave Christians did far more than compare these two heroes; they conflated them, producing out of the two figures one liberator who promised individual deliverance from sins and collective deliverance from slavery. As a Union soldier observed in 1864, "There is no part of the Bible with which they are so familiar as the story of the deliverance of the children of Israel. Moses is their *ideal* of all that is high, and noble, and perfect, in man. I think they have been accustomed to regard Christ not so much in the light of a *spiritual* Deliverer, *as* that of a second Moses who could eventually lead *them* out of their prison-house of bondage."[21]

Historian Eugene Genovese has found this fusion of Jesus and Moses in the sermons of black preachers and slave spirituals. For example, "O the Dying Lamb!" brings together the actions of Moses with the symbol of Jesus as the Lamb who was slain:

> *I wants to go where Moses trod,*
> *O de dying Lamb!*

For Moses gone to de promised land,
O de dying Lamb!

"The Ship of Zion" places Jesus at the center of the Exodus story—at the helm of "de good ole ship o' Zion" bound for the promised land:

King Jesus is de captain, captain, captain,
And she's makin' for de Promise Land.

Another spiritual, "My Army Cross Over," runs the site of Moses's greatest miracle (the Red Sea) into the site of Jesus' baptism (the Jordan River), as if they were one body of water:

My army cross over,
My army cross over.
O, Pharaoh's army drownded!
My army cross over.

We'll cross de mighty river,
My army cross over;
We'll cross de river Jordan,
My army cross over.[22]

Slave Christians frequently described Jesus in personal language, as a comforter and friend who suffered with them under the lash. Yet they also described Jesus in more public terms, as an Old Testament king and warrior whose divine power overwhelmed even the power of the slaveholding South. This "Massa Jesus" would free them from slavery as surely as Moses had delivered the Israelites from bondage. But he wouldn't do just that. He would also save them, New Testment–style, from their sins. Or, as a later gospel hymn, "Jesus, I'll Never Forget," put it:

Jesus, I'll never forget when way down in Egypt's land,
How you brought me out with a mighty outstretched hand,
Broke the bonds of sin and set me free,
Gave me joy and peace and victory.[23]

To slave Christians, Jesus was both savior (from sins) and deliverer (from slavery). Like the spirituals themselves, he gave voice to the need to endure suffering as well as the hope of escaping it. At least in the world the slave Christians made, Jesus was both a this-worldly and an otherworldly liberator.

This Mosaic Jesus helped to transform black Christianity into an effective vehicle for political resistance and social reform. As Eugene Genovese argued in *Roll, Jordan, Roll*, the slaves' creative conflation of Moses and Jesus brought together the saving grace of the New Testament and the transforming justice of the Old. As Moses mutated into Jesus and Jesus into Moses, the Hebraic message of "an eye for an eye" entered into negotiations with the Christian message of "love your neighbor." As Genovese put it: "Jesus, once become Moses, underwent a transubstantiation that carried with it the promise of this-worldly salvation without suicidal adventures. The assimilation solved the problem of how to achieve spiritual freedom, retain faith in earthly deliverance, instill a spirit of price and love in each other, and make peace with a political reality within which revolutionary solutions no longer had much prospect."[24]

This new understanding of Jesus, born in the "hush harbors" of the slave plantations, spread as more African Americans converted to Christianity. The revivalists of the Great Awakening of the 1730s and 1740s produced some black converts, but the catechizing of the Anglicans (still dominant in the South) failed to make many new Christians. By the end of the eighteenth century only about 5 percent of African Americans were church members. During the half century after the Revolutionary War, Baptist and Methodists brought a more experiential style to slaves in the South and free blacks in the North, and they proved adept at winning what NAACP founder W.E.B. Du Bois later called "the souls of black folk." Black preachers founded independent black congregations as early as the 1780s, and their efforts paved the way for the new African-American denominations, such as the African Methodist Episcopal Church (established 1816) and the African Methodist Episcopal Zion Church (established 1821). In these institutions, black Christians shaped and sustained a creole Christianity that blended their own experiences with a combination of West African, Jewish, and Christian elements to create an extraordinary popular religious culture.

This creole culture was Hebraic to the bone. While white Christians were busy crafting a form of Christianity rooted almost entirely in the New Testament, black Christians exhibited what Lawrence Levine has recognized as an "Old Testament bias," gravitating toward heroic accounts of Daniel, David, Joshua, Noah, Moses, and other Hebrew patriarchs.[25] Moreover, rather than carefully discriminating (as most white Christians did) between the old dispensation and the new, and between biblical times and their own, black Christians merged the two, inviting biblical figures to toil alongside them in the cotton fields of Mississippi and the factories of Detroit. As Christians, these believers could not neglect Jesus. So the Coming King of Revelation and the Suffering Servant of the passion narratives became staples of black preaching and hymnody. But the Jesus of the black church was first and foremost a Hebraic hero. Rather than resurrecting Jesus inside the New Testament world of white Christians, black believers reincarnated him in a world of their own making: African Americans were God's chosen people and, thanks to Jesus, whatever bondage they experienced would someday give way to freedom.

COLORING JESUS BLACK

Perhaps because of this conflation of Moses and Jesus, the New Testament and the Old, nineteenth-century black believers did not typically color their liberator black. A number of slave narratives describe Jesus as a white man wearing a white robe—an image that endures today in the art of Sister Gertrude Morgan (whose paintings repeatedly depict Jesus as a bridegroom and Morgan as his bride). And at least one ex-slave explicitly rejected the black Christ. When asked decades after the Civil War whether Jesus was black, that former slave answered, "How can we believe it; the Lord must be white, because I never saw any other kind of people rise and redeem. If de Lord was a big black man, white people would sure haf to run from him. I for one would run from him."[26]

One of the first African Americans to color Jesus black was Cassius Clay. Today that name evokes the life of the flamboyant heavy-weight boxing champion who after becoming a Black Muslim rejected his "slave name" and became Muhammad Ali. During the nineteenth century, however, it belonged most famously to the abolitionist Cassius Clay, who used his paper, *The True American* (established in Lexington, Kentucky, in 1845), to document the sins of slavery. In 1893, Clay intimated that Jesus was black. "Christ was not of the Caucasian race or races," he wrote, "but if He were living in Kentucky today, would be cooped up in the 'Jim Crow' cars."[27]

The Reverend Henry McNeal Turner, an influential bishop in the African Methodist Episcopal Church, paved the way for greater acceptance of a Black Jesus when he affirmed that "God is a Negro" later in the 1890s. An early advocate of black colonization, an effort of "Back to Africa" groups such as the African Colonization Society (established in 1816) to create a black homeland in Africa, Turner was also the editor of the A.M.E. Journal *Voice of Missions*. After Turner described God as a "Negro" in the pages of that journal, one white reader objected, declaring Jesus white and Turner "demented." Then Turner dug in. In an oft-quoted editorial from that same journal in 1898, he argued for an end to the white monopoly on imaging God (without attempting to replace it with a black monopoly):

> We have as much right Biblically and otherwise to believe that god is a Negro, as you buckra, or white, people have to believe that God is a fine looking, symmetrical and ornamented white man. For the bulk of you, and all the fool Negroes of the country, believe that God is white-skinned, blue-eyed, straight-haired, projecting-nosed, compressed-lipped and finely-robed *white* gentleman, sitting upon a throne somewhere in the heavens. Every race of people since time began who have attempted to describe their God by words, or by paintings, or by carvings, or by any other form or figure, have conveyed the idea that the God who made them and shaped their destinies was symbolized in themselves, and why should not the Negro believe that he resembles God as much so as other people? We do not believe that there is any hope for a race of people who do not believe that they look like God.[28]

Turner's views reached a huge audience through the efforts of
Marcus Mosiah Garvey, Jr. (1887–1940), the Jamaica-born founder of
the Universal Negro Improvement Association (UNIA) and the leader
of the earliest and largest mass movement in African-American history. Widely acclaimed as "the Moses of the Negro Race," Garvey
called on African Americans to flee from bondage in the United
States and venture across the wilderness of the Atlantic to freedom
in Africa.[29] Garvey even established a Black Star Line of steamships
to transform that hope into a reality. Through Garvey's influence,
Ethiopianism emerged as a major force in African-American life. This
impulse—rooted in Psalm 68:31: "Princes shall come out of Egypt:
Ethiopia shall soon stretch forth her hands unto God"—yoked the Exodus story to black nationalist aspirations.

Convinced that blacks would never truly respect themselves as
long as they were worshiping a white Savior, Garvey told his UNIA
followers to look at God "through our own spectacles." He then
branded all African Americans who refused to do so kow-towing Uncle Toms. Although some have seen Garvey's UNIA as a secular organization (in part because Garvey rejected overtures to turn it into a
Christian denomination), the group was thoroughly drenched in religion. In keeping with Garvey's keen interest in Roman Catholicism,
UNIA meetings were high-church affairs. They typically included the
Lord's Prayer, a hymn such as "Onward Christian Soldiers" or the
"Universal Negro Anthem," and a reading of Garvey's beloved Psalm
68:31. In his speeches, Garvey popularized arguments about Africans
and the Bible that would become commonplace during the Afrocentrist vogue of the 1980s and 1990s. Civilization appeared first in
Africa, he informed his followers, and Adam and Eve were as dark as
night.[30]

Following Bishop Henry McNeal Turner, Garvey insisted that God
was black, and proud. Whereas Turner saw God's blackness as
metaphorical (and was, in his own words, "no stickler as to God's
color"), Garvey affirmed the literal blackness of Jesus. "Never admit
that Jesus Christ was a white man," he told his followers. "Jesus
Christ had the blood of all races in his veins, and tracing the Jewish
race back to Abraham and to Moses, from which Jesus sprang
through the line of Jesse, you will find Negro blood everywhere, so Je-

sus had much of Negro blood in him." In 1924, the UNIA–sponsored Fourth International Convention of Negroes of the World canonized this line of interpretation, anointing Jesus as the "Black Man of Sorrows" and his mother Mary as the "Black Madonna." At the same convention, Archbishop George Alexander McGuire, a former UNIA chaplain who had organized the African Orthodox Church in 1921 as a religious outlet for Garveyite views, urged UNIA members to tear down and burn the white Madonna and white Jesus pictures in their homes; "Then let us start our negro painters getting busy, and supply a black Madonna and a black Christ for the training of our children."[31]

After an ill-advised meeting in 1922 with the Acting Imperial Wizard of the Ku Klux Klan (to discuss a shared disdain for integration and miscegenation), Garvey was pilloried by black intellectuals. W.E.B. Du Bois labeled him "the most dangerous enemy of the Negro race in America and in the world." New York City's *Messenger*, a socialist organ that billed itself as "The Only Radical Negro Magazine in America," was less charitable, branding Garvey a "Supreme Negro Jamaican jackass" and the UNIA the "Uninformed Negroes Infamous Association." The editors at the *Messenger* also worked hard to have Garvey deported. That work paid off when he was indicted for mail fraud, then deported to Jamaica in 1927. Garvey died in poverty and obscurity in London in 1940, but his vision endures in movements as disparate as Pentecostalism, Black Judaism, and the Nation of Islam.[32]

Pentecostalism, a form of Christianity characterized by speaking in tongues, began in 1906 at an integrated church on Azusa Street in Los Angeles, but it quickly split into a dizzying array of white and black denominations. One of those groups, now known as "Jesus Only" (or Oneness) Pentecostals, split from the Assemblies of God in 1916 largely over its insistence that individuals baptized according to the standard trinitarian formula be rebaptized in Jesus' name alone. Pushing Jesus-onlyism to the limit, they insisted that the one divine reality underlying the Father, Son, and Holy Spirit was Jesus. Although Oneness Pentecostals did not typically take a stand on the color of Jesus, one mostly black Pentecostal denomination did. The

Church of the Living God adopted the blackness of Jesus as an official doctrine. Its catechism reads:

> *Was Jesus a member of the black race?*
> *Yes. Matthew 1.*
> *How do you know?*
> *Because He was in the line of Abraham and David the king.*
> *Is this assertion sufficient proof that Christ came of the black*
>   *generation?*
> *Yes.*
> *Why?*
> *Because David said he became like a bottle in the smoke.*
>   *Ps. 119:83.*[33]

A REINCARNATION OF MUHAMMAD

The blackness of Jesus is also an article of faith in many black Jewish groups, which carried the African-American preoccupation with Exodus to its logical conclusion. While black Methodists and Baptists drew analogies between African-American and Israelite types, black Jews (also known as black Hebrews and black Israelites), like the Mormons before them, literally identified themselves with the people of Israel.

Black Jewish groups first emerged in the 1880s (in Chattanooga, Tennessee) and 1890s (in Lawrence, Kansas), but flourished in northern cities during the first quarter of the nineteenth century, as African Americans who emigrated from the South during the Great Migration began to interact with Sephardic, Ashkenazic, and Ethiopian Jews in major urban centers. All of these groups followed black church precedents by mixing Christian and Jewish theology with black nationalist themes. Many practiced baptism and footwashing, and heeded the words and example of Jesus. Yet they went beyond the standard creolization of Christianity and Judaism. Most saw African Americans as descendants of the lost tribes of Israel. Some went further, insisting that only black Jews were true Jews, and that Jews of European descent were imposters. Some Jewish leaders responded by dismissing black Jews as inauthentic posers, pointing to their neglect of Jewish Law and the Talmud and their celebration of Christian holidays such as Christmas. But black Jews did observe at least some of the Jewish commandments. Many kept a kosher diet and the Saturday Sabbath. All celebrated Passover, a Jewish high holiday commemorating the deliverance of the Israelites from bondage in Egypt.

The Church of God sounds like a Christian denomination, but it is actually one of the more strident sects in black Judaism. According to F. S. Cherry, the group's founder, both God and Jesus are black. Cherry, who reportedly read Hebrew and Yiddish, was a dynamic speaker. "Jesus Christ was a black man," he would bellow to his congregation, "and I'm offering fifteen hundred dollars cash to anyone who can produce an authentic likeness of Jesus and show I'm wrong." He would then pull out a portrait of a white Christ and sneer, "Who the hell is this? Nobody knows! They say it's Jesus! That's a damned lie! Jesus was black!" Cherry also insisted that Adam and Eve (who were made in God's image) were black. So were all true Jews; the white Jew was a "fraud and interloper." In a clever twist on the racist Hamitic myth (which traced the origins of black people to the biblical curse of Ham), Cherry claimed that the first white person turned that unfortunate color because of a curse.[34]

Many of Cherry's views were echoed by the Nation of Islam, which creatively combined elements from Christianity, Islam, and African-American esoteric groups (including the Moorish Science Temple and the Ahmadiyya movement) into its own syncretic stew. According to NOI doctrine, the first humans were black. White people only emerged when a mad scientist named Yakub produced a morally and physically degenerate race of "blue-eyed devils." Descendants of those devils later stole away the true religion of blacks (Islam) and forced Christianity upon them. But the allotted six-thousand-year reign of those white devils was destined to come to an end in the twentieth century, when a savior would appear and bring blacks back to their ancient glory (and true religion). Black Muslims sneered at Christianity as the white man's religion, and decried the Jews as "a race of devils," but they treated Jesus with kid gloves. Though they denied his divinity and his virgin birth, they embraced him as one of their own—

a Muslim prophet who taught freedom, justice, and equality. And they too rejected the widespread stereotype of the Caucasian Christ. "Christ wasn't white," Malcolm X told *Playboy* in 1963. "Christ was a black man."[35]

The Moorish Science Temple, a precursor to the Nation of Islam, did not depict Jesus as an African American, because its founder, Noble Drew Ali, was attempting to steer blacks toward an alternative identity as "Moors." But this group too called Jesus its own. According to a movement catechism called "Koran Questions for Moorism Americans," Jesus was a "Prophet of Allah" sent "to save the Israelites from the iron-hand oppression of the pale skin nations of Europe who were governing a portion of Palestine at that time." Following his death on the cross, he was reincarnated as the Prophet Muhammad.[36]

ARTISTIC TRANSFIGURATIONS

African-American artists and writers have also created a Jesus they could call their own. During the Harlem Renaissance, which gave expression to a powerful spirit of black pride in the 1920s and 1930s, prints of black Madonnas and black Jesuses began to show up on living room walls across Harlem. Many noted black artists of the era produced black Jesus paintings. In *Catholic New Orleans* (1941), Jacob Lawrence depicted a woman shopping in a store crowded with popular religious art. In this picture, an image of a black Christ hanging on a yellow cross stands out amidst the white crosses and rosaries of this putatively Catholic city. William H. Johnson's *Jesus and Three Marys* (1939) attended to Jesus more directly. This painting is dominated by a black Jesus, hanging on a blue cross and adorned in little more than a yellow halo. His massive hands extend from one side of the canvas to the other, while three black Marys (also in halos) look on with the viewer in horror.

Johnson executed this painting in a style that was self-consciously naive. Other black artists of the twentieth century were unconsciously naive. These practitioners of "outsider art" received none of the formal art training that Lawrence enjoyed in New York and Johnson received in Paris. Yet they created black Jesus images decades before Cleage delivered his Black Messiah sermons. Elijah Pierce of Columbus, Ohio, a barber by trade, was one of the most important African-American sculptors of the twentieth century. He carved bas-relief images in wood and painted them with bright house paints. The son of a Baptist minister (and, like many outsider artists, a minister himself), Pierce produced early in his career some white Jesus sculptures of the Warner Sallman variety, but for the most part he colored Jesus black. In *The Transfiguration* (1936), Pierce outfitted Jesus in white clothing as the Gospel of Matthew 17:2 would seem to require ("his face shone like the sun, and his garments became white as light"), but this Jesus is clearly a black man with dark skin and jet black hair, and his appearance on a mountain in the company of Elijah and Moses exhibits again the African-American tendency to conflate the Old and the New Testaments, Moses and Jesus.

Leroy Almon, a student of Pierce who also worked in bas-relief wood carvings, presented Jesus as an African American too. In a striking crucifixion scene clearly influenced by the black theology of the 1970s, Almon (who was also a lay minister) transformed the two criminals who accompanied Jesus on Golgotha into a white man and a devil. His Jesus is a muscular, dark-skinned black man with black hair and a black beard. Other Almon works, including *The Last Supper* and *Nativity*, place Jesus in all-black worlds, surrounded by black disciples, a black Mary and Joseph, and in some cases scenes from the black South.

In a series of poems in the twenties, Countee Cullen transfigured Jesus into words rather than wood. "Christ's awful wrong is that he's dark of hue," this Methodist minister's son wrote in "Christ Recrucified" (1922). In "Heritage" (1925), he remade God in his own image, only to wonder whether an apology was in order:

> Lord, I fashion dark gods, too,
> Daring even to give You
> Dark despairing features where,
> Crowned with dark rebellious hair,
> Patience wavers just so much as
> Mortal grief compels, while touches

Quick and hot, of anger rise
To smitten cheek and weary eyes.
Lord forgive me if my need
Sometimes shapes a human creed

Cullen's most complete treatment of this subject was his long narrative poem "The Black Christ" (1929), which interpreted the life and death of Jesus in light of lynching in the South. Although largely dismissed by literary critics (probably because of Cullen's unfortunate choice to execute the entire 963-line poem in a tedious rhymed tetrameter), "The Black Christ" was one of the most extensive early treatments of this subject in African-American literature.[37]

Langston Hughes, a more influential Harlem Renaissance poet, also conflated lynching and the crucifixion. His "Christ in Alabama" first appeared in *Scottsboro Limited* (1932), a collection of Hughes's work published to protest the arrests of the "Scottsboro Boys," nine black teenagers accused of gang raping two white girls in Scottsboro, Alabama. In that volume, "Christ in Alabama" is accompanied by a striking Prentiss Taylor print depicting Jesus as a black man crucified above a mournful Black Mammy and cotton ready for harvest. Hughes's poetic depiction of a Southern Christ crucified is one of the most powerful protest poems in American literature:

Christ is a nigger,
Beaten and black:
O, bare your back.

Mary is His mother:
Mammy of the South,
Silence your Mouth.

God's His Father—
White Master above
Grant us your love.

Most holy bastard
Of the bleeding mouth,

Nigger Christ
On the cross of the South.

Following a trip to the Soviet Union in 1932, Hughes wrote an even
more incendiary piece, which earned him pickets from followers of
the evangelist Aimee Semple McPherson and an investigation by the
House Committee on Un-American Activities. In "Goodbye Christ,"
Hughes called the Bible a dead text and blasted popes and preachers
as money-grubbing hypocrites. He then told Jesus (or, more precisely,
the white man's Jesus) where to go:

> Goodbye,
> Christ Jesus Lord God Jehova,
> Beat it on away from here now.
> Make way for a new guy with no religion at all—
> A real guy named
> Marx Communist Lenin Peasant Stalin Worker ME—
> I said, ME!
>
> Go ahead on now,
> You're getting in the way of things, Lord.
> And please take Saint Ghandi with you when you go,
> And Saint Pope Pius,
> And Saint Aimee McPherson,
> And big black Saint Becton
> Of the Consecrated Dime.
> And step on the gas, Christ!
> Move![38]

Of course not all African Americans accepted this black Jesus.
The pioneering black scientist Kelly Miller called Marcus Garvey's
Black God "revolting even to the Negro."[39] Today some African-
American artists continue to depict Jesus with blond hair and
blue eyes, and Warner Sallman's Caucasian Christ can be found in
African-American homes and churches across the country. But black
Jesus pictures are no longer rare, and for most African Americans they
seem to invoke pride rather than revulsion.

Black Jesus images began showing up on stained-glass windows, paintings, and murals in black churches during the 1980s as Afrocentrist thinking spread from campuses to congregations and more and more African Americans came to see Africa as the fountainhead of both Judaism and Christianity. In the 1990s, those images proliferated in Bibles specifically designed for black Americans, including *The Original African Heritage Study Bible* (1993) and the *African American Jubilee Edition* (1999). "We look at this as a major movement," explained Maurice Jenkins, an artist responsible for a black Jesus mural in Ebenezer African Methodist Church in Fort Washington, Maryland. "The slave trade took away our culture and our religion, and now this is a natural progression for the black church to revitalize the African traditions that were taken away."[40]

While some activists produced and distributed images of a black Jesus, others worked on uprooting images of the "honky Christ." During the late 1970s, a group called the Committee to Remove All Images of the Divine (CRAID), founded by Wallace D. Muhammad—the son and successor to Elijah Muhammad of the Nation of Islam—took a page out of the book of former UNIA chaplain Archbishop George Alexander McGuire when it organized protests against white Jesus images, though in this case they objected on both racial and Islamic grounds. In the 1990s, Archbishop George A. Stallings, Jr., an excommunicated Afrocentrist Roman Catholic priest and leader of the breakaway denomination the African-American Catholic Congregation, stood in Freedom Plaza in Washington, D.C., and held a lighter to an image of a white Jesus. In an effort to publicize his Black Church/Black Christ Project, which aimed to place black images of Jesus in black churches across the country, Stallings called on his followers to deposit other graven images of a blue-eyed, blond-haired Jesus—including Sallman's *Head of Christ*—in a coffin, and put that imposter forever to rest. "Burn the lie. Burn the lie," Stallings said, adding, "The black Jesus is coming back again." Three days later, on Easter, that black Jesus rose from the dead as promised when Stallings unveiled a portrait of Jesus as an "Afro-Asiatic Jew" at his Imani Temple in Washington, D.C.[41]

During the 1990s and 2000s, Black Jesus pictures also proliferated outside the churches in the art world. Janet McKenzie won the "Jesus

2000" contest sponsored by the *National Catholic Reporter* with an oil painting of a New Age Jesus, framed by a yin-yang symbol on the left and a feather symbolizing Native American spirituality on the right. Although the African features of McKenzie's *Jesus of the People* were unmistakable, the gender of her Jesus was ambiguous, thanks in part to an oversized black and white cassock that covered his/her body. Not so for the gender-bending Jesus of Renee Cox's *Yo Mama's Last Supper*, which created yet another Jesus flap when the Brooklyn Museum of Art put it on display in 2001.

YO MAMA'S BLACK JESUS

Inside the African-American community, "Yo Mama" jokes abound. "Yo Mama's so old," goes one, "she owes Moses a quarter." "Yo Mama's so old," goes another, "she was a waitress at the Last Supper." So Cox's controversial work is an inside joke of sorts. It too places Jesus at the Last Supper, but this Jesus is not taking orders. *Yo Mama's Last Supper* (1996) consists of five large color photographic panels, depicting twelve men at the supper table: eleven black men (one garbed in a nun's habit) and a white Judas. In the center panel stands a black Jesus, arms outstretched, but only belly high, in a gesture that suggests both the crucifixion and the celebration of the Eucharist. Unlike McKenzie's fully clothed *Jesus of the People*, Cox's Jesus is naked except for a pure white stole wrapped around both wrists (recalling, perhaps, the chains of slave Christianity). And her full-breasted Jesus is obviously female. In fact, she is Cox herself.

 Yo Mama's Last Supper was intended to shock. Renee Cox had seen the fame (and infamy) that fell on Andres Serrano after he showed *Piss Christ*, a photograph of a crucifix submerged in his urine, in the late 1980s. And she had tasted a bit of that celebrity herself after she appeared on the cover of *Le Monde*, as a comic book superheroine liberating Uncle Ben and Aunt Jemima from racist stereotypes. Cox knew that Jesus was a powerful icon and that, in a society with fewer and fewer taboos, startling images of him could still scandalize. Nonetheless, her *Last Supper* might have shocked only a few dozen people were it not for New York City's mayor, Rudolph Giuliani, who made Cox's career (as Senator Jesse Helms had earlier made Andres Serrano's) when he lambasted the picture as anti-Catholic. "If you want to desecrate religion in a disgusting way, if you want to promote racism, if you want to promote anti-Semitism, if you want to promote anti-Catholicism, if you want to promote anti-Islamism, then do it on your own money," the mayor said. "Don't use the taxpayers' money to do that." Once Giuliani got into the scrum, other traditionalists piled on. William Donohue, president of the Catholic League, derided Cox's "shock art" as "Catholic bashing" of the worst sort. Edward M. Egan, the Archbishop of New York, personalized the attack, diagnosing Cox as a "pathetic individual." "Sophisticates say this art is fine," he said from the pulpit of New York City's historic St. Patrick's Cathedral. "We stand for what is right and decent. We live the life of Jesus Christ against the tide without applause and only ridicule."[42]

Cox, who was born in Jamaica and grew up in the Catholic Church, characterized the controversy as much ado about skin color. "There are plenty of images of a nude Christ," she said. "My guess after all of this hoopla is that it is a question of race. People have a problem with the fact that it's an African-American woman at the head of the dinner table." Following African-American interpreters from Turner to Cleage, who traced their black God all the way back to Genesis 1:27 ("So God created man in his own image"), Cox contended, "We are all created in the likeness of God; there shouldn't be any problem with anyone presenting themselves as such."[43]

Although Cox's work is part of a broader contemporary impulse to shock patrons of the arts, it stands as well in a long line of African-American reinterpretations of Jesus. Cox calls her broader effort to inject black actors into biblical dramas "flippin' the script."[44] Others call it "conjure" and trace the practice back to West African conjure men, trained in the art of using toxic herbs to tonic effect. A more proximate influence on Cox's work is likely womanist theology. Cox spent considerable time reading about black history at the Schomburg Center for Research in Black Culture in New York City, and she is fond of quoting womanist thinkers such as bell hooks. *Yo Mama's Last Supper* can be understood, therefore, as a reinterpretation not only of Da Vinci's classic but also of womanist theology—a translation of Alice

Walker's call for "outrageous, audacious, courageous, or *willful* behavior" into the visual arts.

Another key influence on Cox's work is America's Black Jesus tradition, which has been conjuring Jesus for freedom for centuries. Like Marcus Garvey (who also hailed from Jamaica), Cox was influenced by Roman Catholicism but has by her own account moved beyond it. In fact, she has rejected organized religion entirely. Nonetheless, she appreciates the iconic power of Jesus (and the power of iconoclasm as well).

Given the history of slavery and segregation, and of efforts by Christians to baptize both as godly institutions, it may be surprising that more African Americans have not followed Cox in a mass exodus out of "white man's religion." African Americans turned to Protestantism en masse during late-eighteenth-century revivals, in part because evangelicalism seemed to echo key beliefs, practices, and sensibilities of West African religious traditions. Today they remain extraordinarily Christianized—more likely than whites to attend church, read the Bible, and report a close relationship with Jesus. Blacks did not become or remain Christians because they were duped. They did so because they were able to make Christianity their own. In *Narrative of the Life of Frederick Douglass, an American Slave* (1845), perhaps the most influential slave narrative in American history, the abolitionist orator Frederick Douglass came close to rejecting Christianity. He fiercely attacked as hypocritical the faith that had produced "men-stealers for ministers, women-whippers for missionaries, and cradle-plunderers for church members." And for his attacks, some branded him an infidel. But Douglass was no more an infidel than Thomas Jefferson. Like Jefferson, he distinguished between "the Christianity of this land, and the Christianity of Christ," recognizing "the widest possible distance" between the two. American religion, Douglass wrote, was "the climax of all misnomers, the boldest of all frauds, and the grossest of all libels." He hated "the corrupt, slaveholding, women-whipping, cradle-plundering, partial and hypocritical Christianity of this land." But that hatred only made him love "the pure, peaceable, and impartial Christianity of Christ" all the more.[45]

As Douglass and other African Americans tailored the Christian tradition to fit their New World circumstances and West African roots, a new form of Christianity emerged. One of the distinguishing marks of the black church today is its thoroughgoing biblicism. While *sola scriptura* gave way to *solus Jesus* in many mainline Protestant congregations in the late nineteenth century, black believers held fast to both Jesus and the Bible, reading the Bible through the person of Jesus and Jesus through the books of the Bible. Popular pictures of Jesus by African-American artists typically present their subject in a recognizable Bible story, eschewing the head-and-shoulders portraits that came to dominate most Jesus art after World War II. Fred Carter's *Jesus Praying in the Garden* (1987), for example, concedes something to the popular portrait genre by presenting a closeup of his black Jesus, but the setting is plainly the Garden of Gethsemane and the moment is when Jesus prayed, "Let this cup pass from me" (Matthew 26:39).

Although African Americans typically depict Jesus in New Testament scenes, they continue to see him as an heir of the kings and prophets of the Old Testament. Like many other Christians, black Christians see Jesus as a Suffering Servant who by carrying their sins onto the cross made salvation possible. But they merge that New Testament Jesus with the Old Testament Moses, creating one Black Moses who cares about this world as much as the next, who delivers them from oppression as well as sin. Then, as if to ensure that this Redeemer truly lives, they reincarnate him, again and again, in black women and men as diverse as Marcus Garvey, Harriet Tubman, and the Reverend Martin Luther King, Jr.

This commitment to reincarnating Jesus is powerfully on display in a Last Supper mural at Union Temple Baptist Church, a congregation of some 7,000 in the nation's capital. Like the dome unveiled at St. Cecelia's in Detroit in 1968, this massive 19-by-30-foot mural places a black Jesus in the company of angels. Only this time all the angels are black. Here Garvey, Tubman, and King appear in a pantheon of black saints surrounding a militant black Jesus ascending to heaven. This Jesus, described on the church's Web site as "a Black Man of African Hebrew Descent," is both massive and muscular. His eyes are fiery. His hands, recalling those in Johnson's *Jesus and the Three*

Marys, are huge. He looks, in other words, as if he could easily play the part assigned to him by Charlie Braxton in the 1990 poem "Apocalypse":

> *beware*
> *jesus is a big mean assed black man*
> *painted smokey grey*
> *and boy is he mad pissed off*[46]

Below this martial Jesus—part Hebrew patriarch, part apocalyptic warrior—twelve apostles of black history sit or stand as if at the Last Supper, many clad in traditional African clothing that mirrors the pattern on the stole draped across Jesus' strong left shoulder. Garvey, Tubman, and King are accompanied by Frederick Douglass and Nelson Mandela. Elijah Muhammad, Malcolm X, and Louis Farrakhan of the Nation of Islam are there too, transformed by the artist's imagination into disciples of Jesus. In a nod to womanist theology (and the civil rights movement), Rosa Parks and Dorothy Height also have an honored place at the table.

This image testifies not only to the tendency of African Americans to color Jesus black but also to the determination, born on slave plantations, to see Jesus reincarnated, over and over again, in the experiences of African Americans. For centuries, African Americans have embraced Jesus as a Savior who by carrying their sins on the cross made possible their salvation. But they have not simply adopted a white Jesus into their black families. Like the conjure men of West Africa, they have transformed the toxin of the blond-haired, blue-eyed Jesus into the tonic of a black Moses who delivers them not only from sin but also from oppression, and not only via his own body but also in the bodies of the faithful.

Seven

RABBI

President John F. Kennedy once called Christmas "the universal holiday of all men," adding that "Moslems, Hindus, Buddhists, as well as Christians, pause from their labors on the 25th day of December to celebrate the birthday of the Prince of Peace."[1] Conveniently, he left out Jews, who have not traditionally commemorated Jesus' birthday. But as Kennedy's remarks indicate (and U.S. Supreme Court rulings affirm), Christmas has become both a holy day and a holiday in the United States, and the line between its spiritual and its secular purposes seems harder to draw each year. As a result, Jewish Americans struggle at Christmastime with how to stay faithful to both their religious tradition and their nation. Should they decorate trees? Exchange gifts? Open their homes to Santa Claus? And what should they make of Jesus?

On the Sunday before Christmas in 1925 a crowd of about three thousand people gathered in Carnegie Hall in New York City to hear Rabbi Stephen S. Wise speak on "A Jew's View of Jesus." Wise began by affirming the reality of the historical Jesus: "For years I have been led to believe, like thousands of other Jews, that Jesus never existed

. . . I say this is not so. Jesus was."[2] Jesus was a Jew, not a Christian, he continued, and Jews should accept him as one of their own. Wise's remarks sparked a firestorm in the faith, prompting a reevaluation of the place of Jesus in American Judaism and of Judaism in American culture. Was Jesus really a Jew? Was Wise following in the footsteps of Paul, the original apostate? How far would Jews go in accommodating themselves to American culture and its Christian majority? How far should they go?

Wise (1874–1949) was born in Budapest, and came to New York with his family as an infant. Like his father and grandfather before him, he studied for the rabbinate and was ordained. Aligning himself with Reform Judaism, he worked to accommodate the Jewish tradition to the facts of science, the rules of reason, and the reality of progress. But he distinguished himself from most of his Reform colleagues by affirming enthusiastically the Zionist cause. While other Reformers argued that pining for another homeland would invite anti-Semitism and prevent Jews from becoming full participants in American society, Wise affirmed the sentiment of his friend, the U.S. Supreme Court Justice Louis Brandeis, who said that "to be good Americans, we must be better Jews, and to be better Jews, we must become Zionists."[3] By 1925, Wise was running the United Palestine Appeal, a new Zionist organization dedicated to raising the unprecedented sum of $5 million in its inaugural campaign.

As Wise rose to prominence in American Judaism and the international Zionist movement, he worked closely with leading Democratic Party politicians and liberal Protestant ministers. Embracing a version of the Social Gospel that placed social activism at the center of the religious life, he assisted in the foundation of both the National Association for the Advancement of Colored People (NAACP) in 1919 and the American Civil Liberties Union (ACLU) in 1920. In 1922 in New York City, he established a Reform seminary called the Jewish Institute of Religion.

Though a mover and shaker in political circles, Wise made his reputation as an orator. In 1906, he was courted for a prestigious post at Temple Emanu-El, New York City's oldest Reform temple and now putatively the largest Reform congregation in the world. But after learning that the temple's board of trustees insisted on controlling the pulpit, he boldly withdrew his name. He then sent a letter to *The New York Times* explaining his decision, and his commitment to the open pulpit. "The chief office of the minister, I take it, is not to represent the view of the congregation, but to proclaim the truth as he sees it," Wise wrote. "In the pursuit of the duties of his office, the minister may from time to time be under the necessity of giving expression to views at variance with the views of some, or even many, members of the congregation."[4]

In order to give free expression to his often controversial views, Wise founded the Free Synagogue, which met in a theater and later a Universalist sanctuary before settling in 1910 in Carnegie Hall, which was then typically dark on Sunday mornings. That grand venue, along with Wise's oratorical gifts, attracted a few thousand congregants on some weeks (as well as curious journalists), turning Wise into the best-known rabbi in the United States—the Billy Sunday of American Judaism. One distinguishing mark of the Free Synagogue was its Sunday morning meetings, which were designed as an alternative to what Wise saw as the pulseless services traditionally held on the Saturday Sabbath. During one of those Sunday gatherings, on December 20, 1925, Wise delivered his most notorious sermon.

"A JEW'S VIEW OF JESUS"

"A Jew's View of Jesus" was in large measure an appreciative review of an important book on Jesus written by a pro-Zionist scholar at Hebrew University in Jerusalem. Joseph Klausner's *Jesus of Nazareth*, published in Hebrew in 1922 and in English in 1925, rejected claims by scholars such as Ernest Renan that there was no Judaism in Jesus, and by racists such as Houston Stewart Chamberlain that Jesus was an Aryan. Jesus, it argued, was drenched in the Jewish culture of Palestine. Klausner criticized Jesus for possessing "exaggerated self-confidence" bordering on "self-veneration," but praised him too—as "a great teacher of morality and an artist in parable" and "a true Jew of the Jewish family." Neither God nor the Messiah, his Jesus was a powerful teacher whose ethical precepts, while at times impracticable and otherworldly, evinced nonetheless "a sublimity, distinctiveness and originality in form unparalleled in any other Hebrew ethical code." Echoing Jefferson, Klausner depicted Jesus as a "moralist and world-reformer," and the rhetorical flourish that closed his book somehow seemed to indicate both the debt that Klausner owed to the Sage of Monticello and his ignorance of the Jefferson Bible: "If ever the day should come and [Jesus'] ethical code be stripped of its wrappings of miracles and mysticism," he wrote, "the Book of the Ethics of Jesus will be one of the choicest treasures in the literature of Israel for all time."[5]

At Carnegie Hall that day, Wise also reclaimed Jesus for Judaism. He began by repudiating the view, promulgated by the nineteenth-century German scholar Bruno Bauer, that Jesus never existed. On the contrary, Wise affirmed, "Jesus was." But what exactly was he? According to Wise, a fairly typical Jew. The Jesus of history belonged in his view not at the right hand of God, but in a line of great Jewish teachers running from Abraham and Moses to Micah and Amos. Unfortunately, Christians had failed to accept Jesus for who he really was. But American Jews could do better, accepting the rabbi from Nazareth as a Jewish prophet who, like Jeremiah (and, for that matter, Wise himself) called down God's righteous wrath on injustice and oppression.

"A Jew's View of Jesus" provoked a barrage of criticism from American Jews and attracted a long line of rubbernecking Christians keen to glimpse the carnage Wise had wrought. Perhaps because of the emotions the talk stirred up, many U.S. newspapers and magazines misunderstood the controversy. Editors at *The New York Times*, for example, mistakenly thought the debate was about whether Jesus had actually lived. The "Jesus myth" theory had undergone a modest revival around the turn of the century in Europe, but it never gained much traction in the United States. So the existence of the historical Jesus was not the real issue. Neither did the controversy turn on Wise's proclamation of Jesus' Jewishness, since that too was old news, at least in Reform circles. The real question was the direction American Judaism was heading.

Then, as now, American Judaism was divided into three main branches: Reform, Conservative, and Orthodox. In each community, the key dilemma was reconciling Jewishness and Americanness—finding the right balance between integration and segregation. As a rule, Reform Jews eagerly adapted their tradition to American circumstances, while the Orthodox fiercely opposed assimilation. The Conservatives split the difference, siding with the Reformers on some matters (Biblical criticism and mixed gender synagogue seating, for example) and with the Orthodox on others (such as the authority of Jewish Law, and the necessity of circumcision).

Jews also divided over their views of the United States, and the possibility and desirability of becoming full participants in American society. Reformers, embracing the promises of religious freedom and the separation of church and state, typically saw the United States as a secular country, and they remained optimistic about the willingness of Christians to accept Jews as equal participants in it. The Orthodox usually saw the United States as a Christian country, where anti-Semitism was rife and the hope for integration naive. Fierce opponents of Americanization, they saw the Reformers as a gang of David Levinskys, eager accommodaters who, like the title character in Abraham Cahan's *The Rise of David Levinsky* (1917), would happily sacrifice Jewish Law (and identity) on the altar of American success. From their perspective, the overeager assimilationism of the Reformers would result in a litany of liberal horrors, including intermarriage and conversions to Christianity.

These divergent views were rooted, of course, in different social and economic circumstances. The Orthodox were dominated by new arrivals from Eastern Europe, many of them poor, and many able to speak only Yiddish. The Reformers had typically come from Germany much earlier in the nineteenth century, spoke fluent English, and had achieved for themselves some measure of economic success and social acceptance. They did not want strict observance of the Levitical codes to prevent them from enjoying closer relations with their Christian neighbors.

As of 1925, Reform Judaism was the dominant branch in American Jewry. But the arrival of roughly 2.5 million Jews, mostly from Eastern Europe, over the prior half century threatened that dominance, as did the rapid growth of the Conservative option, which many were coming to see as a classic compromise between those who never saw an Americanization they didn't like and those who viewed the United States as a *trefa medinah* (an unclean land).[6]

The fiercest attacks on Wise came from the Orthodox-run and New York–based Yiddish newspapers, which argued that he was flirting with the idols of Americanism, including the Christian God. *Der Morgen Journal* ran an anti-Wise editorial with a thick black border. This symbol of mourning intimated that this renegade rabbi, if unchecked, would preside over the death of American Judaism (or, perhaps, that its editors were already sitting shiva for Wise the apostate). *Tageblatt* said Wise was luring "the younger generation to the baptismal font." *Der Tag* flayed him for treating Jesus like family. "Does not Doctor Wise know how much of our blood has been shed for the God whom he now wants to adopt?" Before long, rabbinic groups formally censured Wise. The Union of Orthodox Rabbis chastised him for threatening to "drive our children to conversion." Young Israel, an organization of Orthodox youth, passed a resolution characterizing Wise's sermon as a "grave menace to Judaism." Agudath Harabonim, a particularly strict group of Orthodox rabbis, effectively excommunicated him.[7]

Although the fiercest invective came from the Orthodox camp, some Reformers, mistaking Wise's call for the conversion of Jesus to Judaism for a call for the conversion of Jews to Christianity, turned on him too. Rabbi George Solomon of Temple Mickve Israel in Savannah, Georgia, one of the oldest Jewish congregations in the United States, chastised his colleague for thinking "more of the continued glory of Stephen S. Wise than of the cause which he is serving." Dr. Henry Leffmann of Philadelphia said that Wise's remarks, rather than undercutting anti-Semitism, would "simply put ammunition into the hands of the KKK." The most acerbic Reform critique came from Rabbi Samuel Schulman of Temple Beth-El in New York City who, like Solomon, accused his rival of grandstanding. "The sensationalist of the Jewish Pulpit is again on the rampage," he told *The New York Times*. "Rabbi Wise's remarks were entirely uncalled for. It is an indisputable fact that to the consciousness of Christendom Jesus is more than a man. He is therefore impossible for any Jew. When Christians will cease calling Jesus God, Israel will know what to do with him as a man."[8]

In a sermon on "Judaism, Jesus and the Decadence in the Reform Jewish Pulpit," Schulman ratcheted up his rhetoric, labeling Wise's homily an "outrage" and characterizing as "indelicate and undignified" Wise's propensity for giving birth to Jesus every Christmas and resurrecting him each Easter. Although Schulman did not say that Wise intended to convert his listeners to Christianity, he insisted that the slope from lauding Jesus to embracing Christianity was as slippery as it was steep. Whereas Wise had drawn a sharp distinction between the "religion of Jesus" (which he valued) and the "religion about Jesus" (which he criticized), Schulman insisted that the two were one and the same. "Conversion to Jesus" was in his view "the first step in the conversion to Christianity." In fact, "any Jewish Congregation that accepted Jesus as teacher," Schulman prophesied, "would be merged in Christianity within a generation."[9]

Toward the end of this sermon, Schulman may have revealed his hand when he labeled Wise an "intense Jewish Nationalist and racialist and Zionist."[10] By the 1920s, many Reform rabbis in the United States had come around to supporting Zionism. But Schulman argued that their Zionism would only produce a secular Israel, something he could never countenance. Clearly this denunciation of "decadence in the Reform Jewish pulpit" was in some measure a judgment against the "Americanized Zionism" of the Brandeis camp. So was the decision by Mizrachi, a lay organization promoting religious Zionism, to call for Wise to resign as chairman of the United Palestine Appeal. Wise responded to that demand, first, by describing the whole affair as a huge misunderstanding and, second, by tendering his resignation, an action that immediately rallied the troops to his cause.

During the Jesus controversy, as it came to be known, many Reform rabbis delivered sermons echoing Wise's views. Rabbi Sidney S. Tedesche of New Haven praised Jesus as a "great moral teacher," and Rabbi Samuel M. Gup of Providence called him "a religious genius of the first rank." In another Christmas sermon, Rabbi Lewis Browne of Newark, New Jersey, said, "I believe that Jesus lived, that he was a Jew, and that he preached Jewish doctrines." Rabbi Hyman Enelow may have presented the most vigorous defense. He began a sermon at Temple Emanu-El (where Wise had turned down a post) by criticizing Jews who exhibited "an excessive admiration for Jesus" by going "into ecstasies over his teachings." He then proceeded to wax ecstatic himself, exceeding even Wise in rhapsodizing about Jesus the Jew. "Jesus

has become the most eminent personage in the religious life of western civilization, and possibly of the whole civilized world," Enelow
told his congregation, adding that Jesus was nonetheless "a loyal
member and lover of the Jewish faith."[11]

Liberal Protestants, eager for closer ties between Jews and Christians in an era beset with anti-Semitism, also came to Wise's defense.
Christian Century, Christian Advocate, Churchman, and *Independent*
all published pro-Wise pieces, and many Protestant ministers delivered sermons defending the rabbi's views of Jesus. In a letter to *The
New York Times,* Edwin Knox Mitchell of Hartford Theological Seminary wrote, "Rabbi Wise of New York has done a noble and courageous thing in accepting the moral and spiritual leadership of Jesus. It
is a first step toward religious toleration and racial reconciliation. And
Christians of all creeds ought to welcome this manifestation of the
spirit of the founder of their faith." Harry Emerson Fosdick, one of
the leading spokesmen for liberal Protestantism in this period, called
the rabbi "the best Christian in New York." Such support was a mixed
blessing for Wise, since it only reinforced his critics' claim that he had
all but embraced Christianity. Looking back later on criticism by Orthodox rabbis and support from Christian ministers, he wrote, "I
know not which was more hurtful—the acceptance of me as brother
and welcoming me into the Christian fold or the violent diatribe of a
fellow rabbi."[12]

On top of this outpouring of Reform and Protestant support came
a sprinkle of Conservative Jewish approbation. In a letter to Wise,
Solomon Goldman, a Conservative rabbi from Cleveland (and a fellow Zionist), wrote, "No sane Jew doubts your loyalty to the eternal
ideals of Israel." Rabbi Max D. Klein of Philadelphia, speaking on behalf of the Rabbinical Assembly of the Jewish Theological Seminary
(a Conservative stronghold), said that both Wise and the Agudath
Harabonim had sinned, but that Wise should stay on "for the sake of
Zionism." Wise's most important defender, however, was the Macy's
owner and Jewish philanthropist Nathan Straus, who on Christmas
Day wrote to Wise urging him to stay on as chairman of the United
Palestine Appeal and announcing a gift of $650,000 for welfare work
in Palestine.[13]

In the end, supporters such as Straus saved Wise's position. When the *Jewish Daily Bulletin* conducted a straw poll of 205 Zionist leaders, 190 said they wanted Wise to continue as chairman. The Zionist Organization of America voted overwhelmingly (71–1) for him to stay on. The most decisive ballot came on January 3, 1926, when the executive committee of the UPA officially refused, by a margin of 59–9, to accept Wise's resignation. Later that day, Wise rose to thank his colleagues, concluding his brief talk with this Hebrew affirmation from the biblical book of Jonah: *"Ivri Anochi"*—"I am a Hebrew."[14]

NOTHING NEW

Wise's opponents acted as if the middle-aged rabbi were an *enfant terrible* who had committed the unprecedented sin of sidling up to Jesus. Yet nothing Wise said about Jesus was groundbreaking. In fact, virtually all his arguments had been advanced by other American rabbis many times before.

During the middle ages, European Jews had responded to Jesus largely by ignoring him. In an era where Christians routinely charged Jews with the crime of deicide, even the name of Jesus was taboo in most Jewish circles. Jewish texts that dared to mention him typically referred to Jesus as "that man" or "the hanged one," and their judgment of the man was nearly as harsh as the Christians' depiction of Jews as "Christ-killers." The classic medieval treatment was *Toledoth Yeshu*, a popular life of Jesus that likely circulated as folklore as early as the sixth century before being put on paper around the tenth. In this incendiary text, Jesus is an illegitimate child conceived by rape who grows up to become a sorcerer adept at black magic. Klausner dismissed *Toledoth Yeshu* as a fable, yet even as fable the text exemplifies the hostility of pre-modern Jews to Jesus, a hostility rooted, it should be noted, in centuries of violence against Jews by Christians.

With the Enlightenment of the eighteenth century and increasing freedom for European Jews came more generous interpretations of Jesus. Most in the Orthodox community continued to treat Jesus as a pariah. In fact, as late as the 1920s, the Orthodox scholar Aaron Kaminka, writing about Klausner's book in the New York–based *Ha-Toren*, would refer to Jesus only as "that man."[15] But as Jews gained civil rights and Jewish-Christian relations improved in many European countries, some liberal Jews began to speak his name and laud his teachings.

Joseph Salvador, a French Jew, began the reclamation process with *Jésus-Christ et sa doctrine* ("Jesus Christ and His Teachings"), a two-volume study published in Paris in 1838, only three years after D. F. Strauss's *Life of Jesus*. While Strauss had prepared the way for modern biblical criticism, Salvador inaugurated the modern Jewish view of Jesus—as a Jew tragically miscast as a Christian. Soon the thesis of Jesus' Jewishness was so widespread in European Jewish circles that the only debate about him seemed to be what sort of Jew he had been. Was he a rabbi of the Pharisaic school, as the German scholar Abraham Geiger argued? A member of the breakaway ascetic community the Essenes, as Geiger's countryman Heinrich Graetz (and Salvador) contended? Or the spiritual original that Claude Montefiore of England made him out to be?

In the United States, Wise also had forerunners. One of the most important was Isaac Mayer Wise (no relation), a key transitional figure who began his career doubting the existence of Jesus and concluded it with a string of sermons and books on the man he had come to respect as a "Pharisean doctor of the Hillel school."[16] Widely regarded as the father of Reform Judaism in the United States, Wise (1819–1900) played a key role in the founding of the Union of American Hebrew Congregations (in 1873), Hebrew Union College (in 1875), and the Central Conference of American Rabbis (in 1889). He also presided over the drafting of the famed Pittsburgh Platform (1885)—Judaism's "Declaration of Independence," in Wise's oft-quoted formulation—which definitively allied his brand of Judaism with reason rather than revelation, ethics rather than rites, science rather than superstition, and prophets rather than priests.

Like other Reform leaders of his generation, Wise was intent on integrating Jews into American culture, and he understood that rabbis needed to weigh in on Christianity if their people were ever going to move into the religious and cultural mainstream. Wise wrote a series of books on Christianity, and published an important collection of essays called "Jesus Himself," initiated in 1869 in his weekly *The Israelite*. In many respects the arc of his theology mirrored Thomas Jefferson's theological development. Like Jefferson, Wise initially dismissed Jesus, in part because he could not imagine a Jesus liberated from Christian dogmatism and scriptural half-truths. But once he felt empowered to distinguish the religion of Jesus from the religion about Jesus, he embraced the Galilean rabbi as one of his own. For Jefferson, of course, this unbound Jesus was an enlightened sage and a fierce critic of Jewish authorities. For Wise, he was a Jewish Pharisee and patriot martyred not by the Jews but by the Romans (because of his agitation for the liberation of his people from Roman occupation). Wise also resembled Jefferson in his homespun approach to biblical criticism. Though he was familiar with German scholarship on the New Testament (by Christians and Jews alike), he was no Bible scholar himself. As one biographer put it, he was "a shrewd, self-taught homiletician who wrote farfetched things."[17]

The work of Isaac Mayer Wise represented a major step toward the appreciative view of Jesus that would dominate Reform Judaism in the United States by the end of the nineteenth century. While prior American Jewish thinkers had largely ignored the central symbol of Christianity, Wise rightly discerned that in modern America Jesus was an unavoidable presence. Then, as today, to be an American was to reckon with Jesus. If Jews ignored him, Wise reasoned, they would forfeit their claim on mainstream status and leave defining the symbol of Jesus (and wielding its power) to Christians alone. And so, while Bushnell and Beecher were making Jesus into a sentimental Protestant, Wise recast him as a Jew. His restoration of Jesus' Jewishness stopped shy of embracing Jesus with pride. But in time American Jewish attitudes toward Jesus would move beyond restoration to reclamation, and Jesus would be recast as one of the greatest rabbis of all time.

"A PEOPLE OF CHRISTS"

Though rooted in earlier work by Salvador in France, Geiger and Graetz in Germany, and Montefiore in England, this reclamation process flowered in the United States, spurred on by scholarship in the first quest for the historical Jesus. The key decade was the 1890s, which saw an outpouring of writing on Jesus by Reform rabbis. Two of the most notable contributors were Kaufmann Kohler and his brother-in-law Emil G. Hirsch, who together cast Jesus as a proto-Reform Jew—a prophetic figure who, like themselves, labored to push the tradition from tribalism to universalism, ritualism to freedom.

Born in Bavaria, Kohler (1843–1926) came to the United States in 1869 to serve the Beth-El Congregation in Detroit, and quickly emerged as a major voice in the U.S. Reform community. He spear-headed the adoption of the Pittsburgh Platform in 1885, and suc-ceeded Isaac Mayer Wise as president of Hebrew Union College in 1903. Hirsch (1851–1923), who was born in Luxembourg, was influ-enced as a university student by the *Wissenschaft des Judentums* ("Sci-ence of Judaism") school and its critical analysis of Jewish history and scriptures. After coming to the United States in 1869, he served as a rabbi in Baltimore and Louisville before succeeding Kohler in the pul-pit at Chicago Sinai Congregation. In 1892 he took a position as pro-fessor of rabbinic literature and philosophy at the University of Chicago. For more than three decades he edited the *Reform Advocate*, an important organ for the U.S. Reform community. Both Kohler and Hirsch were keenly interested in Jewish-Christian dialogue, a cause they advanced as representatives of the Jewish community at the World's Parliament of Religions in Chicago in 1893.

Kaufmann Kohler, in works such as *Moses and Jesus* (1892) and *Je-sus of Nazareth from a Jewish Point of View* (1899), drew a sharp con-trast between Jesus and Paul. In fact, he traced all that was wrong in Christianity to Paul, whom he described as an "irritable, ghost-seeing fanatic from the Greek isle of Tarsos, who acted like an infuriated zealot when in Judea, and poured forth all the wrath of his hot temper against the Jews." Jesus, by contrast, Kohler welcomed as "one of the best and truest sons of the Synagogue." Following Graetz, he saw Je-sus as an Essene rather than a Pharisee. He focused, however, not on Jesus' asceticism but on his love of ordinary people. For Kohler, Jesus was a "helper of the poor" and a "sympathizing friend of the fallen." Admittedly, he was a tad overcivilized, lacking "the element of stern justice expressed so forcibly in the Law and in the Old Testament characters, the firmness of self-assertion so necessary to the full de-velopment of manhood, and all those social qualities which build up home and society, industry and worldly progress." But he was none-theless a "unique exponent of the principle of redeeming love."[18]

Hirsch could not resist criticizing Jesus for not marrying, yet he too praised him as a magnetic man of the people and an orator of beauty. In *The Jews and Jesus* (1893), Hirsch denounced the *Toledoth Yeshu* as "a pasquille of the vilest sort" and "a cesspool of all nastiness." Calling Jesus "a noble character," he reclaimed him as a Jew. "The Jew, of whatever shade of opinion, is willing to acknowledge the charm, the beauty, the whole-souled perfection of the great prophet of Nazareth," Hirsch wrote. "He belongs to us; we have not rejected him." Following Geiger (with whom he had studied in Europe) and his own father, Samuel Hirsch (who had also written on Jesus), Hirsch insisted that Jesus' teachings were neither unique nor original, at least in terms of content, since what he taught was "the echo of the doctrines he himself had heard from the lips of his own Jewish masters." Jesus' impatience with legalistic moralizing, his disdain for empty ceremony, and his attention to intention in ethics were all inheritances from Judaism rather than gifts to it. The Sermon on the Mount was a Jewish sermon, firmly rooted in the disputations of the Talmud. The Lord's Prayer, which contained "not a single gem but had graced in some form or other the crown worn by the synagogue," was a revision of the Kaddish supplication. Even the Golden Rule was borrowed—from Confucius and the great Talmudic sage Hillel.[19]

Hirsch did grant, however, that Jesus expressed that old content in a new way: "His words have the stamp of great genius; not so much for what they say, as for the manner in which they are put forth." While the Pharisees, Sadducees, and Essenes of his day all considered themselves above ordinary folk, Jesus spoke a language common people could understand. And because of the new wineskins in which he put the old wine of his Jewish youth, "his words became the ready moral currency of the world."[20]

Of all the nineteenth-century arguments for reclaiming Jesus, this one from Hirsch's "The Doctrines of Jesus" may summarize the Reformers' position most eloquently and succinctly:

> He was of us; he is of us. We quote the rabbis of the Talmud; shall we then, not also quote the rabbi of Bethlehem? Shall not he in whom there burned, if it burned in any one, the spirit and the light of Judaism, be reclaimed by the synagogue? . . . Happy

this day when Judaism finds again her son, the son comes back to the mother laden with the rich reward of this quest. The New Testament in the gospels presents Jewish thought, Jewish religion, Jewish universalism. Not an advance beyond Judaism, but a correspondence with Judaism, we have in the doctrine of Jesus, who was Jew and man.[21]

The Prodigal Son is, of course, a New Testament parable, typically interpreted by Christian clerics as a message about the mercy offered by God to all sinners. Here Hirsch places a Jewish Jesus into that Christian story, casting him as son who had forsaken his mother's home, and reinterpreting his reunion with his Jewish family as a tale of exile and return.

The broad context for such reincarnations of Jesus was Christian missions to the Jews. "Why do you reject Jesus?" the Christians asked. To which Hirsch and his colleagues replied, "We don't." They then went to some lengths to explain precisely whom they were accepting (Jesus the *mensch*) and whom not (Jesus the Messiah). Another context for these reincarnations was Christian anti-Semitism, especially the ancient accusation that the Jews had killed Jesus. During the medieval period, some Jews had responded to this charge by claiming that they had indeed killed Jesus, and would happily do so again, given his false claims of divinity and messiahship. Salvador had argued a similar line in his 1838 book. But Hirsch, Kohler, and Isaac Mayer Wise denied accusations of deicide as the basest slander, drawing on the new tools of biblical criticism to support their position that the Romans were at fault. "The pack of howling fanatics who still cry at the heels of the Jew, 'Christ Killer,' have yet to learn to read and understand the gospels correctly," Wise wrote.[22] But it was Rabbi Joseph Krauskopf of Congregation Keneseth Israel in Philadelphia who developed this modern position most carefully, in *A Rabbi's Impressions of the Oberammergau Passion Play* (1901).

This popular pássion play, held every ten years outside Munich in the Bavarian Alps, had depicted the Jews as money-grubbing Christ killers since it was first performed in 1634, making it by many accounts the world's most popular and persistent showcase for anti-Semitism. During the late twentieth century, the local residents who produce the play would tone down that anti-Semitism (taking the horned hats off the Jews, for example, and calling Jesus "Yeshua"), but upon Krauskopf's visit in 1900 they were still glorying in displaying, as Adolf Hitler would later put it, "the whole muck and mire of Jewry."[23] That same anti-Semitic spirit animated *The Passion Play of Oberammergau*, the first American film on Jesus, which opened just two years before Krauskopf went to see the live production firsthand, and likely inspired his trip.

The production Krauskopf witnessed in Bavaria was in his judgment "dramatically thrilling" but "historically false"—"a mass of falsehoods, of base inventions against the Jews, that obviously never happened, never could have happened, that are flagrantly self-contradictory, that violently outrage the history and law and religion and constitution of the Jew." Jesus was Jewish through and through, Krauskopf argued, so Jews had no reason to quarrel with him, much less to try, convict, and kill him. Jesus' blood was on the hands of Rome alone, which executed him for political reasons (as a Jewish nationalist). The earliest Christian writings were, Krauskopf noted, relatively favorable to the Jews. Only later did the Christians turn against their mother religion, inserting calumnies against Jews into their scriptures, and turning Jesus "from a hater of Rome to a champion of it," "from a patriot of Israel to an opponent of it." The real Jesus was not the "Divinity without Humanity" of Christian theology, but the humble Jewish "teacher of the Golden Rule."[24]

For centuries, other Jews had made similar claims in disputations with Christians. Krauskopf gave those arguments a new sophistication, however, bolstering his position with references to scholarship on the Bible and adding plaudits for Jesus along the way. The careful attention Krauskopf gave to the subject of the crucifixion—also evident in texts such as Wise's *The Martyrdom of Jesus of Nazareth* (1874) and Hirsch's "The Crucifixion Viewed from a Jewish Standpoint" (1892)—suggests that the reclamation project was motivated in part by a desire to show that Jews harbored no animosity toward Jesus. But another, more daring, motivation also seems to have been at work, namely presenting the Jews as a crucified rather than a crucifying people. It was the Christians, not the Jews, who were the crucifiers, Krauskopf and his fellow rabbis argued. "The thorny crown; who wears it? . . . The lash; who felt it?" Hirsch asked. Not just Jesus, but also the Jews. "We bore a cross, the weight of which was a thousand-fold heavier than that which Jesus carried to the place of his execution." "The Jews," Kohler concluded, "are a people of Christs."[25]

A MOST FASCINATING FIGURE

By the time Krauskopf went to Oberammergau, Jesus was revered not only in Reform pulpits but also in the pews. A survey of attitudes to Jesus among American Jewish leaders, instigated by Kohler in 1899, found none of the hostility to Jesus common in medieval Europe. Rabbi Henry Berkowitz of the Rodeph Sholem Congregation in Philadelphia called him "the gentlest and noblest rabbi of them all." Rabbi David Philipson, a Hebrew Union College professor, praised both "the sweetness of his character" and "the power of his genius." Isidor Singer, who published the findings, concluded that Jesus had become a welcome guest in Reform temples across the United States. "Thousands, yea, tens of thousands, of educated and noble-minded Jews in our day," he wrote, "are gradually giving up the attitude of their forefathers toward the central figure of Christianity." A modern spirit of esteem had replaced the "ignorance, antipathy and fear" of medieval times. Now "it is not strange in many synagogues, especially in this country," he wrote, "to hear sermons preached eulogizing this same Jesus," and few Jews question the widespread consensus that Jesus is "one of the noblest twigs of the old branch of Judah."[26]

Harris Weinstock, a progressive Jewish businessman from California, traced this "change of sentiment toward Jesus" to "the intelligent and progressive preaching of our modern rabbis, who seem to appreciate the glory Jesus has shed upon the Jewish name." In *Jesus the Jew* (1902) he illustrated this transformation with a story from his youth. Apparently, a Jewish friend of Weinstock had brought a book about Jesus one day into Sabbath school. "Sacrilege! Sacrilege!" the rabbi cried, so repulsed by the book that he "seemed to be afraid to touch it." Rather than teaching Weinstock to shun Jesus, however, the incident piqued his curiosity. He began to read the New Testament, where he discovered that, "according to New-Testament traditions,

Jesus was born a Jew, lived a Jew, died a Jew." He found "that the high morality which he preached was Judaism in its purest form . . . that the thought of establishing a new belief, or even a new sect, was the farthest from his mind." Weinstock also concluded, on the basis of his New Testament research, that Jesus did not teach Christian doctrines such as the atonement, election, or predestination, and by the turn of the century other Reformers were reaching the same conclusions. Old taboos about Jesus were, in Weinstock's words, "speedily being replaced in the modern Jewish mind by a keen appreciation of the beauty and the nobleness of the character of Jesus," and many Sabbath schools were introducing young people to the life of the man Weinstock described as "one of the greatest gifts that Israel has given to the world."[27]

Weinstock hoped that a Jewish Jesus, reincarnated by Jews yet still revered by Christians, could become "the connecting link between the divine mother-religion, Judaism, and her noble daughter, Christianity." In a remarkable passage that recalls both the genealogies of the Hebrew Bible and Protestant myths of America, Weinstock brought Judaism, Christianity, and America together in common cause:

> Had there been no Abraham, there would have been no Moses. Had there been no Moses, there would have been no Jesus. Had there been no Jesus, there would have been no Paul. Had there been no Paul, there would have been no Christianity. Had there been no Christianity, there would have been no Luther. Had there been no Luther, there would have been no Pilgrim fathers to land on these shores with the Jewish Bible under their arms. Had there been no Pilgrim fathers, there would have been no civil or religious liberty. Had there been no civil or religious liberty, tyranny and despotism would still rule the earth, and the human family would still live in mental, moral, and physical bondage.[28]

The views of lay people such as Weinstock and rabbis such as Wise, Kohler, Hirsch, and Krauskopf reached a larger audience with the appearance of the *Jewish Encyclopedia*, a twelve-volume work published between 1901 and 1906. They also began to move beyond Reform Judaism, since the *Jewish Encyclopedia* was a joint effort of Reform and Conservative Jews. The encyclopedia's extensive article on "Jesus of Nazareth" included a section on Jesus in theology by Kohler and on Jesus in history by Joseph Jacobs (a Conservative Jew who emigrated from England to the United States in 1900 and went on to teach at Jewish Theological Seminary). The encyclopedia expressed grave skepticism about the historical reliability of the Gospels, which in its view presented not the real Jesus of history but a series of theological Jesuses made in the peculiar images of the four evangelists. Its Jesus was a faithful Jew, so faithful that he taught nothing original. He attracted followers for psychological rather than theological reasons—not because of the uniqueness of his teachings but because of the power of his "magnetic personality." In an effort to describe that personality, the encyclopedists flirted with the new psychological approach to religion made popular by the publication of William James's *Varieties of Religious Experience* (1902). Jesus was a healer and mystic, they argued, who exhibited a "tendency to ecstatic abstraction," a tendency common "in other great leaders of men, like Socrates, Mohammed, and Napoleon, being accompanied in their cases by hallucinations." Readers searching for the origins of Christianity were directed once again not to Jesus but to the apostate Paul, who by focusing on Jesus' death rather than his life set the Christian tradition on a fateful march from its Jewish roots to modern-day anti-Semitism.[29]

The encyclopedists' description of Jesus as a "magnetic personality" reveals the debt these writers owed to the culture of personality. "Fascinating" and "magnetic," "dominant" and "forceful" were, according to Warren Susman, keywords of this new culture of self-assertion, which took shape in the 1890s (when writing on Jesus by Reform rabbis took off) and matured in the 1920s and 1930s (when Jewish interest in Jesus peaked). And while most Reform rabbis followed the encyclopedia in refusing to ascribe originality to Jesus' teachings, they drew nonetheless on the culture of personality in speaking (as both Hirsch and Kohler did) of his "charm." No one submerged Jesus deeper in that culture, however, than Temple Emanu-El's Rabbi Enelow.[30]

In *A Jewish View of Jesus* (1920), Enelow extolled Jesus as "the most fascinating figure in history." Though he followed the now standard line in portraying Jesus as a faithful Jew with no intention of establishing a new religion (that was Paul's doing), he granted considerable originality to Jesus, whom he described as "a unique religious teacher." "Supreme personality is greatest originality," he wrote, and his Jesus had both in spades. Dismissing earlier efforts to align Jesus with the Essenes, he portrayed Jesus as a mercurial mystic who distinguished himself from the masses even as he held sway over them. "Like all great personalities," he wrote, "Jesus was no party man; he was himself: he never really belonged to a crowd, nor could he attach himself to one." What made Jesus unique was his insistence that religion was personal. Yes, Jesus taught the traditions and ideals of Judaism. But his genius lay in "giving to those traditions and ideals a new expression, a new emphasis, and in endowing them with the perennial appeal of a fascinating personality." While earlier Jewish teachers "taught impersonally," Jesus "taught personally." He brought religion down from the realm of principles to the realities of people.[31]

A final Jewish thinker who reclaimed Jesus before the Jesus controversy of 1925 was Stephen Wise himself. In 1900, Wise had supported a campaign led by Harris Weinstock to introduce teaching about Jesus the Jew into Sabbath schools across the United States. Such teaching, Wise had written in a letter endorsing the proposal, would introduce Jewish children to the fact "that Jesus was a Jew of the Jews, an earnest, high-minded teacher of the Jewish faith." Most of Wise's earlier pronouncements about Jesus, however, were made before Christian audiences. Like other Reform rabbis of his time, Wise preached regularly in churches, where his approach reversed the Lutheran pattern of hitting the congregants first with sin and then with grace. Typically Wise began by lauding Jesus. Then he chastised his audience for failing to live up to Jesus' lofty moral teachings.[32]

In 1913 in the liberal Protestant magazine *The Outlook*, Wise lavished even greater praise on his Jesus—whom he called, as Mormons then did, his "elder brother"—than he would in his 1925 sermon. "Jesus," he wrote, "was not only *a* Jew but he was *the* Jew, the Jew of Jews." Other Jews, he added, "accept Jesus for that which he was, not for that which Christianity has mistakenly sought to make of him—a Jewish teacher, a Jewish leader, a prophet in Israel, clear-visioned, tenderly loving, selfless, Godlike, though not uniquely Godly." Paul' had buried Jesus in a mountain of Hellenistic confusion, he wrote. Now Jews were effecting a "resurrection of the body of the teachings of Jesus from the tomb of dogmatic Christianity," reclaiming Jesus as their own. Jews were the true guardians of the legacy of Jesus and in the future, Wise prophesied, they would be remembered not as "Christ-killers" but "Christ-bearers."[33]

AUDACITY AND ASSIMILATION

Given Wise's many debts to his predecessors, to say nothing of his earlier (and more provocative) pronouncements on the Jewishness of Jesus, the strong reaction to his 1925 sermon is something of a puzzle. As has been noted, the complex politics of Zionism likely magnified the dispute. The fact that the sermon was delivered in New York also mattered. At the time, just under half of all Jewish Americans resided in New York City, so Jews in the area played a disproportionate role in shaping American Judaism. That the sermon was delivered to Jews was also a factor. It is one thing for a rabbi to stand in a church and challenge his listeners to live up to the teachings of Jesus—as Wise had repeatedly done—and quite another for him to stand in a synagogue and do the same. Finally, it was significant that the words came from Wise, who by the mid-1920s was, as *The American Israelite* observed, "undisputably the most popular Rabbi in America."[34]

Another spark was the remarkable convergence of liberal Protestantism and Reform Judaism in the 1920s. During the last three decades of the nineteenth century, Reform rabbis and Unitarian ministers had explored closer ties between their liberal faiths. Some had even considered a merger, wondering whether Jews and Christians could celebrate Hanukkah and Christmas together as one national holy day, and whether Moses or Jesus was the most appropriate standardbearer for their aborning universalism. But as liberal Protestantism edged in the Unitarian direction in the early twentieth century, a broader and bolder rapprochement seemed possible.[35]

In 1924, a pivotal year in the history of American Judaism, the U.S. Congress cut the torrent of Jewish immigration to a trickle with the passage of the Johnson-Reed Act. Over the prior half century, Jewish immigrants, mostly Eastern European and Orthodox, had flooded into the country, challenging the authority of earlier generations of German-born Reform rabbis, and leading Rabbi Martin Meyer of San Francisco to prophesy that "the future of the Jew in America will be in the hands of the Russian-descended contingent . . . because of the preponderance of the numbers."[36] By the time Wise set off his Jesus controversy, Jewish immigration had all but ended, and the 4.5 million Jews living in the United States were coming to realize that the future of American Judaism was in their hands, and those of their U.S.–born children. Rather than the vagaries of immigration policy and patterns, the choices of Jewish Americans would determine what American Jewry would become. And contestants on both sides of the Wise debate strained to push it in the proper direction. For Wise and the ascendant German-American Reformers, it was time to reassert their leadership by moving forcefully toward America's cultural and religious mainstream (and accommodating the Eastern Europeans when possible). For the Orthodox, it was time to step up their resistance. The Orthodox opposition to Wise was in part a rear-guard reaction against the remarkable success of the Reform cause—success which was all but assured when President Calvin Coolidge signed the Johnson-Reed Act into law.

Opposition to Wise must also be understood as a response to the newfound celebrity of Jesus, who mattered more in the United States in the 1920s than he had when Wise's predecessors were writing during the last half of the nineteenth century. As the title of The Inescapable Christ (1925) suggests, Jesus was impossible to overlook in 1920s America. In 1925, Metro-Goldwyn-Mayer released Ben-Hur, and while MGM founder Louis B. Mayer billed the film as "The Picture Every Christian Ought to See!" it was seen as well by many Jews, who took considerable pride in the fact that Mayer was one of their own. Meanwhile, Barton's The Man Nobody Knows and Papini's The Life of Christ were at or near the top of the bestseller list, and it wasn't just Christians who were reading them either.

Although the public power of mainline Protestantism had peaked,

Jesus' cultural authority was hitting new highs during the Roaring Twenties. Inside most mainline Protestant churches, Jesus had replaced the Bible as the leading religious authority. But the Jesus lauded in those churches had also been fairly well de-christianized, as liberals had taken away his miracle-making power and distanced him from controversial doctrines such as the virgin birth, the vicarious atonement, and the resurrection. Some Protestants had even come to see Jesus, like Rabbi Solomon H. Sonneschein did, as "*one* of the *Great* and sainted saviors of the race, but . . . not *The Savior!*" Meanwhile, Reformers were eliminating much of Judaism's distinctiveness, downplaying the notion of Jewish chosenness and eliminating many ritual observances—what Krauskopf called Judaism's "obstructive exclusiveness and ceremonialism." By the mid-1920s another rabbi's prediction "that the Jewish world will move toward a progressive appreciation of Jesus in proportion as the Christian world turns its back on the whole abracadabra of medieval theology" seemed to be coming true. To some liberal Christians and Reform Jews, it looked as if Christianity and Judaism were converging, and the point of convergence seemed to be Jesus himself.[37]

When faced with a Jesus who was rapidly moving beyond his Christian home into American culture at large, and with the prospect of closer ties with American Christians, Jewish Americans were faced with two important choices. First, they had to decide whether Christians had the exclusive right to define the meaning of Jesus. Second, they had to decide whether to say yes or no to him. In each case, Orthodox and Reform Jews made very different choices.

The Orthodox ceded to the Christians the right to define Jesus. To be more precise, they accepted what they thought was the standard Christian definition of him, as a miracle-working God-man and Messiah (a view becoming more obsolete by the minute inside mainline Protestantism). Given their standing as religious outsiders, they harbored neither the hope nor the desire that they could shape American views of this national celebrity, who was as untouchable to them as Babe Ruth's pitching. So they saw Jesus as the source of all the anti-Semitic horrors of Christendom, and rejected both him and his religion.

Reform Jews, by contrast, refused to concede to Christians the right to fix the meaning of Christian keywords. Taking a page out of *Alice in Wonderland*, they were intrepid enough to believe, as Humpty Dumpty did, that when they used contested words—even ones as loaded as *Jesus* and *Christianity*—those words would mean exactly what they told them to mean. And though they were no doubt motivated in part by a wish to be accepted by Christians, the results were anything but flattering to Christianity. Talking about Jesus surely signaled the Reformers' Americanness, but talking about him the way they did demonstrated unequivocally their Jewishness. Because Jesus was a Jew, as Klausner wrote, "to his finger-tips,"[38] Jews had the inside track when it came to understanding his teachings. And a close examination of those precepts revealed a wide gap between what Jesus had taught and how Paul and the rest of Christendom had acted. There was no need for Jews to convert to Christianity, the Reformers intimated. The crying need was for Christians to start acting like the man they called their Savior.

It is hard to judge which of these approaches was more audacious. The Orthodox defied an overwhelmingly Christian culture by refusing to affirm its key symbol, and in many cases even refusing to utter his name. Yet the Reformers may have showed more chutzpah, since implicit in their approach was the claim that the history of Christendom was a sordid tale of the betrayal of Jesus. To be sure, the Reformers' agenda was assimilationist, motivated by a desire to be accepted in Christian circles. But they by no means gave away the store. Like other reincarnators of Jesus, they interpreted the Nazarene carpenter not as the one and only Risen Lord but as one great Jewish thinker among many. They too extracted Jesus from his Christian milieu, relocating him inside their own religious world, and then drawing on his cultural authority to criticize the very Christians whose favor they were supposedly currying. The historian Susannah Heschel, in a study of Abraham Geiger's writings on Jesus, calls this process "reversing the gaze." In the African-American tradition it is called tricksterism or conjure. By any name, it is surely something other than the sycophancy the Orthodox denounced, or even the bland assimilationism many have attributed to the American Reform tradition. The aim of Rabbi Stephen Wise was not to make Judaism more Christian but to make Christianity more Jewish. In that regard, he may have accommodated himself *less* to American Christianity than did his Orthodox opponents.[39]

AN OPEN LETTER TO JEWS AND CHRISTIANS

In the decades that followed the Jesus controversy, efforts to reclaim Jesus for Judaism spread. A review of modern Jewish attitudes toward Jesus published in 1934 confirmed that neither Jesus nor the culture of personality was dying when it reported that "the Modern Jew sees in him a noble and magnetic personality, a defender of the common people."[40] In 1937 the French priest Joseph Bonsirven saw into print *Les Juifs et Jésus; attitudes nouvelles* ("The Jews and Jesus: New Attitudes"). After an extensive review of sermons by American rabbis, Bonsirven concluded that antipathy toward Jesus had given way to a strategy of reclamation. The reclamation project reached its apex, however, not in sermons by Reform rabbis but in books by Jewish novelists. During the 1930s, *An Open Letter to Jews and Christians* (1938) by the Russian-born writer John Cournos and *The Nazarene* (1939) by the controversial Yiddish novelist Sholem Asch pushed the reclamation project to the limit.

Cournos's book, which first ran as an article in the December 1937 *Atlantic Monthly*, followed Harris Weinstock by invoking a childhood memory as a foil. Cournos began his *Open Letter* by recalling the Christ of neighborhood bigots who, by branding him a "Christ-killer," turned Jesus into "a name to be loathed and execrated, evoking anathema instead of blessing." In keeping with the well-established pattern, Cournos drew a sharp distinction between the true Christianity of Jesus (which he called "Jesusism") and the false Christianity of Paul and the neighborhood bigots. He then presented the most fawning effort yet to reclaim Jesus for American Jewry. Jesus was greater than Moses, Cournos argued, because he redirected the focus of Jewish life "from tribalism (call it nationalism) to universality, from formalism to freedom, from the letter to the spirit"—in short, because he seemed to anticipate the transformations Reform Jews would fight for in the nineteenth and twentieth centuries. As the singular genius of Judaism—"the apex and the acme of Jewish teaching"—Jesus deserved not only the respect but also the love of every Jew. And Cournos's own love of Jesus seemed boundless. "If there were no Jesus, if Jesus were a myth," Cournos wrote, he "would have to be invented. Without him, without all he stands for, Western humanity would be wholly bankrupt." To deny such a man was in his view not simply to take on the shame of Peter's denial. It was "to reject the Jewish heritage, to betray what was best in Israel." Those who did not embrace "the greatest Jew who ever lived" were, to put it bluntly, bad Jews.[41]

Cournos's letter seemed to offend everyone. The Reverend Edmund A. Walsh, a Jesuit priest, welcomed Cournos's openness to Jesus but insisted on the right of the Catholic Church to define its Savior. "To accept Christ means to accept the whole Christ," he wrote. "If Jewry accepts the invitation to consider Christ hereafter as its greatest prophet, Judaism must accept the prophet's two major contentions, that He was the son of God and the Messiah." The most biting critique of Cournos came from a fellow Jew, Rabbi Louis I. Newman of New York, who blasted him for selling out for the blood money of Christians. Cournos's effort to win the goodwill of Christians by embracing Jesus as Judaism's greatest prophet, wrote Newman, is "an obnoxious bargain" that "meets with no approval among informed and self-respecting Jews." There is a reason, Newman continued, why no one knows where Moses is buried. And that reason is that Jewish monotheism worships God alone.[42]

As Newman perceived, Cournos's *Open Letter* was in part an effort to make a place for Jews at the American table by minimizing the distance between Christianity and Judaism. However, it was also a daring effort to interpret Jesus and Christianity in a Jewish light. Like Americans from Thomas Jefferson to Stephen Wise, Cournos embraced a Jesus disentangled from Christian dogmatism, a wholly human teacher "*sans* halo, *sans* miraculous birth, *sans* miracles." Though Cournos rejected the dogmas of the atonement and the resurrection, he drew on the rhetoric of both to make perhaps his boldest claim. The "real crucifixion," he argued, occurred long after Jesus' death, and the real "Christ-killers" were not Jews but Christians—Paul and other dogmatizers who encrusted the living spirit of Jesus into dead doctrines and empty rites. The true resurrection, he wrote, would come when Jesus—the Jewish Jesus—was raised "from the sepulchre of dogma and outward forms."[43]

Among those outward forms, Cournos continued, were the multitudes of European Christs hanging in European museums. Depictions of Jesus by European artists, he wrote, have been "pagan, or feminine, or Hellenic, or medieval; often saccharine, and too often tortured and emaciated," but "scarcely one of them is Jewish, and scarcely one conveys a living reality to the Jew." "Is it not possible," he asked, "that only a Jew can paint him or carve him or write a biography of him?" Cournos may have been thinking of the Jewish sculptor Jacob Epstein, whom Cournos described earlier—in a review of his sculpture of a plainly Semitic Christ—as "the greatest artist of our age." But it is more likely that the Yiddish novelist Sholem Asch was uppermost in his mind, since later in his *Open Letter* he reported that Asch was working on just such a biography. "If I know anything of Sholem Asch," Cournos prophesied, "it will be a portrait to startle his co-religionists."[44]

THE NAZARENE

Born in Poland, Asch (1880–1957) came to the United States in 1910 and became a naturalized U.S. citizen a decade later. He began his career writing in Hebrew, but switched to Yiddish early on, and quickly became the first Yiddish writer to achieve international acclaim. Although he wrote his novels, plays, short stories, and essays in that language, they were widely read in his adopted homeland in English translation (and, of course, in Yiddish as well). Asch's work focused primarily on Jewish life in Eastern Europe and the United States, but his most controversial works took up Christian themes. Sweeping historical novels on Jesus (*The Nazarene*, 1939), Paul (*The Apostle*, 1943), and Mary (*Mary*, 1949), now referred to as his christological trilogy, all hit the U.S. bestseller list. A 1909 short story, "In a karnival nakht" ("In a Carnival Night"), prompted a spirited debate in Yiddish-speaking circles because of its depiction of Jesus as a sympathetic martyr. But the work that got him in real trouble was *The Nazarene*, which provoked a Jesus controversy inside American Judaism unseen since Wise's Christmas sermon of 1925.

At 698 pages, *The Nazarene* makes Papini's weighty *Life of Christ* look like a novella. But the book is long on details too. Asch reportedly amassed a library of over a thousand works in researching the subject, and the payoff is a work as rich in historical detail as the Jesus paintings of James Tissot. Asch mimics the New Testament in presenting "the Rabbi of Galilee" from multiple perspectives—that of a Roman military man, a Pharisee, and, most daringly, Judas Iscariot himself. Via a jarring plot device, the Roman soldier and the Pharisee are reincarnated in 1930s Poland as an anti-Semitic Orientalist (Pan Viadomsky) and his young assistant (the book's unnamed narrator). Judas's voice is introduced through an ancient manuscript: a fragment of a long-lost gospel attributed to "Judah Ish-Kiriot," recovered and translated by Viadomsky and his assistant. From these competing points of view—the recovered memories of the Roman soldier and the Pharisee, and the apocryphal gospel according to Judas (which alone occupies nearly a third of the book)—an image emerges of Jesus as master of the parable and a sympathetic friend of "the oppressed and the rejected, the abandoned of God and men." This sensitive soul outrages the Sadducees by extending his mission beyond Israel, but remains nonetheless "a pious and observant Jew" who wears a tallith (prayer shawl), reads from the Torah in the synagogue, and interprets the scriptures in the light of Hillel. Rabbi Yeshua ben Joseph, as he is called, is no ordinary Jew, however. He performs miracles and eventually comes to believe that he is the Messiah himself. At least to his contemporaries, this "man of wonders" appears to be "a thousand times higher than a Rabbi." In a textual analog to Marc Chagall's *White Crucifixion*—an oil painting, completed in 1938, of a crucified Jesus wearing a tallith and surrounded by images of pogroms and burning Torahs—Jesus dies a faithful Jewish martyr. With blood clotting in his earlocks, he expends his last breaths reciting the Shema, the most sacred words in Jewish scripture: "Hear, O Israel, the Lord our God, the Lord is One."[45]

Asch follows earlier Jewish reclaimers of Jesus in blaming the Romans for the crucifixion. He takes considerable pains to exonerate Judas, who comes across as overzealous rather than venal, and driven by devotion rather than greed. The novel's other Jewish characters are divided over Jesus. When Pilate asks the crowd whether he should release Jesus or "Bar Abba," the Jews in the assembly do not respond in unison. Instead a great debate breaks out, with some calling him a "blasphemer," others praising him as a "holy man," and still others eagerly awaiting a sign to confirm his standing as the Messiah.[46] Absent a Jewish consensus, Pilate is forced to make up his own mind. In the end, a Pharisee, rather than the Roman procurator, washes his hands of Jesus' blood.

Among Gentile critics of *The Nazarene*, conservatives criticized Asch for playing fast and loose with the Gospels in an effort to exonerate the Jews, while liberal reviewers found *The Nazarene* far too faithful to the original. But the consensus was that the book shone. "The most extraordinary evocation of Jesus since Renan's," gushed *Time*. "Brilliantly penetrating" and "profound" wrote *The New York Times*. *Christian Century* hailed *The Nazarene* as "a great novel by a great author on a great theme," adding that Asch had "performed a mitzvah of such proportions that future generations will call him blessed." Some Jewish writers also praised the book. In a piece in the *Atlantic Monthly*, John Cournos called it a "superb achievement" and commended the author for portraying Jesus as "the finest Jew that ever lived, one worthy of acceptance by the Jews as the crowning figure of their culture and history." A particularly perceptive review came from the literary critic Alfred Kazin, who had grown up speaking Yiddish and also had the chutzpah to take up a foreign tradition (in his case, modern American literature) and make it his own. Writing in the *New Republic*, Kazin refused to judge the novel great, though he did find greatness in it. Calling the book "a very warm and often moving portrait of Yeshua ben Joseph, the forlorn and strangely gifted Rabbi of Nazareth," he praised Asch for approaching his subject "without recrimination or frenzied affection." He deemed the novel intense, and traced the source of that intensity to Asch's rediscovery of a Hebraic Jesus. "Nothing, as it happens, could be more characteristically Yiddish or more imperative in its own way," he concluded, "than this 'Gospel according to *Chaver* Sholem.'"[47]

Many in the Anglo-Jewish press also embraced Asch as a *chaver* ("friend" in Yiddish). *The American Hebrew*, one of the country's most influential organs of Conservative Judaism, saw "great literary and spiritual value" in the novel, and lauded Asch's effort to redeem the Pharisees from longstanding Christian stereotypes. The Philadelphia-based *Jewish Exponent* called it "a historical novel of magnificent sweep and spiritual power," applauding his decision to make the legionary who savagely whips Jesus while carrying his cross to Golgotha—"the most brutal of the Romans"—a native of Germany.[48]

Yiddish critics saw Asch as something less than a *chaver*, panning the book as Christian not only in theme but also in sympathy. The New York–based Yiddish daily the *Forward*, which in Kazin's words previously serialized Asch "as proudly as The Ladies Home Journal serializes Faith Baldwin," refused to run an excerpt, and its reviewer rebuked Asch for hanging the forbidden fruit of conversion before his Jewish readers. The *Forward's* editor was Abraham Cahan, a free-thinking socialist who had made a name for himself as the author of *The Rise of David Lewinsky* (and for Asch by publishing his work). But now Cahan turned on his protégé, devoting two years of his life to stirring up an anti-Asch campaign more vitriolic than what Sigmund Freud endured after the English-language publication of *Moses and Monotheism* (also in 1939). In *Sholem Asch's New Way* (1941), published in Yiddish only, Cahan portrayed Asch as far worse than Lewinsky: a Trojan Horse launching a secret mission to convert the Jews to "Jesusism."[49]

The vilification reached new lows in the work of Herman Lieberman, a writer at the *Forward* (and a recent convert to Orthodoxy), whose fulminations recall the 1989 Iranian fatwa against Salman Rushdie's *The Satanic Verses*, minus the death decree. Lieberman labeled *The Nazarene* "an obvious missionary tract" and assaulted its author for undertaking "a veritable crusade among Jews on behalf of the Christian faith." "Let the Christians crown Asch as a new apostle," Lieberman wrote. "To Jews he is but a desecrator, a misleader and seducer, a traitor to all that is most precious and holy, a corrupter of the house of Israel, an incendiary of the Holy Temple." Lieberman's attack on Asch was so brutal and personal that some who were not otherwise friendly to the novelist were inspired to come to his defense. Rabbi Samuel Sandmel of Hebrew Union College judged Asch's christological novels "tedious" and warned readers that "the Judaism Asch attributes to the age of Jesus is in reality that of premodern Poland," but added that when he read "the merciless attacks" on Asch by Lieberman he "ended up with a deep sympathy for him."[50]

Asch might have responded to criticisms of *The Nazarene* by retreating. During the 1920s, Wise had done just that, attributing his Jesus controversy largely to misinformation spread by the media. But Asch did not retreat. In fact, he became more brazen, championing Jesus as the Jew among Jews even as Hitler rampaged across Europe in the name of an Aryan Christ. In addition to completing his christological trilogy, Asch produced opinion pieces such as *What I Believe* (1941). In that book, he ranked Jesus' teachings "with those of the Psalmist and the Prophets as the highest achievement of the Jewish genius." He summed up his understanding of Jesus in this 1944 interview:

> For Jesus Christ is to me the outstanding personality of all time, all history, both as Son of God and as Son of Man. Everything he ever said or did has value for us today and that is something you can say of no other man, alive or dead. There is no easy middle ground to stroll upon. You either accept Jesus or reject him.[51]

THE JUDEO-CHRISTIAN TRADITION

One reason for Jewish writers' shift into pro-Jesus overdrive in the 1930s was doubtless the emergence of Fascism and Nazism in Europe, and Communism in the Soviet Union. Cournos addressed his *Open Letter* not only to Christians but also to "the Antichrist trinity of Hitler, Stalin, and Mussolini," who together had made Jesus over "in their own Satanic image" as "a tall, lean, strong, light-haired Nordic fighter." According to Cournos, the only effective reply to this anti-Jewish and anti-Christian assault was a united front of Jews and Christians. Cournos referred to his anti-Antichrist phalanx as "Judaeo-Christianity" and saw that combination as the world's last and best hope. "There are two ideas in the world today: Communism and Fascism, which would make us slaves, and Judaeo-Christianity, which would set us free," Cournos wrote. If only Christianity would jettison its dogma and Judaism its exclusiveness, the two religions could make "a single united front in the name of Jesus."[52]

Mark Silk, who has studied the development of the term *Judeo-Christian*, traces its origins to the 1930s, when left-wing Catholics and Protestants used it to differentiate themselves from anti-Semites such as Father Charles Coughlin, a Catholic priest from Michigan who was spewing anti-Jewish invective over the radio in the name of his "Christian Front." In Silk's account, Jewish thinkers appear largely to criticize the idea as a recipe for subordinating the Jewish minority, both theologically and politically, to the Christian majority. But Jewish writers also embraced the concept, in some cases long before the Christian thinkers cited by Silk.[53]

Asch's *One Destiny: An Epistle to the Christians*, written in Yiddish toward the end of World War II and translated into English in 1945, was patterned after Cournos's *Open Letter*, and it struck many of the same chords. It too responded to Nazi might and theology with the urgency and the rhetoric of the biblical book of Revelation. It too yoked the Anti-Christ with anti-Semitism, arguing that "the Nazi beast" was seeking to devour both the Jews and "the Judeo-Christian idea." It too expressed the hope that a generic Jesus would be the salvation of the world. Asch called true Christianity and true Judaism "two parts of a single whole" and prophesied that "no deliverance, no peace, and no salvation can come until the two halves are joined together." While others saw the Holocaust as a sign of the end of constructive Jewish-Christian relations, Asch argued that no other time in the history of the world was as propitious for a rapprochement between the two faiths. Christians, he argued, had been in the forefront of resistance to Nazism. Among Jews, especially American Jews, Asch discerned "a revolutionary change of opinion" about Jesus. Jews and Christians had created western civilization, and a renewal of their "common faith" in one God was according to Asch "the only means of salvation for a world in flames."[54]

After World War II, the "Judeo-Christian tradition" emerged as a key trope in American religious and political life. As godless Communists replaced Nazis as the Great Satan, many Americans came to see themselves as a people in covenant with the one God of Judaism and Christianity. During the 1930s, Asch and Cournos had both hoped that Jesus could serve as a bridge holding the Jewish and Christian traditions together. As literary men, they were imaginative enough to conceive of a Jesus sufficiently liberated from Christianity to appeal to liberal Jews yet sufficiently rooted in Christianity to appeal to liberal Christians. Such plans were dashed on the rocks of the Holocaust.

Of course, some continued to harbor the hope that Jesus could yet function as a link connecting Judaism and Christianity. A group of liberal Roman Catholic intellectuals, led by John M. Oesterreicher (a convert from Judaism), founded the Institute for Judaeo-Christian Studies at Seton Hall University in 1953 and published an influential annual appropriately called *The Bridge*. Their calls for Jewish-Christian understanding helped to prompt the Roman Catholic Church, first, to consider during Vatican II (1962–65) the ways in which its doctrines had stoked the fires of concentration camp crematoriums and, second, to reverse its "theology of contempt" (including the charge of deicide) in 1965 in *Nostra Aetate* ("In Our Times"). Jewish critics, objecting to Oesterreicher's policy of publishing only Catholic authors, called *The Bridge* a one-way street and his attempt to construe Jesus as the connecting link between Jews and Christians a thinly veiled missionary effort.[55]

Back in 1926, Rabbi Schulman had insisted that Jesus was not a uniter but a divider of Judaism and Christianity. Jews and Christians would never coalesce around Jesus, he argued: "If they are ever to be united, the belief in one God will bring about the union." At least in this regard, Schulman turned out to be right. As American Christians and Jews came together in the Cold War, they did so under the banner of monotheism rather than "Jesusism." During the 1950s, the U.S. Congress inserted the words "under God" into the Pledge of Allegiance, not "under Jesus." That same decade, a landmark book called *Protestant, Catholic, Jew* (1955) by the Jewish sociologist Will Herberg proclaimed the good news of generic monotheism, celebrating the fact that both Catholics and Jews had been welcomed into what was once a Protestant-only mainstream. According to Herberg, Protestantism, Catholicism, and Judaism had become the three great branches of a shared national faith. All championed the fatherhood of God and the brotherhood of humanity ("sisterhood" was not yet in cultural currency). All affirmed equality and democracy, and stood fast against godless Communism. Herberg's "triple melting pot" theory said a lot about the place of Jews in American society, but was conspicuously silent on Jesus. After the Holocaust heightened awareness of the bloody history of Christian anti-Semitism, Jesus became a stumbling block rather than a bridge in Jewish-Christian relations, and he wasn't mentioned at all in a high-profile "Jewish Statement on Christians and Christianity" signed by prominent American Jews in 2002.[56]

While Jewish interest in Jesus cooled considerably in the decades following World War II, it did not disappear altogether. The Holocaust, which saw roughly 6 million Jews killed by Hitler's regime, effectively brought the project to reclaim Jesus for Judaism to an end. It also brought on intermittent revivals of medieval Jewish views of Jesus. The British writer Hugh J. Schonfield produced a new translation of the *Toledoth Yeshu* in 1937, and followed it up with *The Passover Plot*, a 1966 bestseller that explained away the resurrection by arguing that Jesus only appeared to die on the cross. Few American Jews said "Amen" to such views but their praise for Jesus was far more tempered after World War II.

A JEWISH QUEST

Beginning in the 1950s and the 1960s, the locus of Jewish interest in Jesus shifted from the synagogue to the university. In 1952, *Ha-Modia*, an Orthodox newspaper in Jerusalem, complained that Reform rabbis in the United States were still delivering sermons on the moral teachings of Jesus. But as a rule scholars were displacing rabbis as the leading interpreters of the Nazarene, in part because the U.S. professorate, long closed to Jewish intellectuals, was finally opening up to them.

During those decades, Rabbi Samuel Sandmel (1911–1979) emerged as the most powerful American Jewish voice on Jesus, and he typified the new tendency to approach Jesus with more skepticism (and more footnotes). Though trained as a rabbi at Hebrew Union College, he earned a Ph.D. in New Testament studies from Yale and became a professor in 1952 at what had become Hebrew Union College/Jewish Institute of Religion. Sandmel's key works, written in the midst of the New Quest for the historical Jesus, were *A Jewish Understanding of the New Testament* (1956) and *We Jews and Jesus* (1965). In the latter book, Sandmel looked back on the first few decades of the twentieth century and observed that Jews and Christians seemed at that time to be "on the threshold of some incipient

common understanding of Jesus." By 1965, however, that shared understanding had eluded them. "Jews and Christians," Sandmel wrote,
"are farther apart today on the question of Jesus than they have been
in the past hundred years." Joseph Klausner's hope of reclaiming Jesus for Judaism had become, in Sandmel's words, a "distant dream."[57]

Sandmel's more cautious views of Jesus fit the post-Holocaust era.
Far more than his predecessors, Sandmel knew the ins and outs of
New Testament criticism. While Stephen Wise was a full-time rabbi
and Sholem Asch a novelist, Sandmel was a college professor with a
Ph.D. in New Testament studies. As a historian, Sandmel was skeptical about the ability of even trained academics to arrive at the Jesus of
history. He poked fun at the tendency of Jewish writers to turn the
story of Christianity into a melodrama in which Jesus plays the hero
and Paul the villain, and he criticized Reformers from Isaac Mayer
Wise to Hyman Enelow for writing about Jesus "as if [he] were a
nineteenth-century American rabbi." Jewish lives of Jesus, even ostensibly nonfiction ones, were in Sandmel's view products of the
imagination, and far too often their authors approached the New Testament naively, as if Jesus had actually said and done everything attributed to him. Sandmel saved some of his most biting words for
John Cournos's claim that Jesus was "the apex and acme" of Judaism.
"It is this sort of thing," he wrote, "which by its unrestrained elasticity
persuades me to remain within the rigid confines of scholarly, pedan-
tic knowledge." In the end, he was kinder to Jesus than he was to
Cournos, but his pronouncements about the Galilean rabbi sounded
less like back-slapping sermons and more like the faint election-night
praise offered by defeated politicians to their opponents. Sandmel
conceded that Jesus was "a great and good man," for example, but he
denied that he "exceeded other great and good men in the excellency
of human virtues."[58]

Today work on Jesus by American Jews is dominated by Sandmel's
heirs in the academy, not Wise's heirs in the pulpit. Since the 1970s,
New Testament scholars of many faiths have been engaged in another
quest for the historical Jesus. One key characteristic distinguishing today's Third Quest from the initial quest (of the nineteenth century)
and the New Quest (begun in the 1950s) is the leadership of U.S.
scholars, who now dominate the field. Another is the active participa-

tion of Jewish scholars, who for the first time are finding themselves at the center of a search for the historical Jesus. When Wise delivered his Christmas sermon in 1925, university professorships were almost entirely closed to Jewish intellectuals and few Christian scholars were interested in what Jews had to say about the origins of Christianity. After the Holocaust, and particularly after Vatican II, interreligious dialogue came to characterize not only the interactions of grassroots priests, ministers, and rabbis but also scholarly work on the New Testament. Moreover, the discovery of the Dead Sea Scrolls and other ancient manuscripts in the 1940s and 1950s, made it plain that the histories of early Christianity and Second Temple Judaism were inextricably tied.

Today readers interested in the historical Jesus can consult books written by eminent Jewish historians such as David Flusser, Geza Vermes, and Paula Fredriksen. The emphasis of these scholars on the Jewishness of Jesus is echoed in works by non-Jews, including E. P. Sanders's *Jesus and Judaism* (1985), James H. Charlesworth's *Jesus Within Judaism* (1988), John P. Meier's *A Marginal Jew* (1991), and Bruce Chilton's *Rabbi Jesus* (2000). In fact, the Jewishness of Jesus is another distinguishing mark of the Third Quest. Jesus scholars don't agree on much, but there is widespread agreement in their ranks about Jesus' Jewish roots. The Jesus Seminar, which depicts a Jesus largely aloof from Jewish culture, is the proverbial exception that proves this rule; the chief scholarly complaint about the work of Robert Funk and his Fellows is their tendency to obscure Jesus' Jewish roots.

Another striking feature of today's Third Quest is how closely it mirrors the writing on Jesus of the Reform rabbis of the late nineteenth and early twentieth centuries. In many cases, recent scholarly works distinguish themselves from Reform sermons on Jesus a hundred years ago chiefly by their polyglot footnotes. With contemporary scholars, as for those rabbis, Jesus is, as Rabbi Stephen Wise put it, "a historic being, not a myth; a man, not a god; a Jew, not a Christian." The hue and cry that arose following Wise's Christmastime sermon is now largely absent, but the key question continues to be what kind of Jew Jesus was. Or, as one scholar put it, "the Jewishness of Jesus is now axiomatic . . . [even for] those New Testament scholars who can only pay lip service to it."[59]

In fact, making Jesus more and more Jewish seems to be a trend in historical Jesus research. *Jesus of Nazareth: King of the Jews* (1999) by Boston University professor Paula Fredriksen depicts Jesus as an observant Jew, well-versed in the Jewish scriptures and immersed in the sacrificial rites of the Temple in Jerusalem. Geza Vermes, a British historian who helped to launch the Third Quest with his depiction of Jesus as a charismatic miracle worker in *Jesus the Jew* (1973), contends in *The Changing Faces of Jesus* (2001) that his subject was a fiercely faithful Jew who taught "the permanent validity of the Torah" and drew inspiration from the writings of the prophets.[60]

Such language plainly recalls earlier efforts by Reform rabbis to reclaim Jesus for Judaism. And though contemporary Jewish scholars tend to be more suspicious of Jesus than were Stephen Wise and his predecessors, they echo that earlier work with remarkable fidelity. Approaching the New Testament with a hermeneutics of suspicion, they draw a sharp distinction between the religion *of* Jesus and the religion *about* Jesus, tracing the genesis of the latter to Paul and other early Christians. They reject claims of Jesus' divinity and messiahship, and place the blame for his crucifixion on Romans rather than Jews. The cumulative effect of this work is to transport Jesus from the Christian world back to Judaism. In that process, Jesus loses nothing of his personality, however, since this recent crop of scholars sees Jesus as a fascinating figure, the enigma of Second Temple Judaism.

Books in the current Jesus quest typically appear in the nonfiction aisle, but they are not immune from the tendency of novelists and visual artists to find in Jesus a mirror image of themselves. "To attempt to fit the historical Jesus into his Jewish setting is to put a somewhat uncertain figure into an uncertain background," Samuel Sandmel has observed. But that uncertainty has deterred few from the task. In fact, it has emboldened Zionists to interpret Jesus as a martyr for the nation and Reform Jews to embrace him as a crusader for social justice. In *Jesus of Nazareth: King of the Jews*, Paula Fredriksen warns against any conception of Jesus that fails to grate on twenty-first-century ears. Anachronism "is the first and last enemy of the historian," she writes, and like Sandmel before her, she scoffs at attempts to turn Jesus into a hippie, a supply-side economist, a feminist, or, for that matter, any modern person at all. But that note of caution has prevented few Jewish thinkers from yanking Jesus away from his Christian handlers and remaking him into a mirror image of themselves.[61]

JESUS CULTURE

A recent book called *Jesus Through Jewish Eyes* (2001) includes essays and poems about Jesus by Jewish rabbis, lay people, and scholars (almost all of whom live and work in the United States). Contemporary American culture, one essayist writes, is "Jesus-culture." In the United States, Jesus is "virtually impossible to avoid," so Americans define themselves at least in part by figuring out what Jesus means to them. "It is time for Christians to accept Jesus as a Jew," another contributor writes. "It is also time for Jews to reclaim him . . . as a brother." One essay in the volume makes this point with a hackneyed joke: "How do we know that Jesus was Jewish? He went into his father's business, lived at home until he was thirty, and had a mother who thought he was God!" The essay ends with some better humor. An aging Jewish woman finds herself in a Catholic hospital with a huge picture of Jesus facing her bed. A passing nun, aware that the woman is Jewish, offers to have the picture removed. "Oh no," the woman replies, "such a success by one of our boys. Leave it up!"[62]

Perhaps humor is not to be taken seriously. But these jokes, and their proliferation outside Jewish circles, suggest at least two important things about the American history of Jesus the Jew. They suggest, first, that efforts to reclaim Jesus for Judaism persist. The project of proudly claiming Jesus for Judaism began in the United States in the 1860s, ramped up in the 1890s, and peaked in the 1920s and 1930s. Though popular interest in Jesus the Jew waned following World War II and the Holocaust, it did not go away in either the U.S. Jewish community or American culture at large. Americans now laugh at these jokes not because a Jewish Jesus is an anomaly but because he is commonplace. Everyone now knows that Jesus was a good Jewish boy.

These jokes suggest, second, that the Jesus question is no longer as hotly contested as it was for earlier generations of Jewish Americans. Jewish Americans who speak or write about Jesus rarely fawn over him the way Cournos did. As heirs of Sandmel rather than Asch, their work generally commands respect rather than disgust. Portraits of Je-

sus as a good Jew can still boil the blood of many Orthodox Jews, who
continue to criticize reclaimers of Jesus as traitors. But for the most
part the rhetoric visited upon Cournos and Asch has been toned
down. Time, among other things, has made it clear that to call Jesus a
Jew is not necessarily to call for Jews to become Christians. Moreover, the subversive spirit of the reclaimers—their reincarnation of Jesus as one Jew among many, and particularly their insistence that they
understand better than the average Christian who Jesus truly was—
has become more evident over time, particularly as Jewish scholars
have crafted prizewinning biographies of Jesus. Why denounce a
Jewish Jesus when he can be such a powerful tool against Christian
missions?

In his insightful book on Jesus and Judaism, Samuel Sandmel distinguished the Jewish Jesus from the Christian Christ. He then proposed a third category: "the Jesus of Western culture."[63] Sandmel said
he had no religious relationship with Jesus, but as a participant in
Western society he saw no reason to try to isolate himself from this
cultural Jesus, who belongs not just to Christians or Jews but to Western culture as a whole. American Jewish thinkers have contributed
mightily to the significance of this "Jesus of Western culture." As they
have welcomed Jesus into Judaism, they have also made him more at
home in the United States. In the process, they have helped to transform American culture into a "Jesus culture."

Perhaps this is what the Orthodox were worried about. Sandmel
was convinced that "Jews can be trusted to discern the difference between the Jesus of religion and the Jesus of western culture."[64] He
was also convinced that they could resist the undeniable power of
celebrity in American life, and avoid redirecting their religion from
principles to personalities. The Orthodox were not so sure, and their
fears may not have been entirely unfounded. Sandmel was able to
keep the distinctions between his various Jesuses straight, in part because his approach to Jesus was entirely secular. But rabbis, novelists,
and scholars alike have blurred those distinctions, giving Jesus a place
not only in the history of culture but also in the history (and perhaps
the practice) of American Judaism.

Eight

ORIENTAL CHRIST

Today in Hindu homes and temples across the United States a striking image of divinity is on display. Dressed in a flowing white robe, his long hair pulled back behind slight shoulders, this holy man sits, half-lotus style, eyes cast down, in meditation. A halo rings his head, and his body is framed, St. Francis–like, by wild animals—a dove gracing his right shoulder, a rabbit preening his left foot, a sleeping snow leopard tucked in behind him. "He was there in the wilderness . . . ," the text in the picture reads, "and was with the wild beasts" (Mark 1:13). Painted in the 1920s by Eugene Theodosia Oliver, a Catholic, in keeping with instructions from a Hindu monk, the image is called *Christ the Yogi*. This Jesus is clearly at peace with nature, with himself, and with God. He knows precisely who he is. And who he is, quite plainly, is a Hindu.

The story behind the diffusion of this image—an image as recognizable in American Hindu circles as Warner Sallman's portraits of Christ are among American Protestants—is the story of America's Vedanta societies. That tale is typically told beginning with the arrival of Swami Vivekananda (1863–1902), the first Hindu missionary to the

United States, at the World's Parliament of Religions, held in Chicago in 1893 in conjunction with the World's Columbian Exposition. But a more useful starting point may be the day nearly two decades earlier when Jesus came to a village in northern India.

The villager who encountered Jesus that day was Ramakrishna, a venerable Indian mystic from West Bengal. As a young man, Ramakrishna (1836–86) had embraced the non-dualistic philosophy of Advaita Vedanta, which affirms the essential unity of Brahman (God) and Atman (Self/Soul) and teaches the unity of all religions. Ramakrishna was not content merely to affirm the unity of all religions, however. He was determined to experience it. So this devotee of the Hindu goddess Kali submitted himself, first, to Allah and, later, to the rigors of Buddhist meditation. In 1874, he turned to Christianity or, to be more precise, to Jesus. A follower described Ramakrishna's Christian experience like this:

One day, while Sri Ramakrishna was seated in the drawing-room of another devotee's home, he saw a picture of the Madonna and Child. Absorbed in contemplation of this picture, he saw it suddenly become living and effulgent. An ecstatic love for Christ filled Sri Ramakrishna's heart, and a vision came to him of a Christian church in which devotees were burning incense and lighting candles before Jesus. For three days Sri Ramakrishna lived under the spell of this experience. On the fourth day, while he was walking in a grove at Dakshineswar, he saw a person of serene countenance approaching him with his gaze fixed on him. From the inmost recesses of Sri Ramakrishna's heart came the realization, "This is Jesus, who poured out his heart's blood for the redemption of mankind. This is none other than Christ, the embodiment of love." The Son of Man then embraced Sri Ramakrishna and entered into him, and Sri Ramakrishna went into samadhi, the state of transcendental consciousness. Thus was Sri Ramakrishna convinced of Christ's divinity.[1]

Soon Ramakrishna's disciples were worshiping Christ as a divinity and attempting to reach this "Jesus state." Many reported similar experiences of mystical union with Jesus.

Shortly after Ramakrishna's death in 1886, a group of followers (twelve according to legend) gathered on Christmas Eve to discuss Jesus, his life of renunciation, and his realization of God-consciousness. Their leader was Swami Vivekananda, an indefatigable organizer who was destined to play the role of Paul in the nascent Ramakrishna movement. Vivekananda told his friends of Jesus' birth, baptism, teaching, death, and resurrection. He described how Paul had "preached the gospel of the Arisen Christ and spread Christianity far and wide." Now it was time for them to do likewise. So they vowed to live as renunciants, denying themselves as Jesus had done. Then Vivekananda and his twelve established the Ramakrishna Order as a way to spread the Jesus-friendly gospel of Ramakrishna.[2]

Vivekananda later went on a pilgrimage around India with a worn copy of *The Imitation of Christ* (by the Roman Catholic monk Thomas à Kempis) in tow. His most celebrated pilgrimage took him to the United States, where he attended the World's Parliament of Religions. In Chicago, Vivekananda won over his listeners with his sharp wit, dashing good looks, and Irish brogue. As he spoke of his religious tradition, Vivekananda forced his listeners to reckon for the first time with Hinduism in the flesh. Here was a living embodiment of the Hindu tradition, and his own faith seemed to have nothing to do with the horrors of widow burning and idol worship emphasized in missionary accounts. Christian missions in India are foolish, Vivekananda contended, since all religions are manifestations of one divine reality.

After the Parliament, Vivekananda lectured widely across the United States, spreading Ramakrishna's gospel of the unity of all religions. He was a regular guest at Green Acre, a spiritual retreat center in Eliot, Maine, where he met practitioners of a wide variety of American religions, including the New Thought leader Ralph Waldo Trine. He also spoke often at the salon of Mrs. Sara Bull in Cambridge, Massachusetts, where he befriended a number of Harvard professors, including the psychologist of religion William James. In 1894 in New York City, Vivekananda established the Vedanta Society, the first major Hindu organization in the United States. When he returned to India in 1897, he left behind Vedanta centers in cities across the country. In those societies, Vedantists celebrated Christmas by reading the story of the Nativity, contemplating the Sermon on the

Mount, listening to lectures on the life of Jesus, singing Christmas carols, and doing *darshan* (sacred seeing) of *Christ the Yogi*. "Meditate on Christ within," worshipers were told, "and feel his living presence."[3] And in Vedanta societies from Boston to San Francisco, they continue to do so today.

AVATAR

Hindus reckoned with Jesus long before Vivekananda came to Chicago in 1893 or Ramakrishna encountered Christ in the Dakshineswar grove in 1874. In fact, they have been retelling his story ever since Portuguese Catholics first came to Goa in the early sixteenth century. The Jesus tradition that the Vedantists brought to the United States is, therefore, quite old in American terms—older, in fact, than the Jesus traditions of home-grown American religions such as the Church of Jesus Christ of Latter-day Saints and the Church of Christ, Scientist.

Ram Mohun Roy (1772–1833), the leader of the religious and social reform society the Brahmo Samaj (established in 1828), helped to bring Indian christology into being as he attempted to reconcile Hinduism with Christianity. Like his contemporary Thomas Jefferson, Roy was a monotheist with Unitarian sympathies who denied the divinity of Jesus while affirming the excellence of his moral teachings. *The Precepts of Jesus: The Guide to Peace and Happiness* (1820), like Jefferson's abridged and expurgated Bible, stripped all supernaturalism from the Gospel accounts.

During the Indian Renaissance of the nineteenth century, Hindu interest in Jesus quickened. In an 1866 lecture on "Jesus Christ: Europe and Asia," Keshub Chunder Sen, an advocate of a reform movement called the "New Dispensation," argued that Jesus was "not a European, but an Asiatic."[4] In *The Oriental Christ* (1883), P. C. Mozoomdar, another Brahmo Samaj leader, followed Sen in describing Jesus as Oriental. He went a step further, however, when he called himself not only a Hindu but also a Jesus devotee.

Inspired by Ramakrishna, on the one hand, and this Indian Jesus tradition on the other, American Vedantists produced hundreds of books, lectures, and articles about Jesus during the twentieth century.

Three of the most important are "Christ, the Messenger" (1900) by Swami Vivekananda; *Christ and Oriental Ideals* (1923) by Swami Paramananda; and *Hindu View of Christ* (1949) by Swami Akhilananda. Swami Paramananda (1884–1940), who established Vedanta centers in Boston and Los Angeles, was one of the most popular Hindu leaders in the United States before the guru explosion of the 1960s and 1970s. Long before the Maharishi Mahesh Yogi was turning seekers on to Transcendental Meditation, Paramananda was instructing Americans in Hinduism. No world-denying renunciant, Paramananda loved fashionable clothes and fast cars; one wag dubbed him the "Hollywood star swami." Swami Akhilananda (1894–1962) established and led the Vedanta Society of Providence, and spearheaded the Boston Vedanta Society after Paramananda's death in 1940. Though not as flashy as Paramananda, he was instrumental in introducing Vedanta to a generation of American intellectuals, particularly Boston-area philosophers and theologians, during and after World War II.

· On first blush, "Christ the Messenger," *Christ and Oriental Ideals*, and *Hindu View of Christ* all look remarkably traditional. While American Jewish interpreters (and Ram Mohun Roy himself) denied his divinity, these three texts all glory in Jesus' godliness. Vivekananda called Jesus "a messenger of light" and a "sannyasin." Akhilananda described him as a miracle-working "yogi." But the most popular Vedantist appellation for Jesus was divine incarnation. Whereas American Jewish admirers of Jesus were careful to call him, simply, Jesus, Vedantists lauded him as Christ.

Vivekananda, Paramananda, and Akhilananda all saw Jesus as an incarnation of God, an embodiment of divinity worthy of worship. Akhilananda, who wrote *Hindu View of Christ* after World War II, when neo-orthodox critiques of Protestant liberalism were in the air, took on not only psychologists who derided Jesus as a psychotic but also wishy-washy liberals who showered him with faint praise (as a great moral teacher). When Jesus said "I and the Father are One," he wasn't speaking metaphorically, Akhilananda insisted. Jesus was nothing less than a "fully enlightened" God-man who knew of his divinity at birth. "If I, as an Oriental, have to worship Jesus of Nazareth," Akhilananda wrote, quoting Vivekananda, "there is only one way left

to me, that is, to worship Him as God and nothing else." Apparently
Akhilananda did a good job of that. Paul Johnson, a professor at
Boston University's School of Theology and a friend of the swami,
called him not only "a devout Hindu" but also "one of the best Christians I have known."[5]

Of course, when Vedantists such as Vivekananda, Paramananda,
and Akhilananda referred to Jesus as an incarnation, they meant
something different by it than what most Christians mean. In the
Christian tradition, incarnation is typically seen as a once-and-for-all
event, the mystery of God taking on a body in the person of Jesus
Christ. The Sanskrit word for incarnation is *avatar*, literally a "descent" of divinity to earth, and according to Hindus this is a recurring
rather than a unique role. Vishnu, for example, is said to have ten
incarnations, descending, among other things, as a tortoise, a fish,
a dwarf, and as both Krishna and the Buddha. Vivekananda, Paramananda, and Akhilananda all quoted a classic proof text from the
Hindu scripture the Bhagavad Gita to underscore the multiplicity of
avatars. "Whenever, wherever virtue declines and vice prevails, then I
embody Myself," Paramananda's translation went. "For the protection
of the good and for the destruction of the evil and for the reestablish-
ment of religion, I am born from age to age."[6]

The key notion here is that God takes on bodies whenever necessary; avatars are many, not one. In the abstract, God is one, but that
abstract God is unknowable, beyond human imagining. Happily, God
incarnates in human bodies in order to make Himself known. Such
divine descents occur whenever humans turn away from God. Because humans turn away from God repeatedly, incarnations of divinity
occur over and over again. So while Jesus is an avatar, he is not to be
mistaken as the only one. Krishna, too, is a divine descent, as is the
Buddha. Or, to put it as the Vedantists often did, Krishna and Buddha
are also Christs. "Let us therefore find God not only in Jesus of
Nazareth but in all the great Ones that have preceded him, in all that
came after him, and in all that are yet to come," wrote Vivekananda.
"They are all manifestations of the same Infinite God."[7]

What is the role in this scheme of such a Christ? It is not to save
humans from sin and deliver them to heaven. In fact, Vedantists em-
phatically reject original sin. "Vedanta forbids us to dwell on the

thought of sin," says Paramananda. "Call no man a sinner. All are children of immortal bliss." According to Vedantists, all human beings are "inherently perfect." The problem is that such perfection is in most of us latent rather than manifest. Humans, in short, are ignorant. And what they are ignorant of is their own divinity. Jesus' role in salvation, then, is not atoning for our sins. "The idea . . . that if we believe in a certain Savior we have only to fold our hands and let Him save us," writes Paramananda, "is a grave mistake." The avatar's purpose, rather, is to embody the divinity of humanity and lead others to perfection. The Christian notion that Jesus " 'taketh away the sin of the world,' " wrote Vivekananda, "means that Christ would show us the way to become perfect," for did not Jesus say, "Be ye therefore perfect, even as your Father which is in Heaven is perfect" (Matt. 5:48)? The role of Jesus, indeed of every avatar, is to inspire us to achieve that perfection—that "direct realization of God" that he enjoyed—and so to be able to say, as Jesus said (in one of the Vedantists' favorite proof texts), "I and the Father are one" (John 10:30).[8]

Of course, the vast majority of modern American Christians hold a very different view of Jesus, insisting on both the reality of sin and the uniqueness of their Savior. But that is the problem, these swamis believed. By affirming the status of Jesus as God's one and only Son, traditional Christians were limiting an infinite God, dogmatizing Jesus, and turning Christians into haters of so-called "heathens." So while traditional Christians clung "to the dogmatic Christ, the creed-bound Christ of organization and institution," Vedantists looked "to that Christ who is the soul of Divinity, who cannot be partitioned off any more than we can partition off the infinite sky."[9]

THE CHRIST IDEAL

Along with Jesus the avatar, Hindus also lauded Jesus the Oriental Christ. This view, first announced in the West in P. C. Mozoomdar's *Oriental Christ*, quickly took on a life of its own, and a variety of different meanings.

In some Vedantist writing, to call Jesus Oriental is to make a claim about his race or ethnicity, to contend that Asian blood coursed through his veins. Swami Vivekananda seemed to affirm this understanding when he excoriated Christian missionaries for their naive "attempts to paint [Jesus] with blue eyes and yellow hair." "The Nazarene," he insisted, was "an Oriental." From another Vedantist perspective, to call Jesus Oriental was to make a historical claim— that Jesus was influenced by Oriental thought or, perhaps, visited India during his youth (or, in some stories, after his crucifixion). Paramananda gave voice to a widespread myth when he asserted that Indian Buddhist missionaries to Palestine inspired the founding of the Essenes, who influenced John the Baptist, who influenced Jesus himself. Other Vedantists, drawing on Notovitch's *The Unknown Life of Jesus Christ*, claimed that Jesus studied in Asia during the "lost years" of his teens and twenties. One purpose of such historical claims was to subvert stereotypes of Asians as heathens: if Jesus sat at the feet of Asian teachers in India and Tibet, then perhaps Asians are worthy of respect. And if Hinduism influenced Christianity at the source, perhaps it deserves respect as well.[10]

Still, when Vivekananda, Paramananda, and Akhilananda referred to Jesus as an Oriental, they were generally making neither a racial nor a historical argument. Rather they were associating Jesus with certain beliefs and values. None of these swamis was particularly interested in the historical Jesus, and all three saw Christ more as a timeless principle than a living person—an embodiment of "Oriental ideals." In an effort to define what they called "the Christ-Ideal," Vivekananda, Paramananda, and Akhilananda all called down stereotypes of East and West, linking Jesus with the Orient rather than the Occident. The three conjured those categories differently, but all portrayed the East as the land of the spirit par excellence, and the West as the land of political, economic, and technological achievement. "The voice of Asia has been the voice of religion," wrote Vivekananda, "The voice of Europe is the voice of politics." Paramananda wrote that "the Eastern heart yearns primarily for spirituality," while, in Akhilananda's words, Western civilization "emphasized the path of pleasure as the solution to the problems of man."[11]

In her *Story of Jesus Christ* (1897), the American novelist Elizabeth Stuart Phelps contrasted her protagonist with the stereotype, propagated in scores of missionary travelogues, of the Oriental holy man as an impractical dreamer. "He did not waste himself in speculation, or lose himself in aimless Oriental reverie," she wrote of her practical Savior. "He sat on no stone pillar with crossed and idle feet, a figure given over to dreams and desolation, a spectacle for curiosity, a scarecrow for common men. He withdrew into no useless trance, no remote psychical experimentation." The Vedantists agreed with this characterization of Jesus, but not with its stereotype of the Oriental sage. "In the West, the preacher who talks the best is the greatest preacher," wrote Vivekananda. But in the East, the true holy man is the one who practices what he preaches. And Jesus, Vivekananda added, was "intensely practical."[12]

When they said Jesus was practical, the Vedantists did not exactly mean that he knew how to change a flat tire or fix a broken faucet. They meant he knew how to apply his faith to daily life. In the West, they argued, Christians are preoccupied with theology rather than practice. But "religion in the East is not a matter of belief in doctrine, dogma, or creed; it is being and becoming; it is actual realization." From this perspective Jesus was characteristically Oriental in that he made manifest the unity of divinity and humanity rather than merely preaching it. And he did so without a hint of the hypocrisy that the Vedantists associated with Christian missionaries. Paramananda illustrated that point with a novel interpretation of a New Testament parable: "It was this which Christ meant when he gave the parable of the two houses: one built on the rock, the other on the sand, typifying the two lines of the religious life, the one of theory or mere belief, the other of practice." The house built on the sand was the house of the dogmas, creeds, and rites of organized religion—the house of going to church and going through the motions. The house built on the rock was the house of the genuine spirituality of Jesus. "One becomes a good Christian," concluded Paramananda, "not by clinging to a special creed, but by living."[13]

The Vedantists' representations of East and West also drew on Victorian stereotypes of the masculine and the feminine. Like many other interpreters, they aligned the East with femininity and the West with masculinity. Here again Jesus was said to be more Eastern than Western. In "If Christ Came Today," a piece written with Charles Sheldon's bestseller, *In His Steps*, in mind, Paramananda asked (as Sheldon did) what Jesus would do if he "came today." Paramananda wrote the article in 1938, with World War II in the offing, and in it he concluded that Jesus would be "the Prince of Peace," blessing the meek, the pure in heart, and the peacemakers. Jesus was a renunciant, Paramananda argued. He was "meek and humble, forgiving and merciful . . . tender and loving." If he returned today he would renounce the descent of civilizations into fruitless violence. He would also renounce decades of efforts to turn him into a macho warrior. Great nations, Paramananda wrote, should stop teaching "young boys to stand up for their rights and to fight back lest they should be called 'sissies.' " Young men should imitate Jesus instead by practicing "true renunciation."[14]

In the contest between the feminizers and the masculinizers of Jesus, the Vedantists cast their lot with the feminizers. Like Ramakrishna, who came to believe in Jesus' divinity after gazing at an image of the Madonna and Child, some U.S. Vedantists focused their adoration on the baby Jesus. Sister Daya, a friend of Paramananda and one of his most valued assistants, wrote an essay comparing the "Christ Child and Child Krishna," and like other women of the late Victorian era she seemed drawn primarily to the infant Jesus. Inside America's Vedanta societies, the key day for remembering Jesus has typically been neither Good Friday nor Easter but Christmas, a holiday that Paramananda described as "a symbol of that infinite tenderness . . . interwoven with everything helpless and childlike."[15]

In organs such as *Vedanta Magazine*, Vedantists often ran images of Jesus to illustrate their Christmas sermons on him. The images they circulated most widely generally emphasized Jesus' infancy over his adulthood, his femininity over his masculinity. Heinrich Hofmann's *Christ in the Temple* (1871) was one such picture, though Vedantists typically reprinted only a close-up of this Jesus' youthful face. A twelve-year-old boy debating fine points of theology with scribes in the Jerusalem Temple (the original context for this narrative painting) evidently did not interest them. What attracted them was, in the words of New York City's Swami Abhedananda, the tender face of "Jesus the Christ" as a "meek and gentle and self-sacrificing Son of Man."[16]

Early in the twentieth century, Vedantists decided they need a Jesus picture of their own. Swami Trigunatita, who led the San Fran-

cisco Vedanta Society and oversaw the building there of the first
Hindu temple in North America, commissioned Eugene Oliver to
paint *Christ the Yogi*. That picture too has all the machismo of a St.
Francis holy card. It evokes a meek rather than a militant Jesus, emphasizing qualities that Teddy Roosevelt and other muscular Christians of the era would have associated with femininity rather than
masculinity.

From the first settlements at Jamestown and Plymouth, immigrants
have shaped their identity as Americans by adapting their religious beliefs and practices to American soil. When Vedantists referred to Jesus as an Oriental, they were saying something not only about his
character but also about theirs. Like us, they were saying, Jesus lives
in America, but his spiritual home is in India. As they relocated and
reinterpreted Jesus, Indian-American swamis and their American-
born followers staked a claim to participate fully in the drama of
American religion. By calling into question widespread stereotypes of
Hinduism, the Vedantists asserted their right to define their own religious heritage, rather than having hostile missionaries define it for
them. If Christ was an Oriental, then perhaps Western stereotypes of
Hinduism were suspect. At the very least, they were not the first and
only word. But these Vedantists were doing something more bold than
asserting a right to define themselves and their religion. They were asserting a right to define Christianity too.

JESUS VS. CHURCHIANITY

The Oriental Christ fashioned by Vedantists was both orthodox and
unorthodox, radical and traditional. In their emphasis on Jesus as an
incarnated divinity, Vivekananda and his successors were more theologically conservative than many of their Protestant contemporaries,
who at the turn of the twentieth century were gravitating toward a liberal form of Christianity that soft-pedaled heaven and hell, accusations of sin, and signs of supernaturalism. While their predecessor
Ram Mohun Roy had courted the Unitarians as fellow travelers, the
Vedantists criticized Unitarians for viewing Jesus as merely a great
man. Jesus, they insisted, was an incarnation of God who was worthy
of both imitation and worship. Vedantists were quite comfortable re-

ferring to Jesus as the Son of God and they attributed to him a variety of miracles. They were also inveterate readers of scripture who could trade Bible verse for Bible verse with the most learned Protestant preachers.

Nonetheless, the Vedantists' understanding of the nature of Jesus' divinity was quite heterodox. While they accepted his miracles, they downplayed their importance, noting that miracle-working was something of a pedestrian skill among Hindu yogis. And while they quoted the Bible repeatedly, they did not typically believe it was divinely inspired. Echoing Brigham Young, Swami Abhedananda gloried in the fact that "the light of scientific investigation" had been shed on the "absurd and meaningless" myths of the Bible.[17] Of course, these views distinguished neither him nor his colleagues much from their liberal Protestant colleagues, who themselves had little interest in miracles or biblical inerrancy. When Vedantists called for a Christianity shorn of empty rites and outmoded creeds—a religion of Jesus alone—they were consenting to the Protestant mainstream, not dissenting from it.

What distinguished the Vedantists from the Christians surrounding them, liberals and fundamentalists alike, was their utter lack of interest in the historical Jesus. Christians have typically affirmed both the historical Jesus and the living Christ, the man who lived in the ancient Mediterranean world and the Savior who lives today in believers' hearts. As a practical matter, however, followers of Jesus have typically emphasized one or the other. Paul of Tarsus and Joseph Smith, for example, each emphasized the living Christ over the historical Jesus. Ramakrishna's American followers also emphasized the ability of that living Christ to enter human hearts. But they did more than ignore the historical Jesus. Many actually denied him.

When Europe witnessed a modest resurgence, around the turn of the century, of the view that Jesus never existed, American Christians typically ignored the theory, and leading Reform rabbis refuted it. Vedantists, by contrast, seemed energized by it. Swami Vivekananda initially believed in the historical Jesus but after a curious dream came to doubt that he ever lived. Yet such doubts did not trouble him a bit. "It does not matter at all whether the New Testament was written within five hundred years of his birth; nor does it matter even how much of that life is true," he wrote. "But there is something behind it, something we want to imitate." Swami Abhedananda conceded that the events of Jesus' life, particularly his youth, were "not based upon historical facts." And he insisted that he was not at all bothered by what he saw as the Gospels' make-believe character:

> The students of Vedanta do not care whether the personality of Jesus was historical or not, whether he was born of a virgin at Bethlehem or not, whether he was the fulfilment of the old prophecy, or of the promise of Yahveh, the tribal God of the house of Israel, or of the Messianic hope of the Jewish people, but the students of Vedanta recognize in the Sublime Character of the Saviour Christ the manifestation of the universal Logos or the Word of God as they do in other incarnations of the same Almighty Being.

Sister Daya made the same point in fewer words. "Even if the Man of Nazareth were proved to be a myth," she wrote, "Christ would yet live!" That was because, for these Vedantists, Jesus was more a principle than a person, an eternal ideal rather than a historical reality.[18]

This lack of interest in the historical Jesus is consistent with traditional Hindu views of the self. While Jews and Christians have typically affirmed Thomas Aquinas's formulation of the person in which "soul and body are one being," Hindus have seen the essence of the person as soul only, dismissing the body as external to the true self. The ancient Greeks shared this conception, viewing the individual as essentially spiritual and the body as a tomb or prison. Influenced by that Greek culture, gnostic Christians affirmed an understanding of Jesus as fully God but not fully human: Jesus only seemed to have a body. The Vedantists adopted this heretical view. Jesus was a "disembodied soul" bereft of "sex ideas," Vivekananda wrote. "That which was crucified was only a semblance, a mirage." Swami Abhedananda described Jesus' body as a "mere shell" and said his soul was "separate" from his body.[19]

Vedantists further distinguished themselves from their Christian neighbors by arguing that all human beings can become Christs. Like Christ the avatar, the Oriental Christ is a recurring reality, not a historical being, and can be found wherever the "supreme state of God-consciousness" resides. "Whoever reaches that state," whether via Christianity, Hinduism, Buddhism, or any other religion, wrote Abhedananda, "becomes a Christ." The differences people see between religions are illusory. To be sure, there are sharp differences in creeds and rites. But if you look beyond those externals to internals, beyond mere appearances to underlying essences, you will see that all the great religions of the world preach the same timeless truths and work toward the same goal of the union of humanity with divinity. Just as the one God appears in many forms, so there is "one religion" with "many aspects." "Truth is one," say the Vedas, in a line quoted regularly by these swamis. "Men call it by different names." Or, as Paramananda put it, "All great faiths are the expression of the one great cosmic Spirit coming down to show him his relationship with the Divine."[20]

At first glance, this approach seems to be wonderfully tolerant. But on further inspection it is shockingly audacious. Vedantists did not merely assert similarities across religions. They asserted their fundamental equivalence. And when it came to describing the one religion shared by all humanity they defined it almost entirely in Hindu terms, bursting with avatars but bereft of creeds. It is "Vedanta, and the Vedanta alone," Vivekananda wrote, "that can become the universal religion of man." And when it came to Christianity, Vedantists were no less assertive. They divided the religion into a true and a false form: "the religion of Jesus the Christ" and "Churchianity." Then they drew on the authority of Jesus—"the universal Christ," not "the dogmatic Christ"—in order to denounce whatever they believed was wrong with the tradition. "The religion of Christ, or true Christianity," Abhedananda wrote, "had no dogma, no creed, no system, no theology. It was a religion of the heart, a religion without any ceremonial, without ritual, without priestcraft." All the abominations of Christianity—including original sin, hell, the vicarious atonement, the resurrection of the body—came later, through Paul and the early Church Fathers, and deserve no place in true Christianity today.[21]

In keeping with Rabbi Kaufmann Kohler and Rabbi Emil Hirsch before them, these Vedantists claimed far more than the right to interpret Jesus, the Bible, and Christmas. They insisted that they understood those symbols better than Christians themselves. And while most of these teachers did not follow their mentor Ramakrishna in claiming to be Christians, many claimed to be able to discern a good Christian (one who "lives the life") from a bad one (who doesn't). Swami Abhedananda, in one of hundreds of Vedantist sermons on Christmas, boldly asserted that "Vedanta alone can help us to understand the spiritual Ideal of Christ and the true meaning of the Spiritual Christmas."[22]

The most intrepid American Vedantist may have been Swami Trigunatita, the San Francisco Vedanta Society leader who commissioned *Christ the Yogi*. In "Jesus of Nazareth from the Hindu Standpoint" (1915–16), he took Vedantist daring to its logical conclusion. Echoing the inveterate Roman Catholic claim that there is "no salvation outside the church," Trigunatita wrote that the Vedantist teaching of self-realization "alone leads you to the truth." "Will your baptism and acceptance of Christ as your Savior be able to save you?" he asked. "No . . . Unless you realize yourself, no Bible, no doctrine, no amount of baptism can ever save you." Trigunatita's position was not that other religious paths were entirely futile. It was possible to realize your own equivalence with God through other faiths. But any person on the path to self-realization was in his view "a true Vedantist."[23]

Much later in the twentieth century, the Roman Catholic theologian Karl Rahner would use the term "anonymous Christian" for practitioners of other religious traditions who in his view were nonetheless saved by the grace of God and the death of Christ. Non-Christians who did not cotton to his condescension rightly took him to task. Yet Trigunatita was no less presumptuous in seeing all true seekers as anonymous Hindus: "No matter by what way, by what method you carry on your religious culture—be you a Christian, be you a Mohammedan, be you a Buddhist—so long as you are a sincere seeker after truth, you are a great Vedantist, you belong to Hinduism," he wrote. "Hinduism is your religion."[24]

YOGI JESUS

When Swami Trigunatita wrote those words, the Vedanta Society was the leading Hindu organization in the United States, both in influence and in numbers. That situation changed with the arrival of Swami Yogananda. Like Vivekananda, who came to the United States to attend the World's Parliament of Religions, Yogananda (1893–1952) came to the country to attend an interreligious conference, in his case the International Congress of Religious Liberals, held in Boston in October 1920. Unlike Vivekananda, who eventually returned to India, Yogananda made his home in the United States (in Los Angeles) and became an American citizen.

A generation younger than his predecessor, Yogananda was a powerful speaker and an able organizer. He was also an eager adapter of Hinduism to American circumstances. He praised Bruce Barton's *The Man Nobody Knows* as a "wonderful book" and drew expertly on the advertising techniques Barton extolled in order to promote his own mission. He also adapted his message to the therapeutic concerns of America's new culture of personality. In addition to lecturing on the cultivation of "Christ Consciousness," he spoke on "The Divine Art of Making Friends," "How to Be More Likable," and "Developing Dynamic Will." He stressed self-denial far less than the Vedantists, and self-fulfillment far more. In "Developing Personality," he described the goal of self-realization as awakening the "divine personality" within. This aggressive adaptation paid off handsomely. His Self-Realization Fellowship (SRF), incorporated in 1935 and now based in Los Angeles, quickly became the largest and most influential Hindu organization in the United States. With the publication of his *Autobiography of a Yogi* (1946), Yogananda's influence spread well beyond the SRF's peak numbers of 150,000 members and 150 centers. That memoir became required reading in the counterculture of the 1960s and 1970s.[25]

In addition to telling the life story of Yogananda and his guru, Sri Yukteswar Giri, *Autobiography of a Yogi* outlines Yogananda's distinctive form of Hindu practice, called Kriya Yoga. Kriya Yoga shares with other Hindu spiritual techniques the goal of liberation from the endless cycle of life, death, and rebirth. Two things set it apart, however. The first is its promise of quick and easy results. Americans like their food fast and their salvation instantaneous, so Yogananda calls his new and improved yoga the "airplane route" to God. "*Kriya Yoga* is an instrument through which human evolution can be quickened," he explains. "One thousand *Kriya* practiced in eight hours gives the yogi, in one day, the equivalent of one thousand years of natural evolution." Kriya Yoga's second distinguishing feature is its scientific technique. Yogananda's breathing technique, transmitted from guru to student, aspires to elevate spiritual power (kundalini) from the base of the spine to the spiritual center at the crown of the head, culminating in a liberating awareness of the unity of the self with the divine. Yogananda calls this practice "the scientific technique of God-realization" and claims it had been utilized by "St. John, St. Paul, and other disciples."[26]

Even more than his counterparts in the Vedanta Society, Yogananda blurred the distinctions between Christianity and Hinduism. He quoted repeatedly from the New Testament, and on his home altar he kept pictures of five avatars, with Jesus in the center. Yogananda also commented extensively on Jesus, who was for him a secret practitioner of Kriya Yoga—a "spiritual giant" who demonstrated his mastery over matter by, among other things, rising from the dead. According to SRF lore, Kriya Yoga's founding avatar Babaji was in constant spiritual communion with Jesus. In fact, Yogananda's mission to America began when Jesus appeared to Babaji and told him to send Yogananda to spread Kriya Yoga in the West.

Like the Vedantists, Yogananda spoke of Jesus as one avatar among many who came to awaken human beings to their essential divinity. While Vedantists typically referred to him as an Oriental, however, Yogananda saw him as at once Oriental and Occidental—a synthesizer of East and West. In "Jesus: A Christ of East and West," a talk he delivered regularly during the 1930s and 1940s, Yogananda called Jesus "a divine colossus standing between Orient and Occident" who embodies their union through his birth in Asia and his acceptance as a guru in America.[27]

Yogananda believed that Jesus had been reincarnated repeatedly, so it should not be surprising that he focused more on the living Christ than the historical Jesus. Like Ramakrishna he reported a mystical encounter with that living Christ, a series of encounters, in fact. Once, while working on what he called "a spiritual interpretation of Christ's life" in his hermitage in Encinitas, California, Yogananda implored Jesus to guide him to just the right words. As he described in his *Autobiography*, his sitting room was suddenly showered with blue light:

> I beheld the radiant form of the blessed Lord Jesus. A young man, he seemed, of about twenty-five, with a sparse beard and moustache; his long black hair, parted in the middle, was haloed by a shimmering gold. His eyes were eternally wondrous; as I gazed, they were infinitely changing. With each divine transition in their expression, I intuitively understood the wisdom that was being conveyed. In his glorious eyes I felt the power that upholds the myriad worlds. A Holy Grail appeared at his mouth; it came down to my lips and then returned to Jesus. After a few moments he spoke to me in beautiful words of reassurance, so personal in their nature that I keep them in my heart.[28]

Here Yogananda too found a way to love Jesus without accepting Christianity. He too drew a sharp distinction between Jesus and Christianity, and insisted on interpreting both in his own way. That he arrived at a Jesus who practiced what Yogananda preached is not surprising. What is worth noting is his bold claim—a claim he shared with thinkers from Thomas Jefferson to Swami Vivekananda—to understand Jesus better than Christians themselves. Yogananda repeatedly referred to "true Christianity," which in his view included time-honored Hindu doctrines such as reincarnation. He also claimed to be able to divine the real meaning of traditional Christian doctrines such as the crucifixion and the resurrection. The true Second Coming of Christ, for example, was according to Yogananda the awakening of the individual to "Christ Consciousness." And the true seat of that consciousness was not in the heart but in the seventh chakra (or "Christ Consciousness center") located between the eyebrows. Yogananda regularly found similarities between Hinduism and Christianity and then boiled those similarities down to equivalences. *Aum*, an ancient Indian mantra that Yogananda described as the universal life force, was the same as the Holy Spirit. The teachings of Jesus in the New Testament had an "exact correspondence" with the teachings of Krishna in the Hindu scripture the Bhagavad Gita.[29]

Along with many other American interpreters of Jesus, Yogananda looked carefully into the mirror and then created Jesus in his own likeness. But he did more than that. He contended that his image was the true image—that he understood Jesus better than Paul or Augustine, that he revered Jesus at least as much as Martin Luther or Jonathan Edwards had. "I am sometimes asked if I believe in Jesus," Yogananda wrote in "Jesus: A Christ of East and West." "I reply: 'Why such a question? We in India reverence Jesus and his teachings, perhaps more than you do.' "[30]

Swami Yogananda died in 1952, but his mission lives on in the SRF centers he established—nearly 500, by the organization's own count, in fifty-four countries. One principle that animates those centers today is the equality of all religions. The Self-Realization Fellowship Lake Shrine outside Los Angeles in Pacific Palisades includes a Court of Religions that encourages visitors to contemplate the truths of Hinduism, Buddhism, Judaism, Christianity, and Islam as they walk meditatively around a lake. At an on-site gift shop, altars that include icons of Yogananda and his guru alongside Krishna and Jesus sell briskly. Devotional images of Jesus (typically as depicted by Hofmann's *Head of Christ*) can also be found at SRF centers across the country, which like U.S. Vedanta societies celebrate the Christmas season as a time to commune with the Oriental Christ.

Through the Vedanta Society and the SRF, Jesus was reincarnated in Hindu America. While Bruce Barton and Warner Sallman were resurrecting him inside American Christianity as the one and only Savior, these pioneering Hindu gurus were giving him life inside a vast Hindu epic populated by millions of gods, each with multiple manifestations. In that cosmic drama, divinity descended into human affairs not once, but over and over and over again.

BUDDHA-TO-BE

American Buddhists do not typically celebrate Christmas, but at least a few revere Jesus, and they too have made Jesus over in their own image. There are perhaps three or four million Buddhists in the United States, and many more sympathizers, who have not formally converted to the religion but nonetheless cultivate a Buddhist practice or see the world through Buddhist eyes. These Buddhists can be divided into two basic categories. On the one hand, there are cultural Buddhists—the "once born" who have inherited rather than chosen their faith. Many of these birth-right Buddhists are immigrants from Asian countries, but this category also includes practitioners from groups such as the Buddhist Churches of America, which have been active in the country for generations. On the other hand, there are countercultural Buddhists—the "twice-born" who were raised Protestants, Catholics, or Jews (or "Other") only to convert to Buddhism or embrace some form of Buddhist practice. Many of these convert Buddhists are serious practitioners, and a few have even become monks and nuns. Others are part-timers who get most of their Buddhism from books and an occasional weekend retreat. This type also includes "once-born" Buddhists in "twice-born" communities—the sons and daughters of 1960s and 1970s converts. Although countercultural Buddhists get most of the press in the United States, cultural Buddhists are far more numerous, constituting about three-quarters of all practitioners.

Inside American Buddhism, as in American Hinduism, interest in Jesus seems to be keenest among the converts, people like the Beat Generation writer Jack Kerouac, who in *Mexico City Blues* (1959) professed his belief in both Jesus and the Buddha. Among so-called "bookstore Buddhists"—those who get most of their Buddhist instruction from texts rather than teachers—demand for Buddhist interpretations of Jesus was particularly strong in the 1990s. Much of that demand was satisfied by two authors, the Dalai Lama and Thich Nhat Hanh.

The Dalai Lama (b. 1935), the exiled spiritual and political leader of the Tibetan people, came to personify Buddhism in the United States during the 1990s Buddhist vogue. In an era in which mainline Protestant preachers were all but banished from the halls of public power (and the cover of *Time* magazine), the Dalai Lama appeared on the cover of *Time* and met a series of U.S. presidents, including George H. W. Bush, Bill Clinton, and George W. Bush. In 1997, his life inspired two big-budget Hollywood films: *Kundun* and *Seven Years in Tibet*.

Active in Buddhist-Christian dialogue for decades, the Dalai Lama discussed contemplative practices with other monks, including the

Catholic writer Thomas Merton, at his home-in-exile in Dharamsala, India, in 1968. But he has shown no interest in Yogananda-style religious unity. Merton once said that at least when "studied as strictures, as systems and religions, Zen and Catholicism don't mix any better than oil and water." The Dalai Lama has equated efforts to yoke Buddhism and Christianity with "trying to put a yak's head on a cow's body."[31]

But at least in America, where Jesus functions as the proverbial elephant in the room, the Dalai Lama has found it impossible to ignore him. Many Christians who have met the Dalai Lama have likened him to Jesus, pointing to his commitment to nonviolence, his humble demeanor, and his seemingly advanced spiritual state. But the Dalai Lama resists such comparisons. "Don't compare me with Jesus," he told *The New York Times* in 1993. "He is a great master." The Dalai Lama's most extensive treatment of Jesus appears in *The Good Heart: A Buddhist Perspective on the Teachings of Jesus* (1996). There he compares the Sermon on the Mount with the first sermon of the Buddha, and notes the tendencies of each founder to teach through stories and parables. Jesus and the Buddha both preached "simplicity and modesty," for example: the Buddha and his monks wandered around India, begging bowls in hand, and Jesus told his disciples "to take nothing for their journey, not food, stick, pack, or money."[32]

The Dalai Lama's ultimate assessment of Jesus is lofty: "For me, as a Buddhist . . . he was either a fully enlightened being or a bodhisattva of a very high spiritual realization."[33] This is a high compliment indeed, since becoming a bodhisattva, a Buddha-to-be who has cultivated perfect compassion, is to many Buddhists the pinnacle of human achievement. It is also yet another clever reinterpretation of Jesus, who in this case is destined not for messiahship but for Buddhahood.

After the Dalai Lama, with whom he is often compared, Thich Nhat Hanh (b. 1926) is the most influential Buddhist figure in the United States. A Vietnamese Zen monk who went into exile in France in 1966 following his criticism of the Vietnam War, Thây (meaning teacher) lives in a Buddhist community called Plum Village in France. He travels regularly to the United States, where he is active in a variety of organizations, including Parallax Press and the Order of Interbeing, both leading institutions of "engaged Buddhism," a term he coined to denote a Buddhist form of the Social Gospel. Thây also met with Thomas Merton, and he too has participated for decades in Buddhist-Christian dialogue. Unlike the Dalai Lama, however, he has no qualms about mixing up religious traditions. He has images of both the Buddha and Jesus on his home altar, and has adopted Jesus as one of his "spiritual ancestors."[34]

Thich Nhat Hanh's writings on Jesus include two of the bestselling Buddhist books of the 1990s: *Living Buddha, Living Christ* (1995) and *Going Home: Jesus and Buddha as Brothers* (1999). In both books, he follows Yogananda in finding similarities between two religions and then collapsing those similarities into identities. So mindfulness is the Holy Spirit, nirvana and God are both the ground of being, and reincarnation and the resurrection are one and the same. Jesus and the Buddha are not quite identical twins, but they are, at a minimum, "brothers," members of the same spiritual community, equally adept at meditation and equally committed to cultivating mindfulness and compassion. According to Thây, the Buddha was "born again," and Jesus was "enlightened"—"very holy, very deep, and very great."[35]

Not many Buddhist writers have the opportunity or chutzpah to rebuke a pope. But Thich Nhat Hanh did just that. *Living Buddha, Living Christ* responded explicitly to John Paul II's *Crossing the Threshold of Hope* (1994). In that book, the pope affirmed his Church's post–Vatican II commitment to interreligious dialogue, but went on to characterize Buddhism as an " 'atheistic' system . . . indifferent to the world" and to warn his readers about the dangers of Buddhist meditation. He also described Jesus as "totally original and unique," the one and only gatekeeper to salvation. Thich Nhat Hanh responded by dismissing the Pope's representation of Jesus as parochial and shallow— insufficiently attentive to "the deep mystery of the oneness of the Trinity." To the Pope's affirmation of Jesus' uniqueness, he replied, "Of course, Christ is unique. But who is not unique? Socrates, Muhammad, the Buddha, you and I are all unique. The idea behind the statement, however, is the notion that Christianity provides the only way of salvation and all other religious traditions are of no use. This attitude excludes dialogue and fosters religious intolerance and discrimination. It does not help."[36]

Here again we have a non-Christian asserting something far more plucky than the right to interpret Jesus as he sees fit. Thich Nhat Hanh is a Buddhist monk purporting to educate a pope on the mysteries of the Trinity, insisting that he has a better understanding of Jesus and his teachings. Whereas the Dalai Lama's book on Jesus is written as a dialogue, and in it the Dalai Lama exhibits the sort of humility he admires in Jesus (by carefully qualifying his remarks), Thây is far bolder. He advances detailed interpretations of what he calls the "Dharma of Jesus," dismissing theological differences between Christianity and Buddhism on matters such as the soul and the afterlife as "superficial" and "not real." "The best theologian," he insists, "is the one who never speaks about God."[37]

In *Going Home*, Thich Nhat Hanh challenges Christians to trade in images of Jesus on the cross for more positive images, including "sitting in the lotus position or doing walking meditation."[38] Of course that is just what the Catholic painter Eugene Oliver did when he produced *Christ the Yogi* for the San Francisco Vedanta Society. Though their medium was textual rather than visual, the Dalai Lama, Thich Nhat Hanh, and swamis from Vivekananda to Yogananda were all engaged in a similar project.

A NATION OF RELIGIONS

In his conclusion to *Jesus Through the Centuries* (1985), Jaroslav Pelikan argued persuasively that Jesus no longer belongs exclusively to the West: Christians in Korea, Japan, and China all call him Lord. Two decades after that book's publication, the point is so manifestly true that it hardly seems worth repeating. What does bear repeating is that, at least in the United States, Jesus no longer belongs exclusively to Christians. Since the late nineteenth century, American Hindus and Buddhists have weighed in on the Jesus question, and their influence has only increased in the wake of the post-1965 immigration boom. Today Americans who follow the Dalai Lama think of Jesus as a bodhisattva. Congregants at the San Francisco Vedanta Society, where *Christ the Yogi* hangs, embrace Jesus as "a great Yogin" with highly developed "psychic powers." Hare Krishnas worship Jesus as an incarnation of their Supreme Lord Krishna, and Taoists call him the "Eternal Tao."[39]

Recall for a minute the audacity of Vivekananda, Trigunatita, and Yogananda, whose worship of Jesus was, in Vivekananda's words, "unbounded and free." Each sought to unbind Jesus from the shackles of Christianity and ancient Palestine, inviting him to take birth in the hearts of modern American Hindus. The Christians' proprietary view of Jesus—as theirs and theirs alone—produced according to Paramananda only "war and intolerance." The Vedantists' more cosmopolitan approach would deliver "perfect harmony and universal tolerance." While each of these gurus preached the unity of religions, each also insisted that the world's religious traditions converged on the truths of Hinduism, rightly understood. Yes, Jesus was a Hindu. But so were all his true followers. Members of the Vedanta Society and the Self-Realization Fellowship did not merely survive in a country that was somehow both pluralistic and Christian. They dared to imagine Jesus as a Hindu hero and the United States as a Hindu nation. A similar daring manifests itself in the work of Thich Nhat Hanh and, to a lesser extent, the Dalai Lama. And so the menu of Jesus images available to Americans has expanded to include the avatar and the yogi, the bodhisattva and the Buddha-to-be.[40]

Jesus is popular in the United States today in part because the overwhelming majority of its citizens are Christians (a fact, it should be noted, that owes much to the myriad resurrections of Jesus effected by nineteenth- and twentieth-century American Christians). But if Christians had retained a monopoly over interpreting Jesus, he would not have become a national icon. His standing as such can be traced in large measure to the audacious efforts of America's freethinkers and Jews, Hindus and Buddhists, who have conspired to steal Jesus away from Christianity, freeing him up to be (in Paul's words) "all things to all people." As a nation of immigrants has become a nation of religions, populated with Sikhs and Hindus, Confucians and Buddhists, the array of available Jesuses has expanded too. Together these Asian religionists are doing more than making Jesus in their own image. They are making Jesus in the likeness of America.

CONCLUSION

In a country where Jesus is as multiform as Proteus, it is difficult to point to any one representation of him and say it is particularly over the top. But the laughing Jesus may fit the bill, particularly because he seems to have been born in a graveyard.

When Dr. Hubert Eaton founded Forest Lawn Memorial Park in Glendale, California, in 1917, his aim was to create a cheerful cemetery. According to Forest Lawn's founding myth, Eaton drove out on New Year's Day 1917 to a decrepit county cemetery that he was managing. As he surveyed the depressing landscape, he vowed to make it new. He jotted down a statement, part promise and part confession, now memorialized as "The Builder's Creed." In it, Eaton committed himself to making his cemetery "as unlike other cemeteries as sunshine is unlike darkness, as Eternal Life is unlike Death . . . a great park, devoid of misshapen monuments and other customary signs of earthly Death, but filled with towering trees, sweeping lawns, splashing fountains, singing birds, beautiful flowers; noble memorial architecture, with interiors full of light and color, and redolent of the world's best history and romances." To this vow he appended a three-part creed to cheerful Christianity: "I believe in a happy eternal life. I believe those of us left behind should be glad in the certain belief that those gone before, who believed in Him, have entered into that happier Life. I believe, most of all, in a Christ who smiles and loves you and me."[1]

Over the next few decades, Eaton transformed Forest Lawn into one of the largest and most profitable cemeteries in the United States. He replaced tombstones with memorial markers flush to the lawn. He built chapels and hosted weddings of the rich and famous. He also banished from his grounds much of the traditional rhetoric of death, referring to the dead as "loved ones" and his cemetery as a "memorial park." For these efforts, Eaton was brutally satirized by Evelyn Waugh (in *The Loved One*, 1948) and Jessica Mitford (in *The American Way of Death*, 1963), both British writers allergic to American cheerfulness. And while many U.S. intellectuals cackled along with their British counterparts, ordinary Americans flocked to the place, making it one of the most popular tourist attractions in southern California. Bruce Barton spoke for many when he praised Forest Lawn as "a noble resting place for the departed, and a perpetual delight for those who live." He spoke for Eaton when he challenged every American cemetery to adopt the Forest Lawn approach. "Not until that happens will we be able to call ourselves a truly Christian nation," Barton wrote. "For we worship a Master who loved and laughed . . . who, on the very night before his death, could say, 'Be of good cheer; I have overcome the world,' and 'because I live, ye shall live also.' "[2]

As Forest Lawn expanded from 55 to 300 acres, Eaton filled it with Jesus art, including a reproduction of Leonardo da Vinci's *Last Supper* (in stained glass) and Jan Styka's massive original painting, *The Crucifixion*. But he still did not have a "Christ who smiles." At some point in the early 1950s, Eaton grew tired of his dour Christs. "It was a tragic error for Christianity to make of Christ a Man of Sorrows, when He was a loving and smiling Saviour," he wrote. So he announced to the Italian art community a contest with a cash prize for the best portrait of a smiling Jesus. No one took the award home, because none of the entries met with Eaton's approval. Many weren't even smiling, and those that were possessed, as Eaton put it, "a kind of sad look and a definitely European face." "Now, what I'm looking for," Eaton explained, "is a Christ filled with radiance and looking upward with an inner light of joy and hope. I want an American-faced Christ."[3]

George Santayana once wrote that "American life is a powerful solvent. It seems to neutralize every intellectual element, however tough and alien it may be, and to fuse it in the native good-will, complacency, thoughtlessness, and optimism."[4] That solvent has had a powerful effect on American Christians, who have for some time been gravitating from spiritual sticks to carrots—from threats of hell to the promise of heaven, from the burden of sin to the gift of grace, from Good Friday to Easter. When Henry Ward Beecher died in 1887, his family refused to mourn. In lieu of a wake, they threw a party—a "flower funeral" complete with roses at his front door instead of the customary black crepe. In the mid-twentieth century, distributors of Christian stuff realized that Americans were no longer enamored of prints of a crucified Christ, so they threw their marketing efforts into head-and-shoulders portraits of a joyful Jesus. A few decades later, marketing surveys told megachurch pastors that their target market was tired of hearing about depravity and death, so they stopped talking about the wages of sin and banished the cross from their churches. Today only about one in every five American Catholics, Methodists, Episcopalians, Lutherans, and Presbyterians believes in the devil, and 77 percent of born-again Christians say that human beings are "basically good."[5]

This cosmic optimism, as familiar to Americans as it is foreign to Europeans, failed to produce a "Christ who smiles" during Eaton's lifetime. Henry Ward Beecher had offered his well-to-do congregants at Brooklyn's Plymouth Congregational Church a "cheerful, companionable, and most winning" Jesus. To follow Jesus, he reassured them, was "to be the happiest person in the world." In *The Man Nobody Knows*, Bruce Barton also elevated the pursuit of happiness to a religious goal. God, Barton wrote, was "a happy God, wanting His sons and daughters to be happy," and Jesus was "the friendliest man who ever lived." But by his death in 1966, Eaton had been unable to locate an artist who dared to deviate so decisively from the "Man of Sorrows" tradition. In 1987, the Catholic monthly *Liguorian* found just such an artist in Ralph Kozak, whose rendition of a guffawing Jesus, his head tilted back, roaring with laughter, appeared on its April cover. At the end of the millennium, smiling Jesuses were widespread enough to be spoofed. In the film *Dogma* (1999), a Catholic cleric committed himself to supplanting old-fashioned crucifixes with an insanely happy "Buddy Christ" who smiles, winks, and otherwise gives life a big thumbs-up.[6]

THE CULTURAL CAPTIVITY OF JESUS

In *The Lonely Crowd* (1950), a landmark study of the American character, sociologist David Riesman (and coauthors Nathan Glazer and Reuel Denney) identified three major personality types: "tradition-directed" people who follow rules written down by their ancestors; "inner-directed" people who follow rules laid down by their parents; and "other-directed" people willing to bend the rules in order to win the approval of their peers. According to Riesman, the first two types have difficulty adjusting to postindustrial, service-oriented societies, while other-directed people thrive in them. At least in the United States, Jesus has been a classic other-directed personality. Ever eager to please, he has been all things to all people, adjusting his message and appearance in order to be loved by his peers. Critics have denounced Henry Ward Beecher for serving as America's weathervane instead of her conscience, but the American Jesus has been even more attuned to shifts in the cultural winds. Lacking any core sense of self, he has seemed most concerned about keeping up with the Joneses, pumping iron in the era of Teddy Roosevelt and letting his hair down in the heyday of the counterculture. Though Americans have hailed Jesus as a personality who stood out from the madding crowd, they have applauded him loudest when he has walked and talked like them. If they were laughing, they wanted him to laugh along.

This is just the sort of thing the Yale Divinity School professor H. Richard Niebuhr had in mind when he denounced the "captivity of the church" to culture in the 1930s.[7] As the American experiment unfolded, Americans gradually liberated Jesus from divinity, dogma, and even Christianity itself. Born as a person in the evangelical awakenings of the nineteenth century, Jesus became a personality and then a celebrity under the aegis of liberal Protestants after the Civil War.

As non-Christians embraced him in the twentieth century, transforming him into a national icon, Jesus left his Christian home and struck out on his own. But this unbound Jesus was never fully free. Liberated from the past, he became captive to the present, bound to sentimental culture, then crusading masculinity, then sixties excess.

In *The Church Against the World* (1935), Niebuhr took on America's love affair with itself, and its Christians' infatuation with American culture. Focusing on the ever-changing relationship between the church and the world, Niebuhr observed a series of pendulum swings, back and forth between conflict and alliance, withdrawal and engagement. Writing in the wake of World War I and in the midst of the Great Depression, Niebuhr contended that in modern times God had become too friendly, the church and civilization too cozy. When the church "enters into inevitable alliance with converted emperors and governors, philosophers and artists, merchants and entrepreneurs, and begins to live at peace in the culture," Niebuhr wrote, "faith loses its force, . . . discipline is relaxed, repentance grows formal, corruption enters with idolatry, and the church, tied to the culture which it sponsored, suffers corruption with it." And so he concluded that "the task of the present generation appears to lie in the liberation of the church from its bondage to a corrupt civilization." Niebuhr nuanced this argument years later in *Christ and Culture* (1951), now a classic in American theology, but his basic critique was in place in the 1930s.[8]

Historians have decried the church's captivity to culture for some time. Ann Douglas lamented the demise of theology that attended the twilight of Calvinism. Christopher Lasch criticized the capitulation of Christianity to the therapeutic culture of consumer capitalism. Asking, "Where are the real religious prophets?" R. Laurence Moore answered his own question with a question: "Can there be any in a country whose self-image rests on fast, friendly, and guiltless consumption?" American religion, he concluded, has lost its "transformative power."[9]

Evangelicals and fundamentalists have in recent decades become the most vocal critics of American Christianity's captivity to culture, in part because the complacent optimism Santayana identified at the heart of American life seems rife as well in born-again circles. Drawing a hard-and-fast distinction between Christianity and civilization, evangelical and fundamentalist critics of this accommodation believe it is the duty of all true believers to withdraw from the impure world. In the 1990s, a group called the Alliance of Confessing Evangelicals formed to combat what it saw as the secularization of American Christianity. "Evangelical churches today," its "Cambridge Declaration" (1996) began, "are increasingly dominated by the spirit of this age rather than by the Spirit of Christ." They teach a "self-esteem gospel" and a "health and wealth gospel" when they should be preaching the good news of the inerrant Bible. In 1997, the Christian musician Steve Camp issued another call for repentance when he posted his "107 Theses" against the Contemporary Christian Music industry on the Web. "In the past several years there has been a non-so-subtle drifting away from Christocentric music to an anthropocentric music," he wrote. "The object of faith is no longer Christ, but our self-esteem; the goal of faith is no longer holiness, but our happiness."[10]

Conservative Christians are particularly distressed about what this loss of nerve has done to belief in Jesus. In *The State of the Church 2002*, the evangelical pollster George Barna found that only one-third of Catholics, Lutherans, and Methodists believe that Jesus was sinless, and only half of born-again Christians are willing to affirm unequivocally the view that Jesus was without sin. According to Gerald McDermott, a professor of religion at Roanoke College and an Episcopal priest, these data point to "an epochal change in popular theology"—a "loss of faith in the divinity of Christ. . . . In the last 30 years American pastors have lost their nerve to preach a theology that goes against the grain of American narcissism." Together they are reducing Jesus "to no more than the Dalai Lama, an admirable kind of guy."[11]

These critics are onto something. In his history of American Methodism, John Wigger recognized that while Methodists co-opted popular culture for their own ends, the co-optation worked in two directions. "Attracting large crowds of ordinary Americans simply was not possible without catering to their most deeply held hopes, fears, and prejudices," Wigger argued.[12] Jesus' popularity has also come at a cost. When Bruce Barton tried to use Jesus to Christianize the secular world of business, he failed to distinguish clearly enough between the God he was evoking and the economic order he was transforming, so the business world ended up co-opting him. Jesus has no doubt transformed the nation, but the nation has also transformed him. At least in the United States, he has been buffeted about by the skepticism of the Enlightenment, the enthusiasm of revivalism, and the therapeutic culture of consumer capitalism. When Americans demanded a feminized hero, he became sweet and submissive. When they demanded a manly warrior, he muscled up and charged into battle. As feminism and the civil rights movement gained momentum and baby boomers tuned into the New Age, he became a black androgyne as comfortable with his yin as he was with his yang.

Under the circumstances, it might be best to allow Jesus to slip out the back door and return to ancient Palestine. And that is just what Henry J. Cadbury proposed in *The Peril of Modernizing Jesus* (1937). A Harvard professor and a staunch pacifist, Cadbury was troubled by efforts to conscript Jesus into war. He told the New Testament story of the Roman soldiers who "stripped him and put on him a scarlet military cloak . . . and mocked him." "The soldiers put on Jesus their own kind of clothes," Cadbury wrote, "and we all tend to clothe him with our thoughts." Cadbury did not make this point explicit, but he seemed to be saying that Americans are mocking Jesus too. They dress him up as Manly Redeemer (or, for that matter, a Sweet Savior or Superstar) and expect him to do their bidding.

In the United States, Jesus is widely hailed as the "King of Kings." But it is a strange sort of sovereign who is so slavishly responsive to his subjects. At least from the perspective of Cadbury and likeminded critics, the American Jesus is more a pawn than a king, pushed around in a complex game of cultural (and countercultural) chess, sacrificed here for this cause and there for another.

"OPTIMUM TENSION"

The problem with this critique is that it assumes an unchanging Jesus, untainted by human history, who is somehow being violated by his many resurrections and reincarnations. From the perspective of theology, an unchanging Jesus may be a necessity (though the doctrine of the incarnation does place Jesus squarely in the scramble of society). From the perspective of cultural and religious history, however, Jesus is anything but unchanging. In the book of Genesis, God creates humans in His own image; in the United States, Americans have created Jesus, over and over again, in theirs.

Christian symbols, including representations of Jesus, may be gifts from God, but they are nonetheless historically conditioned products of particular times and places. To his credit, Niebuhr admitted that all resolutions of the "Christ and culture" problem were socially constructed and pocked by sin. "Christ's answer to the problem of human culture is one thing," Niebuhr wrote, "Christian answers are another." Countee Cullen also recognized the dangers of absolutizing relative conceptions of Jesus. Aware that his "The Black Christ" was at least in part a product of his own desires, he ended his poem "Heritage" with this supplication and confession: "Lord forgive me if my need / Sometimes shapes a human creed."[13]

Of course, Cullen's need is nothing new, and neither is his dilemma. Only dead religions stay the same; living faiths adapt continuously to changes in their environments. There may be purity in the arena of ritual, but not in cultural and religious history, where believers are always negotiating with their environs, mixing and mingling the sacred and the profane. Even the process of translating scripture into a new language is a compromise of sorts; all efforts to tell the story of the Buddha or Confucius, Krishna or Jesus are themselves retellings of earlier tales. The Gospels of Luke and Matthew are based in part on the Gospel of Mark, and Paul's letters represent a radical reinterpretation of those texts—an extension of the aborning Christian movement beyond the limited confines of Judaism (and Jesus' own Aramaic-speaking community) to the Greek-speaking world.

The United States would not have been Christianized as rapidly or broadly as it was if its people hadn't Americanized the Christian tradition as aggressively as Paul and his successors once hellenized it. Charles Finney's "new measures" were crucial to the expansion of Christianity in the Second Great Awakening. The emphasis on a personal relationship with Jesus, so highly prized in born-again circles today, is a mid-nineteenth-century innovation. Even fundamentalism is an American invention, and a recent one at that, since fundamentalists did not articulate the unchanging articles of their faith until the early twentieth century.

Of course, the fact that change is inevitable does not make all change desirable. The sociologist Armand Mauss has argued that new religious movements are always struggling to maintain an "optimum tension" between assimilation into the surrounding culture and resistance to it.[14] While religions can be extinguished if they refuse to adapt, they die a different death if they adapt too freely. The same is true of not-so-new religions, which are engaged as well in a never-ending pas de deux with culture, always seeking the right balance between accommodating too much and accommodating too little. Through the American centuries, Christians have repeatedly calibrated that "optimum tension." In the process, they have drawn and redrawn the line dividing Christian essentials from inessentials. The procedures for that task have been clear cut wherever religious power has been centralized. The Vatican excommunicated; colonial Massachusetts banished; Salem hung. But the freewheeling spiritual marketplace of the United States has had no real authority other than popular opinion and individual conscience. While weak, such authority has not been entirely ineffectual. When the Ku Klux Klan distributed an image portraying Jesus as a Klansman handing out bread marked "Tenets of K.K.K." to the multitudes, Americans of good will were understandably horrified. Their denunciations stopped the diffusion of the Klan's rhetoric of the fiery cross (and the sullying of Jesus' good name). But public opinion comes and goes, and individual conscience is fickle. Moreover, the prophetic voices that might check both with authoritative pronouncements from on high have often been muted, or ignored.

They have not ever been entirely absent, however. It is easy to dismiss the various appearances of the American Jesus as narcissistic and culture-affirming, and many of his resurrections in the United States have been just that. But his reincarnations have often been culture-denying. Frederick Douglass invoked a radical Jesus in the abolitionist cause, as did William Lloyd Garrison, who put Jesus— and his commandment to "love they neighbor"—on the masthead of his newspaper *The Liberator*. Jews have used a Jewish Jesus to combat anti-Semitism and to criticize what Stephen Wise called the "Christlessness of Christianity."[15] Hindus have invoked an "Oriental Christ" in an effort to combat restrictions on immigration from Asia and racist stereotypes of Indian Americans. And evangelicals have appealed to their Savior not only in individual struggles with sin but also in collective battles against materialism and consumerism. Clearly the American Jesus has been an iconoclast as well as an icon.

JESUS NATION

It is highly unlikely that Americans will ever come to any consensus about who Jesus really is, but they have agreed for some time that Jesus really matters. In a country divided by race, ethnicity, gender, class, and religion, Jesus functions as common cultural coin. To be sure, this cultural Jesus is a shadow of the biblical Son of God, but the public is drawn to him nonetheless. In fact, his popularity only seems to have increased as he has become more human. Given that popularity—among Christians and non-Christians, and outside religious circles altogether—it is tempting to conclude on a triumphalist note. "Forget what you have heard about the cross or the tomb," I can almost hear the preacher saying. "Jesus is alive and well and living in America. And everyone is bearing witness to his glory."

The Baptist preacher George Dana Boardman hit that same note in a speech on "Christ the Unifier of Mankind" he delivered at the World's Parliament of Religions. "Jesus of Nazareth is the universal Homo, the essential Vir, the Son of human nature," he told his multireligious audience. "Blending in himself all races, ages, sexes, capacities, temperaments, Jesus is the archetypal man, the ideal hero, the consummate incarnation, the symbol of perfected human nature, the sum total of unfolded, fulfilled humanity, . . . history's true Avatar."[16] After two world wars and the Holocaust, such triumphalism rings false, but in a sense Boardman's vision has come to pass. Although not every American would say "Amen" to his particular understanding of this "archetypal man," Americans as a rule have embraced Jesus as something of an avatar of America. Many have pressed beyond even Boardman, identifying Jesus as a unifier not only of all "races, ages, sexes" but also of all religions.

Consensus history has been out of fashion since the 1960s, and it shows no sign of coming back, but at least in this case Americans appear to have something significant in common underlying their many differences. Jesus is a major figure in American life. Though by most accounts he never set foot in the United States, he has commanded more attention and mobilized more resources than George Washington, Abraham Lincoln, and the Reverend Martin Luther King, Jr., combined. Is this not powerful evidence for the view that the United States is a Christian country?

The problem with this conclusion is that, for many Americans, Jesus is not a Christian at all. To be sure, the cultural authority of Jesus has been used to promote the Christian tradition. But it has also been used to reform and subvert it, both from within and without, by Americans who see the man from Nazareth as a nondoctrinal, nondenominational, non-Christian. When it came to Jesus, Thomas Jefferson, Rabbi Kaufmann Kohler, and Swami Vivekananda employed similar strategies. All drew sharp distinctions between the religion *of* Jesus and the religion *about* Jesus, and all used the former to attack the latter. While other Americans loved Jesus because of Christianity, they loved him despite it. The fact that the United States is a Jesus nation does not make it a Christian one.

Perhaps the American Jesus demonstrates that this is a multireligious country. After all, here Buddhists and Black Jews, Mormons and Muslims have all claimed to understand Christianity better than the nation's cultural and religious insiders. Mormons have claimed superior insight into Jesus based on the Book of Mormon and later revelations. Jews have said they understand Jesus better because he was a Jew. "The Jews are the true Christians," Rabbi Bernhard Felsenthal has written, "and the so-called Christians are not Christians, inasmuch as they profess a number of doctrines totally foreign to the religion of Christ."[17] These are bold claims, but it must be remembered that Jesus is the subject here, not Moses or Joseph Smith. The Buddha, though beloved and worshiped in some circles, is not an American hero, and the nation does not observe his birthday. Plainly, the spotlight that shines on Jesus illuminates American Christianity far more than the country's other religions.

The American Jesus does not demonstrate either that the United States is a Christian country or that it is a multireligious one. He demonstrates that it is both at the same time. Jesus became a major American personality because of the strength of Christianity, but he became a national celebrity only because of the power of religious dissent. Like America's Jesus himself, who was born among Protestants but now lives among Christians and non-Christians alike, the United States has developed from a Protestant country into a nation, secular by law and religious by preference, that is somehow both the most Christian and the most religiously diverse on earth. As one of its people's foremost cultural artifacts, the American Jesus tells us that Christianity predominates in the United States—that practitioners of all faiths, and of no faith at all, must reckon with its central symbols. He also tells us that the public power of Christianity, while undeniable, is not absolute, that Christians do not have a monopoly, even on the central figure of their tradition.

The American Jesus also tells us that in the United States the sacred and the secular are inextricably intertwined. Jesus is a Jewish figure, a Christian figure, and a Muslim figure, but he is a secular figure too. In fact, some of the most intriguing conceptions of him have originated outside religious circles altogether—among unchurched artists, musicians, and novelists. A. J. Langguth's *Jesus Christs* (1968) is not widely known outside the science fiction community (in part because it is stolen so frequently from public libraries), but it may be the most clever Jesus novel of all time. Langguth, who covered the Vietnam War for *The New York Times*, imagines Jesus as a recurring character who darts across time and space more adeptly than Forrest Gump, dying and rising in ancient Palestine, Nazi Germany, and the contemporary United States. In one scene, he is both a death-row prisoner strapped into an electric chair and a chaplain giving himself last rites. *Jesus Christs* pokes fun at the malleability and multiplicity of Jesus in American culture, but it also underscores his ability to live and move and have his being well beyond the confines of religious institutions.

Interest in Jesus is not restricted to the United States, of course. It is no doubt part of a broader process that the French anthropologist Roger Caillois has described as the "internalization of the sacred" and the German philosopher Eric Voegelin has termed the "immanentization" of transcendence. As God has relocated from "up there" to "in here," Jesus has eclipsed his Father in many modern countries. But Americans have taken that process to new heights. If the sociologist

Adam Seligman is right, and the "immanentization" of transcendence is part and parcel of modernity, it might not be unreasonable to expect to see Americans gradually shifting their sights from Jesus to the Holy Spirit, who is after all the most immanent of the Trinity's three Persons. The meteoric rise in the United States of Pentecostalism and other forms of Holy Ghost religion seems to provide evidence for just such a trend, as does the replacement of crosses in some evangelical megachurches with images of the dove.[18]

For the time being, however, most Americans have their eyes squarely set on Jesus. Though the WWJD ("What Would Jesus Do?") craze of the 1990s has passed, Americans continue to read books such as *What Would Jesus Eat?* (2002) and to weigh the propriety of gas-guzzling SUVs by asking, "What Would Jesus Drive?" The "Jesus balloon," a 110-foot-tall, 750-pound hot air balloon of the "King of King, Lord of Lords," continues to lift off each Easter over northern California, preaching the risen Christ to citizens below. And new controversies—most recently, debates about an ancient burial box inscribed "James, son of Joseph, brother of Jesus" and about a gruesome Mel Gibson movie about Jesus' death—seem to arise every year. What would Jesus make of all this? That is anyone's guess. Might he be leaning back and laughing?

TIMELINE

1791 The ratification of the First Amendment makes religion a matter of individual choice rather than federal mandate.

1801–1830s The Second Great Awakening rapidly Christianizes the American population.

1804 Thomas Jefferson produces "The Philosophy of Jesus of Nazareth," a first draft of the Jefferson Bible.

1830 The Book of Mormon is published.

1835 David Friedrich Strauss's *Life of Jesus* appears in English translation.

1841 *Julian: Or, Scenes in Judea* by the Unitarian minister William Ware becomes the first Jesus novel published in the United States.

1842 Joseph Smith, Jr., introduces his fellow Mormons to the new rite of the "endowment," signaling a shift from "textual Mormonism" to "temple Mormonism."

1844 The "King Follett Discourse" by Joseph Smith boldly distances the Church of Jesus Christ of Latter-day Saints from the Christian creeds and earlier Mormonism.

1850s Currier & Ives publishes one of many popular Jesus lithographs, *The True Portrait of Our Blessed Savior*, based on an apocryphal letter attributed to "Publius Lentulus, a resident of Judea in the reign of Tiberius Caesar."

1852 Harriet Beecher Stowe's *Uncle Tom's Cabin* emphasizes Jesus' self-sacrificial love.

1861–65 Civil War

1861 Horace Bushnell's *Character of Jesus* accents the "passive virtues" of Victorian femininity.

1863 Ernest Renan's *Life of Jesus* appears in English translation.

1865 LDS President Brigham Young calls Jesus his "Elder Brother."

1869 Isaac Mayer Wise begins publishing a series of essays on "Jesus Himself" in his weekly *The Israelite*.

1871 The Fisk University Jubilee Singers embark on their first national tour, drawing attention to black spirituals.

Henry Ward Beecher's *The Life of Jesus, the Christ* appears. A second volume will come two decades later.

1875 "What a Friend We Have in Jesus" debuts in the first edition of *Gospel Hymns and Sacred Songs* by P. P. Bliss and Ira Sankey.

1880 *Ben-Hur, a Tale of the Christ* by the Civil War general Lew Wallace is published.

1889 Heinrich Hofmann produces *Head of Christ* (part of a larger canvass called *Christ and the Rich Young Ruler*), which will later become one of the most popular images of Jesus in the United States.

1890 President Wilford Woodruff of the Church of Jesus Christ of Latter-day Saints issues a manifesto effectively outlawing polygamy among Mormons, opening the door to Utah statehood and ushering in a new era in Mormon history.

1893 The World's Parliament of Religions brings the Hindu reformer Swami Vivekananda to the United States, but is also a venue for Jesus piety, thanks to the Presbyterian retailing magnate John Wanamaker, who puts Mihaly Munkácsys's *Christ Before Pilate* (1881) and *Christ on Calvary* (1884) on display.

1894 *The Unknown Life of Jesus Christ* (1894) by the Russian war correspondent Nicholas Notovitch fills in Jesus' "lost years" with a sojourn in India and Tibet.

Swami Vivekananda establishes the Vedanta Society in New York City.

1897 *In His Steps: "What Would Jesus Do?"* by Charles M. Sheldon transforms Jesus into a Social Gospel crusader.

Elizabeth Stuart Phelps casts her protagonist as a feminist in *The Story of Jesus Christ*.

1898 James Jacques Joseph Tissot's *Life of Our Saviour Jesus Christ*, a series of 365 gouaches, opens at the American Galleries in New York City.

The Passion Play of Oberammergau, the first American movie about Jesus, debuts.

"God is a Negro," affirms the A.M.E. bishop Henry McNeal Turner.

1901 Rabbi Joseph Krauskopf denounces Christian anti-Semitism, including accusations that the Jews were "Christ killers," in *A Rabbi's Impressions of the Oberammergau Passion Play*.

1903 *Jesus of Nazareth* by Bruce Barton's father, William Barton, appears.

1904	Thomas Jefferson's *The Life and Morals of Jesus of Nazareth* is published for the first time, by the Library of Congress.
1906	The *Jewish Encyclopedia* describes Jesus as a "magnetic personality."
1908	*The Psychology of Jesus* exemplifies new interest in the mind of Jesus. *The Aquarian Gospel of Jesus the Christ* by the Civil War chaplain Levi H. Dowling is published. Entire chapters will later make their way into *The Holy Koran of the Moorish Science Temple of America* by Noble Drew Ali.
1910–15	*The Fundamentals* defines the essentials of fundamentalism.
1911	The Men and Religion Forward Movement is founded in an effort to bring "missing men" back to the churches.
1913	Harry Emerson Fosdick's *The Manhood of the Master* presents a masculine Jesus.
1914–1919	World War I
1915	James Talmage's Mormon classic, *Jesus the Christ*, identifies Jesus as the Old Testament Jehovah. Warren Conant's *The Virility of Christ* is published.
1917	G. Stanley Hall lauds Jesus as the "world's master psychologist" in *Jesus, the Christ, in the Light of Psychology*.
1920s	Eugene Theodosia Oliver paints *Christ the Yogi* for the San Francisco Vedanta Society.
1920	Swami Yogananda comes to the United States as a delegate to the International Congress of Religious Liberals, held in Boston. In keeping with the new "culture of personality," Rabbi Hyman Enelow's *A Jewish View of Jesus* extolls Jesus as "the most fascinating figure in history."
1922	Upton Sinclair depicts Jesus as a socialist in *They Call Me Carpenter*.
1923	Giovanni Papini's *Life of Christ* provides conservative Catholics with a bestselling Jesus book. Swami Paramananda's *Christ and Oriental Ideals* hails Jesus as an "Oriental Christ."
1924	The Johnson-Reed Act effectively cuts off Jewish and Asian immigration. Marcus Garvey's United Negro Improvement Association anoints Jesus as the "Black Man of Sorrows."
1925	Bruce Barton's *The Man Nobody Knows* portrays Jesus as a manly businessman. The Scopes "Monkey Trial" in Dayton, Tennessee, pits fundamentalists against modernists. Rabbi Stephen Wise's Christmastime sermon in Carnegie Hall touches off a controversy inside American Judaism. *Ben-Hur* debuts on the screen.

1927	*King of Kings*, a film by Cecil B. DeMille, opens.
1929	The stock market crash brings on the Great Depression. Countee Cullen's long narrative poem "The Black Christ" interprets the life and death of Jesus in light of the brutal history of lynching.
1935	Swami Yogananda's Los Angeles–based Self-Realization Fellowship is incorporated.
1938	*An Open Letter to Jews and Christians* by John Cournos calls the wisdom of Jesus "the apex and the acme of Jewish teaching" and evokes "Judaeo-Christianity" as the only sure antidote to Communism and Fascism.
1939	*The Nazarene*, the first novel in Sholem Asch's "christological trilogy," is published.
1939–45	World War II and the Holocaust.
1940	Warner Sallman paints his iconic *Head of Christ*, now the most widely reproduced religious image in the world.
1946	*Autobiography of a Yogi* by Swami Yogananda presents Jesus as a practitioner of Kriya Yoga.
1953	John M. Oesterreicher begins publishing *The Bridge* through his Institute for Judaeo-Christian Studies at Seton Hall University.
1955	The Montgomery bus boycott sets the civil rights movement in motion.
1959	The Beat Generation writer Jack Kerouac affirms his belief in Jesus and the Buddha in *Mexico City Blues*.
1962–65	Vatican II "updates" Roman Catholicism and reorients Jewish-Catholic relations.
1965	The U.S. Congress opens up immigration from Asia.
1966	John Lennon says the Beatles are more popular than Jesus.
1967	Elizabeth and Ted Wise jump-start the Jesus movement when they open The Living Room coffeehouse in San Francisco's Haight-Ashbury district.
1968	The Reverend Martin Luther King, Jr., is assassinated, leading some to understand him as a new Moses and some as a crucified Christ. Albert Cleage's *The Black Messiah* colors Jesus black.
1969	*Ebony* publishes a cover story on "The Quest for a Black Christ." In *Black Theology and Black Power*, James Cone affirms Jesus' blackness.
1970	Larry Norman's *Upon This Rock* announces the arrival of the Jesus rock genre.
1971	A psychedelic hippie Jesus makes the cover of *Time* magazine; two rock musicals, *Jesus Christ Superstar* and *Godspell*, open; and *Christian Century* proclaims it the year of Jesus.

"Jesus was a Feminist," Leonard Swidler writes in *Catholic World*.

1973   *Jesus Christ Superstar* and *Godspell* are both released as movies.

Geza Vermes emphasizes the Jewishness of Jesus in *Jesus the Jew*.

1975   Edwina Sandys creates a sculpture of a bare-breasted Jesus on the cross to commemorate the United Nations' Decade of Women.

1976   "The Year of the Evangelical," according to *Time* and *Newsweek*.

1978   CCM *Magazine* begins covering the Contemporary Christian Music scene.

1979   Monty Python's *Life of Brian* spoofs the biblical epic.

1981   *What It Means to Know Christ* by B.Y.U. professor George W. Pace calls on Mormons to cultivate a "dynamic personal relationship with Christ."

1982   The Book of Mormon acquires a new subtitle: "Another Testament of Jesus Christ."

1984   Del Parson paints *The Lord Jesus Christ*. Commissioned by LDS authorities, this image is now the quasi-canonical "Mormon Jesus."

1985   The Jesus Seminar convenes.

1987   A laughing Jesus appears on the cover of the Catholic magazine *Liguorian*.

1988   *The Last Temptation of Christ*, a film depicting Jesus as a sexual being, sparks protests across the country.

1993   The Jesus Seminar produces *The Five Gospels: The Search for the Authentic Sayings of Jesus*, calling into question the genuineness of the vast majority of Jesus' sayings.

The Original African Heritage Study Bible includes images of a black Jesus.

1995   Latter-day Saints officials increase the size of the words *Jesus Christ* on their official logo to more than twice the height of the surrounding type.

Thich Nhat Hanh weighs in on the "Dharma of Jesus" in *Living Buddha, Living Christ*.

1996   The Dalai Lama interprets the Sermon on the Mount in *The Good Heart: A Buddhist Perspective on the Teachings of Jesus*.

1998   The Christian musician Steve Camp posts his 107 Theses online, urging the CCM industry to repent of its androcentrism and return to "Christocentric music."

1999   "Jesus of the People," Janet McKenzie's painting of an androgynous African-American Jesus, wins the "Jesus 2000" contest sponsored by *National Catholic Reporter*.

The movie *Dogma* satirizes overoptimistic Christianity via an insanely cheery "Buddy Christ."

2000   The Church of Jesus Christ of Latter-day Saints celebrates the millennium by issuing a new statement, "The Living Christ," affirming its commitment to a high christology.

2001   In anticipation of the upcoming Winter Olympic Games in Salt Lake City, LDS officials ask the media to stop referring to the "Mormon Church" and to call their organization instead "The Church of Jesus Christ" or "The Church."

Renee Cox's *Yo Mama's Last Supper* stirs controversy at the Brooklyn Museum of Art for its depiction of the Last Supper with Jesus as a nude black woman.

2002   The discovery of an ancient burial box, inscribed "James, son of Joseph, brother of Jesus," renews debate about the historical Jesus.

2003   Mel Gibson films a new movie about the last day of Jesus' life while Jewish and Catholic critics denounce his *Passion* as anti-Semitic.

NOTES

INTRODUCTION

1. Hunter Miller, ed., *Treaties and Other International Acts of the United States of America*, vol. 2. Documents 1–40, 1776–1818 (Washington: Government Printing Office, 1931), p. 365; *Holy Trinity Church v. U.S.*, 143 U.S. 457 (1892).
2. *United States v. Seeger*, 380 U.S. 163 (1965).
3. Diana L. Eck, *A New Religious America: How a "Christian Country" Has Become the World's Most Religiously Diverse Nation* (San Francisco: HarperSanFrancisco, 2001), pp. 4, 46.
4. Philip Jenkins, "A New Religious America," *First Things* 125 (August/September 2002), pp. 25–28; see also John Neuhaus, "One Nation Under Many Gods," *First Things* 116 (October 2001), pp. 71–79.
5. Humphrey Taylor, "Large Majority of People Believe They Will Go to Heaven; Only One in Fifty Thinks They Will Go to Hell" (Harris Poll #41, August 12, 1998), *HarrisInteractive*, http://www.harrisinteractive.com/harris_poll/index.asp?PID=167.
6. Alexis de Tocqueville, *Democracy in America* (trans. Henry Reeve; London: Saunders and Otley, 1835), chapter 17, http://xroads.virginia.edu/~HYPER/DETOC/religion/ch1_17.htm.
7. Samuel Sandmel, "Isaac Mayer Wise's 'Jesus Himself,' " in American Jewish Archives, ed., *Essays in American Jewish History* (New York: Ktav Publishing House, 1975), p. 357.
8. Jonathan Edwards, "The Excellency of Christ," in Thomas H. Johnson and Clarence H. Faust, eds., *Jonathan Edwards: Representative Selections* (New York: American Book Company, 1935), pp. 121, 123.
9. Magnus Hagevi, "Religiosity and Swedish Opinion on the European Union," *Journal for the Scientific Study of Religion* 41:4 (2002), p. 763; "More Evidence that Britain Lacks Faith," *Catholic World News* (December 16, 1999), http://www.cwnews.com/Browse/1999/12/11822.htm; George Barna, *The Index of Leading Spiritual Indicators* (Dallas: Word Publishing,

1996), p. 3; George Gallup, Jr., and George O'Connell, *Who Do Americans Say That I Am?* (Philadelphia: Westminster Press, 1986), p. 119.
10. Gallup and O'Connell, *Who Do Americans Say That I Am?*, pp. 69, 83; Taylor, "Large Majority of People Believe They Will Go to Heaven."
11. Mary Baker Eddy, *Science and Health with Key to the Scriptures* (Boston: The First Church of Christ, Scientist, 1994), p. 313.

CHAPTER ONE: ENLIGHTENED SAGE

1. William Linn, *Serious Considerations on the Election of a President: Addressed to the Citizens of the United States* (New York: John Furman, 1800), pp. 24–27; Abraham Bishop, *Oration Delivered in Wallingford on the 11th of March 1801, Before the Republicans of the State of Connecticut, at Their General Thanksgiving for the Election of Thomas Jefferson* (New Haven: William W. Morse, 1801), p. 7.
2. Dickinson W. Adams, ed., *Jefferson's Extracts from the Gospels* (Princeton, N.J.: Princeton University Press, 1983), p. 360.
3. Linn, *Serious Considerations*, p. 19; Adams, ed., *Jefferson's Extracts*, p. 11.
4. Edwin S. Gaustad, *Sworn on the Altar of God: A Religious Biography of Thomas Jefferson* (Grand Rapids, Mich.: Eerdmans, 1996), p. xiii.
5. Adams, ed., *Jefferson's Extracts*, pp. 333, 347, 345.
6. Ibid., p. 369.
7. Ibid., pp. 333, 413.
8. Ibid., pp. 352, 392, 352.
9. Ibid., pp. 55, 375, 369.
10. Ibid., p. 365.
11. The text has been meticulously pieced together by Dickinson W. Adams, based on a variety of sources, including the Bibles Jefferson used when creating the book, and a surviving list of the verses he included in the volume; see Adams, ed., *Jefferson's Extracts*, pp. 45–53.
12. Adams, ed., *Jefferson's Extracts*, p. 396.
13. Ibid., pp. 365, 331.
14. Ibid., pp. 375, 409, 401, 353.
15. Milton C. Sernett, ed., *Afro-American Religious History* (Durham, N.C.: Duke University Press, 1985), p. 104; H. Shelton Smith et al., eds., *American Christianity: An Historical Interpretation with Representative Documents* (New York: Charles Scribner's Sons, 1963), 2.349.
16. Adams, ed., *Jefferson's Extracts*, pp. 405, 375, 345.
17. Ibid., p. 403.
18. Isaac Kramnick and R. Laurence Moore, *The Godless Constitution: The Case Against Religious Correctness* (New York: W. W. Norton, 1996), p. 95; Gaustad, *Sworn on the Altar of God*, p. 131.
19. Adams, ed., *Jefferson's Extracts*, p. 410.
20. Ibid., pp. 381, 330.
21. Ibid., pp. 396, 391, 334, 330.
22. Ibid., p. 414.
23. Ibid., p. 362.

24. Ibid., p. 410.
25. Ibid., pp. 385, 406.
26. Conrad Wright, *The Liberal Christians: Essays on American Unitarian History* (Boston: Unitarian Universalist Association, 1970), p. 16.
27. Adams, ed., *Jefferson's Extracts*, p. 387.
28. Nancy Ammerman, "Golden Rule Christianity: Lived Religion in the American Mainstream," in David D. Hall, ed., *Lived Religion in America: Toward a History of Practice* (Princeton, N.J.: Princeton University Press, 1997), pp. 196–216.
29. Robert W. Funk, *Honest to Jesus: Jesus for a New Millennium* (San Francisco: HarperSanFrancisco, 1966), p. 19.
30. Ibid., p. 306; "The Opening Remarks of Jesus Seminar Founder Robert Funk," http://www.westarinstitute.org/Jesus_Seminar/Remarks/remarks.html.
31. George Tyrrell, *Christianity at the Crossroads* (London: George Allen and Unwin, 1963), p. 22.
32. Funk, *Honest to Jesus*, p. 313; "Jesus and the New Christianity According to Funk," Radio National transcript (January 10, 2000), http://www.abc.net.au/rn/relig/spirit/stories/s196417.htm.
33. Funk, *Honest to Jesus*, p. 8.
34. Ibid., p. 302; "Readers React to Jesus Story," *USA Weekend* (February 7, 1993), p. 13.
35. Jeffery L. Sheler, "What Did Jesus Really Say?" *U.S. News & World Report* (July 1, 1991), p. 57; Associated Press, "Biblical Scholars Vote on Origins of Parables" (March 10, 1986); Ben Witherington III, *The Jesus Quest: The Third Search for the Jew of Nazareth*, 2d ed. (Downers Grove, Ill.: InterVarsity Press, 1997), p. 57; "Jesus Seminar Awarded Scrooge Award by Group," *Arizona Republic* (December 24, 1994), p. B4.
36. Birger A. Pearson, "The Gospel According to the Jesus Seminar," http://id-www.ucsb.edu/fscf/library/pearson/seminar/js7.html.
37. Funk, *Honest to Jesus*, pp. 204, 192, 302, 59, 196; Robert W. Funk and the Jesus Seminar, *The Acts of Jesus: The Search for the Authentic Deeds of Jesus* (San Francisco: HarperSanFrancisco, 1998), pp. 36, 33, 32.
38. Funk, *Honest to Jesus*, pp. 302, 298, 9, 304.
39. Ibid., pp. 306, 20, 19.
40. Robert W. Funk, "The Coming Radical Reformation: Twenty-one Theses," http://www.westarinstitute.org/Periodicals/4R_Articles/Funk_Theses/funk_theses.html; Funk, *Honest to Jesus*, p. 305.
41. Robert W. Funk, Roy W. Hoover, and the Jesus Seminar, *The Five Gospels: The Search for the Authentic Words of Jesus: New Translation and Commentary* (New York: Macmillan, 1993), p. v.
42. Joseph J. Ellis, *American Sphinx: The Character of Thomas Jefferson* (New York: Alfred A. Knopf, 1997).

CHAPTER TWO: SWEET SAVIOR

1. Jon Butler, "Enthusiasm Described and Decried: The Great Awakening as Interpretive Fiction," in Jon Butler and Harry S. Stout, eds., *Religion in*

American History: A Reader (New York: Oxford University Press, 1998), p. 112. On colonial church membership, see Finke and Stark, *The Churching of America* (New Brunswick, N.J.: Rutgers University Press, 1992), pp. 22–53.

2. Sydney Ahlstrom, *A Religious History of the American People* (New Haven: Yale University Press, 1972), p. 124. Not all the Puritans thought alike either. For variants inside the Puritan way, see David D. Hall, *Worlds of Wonder, Days of Judgment: Popular Religious Belief in Early New England* (New York: Alfred A. Knopf, 1989); and Janice Knight, *Orthodoxies in Massachusetts: Rereading American Puritanism* (Cambridge: Harvard University Press, 1994).

3. Ralph Waldo Emerson, *The Journals and Miscellaneous Notebooks of Ralph Waldo Emerson, Volume III, 1826–1832* (W. H. Gilman and A. R. Ferguson, eds.; Cambridge: Harvard University Press, 1963), p. 70.

4. Nancy F. Cott, *The Bonds of Womanhood: "Woman's Sphere" in Nineteenth-Century New England, 1780–1835* (New Haven: Yale University Press, 1977), p. 186. According to Daniel L. Pals, Edwards "seems determined to move beyond Jesus . . . to a Christ of cosmic proportions. And he seems equally concerned to proceed through Christ to a pure and direct apprehension of God" ("Several Christologies of the Great Awakening," *Anglican Theological Review* 72.4 [Fall 1990], p. 421).

5. Karl Barth, *The Epistle to the Romans* (trans. Edwyn C. Hoskyns; New York: Oxford University Press, 1933), p. 10.

6. William R. Hutchison, *Religious Pluralism in America: The Contentious History of a Founding Ideal* (New Haven: Yale University Press, 2003), pp. 19–24.

7. William R. Hutchison, "Diversity and the Pluralist Ideal," in Peter W. Williams, *Perspectives on American Religion and Culture* (Boston: Blackwell Publishers, 1999), pp. 36–37.

8. Robert Richardson, *Memoirs of Alexander Campbell* (Philadelphia: J. B. Lippincott, 1868), 1:352; Paul Keith Conkin, *American Originals: Homemade Varieties of Christianity* (Chapel Hill: University of North Carolina Press, 1997).

9. Frances Trollope, *Domestic Manners of the Americans* (New York: Alfred A. Knopf, 1949), p. 108; Nathan O. Hatch, *The Democratization of American Christianity* (New Haven: Yale University Press, 1989), p. 15.

10. Alexis de Tocqueville, *Democracy in America*, chapter 17, http://xroads.virginia.edu/~HYPER/DETOC/1_ch17.htm.

11. John H. Wigger, *Taking Heaven by Storm: Methodism and the Rise of Popular Christianity in America* (New York: Oxford University Press, 1998), pp. 79, 5.

12. Richard J. Carwardine, *Evangelicals and Politics in Antebellum America*, (New Haven: Yale University Press, 1993), p. 44; Mark A. Noll, *America's God: From Jonathan Edwards to Abraham Lincoln* (New York: Oxford University Press, 2002), p. 197.

13. Paul C. Gutjahr, *An American Bible: A History of the Good Book in the*

United States, 1777–1880 (Stanford: Stanford University Press, 1999), p. 102; Daniel A. Payne, *Recollections of Seventy Years* (New York: Arno Press, 1968), p. 234.

14. W.E.B. Du Bois, *The Souls of Black Folk*, chapter 10, http://xroads. virginia.edu/~HYPER/DUBOIS/ch10.html.

15. Adams, ed., *Jefferson's Extracts*, p. 413.

16. Hatch, *Democratization*, pp. 125, 9.

17. David S. Reynolds, "From Doctrine to Narrative: The Rise of Pulpit Storytelling in America," *American Quarterly* 32.5 (Winter 1980), pp. 487, 490.

18. Hatch, *Democratization*, p. 67.

19. Ralph Waldo Emerson, "Divinity School Address" (1838), http://www. emersoncentral.com/divaddr.htm; Emerson, *The Journals and Miscellaneous Notebooks of Ralph Waldo Emerson, Volume VII: 1838–1842* (A. W. Plumstead and Harrison Hayford, eds.; Cambridge: Harvard University Press, 1969), p. 348; Emerson, *The Journals and Miscellaneous Notebooks of Ralph Waldo Emerson, Volume VIII: 1841–1843* (William H. Gilman and J. E. Parsons, eds.; Cambridge: Harvard University Press, 1970), p. 337. On Emerson's Jesus, see Richard Wightman Fox, "Jefferson, Emerson, and Jesus," *Raritan* 22.2 (Fall 2002), pp. 70–72.

20. Donald Scott, *From Office to Profession: The New England Ministry, 1750–1850* (Philadelphia: University of Pennsylvania Press, 1978), p. 178; Noll, *America's God*, p. 245; Richard Rabinowitz, *The Spiritual Self in Everyday Life: The Transformation of Personal Religious Experience in Nineteenth-Century New England* (Boston: Northeastern University Press, 1989), pp. 200, 178.

21. Rabinowitz, *The Spiritual Self*, p. 177.

22. Horace Bushnell, *The Character of Jesus* (New York: Chautauqua Press, 1888), pp. 7, 86; James Herman Whitmore, *Testimony of Nineteen Centuries to Jesus of Nazareth* (Norwich, Conn.: Henry Bill Publishing Company, 1892), pp. 647, 385; Harriet Beecher Stowe, *Dred: A Tale of the Great Dismal Swamp* (New York: Penguin Books, 2000), p. 347; William G. McLoughlin, *The Meaning of Henry Ward Beecher: An Essay on the Shifting Values of Mid-Victorian America, 1840–1870* (New York: Alfred A. Knopf, 1970), p. 29; Henry Ward Beecher, "A Conversation about Christ," *Homiletic Review* 45.6 (June 1913), p. 490.

23. *Joseph Smith—History* 1:10, in *Pearl of Great Price*.

24. Cotton Mather, *Ornaments for the Daughters of Zion* (Boston: Samuel Phillips, 1691), pp. 56–57; Richard D. Shiels, "The Feminization of American Congregationalism, 1730–1835," *American Quarterly* 33.1 (Spring 1981), pp. 46–62. See also Ann Braude, *Women and American Religion* (New York: Oxford University Press, 2000).

25. Classic formulations of the "separate spheres" story include Barbara Welter, "The Cult of True Womanhood: 1820–1860," *American Quarterly* 18.2 (Summer 1966), pp. 151–74; and Linda K. Kerber, "Separate Spheres, Female Worlds, Woman's Place: The Rhetoric of Women's History," *Journal of American History* 75.1 (June 1988), pp. 9–39.

26. See Ann Douglas, *The Feminization of American Culture* (New York: Alfred A. Knopf, 1977); and Barbara Welter, "The Feminization of American Religion 1800–1860," in her *Dimity Convictions: The American Woman in the Nineteenth Century* (Athens: Ohio University Press, 1976), pp. 83–102.

27. Samuel Miller, *Letters on Clerical Manners and Habits* (New York: n.p., 1827), pp. 93–94; Welter, "The Cult of True Womanhood," p. 162. On women preachers, see Catherine A. Brekus, *Strangers and Pilgrims: Female Preaching in America, 1740–1845* (Chapel Hill: University of North Carolina Press, 1998).

28. Stephen Marini, "Hymnody as History: Early Evangelical Hymns and the Recovery of American Popular Religion," *Church History* 71.2 (June 2002), p. 305.

29. Gary Dorrien, *The Making of American Liberal Theology: Imagining Progressive Religion, 1805–1900* (Louisville, Ky.: Westminster John Knox Press, 2001), p. 185.

30. Leigh Eric Schmidt, *Consumer Rites: The Buying and Selling of American Holidays* (Princeton, N. J.: Princeton University Press, 1995), p. 182.

31. David Morgan, *Protestants & Pictures: Religion, Visual Culture, and the Age of American Mass Production* (New York: Oxford University Press, 1999), p. 181.

32. Bushnell, *The Character of Jesus*, p. 38; Wigger, *Taking Heaven by Storm*, p. 48.

33. Horace Bushnell, *Sermons for the New Life* (New York: Charles Scribner, 1858), p. 200.

34. Smith et al., eds., *American Christianity*, 2.273.

35. Bushnell, *The Character of Jesus*, pp. 36, 10, 17.

36. Ibid., pp. 44, 15, 17, 27.

37. Henry Steele Commager, *The American Mind* (New Haven: Yale University Press, 1950), p. 165; Douglas, *The Feminization of American Culture*, pp. 121–64.

38. Harriet Beecher Stowe, *My Wife and I* (New York: J. B. Ford and Company, 1871), pp. 1–2; Phillips Brooks, *On Preaching* (New York: Seabury Press, 1964), p. 12.

39. David Paul Nord, "The Evangelical Origins of Mass Media in America, 1815–1835," *Journalism Monographs* 88 (May 1984), p. 22.

40. Gutjahr, *An American Bible*, p. 37.

41. Harriet Beecher Stowe, *Uncle Tom's Cabin: Or Life Among the Lowly* (1852; New York: Penguin Books, 1986), chapters 45, 14, 16, http://xroads. virginia.edu/~HYPER/STOWE/stowe.html.

42. See Dan McKanan, *Identifying the Image of God: Radical Christians and Nonviolent Power in the Antebellum United States* (New York: Oxford University Press, 2002).

43. Allene Stuart Phy, "Retelling the Greatest Story Ever Told: Jesus in Popular Fiction," in Allene Stuart Phy, ed., *The Bible and Popular Culture in America* (Philadelphia: Fortress Press, 1985), p. 48; Lew Wallace, *Ben-Hur: A Tale of the Christ* (New York: Harper and Brothers, 1880), pp. 523, 528.

44. Richard Wightman Fox, *Trials of Intimacy: Love and Loss in the Beecher-Tilton Scandal* (Chicago: University of Chicago Press, 1999), p. 208.; Henry Ward Beecher, *The Life of Jesus, the Christ* (New York: J. B. Ford and Company, 1871), pp. 53, 145.

45. Henry Ward Beecher, *Norwood, or, Village Life in New England* (New York: C. Scribner and Co., 1868), pp. 58, 60.

46. Beecher, *The Life of Jesus*, pp. 145, 178.

47. Ibid., pp. 246, 290, 341, 249.

48. Ibid., p. 343.

49. Ibid., pp. 194–95, 395, 252, 294, 304, 149, 302.

50. Ibid., p. 52.

51. Wigger, *Taking Heaven by Storm*, p. 105; Stephen A. Marini, "From Classical to Modern: Hymnody and the Development of American Evangelicalism, 1737–1970," unpublished essay.

52. See Stephen A. Marini, *Sacred Song in America: Religion, Music, and Public Culture* (Urbana: University of Illinois Press, 2003). A similar preoccupation with Jesus can be found in early Pentecostal hymns, where according to one count Jesus is invoked three times more often than God the Father; see Nils Bloch-Hoell, *The Pentecostal Movement: Its Origin, Development, and Distinctive Character* (New York: Humanities Press, 1964), p. 109.

53. Dwight L. Moody, *Conversion, Service, and Glory* (London: Morgan and Scott, n.d.), p. 301.

54. Henry Wilder Foote, *Three Centuries of American Hymnody* (Cambridge: Harvard University Press, 1940), p. 267.

55. Christopher Lasch, *Haven in a Heartless World: The Family Besieged* (New York: Basic Books, 1995).

56. E. J. Goodspeed, *A Full History of the Wonderful Career of Moody and Sankey in Great Britain and America* (New York: H. S. Goodspeed, 1876), p. 71.

57. Ira D. Sankey, *Sacred Songs and Solos: With Standard Hymns, Combined, 750 Pieces* (London: Morgan and Scott, n.d.), p. 448. On cyberhymnal.com, "Amazing Grace" is the most visited site (http://www.cyberhymnal.org/misc/trivia.htm).

58. Marini, "From Classical to Modern."

59. "In the Garden," http://www.cyberhymnal.org/htm/i/t/itgarden.htm; Sankey, *Sacred Songs and Solos*, p. 565.

60. Sankey, *Sacred Songs and Solos*, pp. 322, 596, 168; http://www.cyberhymnal.org/htm/w/o/wonpeac1.htm. A recent *Christianity Today* survey named "What a Friend We Have in Jesus" one of the top ten worship songs of all time: Bonne Steffen, "The Ten Best Worship Songs," *Christianity Today* 39.5 (September / October 2001), p. 48.

61. Thomas Wentworth Higginson, "Negro Spirituals," *Atlantic Monthly* (June 1867), http://wsrv.clas.virginia.edu/~jmp7u/Higg.html#jesus.

62. Martin Marty, *Religion and Republic: The American Circumstance* (Boston: Beacon Press, 1987), p. 165.

63. Winthrop S. Hudson and John Corrigan, *Religion in America*, 6th ed. (Upper Saddle River, N.J.: Prentice Hall, 1998), p. 262; Smith et al., *American Christianity*, 2.279–80.

64. A. V. G. Allen, "The Continuity of Christian Thought," in William R. Hutchison, ed., *American Protestant Thought: The Liberal Era* (New York: Harper and Row, 1968), p. 57.

65. Mark G. Toulouse and James O. Duke, eds., *Sources of Christian Theology in America* (Nashville: Abingdon Press, 1999), p. 327.

66. Toulouse and Duke, eds., *Sources of Christian Theology*, p. 272.

67. Elizabeth Stuart Phelps, *The Story of Jesus Christ: An Interpretation* (Boston: Houghton, Mifflin, 1897), pp. 11, 311, 200, 112, 387.

68. Phelps, *The Story of Jesus Christ*, pp. 411, ix, 102; 67, 385, 142.

69. See Leonard Swidler, "Jesus was a Feminist," *Catholic World* 212 (January 1971), pp. 177–83.

70. Phelps, *The Story of Jesus Christ*, pp. 143, 197; Sankey, *Sacred Songs and Solos*, pp. 554, 560.

71. Whitmore, *Testimony of Nineteen Centuries to Jesus*, 348–49; Beecher, *The Life of Jesus*, pp. 148, 381, 278, 380; Beecher, "A Conversation about Christ," p. 490.

72. Whitmore, *Testimony of Nineteen Centuries to Jesus*, p. 130.

CHAPTER THREE: MANLY REDEEMER

1. "A Believer's Pictures of Christ," *The New York Times Illustrated Magazine* (December 11, 1898), p. 7.

2. Herman Melville, *Moby Dick* (New York: Bantam Books, 1967), p. 348; Kate P. Hampton, "The Face of Christ in Art: Is the Portraiture of Jesus Strong or Weak?" *Outlook* 61.13 (April 1, 1899), pp. 746, 736, 738, 742; George Reynolds, "The Personal Appearance of the Savior," *Juvenile Instructor* 39 (August 15, 1904), pp. 498–99.

3. Gail Bederman, *Manliness and Civilization: A Cultural History of Gender and Race in the United States, 1880–1917* (Chicago: University of Chicago Press, 1995), pp. 100, 77, 100.

4. Theodore Roosevelt, "The Strenuous Life" (1899), http://www.theodore roosevelt.org/research/speech%20strenuous.htm.

5. T. J. Jackson Lears, "From Salvation to Self-Realization: Advertising and the Therapeutic Roots of the Consumer Culture, 1880–1930," in Richard Wightman Fox and T. J. Jackson Lears, eds., *The Culture of Consumption: Critical Essays in American History, 1880–1980* (New York: Pantheon Books, 1983), pp. 1–38.

6. Orestes Augustus Brownson, *The Works of Orestes A. Brownson* (Detroit: T. Nourse, 1882–1887), 19.421; Henry James, *The Bostonians* (New York: Macmillan, 1886), chapter 34, http://www.online-literature.com/henry_james/bostonians/34/.

7. Charles Reagan Wilson, *Baptized in Blood: The Religion of the Lost Cause, 1865–1920* (Athens: University of Georgia Press, 1980).

8. Albert G. Lawson, "Why Are There Not More Men in Our Churches?"

Watchman 73.38 (September 22, 1892), p. 1; Fred S. Goodman, "A Survey of Typical Church Bible Classes for Boys and Men," *Religious Education* 5.4 (October 1910), pp. 363–65.

9. Carl Delos Case, *The Masculine in Religion* (Philadelphia: American Baptist Publication Society, 1906), p. 85; Theodore P. Greene, *America's Heroes: The Changing Models of Success in American Magazines* (New York: Oxford University Press, 1970), p. 78. See also Case's *My Christ* (Philadelphia: Griffith and Rowland, 1915).

10. Betty A. DeBerg, *Ungodly Women: Gender and the First Wave of American Fundamentalism* (Minneapolis: Fortress Press, 1990), p. 89; William G. McLoughlin, Jr., *Billy Sunday Was His Real Name* (Chicago: University of Chicago Press, 1955), p. 179.

11. Martin Marty, *Righteous Empire* (New York: Dial Press, 1970), pp. 177–87; "Emasculated Christianity," *King's Business* 13.4 (April 1922), p. 330; William Elliot Griffis, "Jesus the Soldier," *Homiletics Review* 46.5 (November 1918), p. 349.

12. Janet Forsythe Fishburn, *The Fatherhood of God and the Victorian Family: The Social Gospel in America* (Philadelphia: Fortress Press, 1981), pp. 32, 169.

13. Lyman Abbott, *What Christianity Means to Me* (New York: Macmillan, 1921), pp. 5–10; Susan Curtis, *A Consuming Faith: The Social Gospel and Modern American Culture* (Baltimore: Johns Hopkins University Press, 1991), p. 86.

14. I. H. Meredith and Grant Colfax Tullar, eds., *Manly Songs for Christian Men* (New York: Tullar-Meredith, 1910), p. 27; Curtis, *A Consuming Faith*, p. 81.

15. Toulouse and Duke, eds., *Sources of Christian Theology*, p. 297; Case, *The Masculine in Religion*, p. 118; Mabel Hay Barrows Mussey, *Social Hymns of Brotherhood and Aspiration* (New York: A. S. Barnes, 1914), p. 43; Christian F. Reisner, *Roosevelt's Religion* (New York: Abingdon Press, 1922), 245.

16. Elizabeth Stuart Phelps, *A Singular Life* (Boston: Houghton, Mifflin, 1898), p. 153.

17. Charles Sheldon, *In His Steps* (1897), chapter 31, http://www.kancoll.org/books/sheldon/shchap31.htm.

18. William E. Barton, *Jesus of Nazareth* (Boston: Pilgrim Press, 1903), pp. 506, 504. On Jesus as a bearded lady, see David Morgan, "Absent Fathers and Women with Beards: Religion and Gender in Popular Imagery of the Nineteenth Century," in David Holloway and John Beck, eds., *American Visual Cultures* (New York: Continuum, forthcoming).

19. Barton, *Jesus of Nazareth*, pp. 540, 544.

20. Bruce Barton, *A Young Man's Jesus* (Boston: Pilgrim Press, 1914), pp. ix–x.

21. Ibid., pp. xii, 18, 29, 12, xii.

22. Dr. R. Warren Conant, *The Virility of Christ: A New View*, 2d ed. (Chicago: Dr. R. Warren Conant, 1915), pp. 13, 19, 29, 104, 103.

23. G. Stanley Hall, *Jesus, the Christ, in the Light of Psychology*, (Garden City, N.Y.: Doubleday, Page, 1917), 1.129.

24. Ibid., pp. 22, 23, 92–93.
25. Ibid., pp. 37, 34–35.
26. Bruce Barton, The Man Nobody Knows: A Discovery of the Real Jesus (Indianapolis: Bobbs-Merrill, 1925), preface.
27. Ibid., preface, pp. 107, 19.
28. Ibid., preface, pp. 43, 37, 32, 57, 86, 75, preface.
29. Gilbert Seldes, "The Living Christ," New Republic 43 (June 24, 1925), p. 127; Samuel Sandmel, A Jewish Understanding of the New Testament (Cincinnati: Hebrew Union College Press, 1956), p. 194; Walker Percy, "How to Succeed in Business Without Thinking About Money," Commonweal 77.22 (February 22, 1963), p. 558.
30. Barton, The Man Nobody Knows, pp. 160–61. The Bible passages here are from the King James version, which Barton used.
31. Ibid., pp. 161, 179–80; the Bushnell quote is from Bushnell's Moral Uses of Dark Things (New York: C. Scribner and Co., 1868), pp. 39–40.
32. Edrene Stephens Montgomery, "Bruce Barton and the Twentieth Century Menace of Unreality" (Ph.D. diss.; University of Arkansas, 1984), pp. 115, 116, 114.
33. Montgomery, "Bruce Barton," pp. 119, 116.
34. William R. Hutchison, The Modernist Impulse in American Protestantism (New York: Oxford University Press, 1982), p. 2; Barton, The Man Nobody Knows, p. 188.
35. Barton, The Man Nobody Knows, pp. 181, 136.
36. Montgomery, "Bruce Barton," p. 112.
37. Albert R. Bandini, "A New Life of Christ," Catholic World 113.677 (August 1921), p. 658.
38. Warren I. Susman, " 'Personality' and the Making of Twentieth-Century Culture," in his Culture as History: The Transformation of American Society in the Twentieth Century (New York: Pantheon Books, 1984), pp. 271–85; Susman quotes Emerson on p. 274.
39. Henry Laurent, Personality: How to Build It (New York: Funk and Wagnalls Co., 1915), p. 25; Shailer Mathews, The Message of Jesus to Our Modern Life (Chicago: University of Chicago Press, 1915), p. 39; Susman, " 'Personality' and the Making," pp. 273–74, 277.
40. Harry Emerson Fosdick, The Power to See It Through (New York: Harper and Brothers, 1935), p. 35.
41. T. J. Jackson Lears, "Sherwood Anderson: Looking for the White Spot," in Richard Wightman Fox and T. J. Jackson Lears, The Power of Culture: Critical Essays in American History (Chicago: University of Chicago Press, 1993), pp. 13–37.
42. Barton, The Man Nobody Knows, p. 19.
43. E. Brooks Holifield, A History of Pastoral Care in America: From Salvation to Self-Realization (Nashville: Abingdon Press, 1983), p. 168.
44. Smith et al., eds., American Christianity, p. 2.300; Robert Moats Miller, Harry Emerson Fosdick: Pastor, Preacher, Prophet (New York: Oxford University Press, 1985), p. 407.

45. Susman, *Culture as History*, pp. 146, 142.

46. Robert T. Handy, *A Christian America: Protestant Hopes and Historical Realities*, 2d ed. (New York: Oxford University Press, 1984), pp. 159–84; Grant Wacker, "The Demise of Biblical Civilization," in Nathan O. Hatch and Mark A. Noll, eds., *The Bible in America: Essays in Cultural History* (New York: Oxford University Press, 1982), pp. 121–38.

47. Handy, *A Christian America*, pp. 159–84; Harry Emerson Fosdick, "Recent Gains in Religion," in Kirby Page, ed., *Recent Gains in American Civilization* (New York: Harcourt, 1928), p. 238; J. Gresham Machen, *Christianity and Liberalism* (New York: Macmillan, 1923), pp. 6–7.

48. Reinhold Niebuhr, *Does Civilization Need Religion?: A Study in the Social Resources and Limitations of Religion in Modern Life* (New York: Macmillan, 1927), p. 2; H. Richard Niebuhr, Wilhelm Pauck, Francis P. Miller, *The Church Against the World* (Chicago: Willett, Clark, 1935), p. 124.

49. Shailer Mathews, *The Faith of Modernism* (New York: Macmillan, 1924), p. 146.

50. David Morgan, ed., *Icons of American Protestantism: The Art of Warner Sallman* (New Haven: Yale University Press, 1996), pp. 62, 80, 185.

51. Jack R. Lundbom, *Master Painter: Warner E. Sallman* (Macon, Ga.: Mercer University Press, 1999), p. 136.

52. David Morgan, *Visual Piety: A History and Theory of Popular Religious Images* (Berkeley: University of California Press, 1998), pp. 43, 34, 56; the miracle stories are from Morgan, ed., *Icons of American Protestantism*, pp. 189, 237.

53. Morgan, *Visual Piety*, p. 121.

54. Charles Blakeman, "The Problem of Church Art," *Clergy Review* 48 (1955), p. 27; E. M. Catich, "Sentimentality in Christian Art," *The Furrow* 10 (1959), p. 514; Richard Charles Muehlberger, "Sacred Art: A Critique on the Contemporary Situation," *Liturgical Arts* 28 (1960), p. 70; all are quoted in Colleen McDannell, *Material Christianity: Religion and Popular Culture in America* (New Haven: Yale University Press, 1995), pp. 174, 180, 189.

55. Morgan, ed., *Icons of American Protestantism*, p. 93; "Not Frail, Not Pale," *Time* (November 22, 1948), p. 70; Robert Paul Roth, "Christ and the Muses," *Christianity Today* 11.11 (March 3, 1958), p. 9; "As Ugly as a Rented Bowling Shoe," *Context* (February 15, 1990), p. 4. For an influential discussion of the "feminine gender" of kitsch, see Colleen McDannell, "Christian Kitsch and the Rhetoric of Bad Taste," in her *Material Christianity*, pp. 163–97.

56. Jane W. Lauber, "Are We Losing Our Artist Heritage?" *Christianity Today* 10.23 (September 2, 1966), p. 24; " 'In' and 'Out,' " *Christian Century* 79.23 (June 6, 1962), p. 731.

57. Leonard Sweet, " 'Personal Lord and Savior': Christology and the Devotional Image," http://www.leonardsweet.com/includes/ShowSweetened Articles.asp?articleID=92.

CHAPTER FOUR: SUPERSTAR

1. Robert S. Ellwood, *The Sixties Spiritual Awakening: American Religion Moving from Modern to Postmodern* (New Brunswick, N.J.: Rutgers University Press, 1994).

2. Two Brothers from Berkeley, *Letters to Street Christians* (Grand Rapids, Mich.: Zondervan, 1971), pp. 175, 80, 101.

3. Ronald M. Enroth, Edward E. Ericson, Jr., and C. Breckenridge Peters, *The Jesus People: Old-Time Religion in the Age of Aquarius* (Grand Rapids, Mich.: Eerdmans, 1972), p. 73; Michael Jacob, *Pop Goes Jesus: An Investigation of Pop Religion in Britain and America* (Oxford, England: Mowbrays, 1972), p. 36; Enroth et al., *The Jesus People*, p. 69.

4. Enroth et al., *The Jesus People*, pp. 77, 76.

5. Julian Wagner, "The New Rebel Cry: Jesus Is Coming!" *Time* (June 21, 1971), p. 56.

6. "Reward for Information Leading to the Apprehension of Jesus Christ," poster in the collection of the author.

7. Duane Pederson, with Bob Owen, *Jesus People* (Glendale, Calif.: Regal Books, 1971), p. 31.

8. Wagner, "The New Rebel Cry," p. 56; "Reward" poster.

9. Billy Graham, *The Jesus Generation* (Grand Rapids, Mich.: Zondervan, 1971), p. 13.

10. "Now That Jesus Is 'In' Again," *Christian Century* (June 23, 1971), 767.

11. Wagner, "The New Rebel Cry," 61; Jack Kroll, "Theater," *Newsweek* (October 25, 1971), p. 84.

12. Richard Watts, "The Passion in a Rock Beat," *New York Post* (October 13, 1971); Dan Morgenstern, "Superstar: Beyond Redemption," *Downbeat* (December 9, 1971), front cover.

13. Tom Prideaux, "On This Rock, A Little Miracle," *Life* (August 4, 1972), p. 20.

14. Joseph Barton, "The Godspell Story," http://www.geocities.com/Broadway/Lobby/4209/america.html.

15. Stephen Schwartz, "Bless the Lord," *Godspell*.

16. H. Elliott Wright, "Jesus on Stage: A Reappraisal," *Christian Century* 89.27 (July 19, 1972), p. 785; Ashley Leach, "An Interview with Stephen Schwartz," http://www.geocities.com/Broadway/Lobby/4209/interview.html; Dennis Polkow, "Andrew Lloyd Webber: From Superstar to Requiem," http://www.religion-online.org/cgi-bin/relsearchd.dll/showarticle?item_id=1011.

17. Steve Rabey, "Age to Age," *CCM Magazine* (July 1998), http://www.ccmcom.com/Archives/fullstory_cont2.asp?Id=55.

18. "Jesus Movement?" *For Real* (March 1971), http://www.oneway.org/lovesong/movement.htm.

19. Paul Baker, "Love Song," http://www.one-way.org/lovesong/baker.htm.

20. Timothy Miller, *The 60s Communes: Hippies and Beyond* (Syracuse, N.Y.: Syracuse University Press, 1999), pp. xviii, 94.

21. Enroth et al., *The Jesus People*, p. 98.

22. Ibid., p. 76.
23. "The Explo Story," *Life* (June 30, 1972), http://oneway.org/jesus movement/explo/explo1.htm.
24. Edward E. Plowman, "Whatever Happened to the Jesus Movement?" *Christianity Today* 20.2 (October 24, 1975), pp. 46–48; Rebecca M. White, "The Jesus Movement," http://webbhelper.com/jp/library/becky white/article.html.
25. Donald E. Miller, *Reinventing American Protestantism: Christianity in the New Millennium* (Berkeley: University of California Press, 1997), pp. 1–2.
26. Hatch, *Democratization*, pp. 4–5.
27. VineyardUSA, "The Columbus Accords," http://www.vineyardusa.org/about/history/columbus_accords.htm.
28. Randall Balmer, *Mine Eyes Have Seen the Glory: A Journey into the Evangelical Subculture in America*, expanded ed., (New York: Oxford University Press, 1993), pp. 12–13; Miller, *Reinventing American Protestantism*, pp. 29, 30.
29. Ibid., p. 128.
30. Hutchison, *The Modernist Impulse*, pp. 2, 6.
31. "Face to Face: Paul Davis Interviews Larry Norman," *New Music* 3 (March 1977), http://www.members.iinet.net.au/~wpe/larry/intvw76.html.
32. Jonathan Edwards, *A Treatise Concerning Religious Affections* (Boston: Kneeland and Green, 1746), part 3, section 12, http://www.revival library.org/catalogues/theology/edwards-religiousaffections/part3-12.html. It should be noted that in the same treatise Edwards also wrote of "the great duty of self-denial for Christ," insisting on "hating our dearest earthly enjoyments, even our own lives, for Christ, giving up ourselves, with all that we have, wholly and forever, unto Christ, without keeping back any thing, or making any reserve . . . As it were, disowning and renouncing ourselves for him, making ourselves nothing that he may be all." At least on this score, virtually all Americans today (and most of Edwards's contemporaries) would no doubt fall short.

CHAPTER FIVE: MORMON ELDER BROTHER

1. *The Copy of a Letter Written by Our Blessed Lord and Saviour Jesus Christ* (Philadelphia: Andrew Steuart, 1761), p. 4.
2. "Publius Lentulus," *Catholic Encyclopedia*, http://www.newadvent.org/cathen/09154a.htm.
3. Albert Schweitzer, *The Quest of the Historical Jesus* (London: A. and C. Black, 1910), p. 328; Hall, *Jesus, the Christ*, p. 1.105.
4. Levi H. Dowling, *The Aquarian Gospel of Jesus the Christ* (Santa Monica, Calif.: DeVorss, 1972), p. 17; *Holy Koran of the Moorish Science Temple of America* 46:3, http://www.geocities.com/Athens/Delphi/2705/koran index.html. Another variant on the Jesus-in-India theme is *The Crucifixion, by an Eye-Witness* (Chicago: Indo-American Book Co., 1907), an anonymous text said to have been written seven years after the crucifixion and sent to the ascetic Jewish sect, the Essenes. While Notovitch and

Dowling place Jesus in India before his ministry, the Essene letter places him in Asia after it. According to this letter, Jesus survived his crucifixion and headed east, where he lived to a ripe old age and was buried in Kashmir. The Ahmadiyya movement, an Islamic sect that emerged in the Indian Punjab in the late nineteenth century and reveres its founder, Mirza Ghulam Ahmad, as the true messiah, continues to propagate this story. Rejecting the standard Muslim view that Jesus was not crucified but was raised up to heaven while still alive, Ahmadis in the United States and abroad appeal to this day to *The Crucifixion by an Eye-Witness* to support their position.

5. Ether 2:10.
6. *Doctrine and Covenants* 57:2.
7. The most influential treatments of the genesis of Mormonism include Richard L. Bushman, *Joseph Smith and the Beginnings of Mormonism* (Urbana: University of Illinois Press, 1984); Jan Shipps, *Mormonism: The Story of a New Religious Tradition* (Urbana: University of Illinois Press, 1985); Grant Underwood, *The Millenarian World of Early Mormonism* (Urbana: University of Illinois Press, 1993); John L. Brooke, *The Refiner's Fire: The Making of Mormon Cosmology, 1644–1844* (New York: Cambridge University Press, 1994); and D. Michael Quinn, *Early Mormonism and the Magic World View*, 2d ed., (Salt Lake City: Signature Books, 1998). For a fine short survey of the movement, see Claudia Lauper Bushman and Richard Lyman Bushman, *Mormons in America* (New York: Oxford University Press, 1999).
8. Winthrop S. Hudson and John Corrigan, *Religion in America*, 6th ed. (Upper Saddle River, N.J.: Prentice Hall, 1999), p. 186; Jon Butler, *Awash in a Sea of Faith: Christianizing the American People* (Cambridge: Harvard University Press, 1990), pp. 225–56.
9. *Joseph Smith—History* 1:10, in *Pearl of Great Price.*
10. Peter L. Berger, "Protestantism and the Quest for Certainty," *Christian Century* (August 26, 1998), p. 782.
11. *Joseph Smith—History* 1:5, in *Pearl of Great Price.*
12. Adams, ed., *Jefferson's Extracts,* p. 414; *Joseph Smith—History* 1:12, in *Pearl of Great Price.*
13. *Joseph Smith—History* 1:10, in *Pearl of Great Price.*
14. *Joseph Smith—History* 1:16–20, in *Pearl of Great Price.*
15. Butler, *Awash in a Sea of Faith;* Mark A. Noll, "The Image of the United States as a Biblical Nation, 1776–1865," in Hatch and Noll, eds., *The Bible in America*, pp. 44, 45. For the importance of the Bible in general, and of Deuteronomy in particular, see Donald S. Lutz, "The Relative Influence of European Writers on Late Eighteenth-Century American Political Thought," *American Political Science Review* 78.1 (March 1984), pp. 189–97.
16. *Doctrines and Covenants* 20. A few weeks after Smith promulgated these precepts, at the first church conference held on June 9, 1830, one believer had a vision that underscored early Mormonism's devotion to Jesus: "he

saw heaven opened, and beheld the Lord Jesus Christ, seated at the right hand of the majesty on high." See Joseph Smith, *History of the Church of Jesus Christ of Latter-day Saints* (B. H. Roberts, ed.; Salt Lake City: Church of Jesus Christ of Latter-day Saints, 1902), http://www.math. byu.edu/~smithw/Lds/LDS/History/History_of_ the_Church/Vol_1.

17. M. Teresa Baer, "Charting the Missionary Work of William E. McLellin: A Content Analysis," in Jan Shipps and John W. Welch, eds., *The Journals of William E. McLellin, 1831–1836* (Urbana and Provo, Utah: University of Illinois Press and BYU Studies, 1994), pp. 379–405, 110. Baer's method actually underemphasizes the Christianness of early Mormon preaching, by subsuming subjects such as the "Lord's Prayer" and "Praise to the Lord" under "General Religious" rather than "General Christian." McLellin was excommunicated from the Church in 1838 for (among other things) rejecting the plurality of gods and baptism for the dead.

18. Michael Hicks, *Mormonism and Music: A History* (Urbana: University of Illinois Press, 1989), p. 11; Emma Hale Smith, *A Collection of Sacred Hymns, for the Church of the Latter Day Saints* (Kirtland, Ohio: F. G. Williams and Co., 1835), pp. 20, 101, 48, 111.

19. *Doctrine and Covenants* 20:9.

20. 3 Nephi 11:11, 15:9, 21:23.

21. Susan Easton Black, *Finding Christ through the Book of Mormon* (Salt Lake City: Deseret Book Co. 1987), p. 36; Hicks, *Mormonism and Music*, p. 12.

22. Shipps, *Mormonism*, p. 74.

23. *Doctrine and Covenants* 88:119.

24. *Doctrine and Covenants* 109:61–64.

25. *Doctrine and Covenants* 110:3, 11–12.

26. Jan Shipps, "Joseph Smith and Mormonism," http://www.lds-mormon. com/shipps_joseph_smith.shtml; *Doctrine and Covenants* 109:8; Shipps, *Mormonism*, p. 82.

27. *Document Containing the Correspondence, Orders, &c, in Relation to the Disturbances with the Mormons* (Fayette, Mo.: Boon's Lick Democrat, 1841), p. 61. This sentence often ends with the phrase "public good" rather than "public peace," but an online image of the original handwritten order (http://www.ldshistory.org/extermination.htm) clearly demonstrates that "public peace" is the correct transcription.

28. For a careful history of Mormon ritualization, see David John Buerger, "The Development of the Mormon Temple Endowment Ceremony," *Dialogue* 20.4 (Winter 1987), pp. 33–76.

29. Joseph Smith, "Church History," *Times and Seasons* (March 1, 1842), p. 710.

30. J. Frederic Voros, Jr., "Was the Book of Mormon Buried with King Follett?" *Sunstone* 11:2 (March 1987), pp. 15–18; the concluding paraphrase is by Mormon president Lorenzo Snow.

31. *Doctrine and Covenants* 132:19, 88:22; Brigham Young, *Journal of Discourses* (Liverpool, England: B. Young, 1867), 2:31; Orson F. Whitney, *Sat-*

urday Night Thoughts (Salt Lake City: Deseret News, 1921), pp. 132–33; *Doctrine and Covenants* 86:10.

32. D. Michael Quinn, trans. and ed., "The First Months of Mormonism: A Contemporary View by Rev. Diedrich Willers," *New York History* 54 (July 1973), p. 327; Mark Twain, *Roughing It* (Hartford, Conn.: American Publishing, 1891), p. 102.

33. Harold Bloom, *American Religion: The Emergence of the Post-Christian Nation* (New York: Simon and Schuster, 1992), p. 108. The figure for Endowment House covers the period from 1855 to 1884, while the data for the temples is for the period from 1877 to 1898; see Buerger, "The Development of the Mormon Temple Endowment Ceremony," pp. 49–52.

34. *Doctrine and Covenants* 20:9.

35. Bloom, *American Religion*, p. 123.

36. Young, *Journal of Discourses*, 11:42; Paul James Toscano, *The Sanctity of Dissent* (Salt Lake City: Signature Books, 1994), p. 158.

37. Theodore Parker, "The Transient and Permanent in Christianity," in Conrad Wright, ed., *Three Prophets of Religious Liberalism* (Boston: Skinner House, 1980), p. 136; Hicks, *Mormonism and Music*, p. 11.

38. Orson Pratt, "Celestial Marriage," *The Seer* 1.11 (November 1853), p. 172.

39. *Official Declaration—1, Doctrine and Covenants*.

40. For a thought-provoking sociological analysis of twentieth-century Mormonism, see Armand L. Mauss, *The Angel and the Beehive: The Mormon Struggle with Assimilation* (Urbana: University of Illinois Press, 1994).

41. *Articles of Faith* 1:8; Smith, "Church History," p. 709; James E. Talmage, *Articles of Faith* (Salt Lake City: Deseret News, 1899), p. 424; Ezra Taft Benson, "The Book of Mormon—The Keystone of Our Religion," *Ensign* 16 (November 1986), p. 4; Black, *Finding Christ*, p. 8.

42. Gordon Shepherd and Gary Shepherd, *A Kingdom Transformed: Themes in the Development of Mormonism* (Salt Lake City: University of Utah Press, 1984), Appendix C, cited in Mauss, *The Angel and the Beehive*, p. 88.

43. Philip L. Barlow, "The Third Transformation of Mormonism," in Peter W. Williams, ed., *Perspectives on American Religion and Culture* (Malden, Mass.: Blackwell, 1999), p. 148. Jan Shipps analyzes this sea change in "From Satyr to Saint: American Perceptions of the Mormons, 1860–1960," in her *Sojourner in the Promised Land: Forty Years Among the Mormons* (Urbana: University of Illinois Press, 2000), pp. 51–97.

44. Shepherd and Shepherd, *A Kingdom Transformed*, appendix C.

45. Smith, "Church History," p. 709; Young, *Journal of Discourses* 1:237. Philip L. Barlow's *Mormons and the Bible: The Place of the Latter-day Saints in American Religion* (New York: Oxford University Press, 1991) ably analyzes shifting LDS views of scripture. On Talmage's Jesus, see Malcolm Thorp, "James E. Talmage and the Tradition of Victorian Lives of Jesus," *Sunstone* 12 (January, 1988), pp. 8–13.

46. James E. Talmage, *Jesus the Christ* (Salt Lake City: Deseret Book Co., 1976), pp. 37, 38.

47. "The Father and the Son," *Improvement Era* (August 1916), pp. 934–42.
48. George W. Pace, *What It Means to Know Christ* (Provo, Utah: Council Press, 1981), p. 1; Bruce McConkie, "What Is Our Relationship to Members of the Godhead?" *Church News* (March 20, 1982), p. 5.
49. "All Are Punished!" *Seventh East Press* (March 14, 1982), p. 8; quoted in T. Allen Lambert, "Developing a Personal Relationship," *Seventh East Press* (May 17, 1982), p. 9; quoted in Lavina Fielding Anderson, "Content and Analysis: 'You Have Heard True Doctrine Taught': Elder Bruce R. McConkie's 1981–82 Addresses," http://www.mormonalliance.org/case reports/volume2/part2/v2p2c06.htm; Toscano, *The Sanctity of Dissent*, p. 116; Bruce R. McConkie, "The Purifying Power of Gethsemane," *Ensign* (May 1985), p. 9.
50. McConkie, "What Is Our Relationship," p. 5; Smith, *A Collection of Sacred Hymns*, p. 98; John W. Welch, "Jesus Christ in the Book of Mormon," in Daniel H. Ludlow, ed., *Encyclopedia of Mormonism* (New York: Macmillan, 1992), 2:748.
51. Stephen E. Robinson, *Are Mormons Christians?* (Salt Lake City: Bookcraft, 1991), p. 114; Daniel C. Peterson and Stephen D. Ricks, *Offenders for a Word: How Anti-Mormons Play Word Games to Attack the Latter-day Saints* (Provo, Utah: F.A.R.M.S., 1992), p. 27; see also Shipps, "Is Mormonism Christian?" in her *Sojourner in the Promised Land*, p. 335–57.
52. Church of Jesus Christ of Latter-day Saints, "Christ in the Church" press release, http://www.lds.org/media/newsrelease/extra/display/0,6025,527-1-126-2,00.html; Boyd K. Packer, "The Peaceable Followers of Christ," http://www.lds.org/library/display/0,4945,113-1-47-7,00.html; David Van Biema, "Kingdom Come," *Time* 150.5 (August 4, 1997), p. 50–57; "Official Name of Church Re-Emphasized," press release (March 5, 2001), http://www.lds.org/media2/newsrelease/0,5637,666-1-4497,00.html.
53. "The Living Christ: The Testimony of the Apostles," http://www.lds.org/library/display/0,4945,163-1-10-1,FF.html.
54. Shipps, *Sojourner in the Promised Land*, p. 112; "The Living Christ: What Think Ye of Christ?" http://www.meridianmagazine.com/arts/010403 living1.html.
55. "Christ in America" pamphlet in collection of author; Reynolds, "The Personal Appearance," p. 498–99.
56. Ronald S. Jackson, "We Would See Jesus: Visual Piety," http://www.byuh. edu/academics/ace/Speeches/Mckay/R_Jackson.html; "What's New: LDS Visual Piety," http://www.byuh.edu/whatsnew/20020214.cfm.
57. Noel A. Carmack, "Images of Christ in Latter-day Saint Visual Culture, 1900–1999," in *BYU Studies* 39.3 (2000), p. 66.
58. *Doctrine and Covenants* 1:30; Young, *Journal of Discourses* 10:230; "Crown of Gospel Is upon Our Heads," *Church News* (June 20, 1998), p. 7.
59. Quoted in John W. Kennedy, "Southern Baptists Take up the Mormon Challenge," *Christianity Today* 42.7 (June 15, 1998), p. 24.

CHAPTER SIX: BLACK MOSES

1. Alex Poinsett, "The Quest for the Black Christ," *Ebony* 24.5 (March 1969), pp. 170–78; see also "Artists Portray a Black Christ," *Ebony* 26.6 (April 1971), pp. 177–80.
2. Albert B. Cleage, Jr., *The Black Messiah* (New York: Sheed and Ward, 1968), pp. 3, 91, 37.
3. Ibid., pp. 86, 4, 214, 73, 24.
4. Ibid., p. 72.
5. Ibid., pp. 42–43.
6. Ibid., pp. 85, 95, 44, 82.
7. Elijah Muhammad, *The True History of Jesus* (Chicago: Coalition for the Remembrance of Elijah, 1992), pp. 10, 19; Elijah Muhammad, *Message to the Blackman in America* (Chicago, Muhammad Mosque of Islam No. 2, 1965), p. 22; see also *The Birth of a Savior* (Chicago: Coalition for the Remembrance of Elijah, 1993) and *Jesus: Only a Prophet* (Atlanta: Messenger Elijah Muhammad Propagation Society, n.d.), both by Elijah Muhammad.
8. Cleage, *The Black Messiah*, p. 193.
9. Ibid., p. 46.
10. Ibid., p. 111.
11. James Cone, *Speaking the Truth: Ecumenism, Liberation, and Black Theology* (Maryknoll, N.Y.: Orbis Books, 1999), p. ix; James Cone, *Black Theology and Black Power* (New York: Seabury Press, 1969), pp. 22, 1, 32.
12. Cone, *Black Theology*, pp. 151, 26.
13. Mary Daly, *Beyond God the Father: Toward a Philosophy of Women's Liberation* (Boston: Beacon Press, 1973), p. 19.
14. Ibid., pp. 69–97.
15. Alice Walker, *In Search of Our Mothers' Gardens: Womanist Prose* (San Diego: Harcourt Brace Jovanovich, 1983), p. xi.
16. Daly, *Beyond God the Father*, pp. 69–97; Sojourner Truth, *Narrative of Sojourner Truth* (Battle Creek, Mich.: The Author, 1878), p. 69.
17. Jacquelyn Grant, *White Women's Christ and Black Women's Jesus: Feminist Christology and Womanist Response* (Atlanta: Scholars Press, 1989), pp. 215, 220.
18. "Jesus: Blond or Black?" *Christian Century* 85.43 (October 23, 1968), pp. 1328–29.
19. Howard Thurman, *Jesus and the Disinherited* (New York: Abingdon-Cokesbury Press, 1949), 31.
20. See Albert J. Raboteau, *Slave Religion: The "Invisible Institution" in the Antebellum South* (New York: Oxford University Press, 1978); and his *Fire in the Bones: Reflections on African-American Religious History* (Boston: Beacon Press, 1995).
21. Raboteau, *Slave Religion*, pp. 311–12.
22. Thomas Wentworth Higginson, "Negro Spirituals" (1867), http://www.theatlantic.com/issues/1867jun/spirit.htm.

23. Jon Michael Spencer, *Black Hymnody: A Hymnological History of the African-American Church* (Knoxville: University of Tennessee Press, 1992), p. 123.

24. Eugene D. Genovese, *Roll, Jordan, Roll: The World the Slaves Made* (New York: Pantheon Books, 1974), pp. 272, 254–55.

25. Lawrence Levine, *Black Culture and Black Consciousness: Afro-American Folk Thought from Slavery to Freedom* (New York: Oxford University Press, 1977), p. 50.

26. George P. Rawick et al., eds., *The American Slave: A Composite Autobiography: Supplement, Series 1* (Westport, Conn.: Greenwood Press, 1977), pp. 281–82.

27. "Christ Jesus Not White," *Cleveland Gazette* (December 16, 1893), p. 1.

28. Toulouse and Duke, eds., *Sources of Christian Theology*, pp. 328–29; see also W. L. Hunter, *Jesus Christ Had Negro Blood in His Veins* (Brooklyn, N. Y.: Nolan Brothers, 1901).

29. "The Moses of the Negro Race Has Come to New York," *New York World* (August 22, 1920), http://www.isop.ucla.edu/mgpp/lifeintr.htm.

30. Amy Jacques-Garvey, *Philosophy and Opinions of Marcus Garvey* (New York: Universal Publishing House, 1923–25), 1.44. On Garvey spirituality, see Randall K. Burkett, *Garveyism as a Religious Movement: The Institutionalization of a Black Civil Religion* (Metuchen, N.J.: Scarecrow, 1978).

31. Toulouse and Duke, eds., *Sources of Christian Theology*, p. 329; Marcus Garvey, "African Fundamentalism," http://www.isop.ucla.edu/mgpp/lifesamp.htm; "Negroes Acclaim a Black Christ," *The New York Times* (August 6, 1924), p. 3.

32. David Van Leeuwen, "Marcus Garvey and the United Negro Improvement Association," http://www.nhc.rtp.nc.us:8080/tserve/twenty/tkeyinfo/garvey.htm.

33. Gayraud S. Wilmore, *Black Religion and Black Radicalism: An Interpretation of the Religious History of African Americans*, 3d ed. (Maryknoll, N.Y.: Orbis Books, 1998), p. 182.

34. Ibid., p. 186.

35. Elijah Muhammad, *Message to the Blackman*, 101:3, http://www.seventhfam.com/temple/books/black_man/blkindex.htm; Muhammad, *The True History of Jesus*, p. 19; Malcolm X (*Playboy* interview May 1963), http://www.malcolm-x.org/docs/playboy.htm. Edward E. Curtis IV does an expert job tracing the esoteric origins of the Nation of Islam in his *Islam in Black America: Identity, Liberation, and Difference in African-American Islamic Thought* (Albany: State University of New York Press, 2002).

36. Noble Drew Ali, "Koran Questions for Moorish Americans" pamphlet, pp. 2, 5.

37. Jean Wagner, *Black Poets of the United States from Paul Lawrence Dunbar to Langston Hughes* (Urbana: University of Illinois Press, 1973), p. 335; Countee Cullen, *On These I Stand* (New York: Harper and Row, 1947), pp. 27–28.

38. Langston Hughes, *Scottsboro Limited: Four Poems and a Play in Verse* (New

York: Golden Stair Press, 1932), unpaginated; Benjamin E. Mays, *The Negro's God as Reflected in His Literature* (New York: Atheneum, 1968), pp. 238–239.

39. William Mosley, *What Color Was Jesus?* (Chicago: African American Images, 1987), p. 24.

40. Laurie Goodstein, "Religion's Changing Face: More Churches Depicting Christ as Black," *The Washington Post* (March 28, 1994), p. A1.

41. Laurie Goodstein, "Stallings Campaign Targets White Depictions of Jesus," *The Washington Post* (April 10, 1993), p. B1.

42. "Photographer Renee Cox and NYC Mayor Giuliani's Call for a Decency Commission," http://www.artistsnetwork.org/news/yomama.html; Aïda Mashaka Croal, "Renee Cox Speaks Out," http://www.africana.com/Daily Articles/index_20010227.htm; William Donohue, "Brooklyn Museum of Art Offends Again," http://www.dailycatholic.org/issue/2001Feb/feb17 nu1.htm; David Schwartz and Lauren Rubin, "Cardinal Draws Art Line," *New York Daily News* (March 5, 2001), p. 3.

43. Schwartz and Rubin, "Cardinal Draws Art Line," p. 3; Karen Croft, "Using her Body," *Salon* (February 22, 2001), http://dir.salon.com/sex/feature/2001/02/22/renee_cox/index.html.

44. Croal, "Renee Cox Speaks Out," http://www.africana.com/DailyArticles/index_20010227.htm.

45. Sernett, *Afro-American Religious History*, p. 104. For a comparison of the salience of Christian beliefs and practice among U.S. blacks and whites, see George Gallup, Jr., and D. Michael Lindsay, *Surveying the Religious Landscape: Trends in U.S. Beliefs* (Harrisburg, Penn.: Morehouse, 1999), pp. 52–54.

46. Kevin Powell and Ras Baraka, eds., *In the Tradition: An Anthology of Young Black Writers* (New York: Harlem River Press, 1992), p. 112.

CHAPTER SEVEN: RABBI

1. Jonathan D. Sarna, "Is Judaism Compatible with American Civil Religion?: The Problem of Christmas and the 'National Faith,' " in Rowland A. Sherrill, *Religion and the Life of the Nation: American Recoveries* (Urbana: University of Illinois Press, 1990), p. 156.

2. "Jesus Lived, Dr. Wise Tells Jews," *The New York Times* (December 21, 1925), p. 24.

3. American Jewish Historical Society, "Justice D. Brandeis and American Zionism," http://www.ajhs.org/publications/chapters/chapter.cfm? documentID=281.

4. Melvin I. Urofsky, *A Voice that Spoke for Justice: The Life and Times of Stephen S. Wise* (Albany: State University of New York Press, 1982), pp. 91–92.

5. Hubert Osborne, ed., *Whom Do Men Say that I Am?* (London: Faber and Faber, 1932), pp. 115, 121, 109, 122, 107, 122.

6. Hasia R. Diner, *Jews in America* (New York: Oxford University Press, 1999), p. 57.

7. Melvin I. Urofsky, "Stephen S. Wise and the 'Jesus Controversy,' " in *Midstream* 36.6 (June / July, 1980), p. 37; Herbert Danby, *The Jew and Christianity* (New York: Macmillan, 1927), 113; "Rabbis See Peril in Wise's Sermon," *The New York Times* (December 29, 1925), p. 9; "Calls Dr. Wise a Menace," *The New York Times* (December 30, 1925), p. 1.

8. "Rabbi Fears Dr. Wise Serves His Own Glory," *The New York Times* (December 27, 1925), p. 18; "Dr. Leffmann Calls Dr. Wise to Account," *Jewish Exponent* (January 1, 1926), p. 2; Urofsky, *A Voice that Spoke for Justice*, p. 196.

9. Rabbi Samuel Schulman, *Judaism, Jesus and the Decadence in the Reform Jewish Pulpit* (New York: Temple Beth-El, 1926), pp. 3, 18, 14.

10. Schulman, *Judaism, Jesus*, p. 13.

11. "Christ as Ethical Light," *The New York Times* (December 26, 1925), p. 3; "Agrees with Dr. Wise," *The New York Times* (December 26, 1925), p. 3; "Jesus a Loyal Jew, Asserts Dr. Enelow," *The New York Times* (December 27, 1925), p. 18.

12. "Jew and Christian Come to Wise's Aid," *The New York Times* (December 28, 1925), p. 3; *The New York Times* (February 4, 1925), p. 18; Stephen Samuel Wise, *Challenging Years: The Autobiography of Stephen Wise* (New York: Putnam's Sons, 1949), p. 283.

13. *Jewish Daily Bulletin* (December 23, 1925), p. 1; "Dr. Wise Vindicated by Zionists," *Jewish Exponent* (January 8, 1926), p. 13.

14. Urofsky, "Stephen S. Wise," p. 40; Urofsky translates this sentence as "I am a Jew," but the term *ivri* really means "Hebrew."

15. Danby, *The Jew and Christianity*, p. 103.

16. Samuel Sandmel, "Isaac Mayer Wise's 'Jesus Himself,' " in American Jewish Archives, ed., *Essays in American Jewish History* (New York: Ktav Publishing House, 1975), p. 354.

17. Sandmel, "Isaac Mayer Wise's, 'Jesus Himself,' " p. 355.

18. Kaufmann Kohler, *Christianity vs. Judaism: A Rejoinder to the Rev. Dr. R. Heber Newton* (New York: n.p., 1890), p. 3; Dr. K. Kohler, "Jesus of Nazareth from a Jewish Point of View," pamphlet (1899).

19. Emil G. Hirsch, *The Jews and Jesus* (Chicago: Bloch and Newman, 1893), pp. 9, 12, 28, 12–13, 13.

20. Emil G. Hirsch, *The Doctrines of Jesus* (Chicago: Bloch and Newman, 1894), p. 20.

21. Ibid., p. 21.

22. Isaac M. Wise, *The Martyrdom of Jesus of Nazareth: A Historic-Critical Treatise on the Last Chapters of the Gospel* (Cincinnati: American Israelite, 1874), p. 131.

23. James S. Shapiro, *Oberammergau: The Troubling Story of the World's Most Famous Passion Play* (New York: Pantheon Books, 2000), p. 168.

24. Joseph Krauskopf, *A Rabbi's Impressions of the Oberammergau Passion Play* (Philadelphia: Edward Stern and Co., 1901), pp. 56, 109, 78, 81, 109; see also Krauskopf's *Jesus—Man or God?: Five Discourses* (Philadelphia: Rayner Publishers, n.d.).

25. Hirsch, *The Jews and Jesus*, p. 26; Kaufman Kohler, *Reform Advocate* 10 (December 21, 1895), p. 745.

26. George L. Berlin, *Defending the Faith: Nineteenth-Century American Jewish Writings on Christianity and Jesus* (Albany: State University of New York Press, 1989), pp. 169, 172; Isidor Singer, "The Attitude of the Jews Toward Jesus," *North American Review* 191.650 (January 1910), pp. 128–29.

27. Singer, "The Attitude of the Jews," p. 132; Harris Weinstock, *Jesus the Jew and Other Addresses* (New York: Funk and Wagnalls, 1902), pp. 12, 14, 34.

28. Weinstock, *Jesus the Jew*, pp. 37, 28.

29. Cyrus Adler et al., eds., *The Jewish Encyclopedia* (New York: Funk and Wagnalls Co., 1906), 7.161; see also Shuly Schwartz, *The Emergence of Jewish Scholarship in America: The Publication of the Jewish Encyclopedia* (Cincinnati: Hebrew Union College Press, 1991).

30. Susman, *Culture as History*, p. 277; Hirsch, *The Jews and Jesus*, p. 28; Kohler, "Jesus of Nazareth", n.p.

31. H. G. Enelow, *A Jewish View of Jesus* (New York: Bloch, 1931), pp. 181, 106, 18, 39, 82, 101.

32. Harris Weinstock, *Shall Jesus of Nazareth Be Taught in the Jewish Sabbath School?* (1900), pp. 18–19. Anagarika Dharmapala, a Buddhist reformer from Ceylon, followed a similar strategy in a talk he gave in a church on the same day and in the same city as Wise's "A Jew's View of Jesus"; see "Buddhist Upbraids Western Christians," *The New York Times* (December 21, 1924), p. 24.

33. Stephen S. Wise, "The Life and Teachings of Jesus the Jew," *Outlook* 104 (June 7, 1913), pp. 295–97.

34. "Flirting with Christianity," *American Israelite* (January 14, 1926), p. 3.

35. This story has been pursued carefully in a series of essays by Benny Kraut, including "Reform Judaism and the Unitarian Challenge," in Jonathan D. Sarna, ed., *The American Jewish Experience* (New York: Holmes and Meier, 1986), pp. 89–96; "The Ambivalent Relations between American Reform Judaism and Unitarianism in the Last Third of the Nineteenth Century," *Journal of Ecumenical Studies* 23.1 (1986), pp. 58–68; and "A Unitarian Rabbi? The Case of Solomon H. Sonneschein," in Todd M. Endelman, ed., *Jewish Apostasy in the Modern World* (New York: Holmes and Meier, 1987), pp. 272–308.

36. Marc Lee Raphael, *Profiles in American Judaism: The Reform, Conservative, Orthodox, and Reconstructionist Traditions in Historical Perspective* (San Francisco: Harper and Row, 1984), p. 39.

37. Letter of Solomon H. Sonneschein to Lewis Godlove, December 29, 1885, in Sonneschein Letterbooks, Vol. III, Box x-132, p. 146, American Jewish Archives, quoted in Kraut, "American Reform Judaism and Unitarianism," pp. 66–67; Krauskopf, *A Rabbi's Impressions*, p. 216; Ernest R. Trattner, *As a Jew Sees Jesus* (New York: Scribner, 1931), p. 180.

38. Thomas Walker, *Jewish Views of Jesus: An Introduction and Appreciation* (New York: Arno Press, 1973), p. 102.

39. Susannah Heschel, *Abraham Geiger and the Jewish Jesus* (Chicago: University of Chicago Press, 1998), pp. 1–22; on conjure, see Theophus Harold Smith, *Conjuring Culture: Biblical Formations of Black America* (New York: Oxford University Press, 1994).

40. Jacob Gartenhaus, *The Jew and Jesus* (Nashville: Sunday School Board of the Southern Baptist Convention, 1934), p. 12.

41. John Cournos, *An Open Letter to Jews and Christians* (New York: Oxford University Press, 1938), pp. 22, 24, 77, 118, 12, 10, 13, 60.

42. Edmund A. Walsh, S.J., "An Epistle to the Romans: Modern Style," *Atlantic Monthly* 161.2 (February 1938), pp. 141, 140; Louis I. Newman, "Biting on Granite: A Jewish Rejoinder," *Atlantic Monthly* 161.2 (February 1938), p. 244.

43. Cournos, *Open Letter*, pp. 152, 159, 127.

44. Cournos, *Open Letter*, p. 44; John Cournos, "Jacob Epstein: Artist-Philosopher," *The Studio* 79.328 (July 16, 1920), p. 174; Cournos, *Open Letter*, p. 181.

45. Sholem Asch, *The Nazarene* (trans. Maurice Samuel; New York: G. P. Putnam's Sons, 1939), pp. 498, 265, 482, 471, 472, 685.

46. Asch, *The Nazarene*, p. 654.

47. "The Nazarene," *Time* (October 23, 1939), p. 41; "Recent Religious Books," *The New York Times* (October 14, 1939), p. 17; Karl M. Chworowsky, "Jesus the Jew," *Christian Century* 57.6 (February 7, 1940), pp. 179–80; John Cournos, "The Nazarene," *Atlantic Monthly* 164.5 (November 1939), n.p.; Alfred Kazin, "Rabbi Yeshua ben Joseph," *New Republic* (November 1, 1939), pp. 375, 376.

48. Emanuel K. Schwartz, "The Nazarene Lives Again," *American Hebrew* (November 10, 1939), p. 4; "A Jewish View of Jesus," *Jewish Exponent* (November 17, 1939), pp. 1, 8.

49. Kazin, "Rabbi Yeshua ben Joseph," p. 375; Hannah Berliner Fischthal, "Scholem Asch and the Shift in His Reputation: The Nazarene as Culprit or Victim" (Ph.D. diss., City University of New York, 1994), p. 115.

50. Chaim Lieberman, *The Christianity of Sholem Asch: An Appraisal from the Jewish Viewpoint* (trans. Abraham Burstein; New York: Philosophical Library, 1953), pp. 7, 1, 85; Samuel Sandmel, *We Jews and Jesus* (New York: Oxford University Press, 1965), p. 117.

51. Sholem Asch, *What I Believe* (trans. Maurice Samuel; New York: G. P. Putnam's Sons, 1941), p. 106; Ben Siegel, *The Controversial Sholem Asch: An Introduction to his Fiction* (Bowling Green, Ohio: Bowling Green University Popular Press, 1976), p. 148.

52. Cournos, *Open Letter*, pp. 10, 114, 172, 29, 61.

53. Mark Silk, "Notes on the Judeo-Christian Tradition in America," *American Quarterly* 36.1 (Spring 1984), pp. 65–85. As Silk points out, the first usage of the term "Judeo-Christian" cited in the *Oxford English Dictionary* came in 1899, though in a very different sense. The first appearance of the term in its modern sense noted in the *OED* is a 1939 reference to "the Judaeo-Christian scheme of morals." But Cournos used "Judaeo-Christianity" in

just that sense at least as early as 1938. Bernhard Felsenthal, a Reform rabbi based in Chicago, referred to first-century Ebionites as "Judeo-Christians" in an 1899 essay. See his "Concerning Jesus, Surnamed 'The Christ,'" in Emma Felsenthal, ed., *Bernhard Felsenthal, Teacher in Israel* (New York: Oxford University Press, 1924), p. 192. For another historical treatment, see Deborah Dash Moore, "Jewish GIs and the Creation of the Judeo-Christian Tradition," *Religion and American Culture* 8.1 (Winter 1998), pp. 31–53.

54. Sholem Asch, *One Destiny: An Epistle to the Christians* (trans. Milton Hindus; New York: G. P. Putnam's Sons, 1945), pp. 33, 8, 9, 82, 83, 87–88.

55. Egal Feldman, *Catholics and Jews in Twentieth-Century America* (Urbana: University of Illinois Press, 2001), pp. 9–14; The Editors, "A Statement of Purpose," in John M. Oesterreicher, ed., *The Bridge: A Yearbook of Judaeo-Christian Studies: Volume I* (New York: Pantheon Books, 1955), n.p. Feldman discusses Oesterreicher and his Institute on pp. 74–83.

56. Schulman, *Judaism, Jesus*, p. 19; "*Dabru Emet*: A Jewish Statement on Christians and Christianity," http://www.icjs.org/what/njsp/dabruemet.html.

57. Sandmel, *We Jews and Jesus*, pp. 103, 104, 111.

58. Ibid., pp. 114, 117, 110.

59. "Orthodox Jews Ask Ousting of Dr. Wise," *The New York Times* (December 31, 1925), p. 2; Paula Fredriksen, "Who He Was," *New Republic* (October 15, 2001), p. 53.

60. Geza Vermes, *The Changing Faces of Jesus* (New York: Viking Compass, 2001), quoted in Richard N. Ostling, "The Jewish View of Jesus in Black and White," Associated Press (June 16, 2001).

61. Paula Fredriksen, *Jesus of Nazareth, King of the Jews* (New York: Alfred A. Knopf, 2000), p. 25. To accusations that she is guilty of anachronism herself, Fredriksen (who was raised Catholic but converted to Judaism) replies: "I'm not a 'devout' Jew. I'm a spiritually inarticulate, twenty-first-century, post-Italian Catholic [gioret], who converted not from Christianity but from atheism, and who was a Zionist back in grade school. Do you really see that transcript informing my portrait of the historical Jesus?" ("A Chat with Paula Fredriksen," http://www.jesusarchive.com/Epistle/01-02/QandA_feb01.html).

62. Beatrice Bruteau, ed., *Jesus through Jewish Eyes: Rabbis and Scholars Engage an Ancient Brother in a New Conversation* (Maryknoll, N.Y.: Orbis Books, 2001), pp. 71, 34, 126, 133.

63. Sandmel, *We Jews and Jesus*, p. 111.

64. Ibid., p. 112.

CHAPTER EIGHT: ORIENTAL CHRIST

1. Swami Prabhavananda, *The Sermon on the Mount According to Vedanta* (Hollywood: Vedanta Press, 1963), p. 15.

2. His Eastern and Western Disciples, *The Life of Swami Vivekananda*, 4th ed. (Mayavati, Almora, Himalayas: Advaita Ashrama, 1949), pp. 159–60;

Swami Nikhilananda, "The Hindu View of Christ," *Message of the East* 27.2 (April–June 1938), pp. 81–83.

3. Prabhavananda, *The Sermon on the Mount*, p. 15.

4. Arvind Sharma, ed., *Neo-Hindu Views of Christianity* (New York: E. J. Brill, 1988), p. 7.

5. Swami Akhilananda, *Hindu View of Christ* (Boston: Branden Press, 1949), pp. 36, 43; Carl T. Jackson, *Vedanta for the West: The Ramakrishna Movement in the United States* (Bloomington: Indiana University Press, 1994), p. 112.

6. Swami Paramananda, *Christ and Oriental Ideals*, 3rd ed. (Boston: Vedanta Centre, 1923), p. 26.

7. Swami Vivekananda, *The Complete Works of Swami Vivekananda* (Mayavati Memorial Edition; Calcutta: Advaita Ashrama, 1997), 4.152.

8. Paramananda, *Christ and Oriental Ideals*, pp. 40–41, 91, 66; Vivekananda, *Complete Works*, 7:4; Akhilananda, *Hindu View of Christ*, p. 53.

9. Paramananda, *Christ and Oriental Ideals*, p. 18.

10. Vivekananda, *Complete Works*, 4.142.

11. Paramananda, *Christ and Oriental Ideals*, p. 44; Vivekananda, *Complete Works*, 4.142; Paramananda, *Christ and Oriental Ideals*, p. 21; Akhilananda, *Hindu View of Christ*, p. 47.

12. Phelps, *The Story of Jesus Christ*, p. 118; Vivekananda, "Christ the Messenger," in Swami Satprakashananda, *Hinduism and Christianity: Jesus Christ and His Teachings in the Light of Vedanta* (St. Louis: Vedanta Society of St. Louis, 1975), p. 71.

13. Paramananda, *Christ and Oriental Ideals*, pp. 37, 23.

14. Swami Paramananda, "If Christ Came Today," *Message of the East* 27.4 (October–December 1938), pp. 197, 198, 199, 203.

15. Swami Paramananda, "Christ: The Divine Talisman," *Message of the East* 21.10 (December 1932), p. 291.

16. Swami Abhedananda, "Christ and Christmas," *Vedanta Magazine* 5.12 (December 1909), p. 197.

17. Abhedananda, "Christ and Christmas," p. 195.

18. Vivekananda, *Complete Works*, 4.146; Abhedananda, "Christ and Christmas," pp. 197, 198; Sister Daya, "Christ-Mass," *Message of the East* 12.10 (December 1923), p. 228.

19. Vivekananda, *Complete Works*, 4.145, 1.328; Swami Abhedananda, "Vedanta and the Teachings of Jesus," *Vedanta Monthly Bulletin* 3.9 (December 1907), p. 153.

20. Swami Abhedananda, *Why a Hindu Accepts Christ and Rejects Churchianity* (New York: Vedanta Society, 1901), p. 15; Paramananda, *Christ and Oriental Ideals*, pp. 31, 19.

21. Vivekananda, *Complete Works*, 3.182; Abhedananda, *Why a Hindu Accepts Christ*, p. 1; Swami Paramananda, "Christ and the New Year," *Message of the East* 42.4 (October / December 1953), p. 196.

22. Abhedananda, "Christ and Christmas," p. 198.

23. Swami Trigunatita, "Jesus of Nazareth from the Hindu Standpoint," *Voice of Freedom* 7.9 (December 1915), pp. 162, 168, 162.

24. Ibid., p. 162.

25. Paramahansa Yogananda, *The Divine Romance* (Los Angeles: Self-Realization Fellowship, 1994), p. 339; Paramahansa Yogananda, *Man's Eternal Quest and Other Talks*, 2d ed. (Los Angeles: Self-Realization Fellowship, 1982), pp. 328, 155–59, 139–48, 420–30, 154.

26. Paramhansa Yogananda, *Autobiography of a Yogi*, 4th ed. (New York: Philosophical Library, 1952), pp. 249, 247, 354, 244.

27. Yogananda, *Divine Romance*, p. 336; Yogananda, *Man's Eternal Quest*, p. 284.

28. Yogananda, *Autobiography of a Yogi*, p. 491.

29. Yogananda, *Divine Romance*, p. 335; Yogananda, *Autobiography of a Yogi*, pp. 332, 370; Yogananda, *Man's Eternal Quest*, p. 285.

30. Yogananda, *Man's Eternal Quest*, p. 289.

31. John W. Healey, "When Christianity and Buddhism Meet," *Commonweal* 124.1 (January 17, 1997), pp. 11–13.

32. Claudia Dreifus, "The Dalai Lama," *The New York Times* (November 28, 1993), 6.52; Dalai Lama, *The Good Heart: A Buddhist Perspective on the Teachings of Jesus* (Boston: Wisdom Publications, 1996), p. 96.

33. Dalai Lama, *The Good Heart*, p. 83.

34. Thich Nhat Hanh, *Going Home: Jesus and Buddha as Brothers* (New York: Riverhead, 1999), p. 195.

35. Nhat Hanh, *Going Home*, p. 91; Thich Nhat Hanh, *Living Buddha, Living Christ* (New York: Riverhead Books, 1995), p. 37.

36. Pope John Paul II, *Crossing the Threshold of Hope* (New York: Alfred A. Knopf, 1994), pp. 86, 45; Nhat Hanh, *Living Buddha*, p. 193.

37. Nhat Hanh, *Going Home*, pp. 140, 15, 8.

38. Ibid., p. 46.

39. Jackson, *Vedanta for the West*, p. 84; Hieromonk Damascene, *Christ the Eternal Tao* (Platina, Calif.: Valaam Books, 1999).

40. Vivekananda, *Complete Works*, 4.152; Paramananda, *Christ and Oriental Ideals*, p. 50.

CONCLUSION

1. Ralph Hancock, *The Forest Lawn Story* (Los Angeles: Academy Publishers, 1955), p. 63.

2. Bruce Barton, "A First Step Up Toward Heaven," in *Art Guide of Forest Lawn* (Glendale, Calif.: Forest Lawn Memorial-Park Association, 1963), p. iii.

3. Hancock, *The Forest Lawn Story*, p. 159; "Wanted: the American Smile," *Time* (May 19, 1952), p. 84.

4. George Santayana, *The Character and Opinion of the United States* (New York: Charles Scribner's Sons, 1920), quoted in John Bartlett, ed., *Familiar Quotations*, 14th ed. (Boston: Little, Brown and Co., 1968), p. 867.

5. "Barna Poll on U.S. Religious Belief—2001," http://www.adherents.com/

misc/BarnaPoll.html; George Barna, *What Americans Believe* (Ventura: Regal, 1991), p. 89.

6. Beecher, *The Life of Jesus*, p. 343; Henry Ward Beecher, *Yale Lectures on Preaching* (New York: Fords, Howard, and Hulbert, 1892), 1.190–91; Barton, *The Man Nobody Knows*, pp. 75, 58.

7. H. Richard Niebuhr, Wilhelm Pauck, and Francis Miller, *The Church Against the World*. (New York: Willet, Clark, 1935), p. 128.

8. Ibid., p. 123–24.

9. R. Laurence Moore, *Selling God: American Religion in the Marketplace of Culture* (New York: Oxford University Press, 1994), pp. 276, 275.

10. "The Cambridge Declaration of the Alliance of Confessing Evangelicals," http://www.alliancenet.org/intro/CamDec.html; Steve Camp, "A Call for Reformation in the Contemporary Christian Music Industry," http://www.worship.com/steve_camp_107_theses.htm.

11. "Barna Poll on U.S. Religious Belief—2001," http://www.adherents.com/misc/BarnaPoll.html.

12. Wigger, *Taking Heaven by Storm*, p. 193.

13. H. Richard Niebuhr, *Christ and Culture* (New York: Harper, 1951), p. 2; Countee Cullen, *On These I Stand* (New York: Harper and Brothers, 1947), p. 28.

14. Mauss, *The Angel and the Beehive*, pp. 3–17.

15. Urofsky, *A Voice that Spoke for Justice*, p. 195.

16. George Dana Boardman, "Christ the Unifier of Mankind," in Richard Seager, ed., *The Dawn of Religious Pluralism: Voices from the World's Parliament of Religions, 1893* (LaSalle, Ill.: Open Court, 1993), pp. 466–67.

17. Felsenthal, *Bernhard Felsenthal*, p. 265.

18. Roger Callois, *Man and the Sacred* (New York: Free Press, 1959), p. 132; Eric Voegelin, *The New Science of Politics, an Introduction* (Chicago: University of Chicago Press, 1952), p. 120; see also Adam B. Seligman's provocative discussion of these matters in his *Modernity's Wager: Authority, the Self, and Transcendence* (Princeton, N.J.: Princeton University Press, 2000).

BIBLIOGRAPHY

PRIMARY WORKS ON JESUS

Abhedananda, Swami. *Why a Hindu Accepts Christ and Rejects Churchianity*. New York: Vedanta Society, 1901.

Akhilananda, Swami. *Hindu View of Christ*. Boston: Branden Press, 1949.

Ali, Drew. *Holy Koran of the Moorish Science Temple of America*. n.p.: n.p., 1978.

Asch, Sholem. *The Nazarene*. Maurice Samuel, trans. New York: G. P. Putnam's Sons, 1939.

Austin, Mary. *A Small Town Man*. New York: Harper and Brothers, 1925.

Barton, Bruce. *The Man Nobody Knows: A Discovery of the Real Jesus*. Indianapolis, Ind.: Bobbs-Merrill, 1925.

————. *A Young Man's Jesus*. Boston: Pilgrim Press, 1914.

Barton, William E. *Jesus of Nazareth*. Boston: Pilgrim Press, 1903.

Beecher, Henry Ward. *The Life of Jesus, the Christ*. New York: J. B. Ford, 1871.

Begbie, Harold. *The Happy Christ*. New York: Dodd, Mead, 1906.

Black, Susan Easton. *Finding Christ through the Book of Mormon*. Salt Lake City: Deseret Book Co., 1987.

Bruteau, Beatrice, ed., *Jesus through Jewish Eyes: Rabbis and Scholars Engage an Ancient Brother in a New Conversation*. Maryknoll, N.Y.: Orbis, 2001.

Bushnell, Horace. *The Character of Jesus*. New York: Chautauqua Press, 1888.

Carus, Paul. *The Crown of Thorns: A Story of the Time of Christ*. Chicago: Open Court, 1901.

Cleage, Albert B., Jr. *The Black Messiah*. New York: Sheed and Ward, 1968.

Conant, R. Warren. *The Virility of Christ: A New View*. Chicago: The Author, 1915.

Cone, James. *Black Theology and Black Power*. New York: Seabury Press, 1969.

Cullen, Countee, *The Black Christ and Other Poems*. New York: Harper and Brothers, 1929.

Dalai Lama. *The Good Heart: A Buddhist Perspective on the Teachings of Jesus*. Boston: Wisdom Publications, 1996.

Dowling, Levi. *The Aquarian Gospel of Jesus the Christ.* Los Angeles: Royal Publishing Company, 1908.

Enelow, H. G. *A Jewish View of Jesus.* New York: Bloch, 1931.

Fosdick, Harry Emerson. *The Manhood of the Master.* New York: Abingdon Press, 1913.

Funk, Robert W. *Honest to Jesus: Jesus for a New Millennium.* San Francisco: HarperSanFrancisco, 1996.

Funk, Robert W., Roy W. Hoover, and the Jesus Seminar. *The Five Gospels: The Search for the Authentic Words of Jesus.* New York: Macmillan, 1993.

Goss, Robert. *Jesus Acted Up: A Gay and Lesbian Manifesto.* San Francisco: HarperSanFrancisco, 1993.

Grant, Jacquelyn. *White Women's Christ and Black Women's Jesus: Feminist Christology and Womanist Response.* Atlanta: Scholars Press, 1989.

Hall, G. Stanley. *Jesus, the Christ, in the Light of Psychology.* 2 vols. Garden City, N.Y.: Doubleday, Page, 1917.

Heyward, Carter. *Speaking of Christ: A Lesbian Feminist Voice.* Ellen C. Davis, ed. New York: Pilgrim Press, 1989.

Hirsch, Emil G. *My Religion.* New York: Macmillan, 1925.

Hunter, W. L. *Jesus Christ Had Negro Blood in His Veins.* Brooklyn, N.Y.: Nolan Brothers, 1901.

Jefferson, Thomas. *Life and Morals of Jesus of Nazareth.* Chicago: Manz Engraving, 1904.

Jones, Laurie Beth. *Jesus, CEO: Using Ancient Wisdom for Visionary Leadership.* New York: Hyperion, 1996.

Klausner, Joseph. *Jesus of Nazareth: His Life, Times, and Teaching.* Herbert Danby, trans. New York: Macmillan, 1925.

Krauskopf, Joseph. *A Rabbi's Impressions of the Oberammergau Passion Play.* Philadelphia: Edward Stern, 1901.

Langguth, A. J. *Jesus Christs.* New York: Harper and Row, 1968.

Mathews, Shailer. *The Message of Jesus to Our Modern Life.* Chicago: University of Chicago Press, 1915.

Muhammad, Elijah. *The True History of Jesus.* Chicago: Coalition for the Remembrance of Elijah, 1992.

Nhat Hanh, Thich. *Going Home: Jesus and Buddha as Brothers.* New York: Riverhead, 1999.

———. *Living Buddha, Living Christ.* New York: Riverhead, 1995.

Notovitch, Nicolas. *The Unknown Life of Christ.* F. Marion Crawford, trans. New York: Macmillan, 1894.

Oursler, Fulton. *The Greatest Story Ever Told: A Tale of the Greatest Life Ever Lived.* Garden City, N.Y.: Doubleday, 1949.

Papini, Giovanni. *Life of Christ.* Dorothy Canfield Fisher, trans. New York: Harcourt, Brace, 1923.

Paramananda, Swami. *Christ and Oriental Ideals.* 3rd ed. Boston: Vedanta Centre, 1923.

Peelman, Achiel. *Christ Is a Native American.* Maryknoll, N.Y.: Orbis, 1995.

Phelps, Elizabeth Stuart. *The Story of Jesus Christ: An Interpretation*. Boston: Houghton Mifflin and Co., 1897.

Prabhavananda, Swami. *The Sermon on the Mount According to Vedanta*. Hollywood: Vedanta Press, 1963.

Sandmel, Samuel. *We Jews and Jesus*. New York: Oxford University Press, 1965.

Sankey, Ira D. *Sacred Songs and Solos: With Standard Hymns, Combined. 750 Pieces*. London: Morgan and Scott, n.d.

Satprakashananda, Swami. *Hinduism and Christianity: Jesus Christ and His Teachings in the Light of Vedanta*. St. Louis: Vedanta Society of St. Louis, 1975.

Sheen, Fulton John. *Life of Christ*. New York: McGraw-Hill, 1958.

Sheldon, Charles Monroe. *In His Steps: "What Would Jesus Do?"* Chicago: Advance Publishing, 1897.

Sinclair, Upton. *They Call Me Carpenter: A Tale of the Second Coming*. New York: Boni and Liveright, 1922.

Smith, Emma. *Collection of Sacred Hymns, for the Church of the Latter Day Saints*. Kirtland, Ohio: F. G. Williams and Co., 1835.

Smith, Joseph, Jr. *The Book of Mormon*. Salt Lake City: Church of Jesus Christ of Latter-day Saints, 1998.

Stead, William T. *If Christ Came to Chicago!* Chicago: Laird and Lee, 1894.

Talmage, James E. *Jesus the Christ*. Salt Lake City: Deseret Book Co., 1976.

Tapp, Sidney C. *Why Jesus Was a Man and Not a Woman*. Kansas City: The Author, 1914.

Tissot, James Jacques Joseph. *The Life of Our Saviour Jesus Christ*. New York: McClure-Tissot Company, 1899.

Wallace, Lew. *Ben-Hur, a Tale of the Christ*. New York: Harper and Brothers, 1880.

Weinstock, Harris. *Jesus the Jew and Other Addresses*. New York: Funk and Wagnalls Co., 1902.

Wise, Isaac Mayer. *The Martyrdom of Jesus: A Historic-Critical Treatise on the Last Chapters of the Gospel*. Cincinnati: American Israelite, 1874.

Yogananda, Paramhansa. *Autobiography of a Yogi*. 4th ed. New York: Philosophical Library, 1952.

SECONDARY WORKS ON JESUS

Adams, Dickinson W., ed. *Jefferson's Extracts from the Gospels*. Princeton, N. J.: Princeton University Press, 1983.

Ayres, Samuel Gardiner. *Jesus Christ Our Lord: An English Bibliography of Christology Comprising over Five Thousand Titles Annotated and Classified*. New York: A. C. Armstrong and Son, 1906.

Baldwin, Lewis V. " 'Deliverance to the Captives': Images of Jesus Christ in the Minds of Afro-American Slaves." *Journal of Religious Studies* 12.2, 1986.

Ben-Chorin, Schalom. *Brother Jesus: The Nazarene through Jewish Eyes*. Jared S. Klein and Max Reinhart, trans. and ed. Athens: University of Georgia Press, 2001.

―――. "The Image of Jesus in Modern Judaism." *Journal of Ecumenical Studies* 11.3, Summer 1974.

Berlin, George L. *Defending the Faith: Nineteenth-Century American Jewish Writings on Christianity and Jesus.* Albany: State University of New York Press, 1989.

Birney, Alice L. *The Literary Lives of Jesus: An International Bibliography of Poetry, Drama, Fiction, and Criticism.* New York: Garland, 1989.

Cadbury, Henry J. *The Peril of Modernizing Jesus.* New York: Macmillan, 1937.

Carmack, Noel A. "Images of Christ in Latter-day Saint Visual Culture, 1900–1999." *BYU Studies* 39.3, 2000.

Case, Shirley Jackson. *Jesus through the Centuries.* Chicago: University of Chicago Press, 1932.

Douglas, Kelly Brown. *The Black Christ.* Maryknoll, N.Y.: Orbis, 1994.

Fischthal, Hannah Berliner. "Scholem Asch and the Shift in his Reputation: The Nazarene as Culprit or Victim." Ph.D. diss., City University of New York, 1994.

Fox, Richard Wightman. "Jefferson, Emerson, and Jesus." *Raritan* 22.2, Fall 2002.

Hagner, Donald A. *The Jewish Reclamation of Jesus: An Analysis and Critique of Modern Jewish Study of Jesus.* Grand Rapids, Mich.: Zondervan, 1984.

Heschel, Susannah. *Abraham Geiger and the Jewish Jesus.* Chicago: University of Chicago Press, 1998.

Kissinger, Warren S. *The Lives of Jesus: A History and Bibliography.* New York: Garland, 1985.

Luccock, Halford E. *Jesus and the American Mind.* New York: Abingdon, 1930.

Metzger, Bruce M., ed. *Index to Periodical Literature on Christ and the Gospels.* Leiden, Netherlands: E. J. Brill, 1962.

Murphy, Cullen. "Who Do Men Say That I Am?" *Atlantic Monthly* 258.6, December 1986.

Pals, Daniel L. *The Victorian "Lives" of Jesus.* San Antonio, Tex.: Trinity University Press, 1982.

Pelikan, Jaroslav. *Jesus through the Centuries: His Place in the History of Culture.* New Haven: Yale University Press, 1985.

Phy, Allene Stuart. "Retelling the Greatest Story Ever Told: Jesus in Popular Fiction." Allene Stuart Phy, ed., *The Bible and Popular Culture in America.* Philadelphia: Fortress Press, 1985.

Pinder, Kymberly N. " 'Our Father, God; Our Brother, Christ; or Are We Bastard Kin?': Images of Christ in African American Painting." *African American Review* 31.2, Summer 1997.

Singer, Isidor. "The Attitude of the Jews Toward Jesus." *North American Review* 191.650, January 1910.

Stephens, Bruce M. *The Prism of Time and Eternity: Images of Christ in American Protestant Thought from Jonathan Edwards to Horace Bushnell.* Lanham, Md.: Scarecrow Press, 1996.

Tatum, W. Barnes. *Jesus at the Movies: A Guide to the First Hundred Years.* Santa Rosa, Calif.: Polebridge Press, 1997.

Terrell, Jo Anne Marie. *Power in the Blood?: The Cross in the African American Experience*. Maryknoll, N. Y.: Orbis, 1998.

Urofsky, Melvin I. *A Voice that Spoke for Justice: The Life and Times of Stephen S. Wise*. Albany: State University of New York Press, 1982.

Walker, Thomas. *Jewish Views of Jesus: An Introduction and an Appreciation*. New York: Macmillan, 1931.

Weaver, Walter P. *The Historical Jesus in the Twentieth Century, 1900–1950*. Harrisburg, Penn: Trinity Press International, 1999.

Whitmore, James Herman. *Testimony of Nineteen Centuries to Jesus of Nazareth*. Norwich, Conn.: Henry Bill Publishing Company, 1892.

Wise, Stephen. *Challenging Years: The Autobiography of Stephen Wise*. New York: G. P. Putnam's Sons, 1949.

Witherington, Ben. *The Jesus Quest: The Third Search for the Jew of Nazareth*. 2d ed. Downers Grove, Ill.: Intervarsity Press, 1997.

GENERAL WORKS IN AMERICAN RELIGION AND CULTURE

Ahlstrom, Sydney E. *A Religious History of the American People*. New Haven: Yale University Press, 1972.

Balmer, Randall. *Mine Eyes Have Seen the Glory: A Journey into the Evangelical Subculture in America*. New York: Oxford University Press, 1989.

Barlow, Philip L. *Mormons and the Bible: The Place of the Latter-day Saints in American Religion*. New York: Oxford University Press, 1991.

Bederman, Gail. *Manliness and Civilization: A Cultural History of Gender and Race in the United States, 1880–1917*. Chicago: University of Chicago Press, 1995.

Bloom, Harold. *American Religion: The Emergence of the Post-Christian Nation*. New York: Simon & Schuster, 1992.

Brooke, John L. *The Refiner's Fire: The Making of Mormon Cosmology, 1644–1844*. New York: Cambridge University Press, 1994.

Bushman, Richard L. *Joseph Smith and the Beginnings of Mormonism*. Urbana: University of Illinois Press, 1984.

Butler, Jon. *Awash in a Sea of Faith: Christianizing the American People*. Cambridge: Harvard University Press, 1990.

Carpenter Joel A. *Revive Us Again: The Reawakening of American Fundamentalism*. New York: Oxford University Press, 1997.

Curtis, Susan. *A Consuming Faith: The Social Gospel and Modern American Culture*. Baltimore: Johns Hopkins University Press, 1991.

DeBerg, Betty A. *Ungodly Women: Gender and the First Wave of American Fundamentalism*. Minneapolis, Minn.: Fortress Press, 1990.

Dorrien, Gary. *The Making of American Liberal Theology: Imagining Progressive Religion, 1805–1900*. Louisville, Ky.: Westminster John Knox Press, 2001.

Douglas, Ann. *The Feminization of American Culture*. New York: Alfred A. Knopf, 1977.

Ellwood, Robert S. *The Sixties Spiritual Awakening: American Religion Moving from Modern to Postmodern*. New Brunswick, N.J.: Rutgers University Press, 1994.

Enroth, Ronald M., Edward E. Ericson, Jr., and C. Breckenridge Peters. *The Jesus People: Old-Time Religion in the Age of Aquarius.* Grand Rapids, Mich.: Eerdmans, 1972.

Finke, Roger, and Rodney Stark. *The Churching of America, 1776–1990: Winners and Losers in Our Religious Economy.* New Brunswick, N.J.: Rutgers University Press, 1992.

Fishburn, Janet Forsythe. *The Fatherhood of God and the Victorian Family: The Social Gospel in America.* Philadelphia: Fortress Press, 1981.

Fox, Richard Wightman, and T. J. Jackson Lears, eds. *The Culture of Consumption: Critical Essays in American History, 1880–1980.* New York: Pantheon Books, 1983.

Gaustad, Edwin S. *Sworn on the Altar of God: A Religious Biography of Thomas Jefferson.* Grand Rapids, Mich.: Eerdmans, 1996.

Givens, Terryl L. *By the Hand of Mormon: The American Scripture that Launched a New World Religion.* New York: Oxford University Press, 2002.

Gutjahr, Paul C. *An American Bible: A History of the Good Book in the United States, 1777–1880.* Stanford: Stanford University Press, 1999.

Hatch, Nathan O. *The Democratization of American Christianity.* New Haven: Yale University Press, 1989.

Hatch, Nathan O., and Mark A. Noll, eds. *The Bible in America: Essays in Cultural History.* New York: Oxford University Press, 1982.

Hicks, Michael. *Mormonism and Music: A History.* Urbana: University of Illinois Press, 1989.

Howe, Daniel Walker. *Making the American Self: Jonathan Edwards to Abraham Lincoln.* Cambridge: Harvard University Press, 1997.

Hutchison, William R. *The Modernist Impulse in American Protestantism.* New York: Oxford University Press, 1982.

Jackson, Carl T. *Vedanta for the West: The Ramakrishna Movement in the United States.* Bloomington: Indiana University Press, 1994.

Mauss, Armand L. *The Angel and the Beehive: The Mormon Struggle with Assimilation.* Urbana: University of Illinois Press, 1994.

McDannell, Colleen. *Material Christianity: Religion and Popular Culture in America.* New Haven: Yale University Press, 1995.

McKanan, Dan. *Identifying the Image of God: Radical Christians and Nonviolent Power in the Antebellum United States.* New York: Oxford University Press, 2002.

Moore, R. Laurence. *Religious Outsiders and the Making of Americans.* New York: Oxford University Press, 1986.

Morgan, David, ed. *Icons of American Protestantism: The Art of Warner Sallman.* New Haven: Yale University Press, 1996.

———. *Protestants and Pictures: Religion, Visual Culture, and the Age of American Mass Production.* New York: Oxford University Press, 1999.

———. *Visual Piety: A History and Theory of Popular Religious Images.* Berkeley: University of California Press, 1998.

Niebuhr, H. Richard. *Christ and Culture.* New York: Harper, 1951.

Noll, Mark. *America's God: From Jonathan Edwards to Abraham Lincoln*. New York: Oxford University Press, 2002.

Quinn, D. Michael. *Early Mormonism and the Magic World View*. 2d ed. Salt Lake City: Signature Books, 1998.

Raboteau, Albert J. *Slave Religion: The "Invisible Institution" in the Antebellum South*. New York: Oxford University Press, 1978.

Reynolds, David S. "From Doctrine to Narrative: The Rise of Pulpit Storytelling in America." *American Quarterly* 32.5, Winter 1980.

Shipps, Jan. *Mormonism: The Story of a New Religious Tradition*. Urbana: University of Illinois Press, 1985.

———. *Sojourner in the Promised Land: Forty Years among the Mormons*. Urbana: University of Illinois Press, 2000.

Shipps, Jan, and John W. Welch, eds. *The Journals of William E. McLellin, 1831–1836*. Urbana and Provo, Utah: University of Illinois Press and BYU Studies, 1994.

Sizer, Sandra S. *Gospel Hymns and Social Religion: The Rhetoric of Nineteenth-Century Revivalism*. Philadelphia: Temple University Press, 1978.

Susman, Warren I. *Culture as History: The Transformation of American Society in the Twentieth Century*. New York: Pantheon, 1984.

Thorp, Malcolm R. "James E. Talmage and the Tradition of the Victorian Lives of Jesus." *Sunstone* 12.1, January 1988.

Tweed, Thomas A., ed., *Retelling U.S. Religious History*. Berkeley: University of California Press, 1997.

Tweed, Thomas A., and Stephen Prothero, eds., *Asian Religions in America: A Documentary History*. New York: Oxford University Press, 1999.

Underwood, Grant. *The Millenarian World of Early Mormonism*. Urbana: University of Illinois Press, 1993.

Wigger, John H. *Taking Heaven by Storm: Methodism and the Rise of Popular Christianity in America*. New York: Oxford University Press, 1998.

ACKNOWLEDGMENTS

While researching and writing this book, I received help from many generous friends and colleagues. Both David Morgan and Phil Barlow exchanged numerous e-mails and phone calls with me about our shared interests, correcting my mistakes along the way. John Clayton, Harvey Cox, Robert Ellwood, Aaron Garrett, Philip Goff, Matt Hoffman, Kate Holbrook, Jonathan Klawans, Michael McClymond, Colleen McDannell, Dan McKanan, Patrick Quinn Mason, Mark Noll, Jonathan Sarna, Richard Seager, Jan Shipps, Swami Tyagananda, Judith Weisenfeld, and Wesley Wildman all read one or more draft chapters and offered useful comments and criticisms. I also benefitted from discussions (and an occasional argument) with Randall Balmer, David L. Chappell, Yvonne Chireau, Betty DeBerg, Hannah Berliner Fischthal, Georgia Frank, Paula Fredriksen, Edwin Gaustad, Marie Griffith, William Hutchison, Gerald McDermott, Steve Marini, Robert Orsi, Anthony Pinn, Jon Roberts, Leigh Schmidt, Adam Seligman, Mark Silk, John Stackhouse, Jr., Harry Stout, Jesse Todd, and Grant Wacker. Richard Wightman Fox, a former teacher and colleague who is working on a book of his own on Jesus in America, has been an invaluable conversation partner. Julie Koven of the American Jewish Historical Society, Bryan Craig of the Jefferson Library, and Doreen Fast and James Stambaugh of the Billy Graham Center Museum all went out of their way to provide me with expert research assistance. I also received help from the staff at Boston University's Interlibrary Loan Office, and at my own Department of Religion and Division of Religious and Theological Studies.

Boston University has allowed me to teach two courses on "Jesus in America," and I have profited from interactions with some exceptional students, particularly Lesleigh Cushing, Patton Dodd, Abe Friedman, Crissy Hutchison, Shanny Luft, Mark Mann, Martyn Oliver, Nora Rubel, Michelle Smith, and Emily Wu. I am also grateful for opportunities to discuss my research with students and colleagues at the University of California at Santa

Barbara, where I completed this project while working as the Capps Distinguished Visiting Professor in the Walter H. Capps Center for the Study of Religion in Public Life.

My agent, Sandra Dijkstra, and her staff helped to bring the book into being. Paul Elie, my editor, whipped it into shape. Paul is one of the keenest observers of American religion I know, and he has been my most trenchant critic.

I am also grateful for the financial assistance I received from my home university. B.U.'s Humanities Foundation, led by Katherine O'Connor, provided me a semester's leave when I was first contemplating the book, and a well-timed sabbatical enable me to finish my research.

When asked what her father does for work, my youngest daughter once said, "He goes down to the basement and writes his story." For enduring my absences and supporting me throughout, I thank my daughters, Molly and Lucy, and my wife, Edye Nesmith.

Finally, I need to acknowledge my parents, S. Richard and Helen Prothero. From my infancy, they instilled in me a love of learning and curiosity about "the Christ Child," the twin engines of this project. I have dedicated this book to them.

INDEX

Aaron, Levitical priesthood of, 174–75

Abbott, Jacob, 86

Abbott, Lyman, 69, 86, 95

Abhedananda, Swami, 276, 278–81

Abraham, 179, 190, 215, 217, 232, 245

Adams, Henry, 32

Adams, John, 19, 20, 30

Advaita Vedanta, see Vedantists

African-American Catholic Congregation, 223

African Americans, 48, 80, 83, 179, 188, 200–28, 251; artistic transfigurations of Jesus by, 219–28; in Great Migration, 217; and Black Judaism, 216, 217–18, 301; images of Jesus and, 121, 122; liberation and "womanist" theology of, 205–8; and "separate spheres" ideology, 57; under slavery, 10, 26–27, 49–50, 66–67, 83, 208–13, 226; spirituals of, 76, 77, 79, 210–11, 228; syncretistic denominations of, 163–64

African Colonization Society, 214

African Methodist Episcopal (A.M.E.) Church, 49, 205, 207, 212, 214

African Methodist Episcopal Zion Church, 212

African Orthodox Church, 216

afterlife, doctrine of, 25, 29, 292; in Mormonism, 181

Agape (rock band), 138

Agudath Harabonim, 234, 236

Agyeman, Jaramogi Abebe, see Cleage, Albert B., Jr.

Ahmadiyya movement, 218, 324n4

Akhilananda, Swami, 271–72, 274

Ali, Muhammad, 214

Ali, Noble Drew, 163, 219

Allen, A.V.G., 83

Alliance of Confessing Evangelicals, 296

All Saved Freak Band, 138

Almon, Leroy, 220

Altizer, Thomas, 39, 40

American Anti-Slavery Society, 58

American Bible Society, 58, 65, 80, 137

American Civil Liberties Union (ACLU), 230

American Revolution, 10, 13, 44, 114, 209

American Sunday School Union, 58

American Temperance Society, 58

American Tract Society, 58, 65, 137

American Unitarian Association, 30, 31

Amos, 232

Lundbom, Jack R., 120
Luther, Martin, 40, 139, 170, 285
Lutherans, 5, 15, 46, 51, 121, 122,
  188, 293, 296

Machen, J. Gresham, 26, 27, 114,
  193
Maharishi Mahesh Yogi, 125, 138,
  271
Malcolm X, 16, 201, 203, 204, 219,
  228
Mandela, Nelson, 228
Man Nobody Knows, The (Barton), 11,
  98, 100–108, 110, 116, 151, 154,
  249, 282, 293; film of, 113
Marantha Music!, 139
March on Washington (1963), 209
Marcion, 7
Marini, Stephen, 59, 74, 77
Mark, Gospel of, 29, 69, 128, 134,
  176, 267, 298
Marty, Martin, 80, 94, 121
Martyrdom of Jesus of Nazareth, The
  (Wise), 243
Mary, 12, 57, 63, 103, 216, 254
Mary Magdalene, 15, 133
Masculine in Religion, The (Case), 93
Mather, Cotton, 45, 56, 166
Mather, Increase, 45
Mathews, Shailer, 109–10, 115
Matthew, Gospel of, 25, 29, 69, 128,
  134, 139, 144, 176, 208, 210, 217,
  220, 227, 273, 298
Matthews, Robert, 172–73
Mayer, Louis B., 249
McConkie, Bruce, 189, 191–92
McCowan, Archibald, 96
McDermott, Gerald, 296
McGeehan, Bill, 112–13
McGuire, George Alexander, 216, 223
McKenzie, Janet, 223–24
McLellin, William E., 175, 181,
  325n17
McNally, Terrence, 15
McPherson, Aimee Semple, 113, 147,
  222

megachurches, 147–51, 153–54, 293
Meier, John P., 263
Melville, Herman, 89
Men and Religion Forward Move-
  ment, 93
Mennonites, 46, 47, 205
Mercersburg Theology, 50, 85–86
Merton, Thomas, 287, 288
Methodists, 6, 44, 48–49, 51, 52, 55,
  108, 167, 174, 193, 293, 296;
  African-American, 203, 212, 217,
  220
Metro-Goldwyn-Mayer (MGM),
  249
Mexico City Blues (Kerouac), 286
Meyer, Martin, 249
Micah, 232
millennialists, 142, 143, 166–67
Miller, Donald, 147, 150
Miller, Kelly, 222
Miller, Perry, 209
Miller, Samuel, 58
Millerites, 55, 166–67
miracles, 23, 24, 32, 40, 63, 108, 118,
  124, 149–50, 250, 278
Mitchell, Edwin Knox, 236
Mitford, Jessica, 292
Mizrachi, 235
Montefiore, Claude, 238, 239
Montgomery bus boycott, 209
Moody, Dwight, 75–77, 136, 156
Moody Bible Institute, 117
Moonies, 145
Moore, R. Laurence, 295
Moorish Science Temple, 218, 219
Moravians, 45, 47
Mordecai, 173
Morgan, David, 61, 118
Morgan, Gertrude, 213
Mormons, 4, 8, 15, 47, 55, 89, 150,
  164–99, 209, 247, 270, 301,
  324n16, 325n17; Christianity of,
  193–99; temple, 178–86; textual,
  172–78; twentieth-century, 186–
  92
Moses, 29, 79, 101, 172, 173, 179,